Communications in Computer and Information Science 2712

Series Editors

Rationale

The CCIS series is devoted to the publication of proceedings of computer science conferences. Its aim is to efficiently disseminate original research results in informatics in printed and electronic form. While the focus is on publication of peer-reviewed full papers presenting mature work, inclusion of reviewed short papers reporting on work in progress is welcome, too. Besides globally relevant meetings with internationally representative program committees guaranteeing a strict peer-reviewing and paper selection process, conferences run by societies or of high regional or national relevance are also considered for publication.

Topics

The topical scope of CCIS spans the entire spectrum of informatics ranging from foundational topics in the theory of computing to information and communications science and technology and a broad variety of interdisciplinary application fields.

Information for Volume Editors and Authors

Publication in CCIS is free of charge. No royalties are paid, however, we offer registered conference participants temporary free access to the online version of the conference proceedings on SpringerLink (http://link.springer.com) by means of an http referrer from the conference website and/or a number of complimentary printed copies, as specified in the official acceptance email of the event.

CCIS proceedings can be published in time for distribution at conferences or as post-proceedings, and delivered in the form of printed books and/or electronically as USBs and/or e-content licenses for accessing proceedings at SpringerLink. Furthermore, CCIS proceedings are included in the CCIS electronic book series hosted in the SpringerLink digital library at http://link.springer.com/bookseries/7899. Conferences publishing in CCIS are allowed to use our online conference service (Meteor) for managing the whole proceedings lifecycle (from submission and reviewing to preparing for publication) free of charge.

Publication process

The language of publication is exclusively English. Authors publishing in CCIS have to sign the Springer CCIS copyright transfer form, however, they are free to use their material published in CCIS for substantially changed, more elaborate subsequent publications elsewhere. For the preparation of the camera-ready papers/files, authors have to strictly adhere to the Springer CCIS Authors' Instructions and are strongly encouraged to use the CCIS LaTeX style files or templates.

Abstracting/Indexing

CCIS is abstracted/indexed in DBLP, Google Scholar, EI-Compendex, Mathematical Reviews, SCImago, Scopus. CCIS volumes are also submitted for the inclusion in ISI Proceedings.

How to start

To start the evaluation of your proposal for inclusion in the CCIS series, please send an e-mail to ccis@springer.com

Lourdes Martínez-Villaseñor ·
Roberto A. Vázquez · Gilberto Ochoa-Ruiz
Editors

Advances in Soft Computing

MICAI 2025 Posters Track

24th Mexican International Conference
on Artificial Intelligence, MICAI 2025
Guanajuato, Mexico, November 3–7, 2025
Proceedings

Springer

Editors
Lourdes Martínez-Villaseñor
Universidad Panamericana
Mexico City, Distrito Federal, Mexico

Roberto A. Vázquez
Universidad La Salle
Mexico City, Mexico

Gilberto Ochoa-Ruiz
Instituto Tecnológico y de Estudios
Superiores de Monterrey
Zapopan, Mexico

ISSN 1865-0929 ISSN 1865-0937 (electronic)
Communications in Computer and Information Science
ISBN 978-3-032-08703-4 ISBN 978-3-032-08704-1 (eBook)
https://doi.org/10.1007/978-3-032-08704-1

This Springer imprint is published by the registered company Springer Nature Switzerland AG
The registered company address is: Gewerbestrasse 11, 6330 Cham, Switzerland

Preface

The Mexican International Conference on Artificial Intelligence (MICAI) is a yearly international conference series that has been organized by the Mexican Society for Artificial Intelligence (SMIA) since 2000. MICAI is an important international artificial intelligence (AI) forum and the main event in the academic life of the growing AI community in the country.

This year, MICAI 2025 was organized by the Mexican Society for Artificial Intelligence (SMIA, Sociedad Mexicana de Inteligencia Artificial) in collaboration with the Centro de Investigaciones en Matemáticas (CIMAT) and the Universidad de Guanajuato (UG).

The MICAI series website is www.MICAI.org. The website of the Mexican Society for Artificial Intelligence, SMIA, is www.SMIA.mx. Contact options and additional information can be found on these websites.

The conference, as is traditional, showcased a wide variety of research fields and topics. Moreover, the conference included cutting-edge keynote lectures, as well as detailed paper presentations and comprehensive hands-on tutorials. Furthermore, thought-provoking panels and niche workshops provided a rich and exciting experience that aimed to cater to a wide audience.

Moreover, we continued the legacy of announcing the José Negrete Award, the SMIA Best Thesis in Artificial Intelligence Contest's results. This year, the historic and culturally rich city of Guanajuato was our chosen destination.

MICAI conferences publish high-quality papers in all areas of AI and its applications. The proceedings of the previous MICAI events have been published by Springer in its Lecture Notes in Artificial Intelligence (LNAI) series (volumes: 1793, 2313, 2972, 3789, 4293, 4827, 5317, 5845, 6437, 6438, 7094, 7095, 7629, 7630, 8265, 8266, 8856, 8857, 9413, 9414, 10061, 10062, 10632, 10633, 11288, 11289, 11835, 12468, 12469, 13067, 13068, 13612, 13613, 14502, 14391, 14392, 15246, 15247, 15464 and 15465). Since its foundation in 2000, the conference has grown in popularity and improved in quality.

The proceedings of MICAI Posters 2025 are published in one volume of the Communications in Computer and Information Science series

This volume contains 24 papers structured into four sections:

- Applications
- Machine Learning
- Natural Language Processing
- Neural Networks

The conference received 119 submissions from 12 countries: Brazil, Ecuador, France, India, Italy, Morocco, Mexico, Paraguay, Peru, Spain, the USA and Vietnam. Gender representation also echoed with 323 male authors and 97 female authors adding their voice. From these submissions, 24 papers were selected for poster presentation and publication in this volume after at least three reviews per submission in a double-blind peer-reviewing process carried out by the international Program Committee.

The international Program Committee consisted of 133 experts from 15 countries: Brazil, Canada, China, the UK, France, India, Ireland, Japan, Luxembourg, Mexico, New Zealand, Peru, Russia, Thailand and the USA.

Five workshops were held jointly with the conference (the last two being new additions to the conference):

- WILE 2025: 18th Workshop on Intelligent Learning Environments
- HIS 2025: 18th Workshop on Hybrid Intelligent Systems
- CIAPP 2025: 7th Workshop on New Trends in Computational Intelligence and Applications
- CHARAL 2025: Challenges in Holistic AI for Real-world Applications and Learning Systems
- ECSI 2025: Workshop on Evolutionary Computation and Swarm Intelligence

Furthermore, the MeDA challenge, which aims to advance research in domain adaptation for medical imaging by tasking participants with developing cross-domain classification algorithms using the MedMNIST v2 dataset was organized a second time. The models submitted were evaluated on their ability to generalize to unseen endoscopic tasks. This challenge seeks to raise the ante in medical imaging research at a conference.

We want to thank all the people involved in the organization of this conference: the authors of the papers published in these two volumes, because it is their research work that gives value to the proceedings, and the organizers for their work. We thank the reviewers for their great effort spent in reviewing the submissions and the Program and Organizing Committee members.

A special acknowledgment to the local committee led by Alejandro Rosales Pérez and Adrian Pastor López Monroy, whose meticulous coordination was instrumental in realizing MICAI 2025 in Guanajuato, Mexico. Our acknowledgments extend to Rafael Herrera Guzmán (Director General, CIMAT), and to Óscar Susano Dalmau Cedeño (Coordinador de Ciencias de la Computación, CIMAT). We are also indebted to the following authorities at Universidad de Guanajuato: Héctor Fabián Gutiérez Rangel (Director de la División de Ciencias Económico Administrativas), Martin Picón Núñez (Rector de Campus Guanajuato, Universidad de Guanajuato) and to Claudia Susana Gómez López (Rectora General) for their invaluable assistance in securing the university facilities to complement the facilities of CIMAT.

In addition, the success of this conference and the breadth of its program are a testament to the collaborative efforts of our organizing and local committees and sponsors.

The entire submission, reviewing, and selection process, as well as the preparation of the proceedings, was supported by Microsoft's Conference Management Toolkit (https://cmt3.research.microsoft.com/). Last but not least, we are grateful to Springer for their patience and help in the preparation of these volumes.

In conclusion, MICAI 2025 was more than just a conference. It was a confluence of minds, a testament to the indefatigable spirit of the AI community, and a beacon for the future of Artificial Intelligence. As you navigate through these proceedings, may you find inspiration, knowledge, and connections that propel you forward in your journey.

November 2025

Lourdes Martínez-Villaseñor
Roberto A. Vazquez
Gilberto Ochoa-Ruiz

Organization

Conference Committee

General Chair

Lourdes Martínez-Villaseñor	Universidad Panamericana, Mexico

Program Chairs

Gilberto Ochoa-Ruiz	Tecnológico de Monterrey, Mexico
Roberto A. Vazquez	Universidad La Salle México, Mexico

Workshop Chair

Iris Mendez	Universidad Autónoma de Ciudad Juárez, Mexico

Tutorials Chair

David Pinto	Benemérita Universidad Autónoma de Puebla, Mexico

Doctoral Consortium Chairs

Miguel González Mendoza	Tecnológico de Monterrey, Mexico
Néstor Valasco Berneo	Experient, USA
Gustavo Arroyo Figueroa	INEEL, Mexico

Keynote Talks Chair

Hugo Jair Escalante	INAOE, Mexico

Publication Chair

Hiram Ponce	Universidad Panamericana, Mexico

Publicity Chairs

Bella Martinez	Instituto Politécnico Nacional, Mexico
Claudia Gonzalez	Instituto Tecnológico de Tijuana, Mexico

Communication and Design Chairs

Iván Olvera	Grupo Software de Alta Calidad, Mexico
Omar Saldivar	Barbarosos, Mexico
Luis Gerardo Téllez	Barbarosos, Mexico

Grant Chair

Leobardo Morales	IBM, Mexico

Local Organizing Committee

Local Chairs

Alejandro Rosales Pérez	Centro de Invetigacion en Matemáticas, México
Adrian Pastor López Monroy	Centro de Invetigacion en Matemáticas, México

Logistics Chairs

Jorge Alberto Soria Alcaraz	Universidad de Guanajuato, México
Marco Aurelio Sotelo Figueroa	Universidad de Guanajuato, México

Program Committee

Abel García Nájera	Universidad Autónoma Metropolitana Unidad Cuajimalpa, Mexico
Alberto Gonzalez-Sanchez	IMTA, Mexico
Alberto Ochoa-Zezzatti	UACJ, Mexico
Aldo Márquez-Grajales	Universidad Veracruzana, Mexico
Alexander V. Bozhenyuk	Southern Federal University, Russia
Ana Laura Lezama-Sánchez	SECIHTI, BUAP, Mexico
Andres Garcia Floriano	Instituto Politécnico Nacional, Mexico
Andrés Espinal	Universidad de Guanajuato, Mexico
Angeles Belém Priego Sánchez	Universidad Autónoma Metropolitana Unidad Azcapotzalco, Mexico

Antonieta Martinez	Universidad Panamericana, Mexico
Antonio Neme	UNAM, Mexico
Ari Y. Barrera Animas	Universidad Panamericana, Mexico
Armando Levid Rodríguez Santiago	Universidad Tecnológica de los Valles Centrales de Oaxaca, Mexico
Asdrúbal López Chau	UAEMex, Mexico
Ashokkumar Baldevbhai Prajapati	Soorajba College of Education, India
Ayanfeoluwa P. Oluyomi	Missouri University of Science and Technology, USA
Bella C. Martinez Seis	IPN, Mexico
Bernardo Corona Domínguez	Universidad Nacional Rosario Castellanos, Mexico
Betania Hernandez-Ocaña	Universidad Juárez Autónoma de Tabasco, Mexico
Camila L. Silva	Universidade Federal de Minas Gerais, Brazil
Chandra Prakash	University of the Cumberlands, USA
Christina A. Garcia	Kyushu Institute of Technology, Japan
Claudia I. Gonzalez	TecNM/Instituto Tecnológico de Tijuana, Mexico
Cosijopii Garcia-Garcia	UNISTMO, Mexico
Daniel Flores Araiza	Monterrey Institute of Technology and Higher Education (ITESM), Mexico
Daniela Alejandra Ochoa	CentroGEO, Mexico
Dante Mújica-Vargas	CENIDET, Mexico
David Pinto	BUAP, Mexico
Dhwanit Agarwal	Adobe Inc, USA
Diego Uribe	TecNM ITL, Mexico
Eddy Sánchez-DelaCruz	Tecnológico Nacional de México - Campus Misantla, Mexico
Eduardo Valdez	IPN, Mexico
Efrén Mezura-Montes	University of Veracruz, Mexico
Elisabetta Crescio	Tecnológico de Monterrey, Mexico
Elva Lilia Reynoso Jardon	Universidad Autónoma de Ciudad Juáre, Mexico
Emmanuel Ovalle-Magallanes	Universidad de La Salle Bajio, Mexico
Eric S. Tellez	CICESE-INFOTEC-CONACyT, Mexico
Erik Molino	IIMAS-UNAM, Mexico
Esmeralda Arreola Marin	TecNM campus Cd. Hidalgo, Mexico
Fernando Gudino	National Autonomous University of Mexico, Mexico
Fevrier Valdez	Tijuana Institute of Technology/TecNM, Mexico
Francisco Lopez-Tiro	Tecnológico de Monterrey, Mexico
Gabriel González-Serna	TecNM/CENIDET, Mexico
Garibaldi Pineda Garcia	Applied AGI, UK
Genoveva Vargas-Solar	Grenoble Alpes University, CNRS, France

Gilberto Ochoa-Ruiz	Tecnológico de Monterrey, Mexico
Gildardo Sanchez-Ante	Tecnológico de Monterrey, Mexico
Grissel Rodríguez Roldán	Instituto Artek, Mexico
Guadalupe Carmona Arroyo	Universidad Veracruzana, Mexico
Guillermo Santamaría-Bonfil	BBVA México, Mexico
Gustavo Arroyo	Instituto Nacional de Electricidad y Energías Limpias, Mexico
Haimei Wen	University of Texas at Dallas, USA
Hiram Calvo	Center for Computing Research - Instituto Politécnico Nacional, Mexico
Hiram Ponce	Universidad Panamericana, Mexico
Hugo Jair Escalante	INAOE, Mexico
Humberto Sossa	CIC-IPN, Mexico
Iris Iddaly Méndez-Gurrola	Universidad Autónoma de Ciudad Juárez, Mexico
Ismael Osuna-Galán	UAEQROO, Mexico
Israel Tabarez	Universidad Autónoma del Estado de México, Mexico
Jaime Cerda	Universidad Michoacana de San Nicolás de Hidalgo, Mexico
Jerusa Marchi	Federal University of Santa Catarina, Brazil
Jesús García-Ramírez	UPIIT-IPN, Mexico
Jesús-Adolfo Mejía-de-Dios	Universidad Autónoma de Coahuila, Mexico
Jiale Li	University of Auckland, New Zealand
Jiechen Zhao	University of Toronto, Canada
Joanna Alvarado Uribe	Tecnológico de Monterrey, Mexico
Jonathan Rojas-Simón	Autonomous University of the State of Mexico, Mexico
Jose D Alanis	Universidad Tecnológica de Puebla, Mexico
Jose Sosa	University of Luxembourg, Luxembourg
Jose Alberto Hernandez-Aguilar	Universidad Autónoma del Estado de Morelos, Mexico
José Carlos Ortiz-Bayliss	Tecnológico de Monterrey, Mexico
José Luis M Reyes	UV, Mexico
José Luis Vilchis Medina	ENSTA Bretagne, France
Jose-Federico Ramirez-Cruz	TecNM - Instituto Tecnológico de Apizaco, Mexico
Juan Martínez-Miranda	CICESE-UT3, Mexico
Juan Villegas-Cortez	Universidad Autónoma Metropolitana-Azcapotzalco, Mexico
Juan Carlos Olivares Rojas	Tecnológico Nacional de México/Instituto Tecnológico de Morelia, Mexico
Juana Isabel Méndez	Tecnológico de Monterrey, Mexico

Juan-Carlos Gonzalez-Islas	Universidad Autónoma del Estado de Hidalgo, Mexico
Julio Santisteban	Universidad Católica San Pablo, Peru
Karina Mariela Figueroa Mora	UMSNH, Mexico
Leticia Flores Pulido	Universidad Autónoma de Tlaxcala, Mexico
Li Yu	Zhejiang University, China
Lourdes Martinez-Villaseñor	Universidad Panamericana, Mexico
Luis M. Torres-Treviño	Universidad Autónoma de Nuevo León, Mexico
Mansoor Ali	Tecnológico de Monterrey, Mexico
Maria de la Concepción Pérez de Celis Herrero	Benemérita Universidad Autónoma de Puebla, Mexico
Maria Lucia Barrón Estrada	TecNM-Instituto Tecnológico de Culiacán, Mexico
Mario Anzures-García	Benemérita Universidad Autónoma de Puebla, Mexico
Masaki Murata	Tottori University, Japan
Miguel Gonzalez-Mendoza	Tecnológico de Monterrey, Mexico
Miguel Sanchez Brito	Instituto Politécnico Nacional, Mexico
Mohd. Saif Wajid	BBD University, India
Nancy Pérez-Castro	Universidad del Papaloapan, Mexico
Nestor Velasco Bermeo	University College Dublin, Ireland
Nidiyare Hevia Montiel	Universidad Nacional Autónoma de México, Mexico
Noé-Alejandro Castro-Sánchez	TecNM-CENIDET, Mexico
Obdulia Pichardo-Lagunas	IPN, Mexico
Omar Velazquez Lopez	UNAM, Mexico
Pagon Gatchalee	Chiang Mai University, Thailand
Pengfei Hu	Stevens Institute of Technology, USA
Qi Chang	Accenture, USA
Quanchao Lu	Georgia tech, USA
Rafael Batres	Tecnológico de Monterrey, Mexico
Rafael Guzman-Cabrera	Universidad de Guanajuato, Mexico
Rafael Rivera-Lopez	Tecnológico Nacional de México/Instituto Tecnológico de Veracruz, Mexico
Ramon F. Brena	Instituto Tecnológico de Sonora, Mexico
Ramón Zatarain Cabada	Tec Culiacán, Mexico
Rashi Dhenia	Hitachi, USA
Raúl Monroy Borja	Tecnológico de Monterrey, Mexico
Ricardo Espinosa	Universidad Panamericana, Mexico
Ricardo Landa	Cinvestav, Mexico
Roberto Antonio Vazquez	Universidad La Salle México, Mexico
Rocio O. Ochoa-Montiel	Universidad Autónoma de Tlaxcala, Mexico

Rosa M. Ortega-Mendoza	UAEH, Mexico
Sabino Miranda	UACM, Mexico
Salvador M. Hinojosa	Tecnológico de Monterrey, Mexico
Samuel Efren Viñas Alvarez	Tecnológico Nacional de México campus Zitácuaro, Mexico
Sandra Leticia Juárez-Osorio	Centro de Investigación y Estudios Avanzados del Politécnico Nacional, Mexico
Sheng Gao	University of Pennsylvania, USA
Shuo Li	Carnegie Mellon University, USA
Sofia N. Galicia-Haro	Universidad Nacional Autónoma de México, Mexico
Stephen A. Sunday	Ohio University, USA
Tania A. Ramirez-delReal	CONACyT-CentroGeo, Mexico
Vadim Borisov	Branch of National Research University "Moscow Power Engineering Institute" in Smolensk, Russia
Valery Solovyev	Kazan Federal University, Russia
Vicente Garcia Jimenez	Universidad Autónoma de Ciudad Juárez, Mexico
Victor Lomas-Barrie	IIMAS-UNAM, Mexico
Víctor J. Ruiz	TecNM/CENIDET, Mexico
Yasmín Hernández	Centro Nacional de Investigación y Desarrollo Tecnológico, Mexico
Yaxk'in U Kan Coronado	Universidad La Salle México, Mexico
Yubo Wang	Meta Platforms, inc., USA
Yucheng Zhou	University of Macau, China

Contents

Natural Language Processing

Neural Networks

Applications

Analysis of the Implementation of an E-Commerce Delivery System

Rogelio Lizárraga-Escobar, Cecilia Paláu-Dávila, and Fernando Elizalde-Ramírez(✉)

School of Engineering and Sciences, Tecnológico de Monterrey, Monterrey, Nuevo León, Mexico
fer_elizalde@tec.mx

Abstract. This paper presents an algorithm for the delivery of products from an e-commerce company, with the aim of significantly improving its logistics and organization by focusing on minimizing total delivery hours. The algorithm considers constraints on delivery route capacity and time. A detailed analysis is carried out through queueing models to determine the optimal number of ramps to install and the transport units needed for the efficient transfer of products. These analyses were performed through simulations using real data, considering order size and product purchases modeled through probability distributions, which are used to simulate the demand of a working day. Monte Carlo simulations were also used, in order to generate client groups with simulated demand and fixed capacity. The delivery of products is formulated as a Capacitated Vehicle Routing Problem (CVRP) with time windows. A solution using Ant Colony Optimization (ACO) algorithms was proposed, using a Genetic Algorithm (GA) as a baseline. This algorithm aims to find feasible routes and schedules that meet delivery requirements, considering the constraints. Thus, the CVRP was solved with feasible solutions, significantly reducing total distance traveled and route duration time, compared to the GA.

Keywords: Vehicle Routing Problem · CVRP · Ant Colony Optimization · Genetic Algorithm · Monte Carlo Simulation · E-commerce logistics

1 Introduction

Today, technology and the digital era have significantly contributed to the digital economy, allowing the redefinition of how products and services are purchased or sold through e-commerce. The pandemic accelerated this shift: global e-commerce grew by an estimated 30% in 2020 and has since surpassed prior trajectory trends . By 2025, global e-commerce retail sales are expected to reach approximately $7.4 trillion, capturing over 24% of total global retail sales [4,9]. This trend has forced companies to rethink their logistics strategies to ensure

L. Martínez-Villaseñor et al. (Eds.): MICAI 2025, CCIS 2712, pp. 3–15, 2025.
https://doi.org/10.1007/978-3-032-08704-1_1

timely deliveries and invest in adequate infrastructure, as any failure in these aspects can affect both their reputation and customer base [6].

To address this challenge and optimize resource management, companies resort to simulations that allow them to anticipate and plan various scenarios related to delivery processes. The main objective of this paper is to develop a mathematical or computational model that simulates product delivery logistics in e-commerce, considering a variety of potential scenarios, focusing on minimizing the total delivery hours the transport units should take.

The use and implementation of simulations allow the modeling and forecasting of various logistical scenarios in e-commerce, enabling companies to make informed decisions, optimize their operations, and stay in constant evolution. Not using simulation tools and opting to test systems physically incurs significant economic costs, exposing companies to risks such as operational inefficiency, unnecessary expenses, delivery delays, and customer loss.

The plan is to generate an algorithm that simulates the product delivery logistics of an e-commerce company to various customers. The objective is to understand the necessary operating capacity, that is, the number of units to be acquired and the number of loading ramps to install, minimizing total route hours while respecting the route time restrictions, no greater than an 8-hour workday.

2 Theoretical Framework

This section delineates key contributions in the optimization of product delivery within e-commerce. It examines distinct methodologies, including the Vehicle Routing Problem (VRP), Monte Carlo simulation, and heuristic and metaheuristic algorithms, such as Ant Colony Optimization (ACO), Genetic Algorithms (GA), and 2-opt local search.

Vehicle Routing Problem (VRP) and Variants. The VRP has evolved significantly as a central topic in logistics and distribution research, given its focus on minimizing the travel distance for fleets delivering products to multiple locations. A prominent variant is the Capacitated Vehicle Routing Problem (CVRP), which introduces constraints related to vehicle capacity. Empirical research has demonstrated that hybrid strategies—combining clustering techniques with routing optimization—yield substantial improvements in both computational efficiency and route effectiveness [2]. Moreover, recent studies have integrated distinct optimization algorithms, such as particle swarm optimization (PSO) and gray wolf optimization (GWO), to address the scalability challenges inherent in large-scale applications of these models [8]. Another notable variant is the Vehicle Routing Problem with Time Windows (VRPTW), which incorporates specific temporal constraints for deliveries—an aspect that is particularly critical in urban environments. Recent investigations applying VRPTW in metropolitan areas such as Austin and Chicago have achieved notable enhancements in energy efficiency and have facilitated the integration of electric vehicles in urban logistics [1].

Monte Carlo Simulation. Monte Carlo simulation has emerged as a robust technique for modeling uncertainties in both demand and delivery times. By incorporating stochastic variations in factors such as product demand and vehicle availability, this approach enables the exploration of multiple operational scenarios. In the context of electronic retail product delivery, Monte Carlo methods have been effectively employed to determine optimal route configurations by accounting for fluctuations in traffic conditions and service durations at delivery points [14]. In doing so, the simulation framework enhances system responsiveness and mitigates the risks associated with route inefficiencies.

Ant Colony Optimization (ACO). Ant Colony Optimization represents a class of metaheuristic algorithms inspired by the collective behavior of ants, which follow the most efficient paths between their nests and food sources. Within the context of the VRP, ACO algorithms have been shown to achieve near-optimal solutions even in complex, large-scale scenarios. Recent research applying ACO to expansive e-commerce distribution networks has reported significant reductions in both delivery times and operational costs under high-demand conditions [5]. Additionally, hybrid approaches that combine ACO with Particle Swarm Optimization have further refined solution quality in complex logistical challenges [3,7].

Genetic Algorithms (GA). Genetic Algorithms remain a standard baseline for routing: individuals encode client permutations, variation uses permutation-safe operators (e.g., order crossover and swap/insert mutations), and fitness evaluates a greedy split under capacity/time budgets. Modern state-of-the-art GA variants for VRP are *hybrid*: they embed powerful local-search neighborhoods (2-opt/2-opt*, relocate, swap) and often add adaptive penalties and diversity control (e.g., the Hybrid Genetic Search, HGS) [10,13]. Recent surveys continue to report strong competitiveness of these hybrid GA/LS designs on large VRP families [15].

2-opt Local Search. 2-opt is a classic edge-exchange move that improves a tour by removing two edges and reconnecting the path without crossings; applied iteratively, it yields large distance reductions at $O(n^2)$ checks per pass. In VRP, 2-opt is used intra-route, while 2-opt* exchanges segments between routes; both remain standard building blocks in modern metaheuristics and open-source toolkits [11,13,15].

3 Modeling and Data Analytics

3.1 Problem Definition

The problem requires deciding how many vehicles to use and the optimal number of loading ramps that should be installed to meet the daily product demand. This is done by considering multiple variables such as fluctuating daily customer demand, vehicle capacity constraints, allowed delivery times, and the number of products transported. Additionally, the goal is to minimize the total time of the delivery routes, optimizing the available resources while complying with the maximum 8-hour workday.

To solve this problem, an Ant Colony Optimization (ACO) algorithm is proposed, which is efficient for combinatorial optimization problems, such as the Capacitated Vehicle Routing Problem (CVRP). The model includes N transport vehicles and M customers.

3.2 Sets

- $V = \{i, j \mid i, j = 1, 2, \ldots, M\}$: Set of nodes.
- $K = \{k \mid k = 1, 2, \ldots, N\}$: Set of vehicles.

3.3 Variables

- x_{ijk}: Indicates if transport k departs from destination i to destination j.

$$x_{ijk} \in \{0, 1\} \tag{1}$$

3.4 Parameters

- M: The total number of customers.
- N: The total number of transports.
- Q_k: The capacity of transport k.
- d_i: The customer demand i.
- c_{ij}: The cost (distance in kilometers) from the destination i to the destination j.

3.5 Objective Function

The goal is to minimize the total distance traveled on vehicle routes:

$$\min \sum_{k=1}^{N} \sum_{i=1}^{M} \sum_{j=1}^{M} c_{ij} \cdot x_{ijk} \tag{2}$$

3.6 Constraints

The constraints of the problem can be modeled as follows:

1. Each vehicle must enter and exit a node once:

$$\sum_{i=1}^{M} x_{ijk} = \sum_{j=1}^{M} x_{jik}, \quad \forall j, k \tag{1}$$

2. Enter each node only once and exit with the same vehicle:

$$\sum_{k=1}^{N}\sum_{i=1}^{M} x_{ijk} = 1, \quad \forall j \in \{2,\ldots,M\} \tag{2}$$

3. All vehicles must depart from the depot:

$$\sum_{j=2}^{M} x_{1jk} = 1, \quad \forall k \tag{3}$$

4. Respect the capacity of each vehicle k :

$$\sum_{i=1}^{M}\sum_{j=1}^{M} d_j \cdot x_{ijk} \leq Q_k, \quad \forall k \tag{4}$$

5. The total time of the routes must not exceed the 8-hour workday, considering an average speed of 50 km/h:

$$\sum_{i=1}^{M}\sum_{j=1}^{M} c_{ij} \cdot x_{ijk} \leq 8 \cdot 50, \quad \forall k \tag{5}$$

6. Miller – Tucker–Zemlin formulation to avoid sub-tours:

$$u_j - u_i \geq q_j - Q_k(1 - x_{ijk}), \quad \forall i,j \in V \setminus \{1\},\ i \neq j \tag{6}$$

3.7 Data Information

For the solution of this problem, there are 356 addresses and one depot, for a total of 357 nodes. As our matrix of variables is a square matrix and we have 357 nodes, there is a total of 127,449 variables.

On the other hand, there are a total of 53,632 products, and purchases vary by customer.

3.8 Probability Distributions

To model which products customers buy, we use the *empirical categorical* distribution derived from historical unit shares. The cumulative shares are shown in Fig. 1 (Fig. 2).

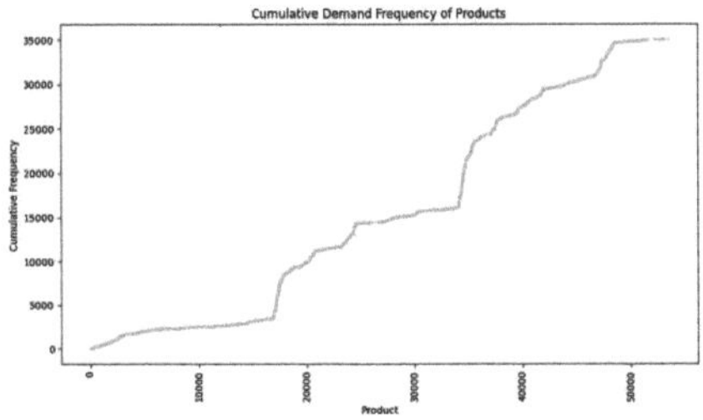

Fig. 1. Cumulative share (CDF) of product demand. The X-axis shows product ID, the Y-axis shows the cumulative share of total units.

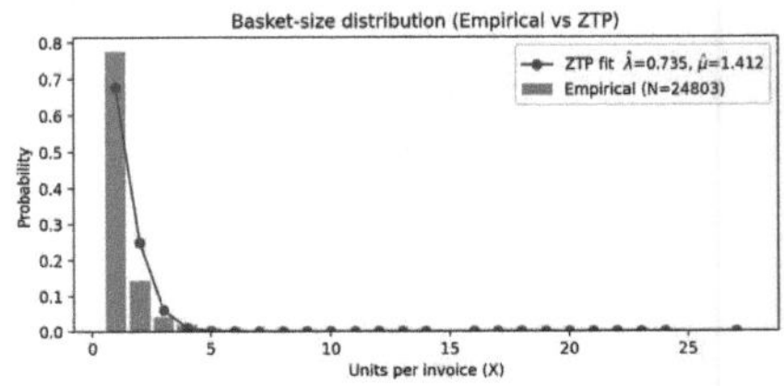

Fig. 2. Zero-truncated Poisson (ZTP) basket-size distribution: histogram of units per customer; Y-axis uses ln counts for readability.

3.9 Resources Used

The program was executed on a Lenovo Yoga 7 running Ubuntu 22.04.5 LTS (partition: 338.1 GB; RAM: 16 GB; CPU: Intel(R) Core(TM) i7-1165G7 @ 2.80 GHz, 8 cores) using Python 3.10.12.

4 Experimentation

4.1 Monte Carlo Demand Simulation

We simulate demand in two parts and express it in cubic meters for routing:

1. **Basket size (units per order).** Every order has at least one item. Thus, each order X is modeled with a ZTP distribution. Its probability mass function and mean are

$$P_{\text{ztp}}(X = x) = \frac{e^{-\lambda}\,\lambda^{x}}{x!\,\left(1 - e^{-\lambda}\right)}, \qquad x \in \{1, 2, \ldots\},$$

$$\mu \equiv \mathbb{E}[X \mid X \geq 1] = \frac{\lambda}{1 - e^{-\lambda}}.$$

   We calibrate λ numerically so that the ZTP mean μ matches the empirical average units per invoice $\hat{\mu}$.
2. **Product mix.** Conditional on X, product IDs are sampled using empirical relative frequencies $p_j \propto$ historical units sold of product j. Each product has a known unit volume (m^3) and its order's volume is the sum of its purchased products.

Then, for each instance with n clients we run T=10,000 Monte Carlo iterations, where each iteration draws baskets, samples product IDs, and then records total units, total volume purchased, and the average units per client. As shown in Table 1, the 95% confidence intervals for the Monte Carlo means are minimal half-widths of 0.23 units, $< 0.12\,\text{m}^3$ total volume, and a minimal difference of average units per client, respectively. By the Central Limit Theorem [12], the standard error of the Monte Carlo estimator scales as $O(T^{-1/2})$. Since the sampling error is already minimal with T = 10,000 iterations, increasing T would yield negligible improvement.

Table 1. Monte Carlo demand summary over T = 10,000 iterations for 300 clients

Statistic	Total units	Total volume (m^3)	Avg. units / client
Mean	423.59	51.78	1.41
Std. dev.	11.74	7.02	0.04
P05	404.00	40.65	1.35
Median	423.00	51.51	1.41
P95	443.00	63.75	1.48
95% CI (mean, lo)	423.36	51.68	1.41
95% CI (mean, hi)	423.82	51.92	1.41

4.2 Creating Groups of Distance Matrices

We evaluate multiple instance sizes (e.g., 200, 250, 300 customers). For each size we use n independent *groups* (distinct client sets and distances) with a single depot at node 0. Each distance file includes depot–client and client–client kilometers. These groups represent different spatial realizations of the same workload size.

4.3 Generating Groups of Purchases

For each (size, group) pair we generate one synthetic purchase table with a fixed pseudo-random seed per group. Thus, distinct lists of purchases were simulated. The procedure is:

- Calibrate the ZTP rate from the historical mean units per invoice.
- For every customer in the group, draw units from the calibrated ZTP.
- Sample product IDs using the empirical probability and sum product volumes to obtain the demand each customer made in m^3.

4.4 Routing Setup and ACO Algorithm

Ant Colony Optimization (ACO). We implemented an ACO for our CVRP with time budgets per route. Each ant builds a permutation of customers using a stochastic transition approach that balances pheromone (τ_{ij}) and heuristic visibility ($\eta_{ij} = 1/d_{ij}$, where d_{ij} is travel distance):

$$P(i \to j) \propto \tau_{ij}^{\alpha}\, \eta_{ij}^{\beta}, \quad \text{with greedy choice probability } q_0.$$

where α, β = pheromone and heuristic visibility weights and q_0 = arg max $\tau_{ij}^{\alpha}\eta_{ij}^{\beta}$. Once our *giant tour* is built we apply *local* pheromone update on traversed edges $\tau_{ij} \leftarrow (1 - \rho_{\text{local}})\, \tau_{ij} + \rho_{\text{local}}\, \tau_0$, where τ_0 is the initial pheromone and $\rho_{\text{local}} \in (0, 1)$ is the local evaporation/deposit rate.

Then, a greedy *split* partitions the permutation into routes subject to capacity and a distance budget per route that takes into account ramp availability. Budget for each route index r is

$$B_r = v \cdot H - \lfloor r/R \rfloor \cdot v \cdot (c/60)$$

with speed v, workday hours H, cadence c minutes, and R ramps. Solutions violating capacity or budget are penalized. Otherwise, the objective is total distance (km) with a strong primary criterion on minimizing vehicles.

After each iteration we apply a *global* pheromone update, with a **Max–Min** logic:

$$\tau_{ij} \leftarrow (1 - \varphi)\, \tau_{ij} + \varphi\, \Delta\tau_{ij}, \quad \Delta\tau_{ij} = \begin{cases} Q/L^* & \text{if } (i, j) \in \psi^*, \\ 0 & \text{otherwise,} \end{cases}$$

Where

$$\begin{aligned} \tau_{ij} &= \text{pheromone level on arc } (i, j), \\ \varphi &= \text{evaporation rate } (0 < \varphi < 1), \\ \Delta\tau_{ij} &= \text{pheromone deposited on } (i, j), \\ Q &= \text{deposit scale } (> Q \text{ for shorter tours}), \\ L^* &= \text{length/cost of the best tour used for the update}, \\ \psi^* &= \text{best tour so far.} \end{aligned}$$

Furthermore, we clamp $\tau_{ij} \in [\tau_{\min}, \tau_{\max}]$ so that we avoid stagnation. Additionally, a 2-opt local search is applied to each route to achieve better results.

Ramp Sweep and Selection. For each group we sweep $R \in \{1, \ldots, 5\}$ (number of ramps). The winner is selected by fewest vehicles and, if tied, lowest total distance. We used fixed seeds for reproducibility across groups and between our algorithms.

Hyperparameters. n_{ants} = 300, iterations = 125, α = 1, β = 1, evaporation $\varphi = 0.2$, $Q = 1.0$, $q_0 = 0.95$, $\rho_{\text{local}} = 0.1$, vehicle fixed cost = 0, speed $v = 50$ km/h, workday $H = 8$ h, cadence $c = 15$ min, trailer capacity = 12.5 m^3.

4.5 Genetic Algorithm (GA Baseline)

As a baseline, we implement a generational Genetic Algorithm that searches over client permutations.

Chromosome and Decoding. A chromosome is a permutation π of the n customers ($\{1, \ldots, n\}$). In order to evaluate π, we build a *giant tour* and apply our greedy split logic used for ACO. The fitness function then prioritizes fewer vehicles and breaks ties by distance:

$$f(\pi) = M \cdot n_r(\pi) + \mathrm{km}(\pi), \quad M = 10^6.$$

Where

$$\begin{aligned} M &= \text{Penalty weight}, \\ n_r &= \text{Number of routes}, \\ \mathrm{km} &= \text{Total distance traveled in km}, \\ \pi &= \text{Client permutation}. \end{aligned}$$

Infeasible additions (capacity or budget) are always rejected by the splitter, whereas single-customer routes are allowed, keeping the GA baseline comparable to ACO on constraints.

Initialization. Let S_n denote all $n!$ permutations of $\{1, \ldots, n\}$. Our search space is then S_n, where each $\pi \in S_n$ encodes a client order prior to splitting into routes. With our population size P_{size}, we seed two heuristics with nearest-neighbor logic (NN) and fill the rest randomly: (i) NN from the depot; (ii) NN starting at the client farthest from the depot; (iii) $P_{\text{size}} - 2$ random permutations (uniform over S_n).

Selection and Replacement. Tournament selection with size k and a generational replacement with *elitism* (best 2 individuals copied as they are to the next generation).

Crossover (Order Crossover, OX). With probability p_{cx}, two distinct cut points $a < b$ are picked uniformly without replacement, from $\{1, \ldots, n\}$. Given parents $A, B \in S_n$, the slice $(A_a, \ldots, A_b)$ is copied into the child C at positions $a, \ldots, b$. Then B is scanned from left to right and fills the remaining positions of C in order, with the elements of B that are not already in the copied slice, switching duplicates. If crossover is not applied, a selected parent is copied.

Mutation. Applied to each offspring with probability p_{mut}. When triggered, we choose one of three light operators: (i) *Swap* two positions ($p_{\text{swap}} = 0.4$); (ii) *Insertion* of one gene into a new position ($p_{\text{insert}} = 0.3$); (iii) *Short segment reversal* ($p_{\text{rev}} = 0.3$). These operators encourage local exploration and prioritize permutation feasibility.

Generations. A total of G generations are run. Patience implemented: If no improvement is achieved after a certain number of generations, the algorithm stops searching for new solutions.

Reproducibility and Ramp Sweep. All runs use fixed seeds aligned with ACO and take the same simulated demand and distance matrices. The best configuration is reported by group.

Hyperparameters. $M = 10^6$, $P_{\text{size}} = 300$, $k = 3$, $p_{\text{cx}} = 0.9$, $p_{\text{mut}} = 0.3$, with mutation mix $(p_{\text{swap}}, p_{\text{insert}}, p_{\text{rev}}) = (0.4, 0.3, 0.3)$, generations = 150, patience = 15, elitism = 2, speed $v = 50$ km/h, workday $H = 8$ h, cadence $c = 15$ min, trailer capacity = 12.5 m^3.

5 Results

5.1 Simulation Results

We evaluated two metaheuristics: Ant Colony Optimization (ACO) and a Genetic Algorithm (GA, used as a baseline), reporting the best configuration found by each algorithm. Per-group outcomes (fleet size, total distance, selected ramps, delivered volume, and workday usage) are shown in Tables 2, 3, 4, 5, 6 and 7. A head-to-head summary at fixed fleet size is reported in Table 8.

Per-Size Comparison (Fixed Fleet). Across all sizes, the Ant Colony Algorithm consistently matches the Genetic Algorithm fleet size, while achieving shorter total distance and lower workday usage:

- **200 customers:** The ACO mean route length is 492.62 km, compared to 568.96 km for GA, a reduction of 76.33 km (**-13.42%**). Route duration drops from 6.27 h to 4.91 h, saving 1.35 h (**-21.67%**), as shown in Tables 2, 3 and Fig. 3.
- **250 customers:** The ACO mean route length is 558.78 km, compared to 644.66 km for GA, a reduction of 85.88 km (**-13.32%**). Route duration is reduced from 6.67 h to 5.16 h, saving 1.59 h (**-22.65%**). See Tables 4 and 5 and Fig. 4.
- **300 customers:** The ACO mean route length is 633.76 km, compared to 727.45 km for GA, a reduction of 93.69 km (**-12.88%**). Route duration is reduced from 5.93 h to 4.83 h, saving 1.09 h (**-18.47%**). See Tables 6 and 7 and Fig. 5.

Statistical Comparison at Fixed Fleet. Across the 200/250/300-client sets (n=10, 10, 9), ACO consistently yields shorter routes than GA: the mean gaps $\Delta\text{km} = \text{GA} - \text{ACO} > 0$ with tight 95% CIs (Table 8). Both the paired t-tests ($p_t < 0.001$) and one-sided Wilcoxon matched-pairs tests ($p < 0.002$) confirm statistical significance.

Table 2. Summary across groups—200 clients (ACO)

n	Vehicles	Cost (km)	Ramps	Volume (m^3)	Route duration (h)
1	4	547.528	3	42.348	4.890
2	3	446.704	1	34.424	5.850
3	3	439.478	3	29.706	4.440
4	2	433.088	2	23.154	6.280
5	4	542.574	3	43.278	4.300
6	3	482.426	3	32.609	5.170
7	3	449.554	4	28.711	5.450
8	3	513.684	4	32.743	4.360
9	4	551.839	3	39.556	3.740
10	3	519.366	2	36.424	4.610
Mean		**492.624**		**34.295**	**4.909**

Table 3. Summary across groups—200 clients (GA)

n	Vehicles	Cost (km)	Ramps	Volume (m^3)	Route duration (h)
1	4	622.035	4	42.348	7.010
2	3	498.640	2	34.424	5.200
3	3	578.692	1	29.706	6.680
4	2	533.168	1	23.154	7.870
5	4	600.240	1	43.278	5.590
6	3	543.650	1	32.609	6.490
7	3	505.312	4	28.711	4.040
8	3	594.253	1	32.743	7.470
9	4	620.008	5	39.556	5.830
10	3	593.572	4	36.424	6.490
Mean		**568.957**		**34.295**	**6.267**

Table 4. Summary across groups—250 clients (ACO)

n	Vehicles	Cost (km)	Ramps	Volume (m^3)	Route duration (h)
1	4	578.456	4	49.876	4.550
2	4	530.170	3	41.808	3.890
3	3	578.243	4	35.713	5.290
4	3	543.462	5	31.604	5.390
5	4	564.516	3	49.812	6.000
6	4	567.534	3	39.113	4.680
7	4	578.994	5	37.965	5.610
8	4	509.546	5	46.821	3.640
9	4	546.464	1	44.334	5.660
10	4	590.369	2	45.387	6.860
Mean		**558.775**		**42.243**	**5.157**

Table 5. Summary across groups—250 clients (GA)

n	Vehicles	Cost (km)	Ramps	Volume (m^3)	Route duration (h)
1	4	653.563	1	49.876	5.770
2	4	643.193	1	41.808	6.310
3	3	670.435	2	35.713	7.070
4	3	633.721	1	31.604	6.790
5	4	637.311	1	49.812	6.680
6	4	625.658	2	39.113	6.720
7	4	671.599	4	37.965	4.860
8	4	615.963	1	46.821	7.600
9	4	625.253	5	44.334	7.200
10	4	669.938	4	45.387	7.670
Mean		**644.663**		**42.243**	**6.667**

Table 6. Summary across groups—300 clients (ACO)

n	Vehicles	Cost (km)	Ramps	Volume (m^3)	Route duration (h)
1	5	657.716	4	50.640	5.670
2	5	654.534	3	55.694	4.330
3	4	605.058	3	44.520	4.090
4	4	608.205	1	45.595	4.860
5	5	663.141	4	51.889	4.750
6	5	607.851	1	51.501	6.500
7	4	631.723	2	44.273	5.060
8	5	641.238	5	59.641	4.820
9	5	634.395	4	53.198	3.410
Mean		**633.762**		**50.772**	**4.832**

Table 7. Summary across groups—300 clients (GA)

n	Vehicles	Cost (km)	Ramps	Volume (m^3)	Route duration (h)
1	5	775.397	4	50.640	5.090
2	5	740.340	2	55.694	6.400
3	4	740.355	2	44.520	7.310
4	4	702.494	2	45.595	6.140
5	5	700.269	2	51.889	5.120
6	5	667.023	2	51.501	6.540
7	4	771.613	3	44.273	6.660
8	5	735.287	5	59.641	4.780
9	5	714.234	1	53.198	5.300
Mean		**727.446**		**50.772**	**5.927**

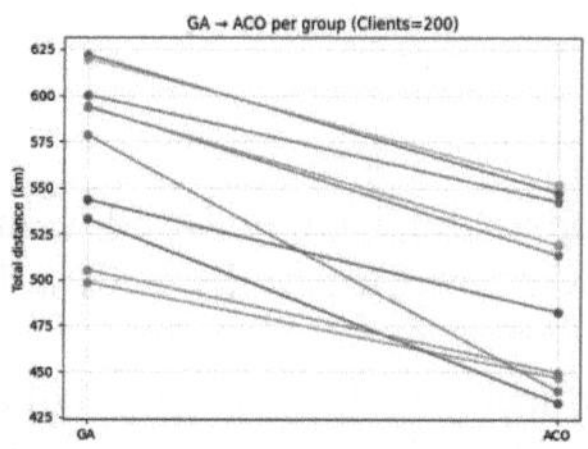

Fig. 3. Total Distance: GA vs ACO (200 clients)

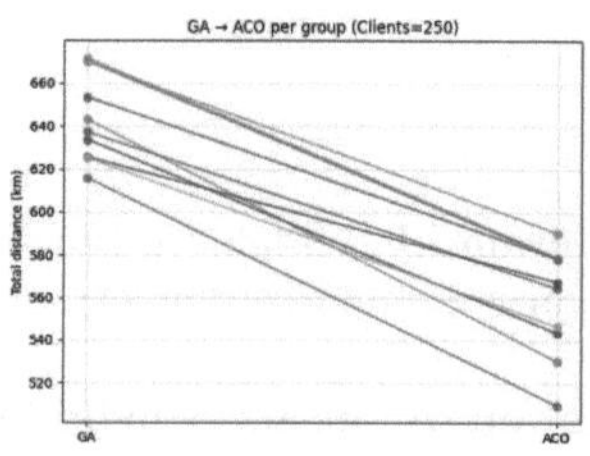

Fig. 4. Total Distance: GA vs ACO (250 clients).

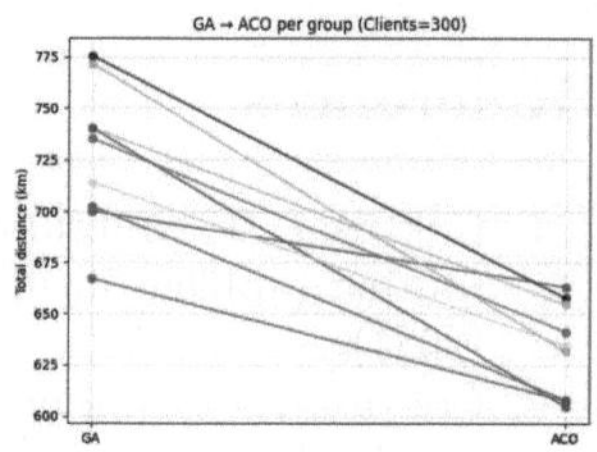

Fig. 5. Total Distance: GA vs ACO (300 clients)

Table 8. Fixed–fleet statistical comparison (GA vs ACO)

Clients	n	$\mu(\Delta\text{km})$	95% CI	t (df)	p_t
200	10	76.33	$[60.1, 92.6]$	9.10 (9)	7.78×10^{-6}
250	10	85.89	$[75.7, 96.0]$	16.60 (9)	4.67×10^{-8}
300	9	93.68	$[71.7, 115.7]$	8.33 (8)	2.23×10^{-5}

Table 9. Wall-clock runtime by instance size

Clients	GA (min)	ACO (min)	Speedup (ACO/GA)	Time saved
200	3.58	140	39.1×	97.4%
250	6.93	160	23.1×	95.7%
300	8.92	190	21.3×	95.3%

Takeaway. ACO delivers better solutions across all sizes and groups, without increasing the number of vehicles. Table 9 reports higher runtimes for ACO, whereas GA saves more than 95% by client size.

6 Discussion and Conclusions

Based on our results, we found three relevant insights.

Quality at Fixed Fleet. Keeping the number of vehicles constant, ACO reduces the total distance and route duration across instance sizes.

Ramp Configuration Matters. The ramp count that yields the best solution is instance dependent (winners span 1–5 ramps across groups).

Demand Held Constant. Since ACO and GA hold the same demand, the significant differences demonstrate algorithmic differences, rather than demand noise. ACO is an effective CVRP-TW solver: in 29 instances, it matched the GA fleet size and reduced total distance in every case under identical constraints, making it the preferred option for tactical planning. Future work: (i) strengthen GA with embedded local search, (ii) incorporate stochastic travel times/time windows, and (iii) model driver breaks and variable speeds.

Acknowledgments. The authors thank the collaborators and reviewers for helpful comments.

Disclosure of Interests. The authors have no competing interests to declare relevant to the content of this article.

References

1. Cokyasar, T., Subramanyam, A., et al.: A time-constrained capacitated vehicle routing problem in urban e-commerce delivery. arXiv preprint arXiv:2201.04036 (2021)
2. Cokyasar, T., Subramanyam, A., et al.: A hybrid solution method for the capacitated vehicle routing problem using a quantum annealer. Front. Logistics Optim. (2023)
3. Dorigo, M., Stützle, T.: Ant Colony Optimization. MIT Press (2004)

4. eMarketer: Global ecommerce sales will hit $7.4 trillion in 2025 (2025). https://www.emarketer.com/content/global-ecommerce-sales-will-hit-7-4-trillion-in-2025
5. Green, T., Gray, L.: Ant colony optimization in vehicle routing problems: a practical approach. Int. J. Metaheuristics (2021)
6. Invesp: The impact of poor customer experience on brand loyalty and revenue (2024). https://www.invespcro.com/blog/ecommerce-customer-experience-statistics/
7. Marinakis, Y., et al.: A hybrid particle swarm optimization algorithm for the vehicle routing problem. Eng. Appl. Artif. Intell. (2023)
8. Son, D.V.T., Tan, P.N.: Capacitated vehicle routing problem—a new clustering approach based on hybridization of adaptive particle swarm optimization and grey wolf optimization. In: Algorithms for Intelligent Systems. Springer (2024)
9. Statista: E-commerce share of total global retail sales from 2015 to 2025 (2025). https://www.statista.com/statistics/534123/e-commerce-share-of-retail-sales-worldwide/
10. van Strien, M., De Maeyer, L., Schüll, A., et al.: PyVRP: a high-performance open-source VRP solver (2023). https://github.com/PyVRP/PyVRP
11. Sun, M., Zhang, Z., Xu, X.: Optimizing multi-echelon delivery routes for perishable goods with joint one- and two-echelon networks. Mathematics **12**(23), 3845 (2024)
12. van der Vaart, A.W.: Asymptotic Statistics. Cambridge University Press (2021). https://doi.org/10.1017/9781108783864
13. Vidal, T.: Hybrid genetic search for the capacitated vehicle routing problem: open-source implementation and swap neighborhood. arXiv prepreint arXiv:2012.10384 (2021)
14. White, D.: Improving inbound logistic planning for large-scale routing problems: a novel ant-colony simulation-based optimization. Euro. Transp. Res. Rev. (2020)
15. Wouda, N.A., Lan, L., Kool, W.: PyVRP: a high-performance vehicle routing problem solver package. INFORMS J. Comput. **36**(4), 943–955 (2024). https://doi.org/10.1287/ijoc.2023.0055

Minimization of Competition Between Flora Species in a Reforestation Area

Fernando Elizalde-Ramirez[1], Cristina Maya-Padron[2](✉), and María-Guadalupe Jimenez-Martínez[3]

[1] Escuela de Ingeniería y Ciencias, Tecnológico de Monterrey, Monterrey, Nuevo León, Mexico
fer_elizalde@tec.mx
[2] Ingeniería en Sistemas Computacionales, Universidad Politécnica de García, García, Nuevo León, Mexico
cristina.maya@upgarcia.edu.mx, kerstin.maya@gmail.com
[3] USPAE-INECOL, Coatepec, Mexico
maria.jimenez@inecol.mx

Abstract. Reforestation plays a crucial role in mitigating climate change and restoring ecological balance [5]. However, high interspecific competition among planted species can significantly affect survival rates and ecosystem resilience. This study addresses the problem of minimizing inter-species competition by optimizing the spatial allocation of tree species in reforestation projects. An exact mathematical programming model was initially developed to determine optimal planting configurations based on species compatibility and resource competition. While the model produced satisfactory solutions for small instances, it exhibited severe computational limitations for larger problem sizes. To overcome these challenges, a Genetic Algorithm (GA) was implemented as a metaheuristic alternative. The GA demonstrated strong scalability, consistently generating feasible and competitive solutions across all problem sizes, including large-scale instances involving hundreds of planting positions and multiple species. Comparative analysis shows that the GA outperforms the exact model in terms of computational efficiency while delivering high-quality solutions. The results support the application of evolutionary algorithms for practical reforestation planning, particularly when exact optimization becomes computationally intractable.

Keywords: Reforestation planning · Species allocation · Interspecific competition · Mathematical programming · Genetic algorithms

1 Introduction

Climate change has become a critical global issue, significantly affecting ecosystems worldwide. In Mexico, deforestation, cattle ranching, and excessive greenhouse gas emissions have contributed to severe environmental consequences, including droughts, wildfires, rising sea levels, floods, and biodiversity loss. As

L. Martínez-Villaseñor et al. (Eds.): MICAI 2025, CCIS 2712, pp. 16–27, 2025.
https://doi.org/10.1007/978-3-032-08704-1_2

part of national environmental policies, reforestation programs have become a strategic response to mitigate these adverse effects and restore ecological balance. Figure 1 shows the strong correlation between high deforestation and drought areas, which creates water stress in these regions and affects access to water for human and agricultural use.

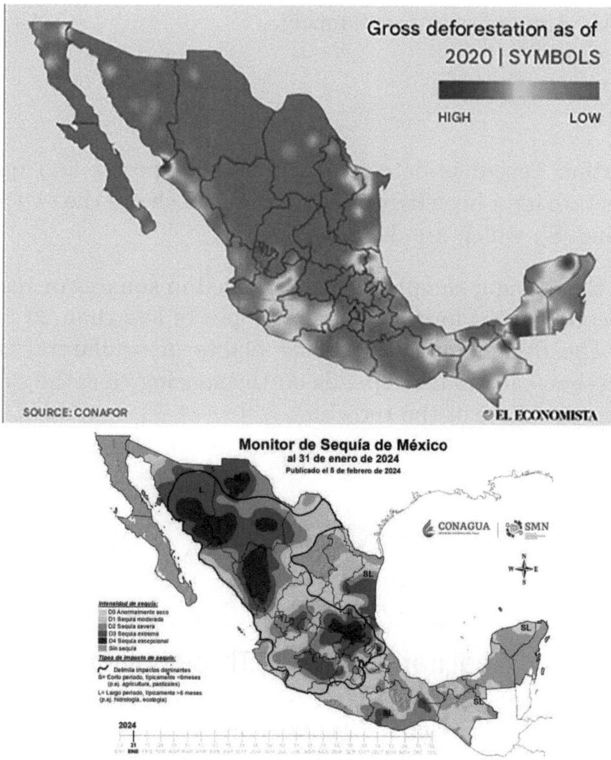

Fig. 1. A comparison of deforested regions and droughts in Mexico.

One of the challenges in reforestation projects is not only the selection of appropriate species and planting schedules, but also the spatial arrangement of plants within the reforestation site. When tree species are placed in close proximity, they often compete for limited resources such as sunlight, water, nutrients, and space, which can compromise the survival rate of the plantation.

According to the criteria established by the General Directorate of Environmental Impact and Risk [10], compensatory reforestation must achieve a minimum survival rate of 80% during the first year, remaining above 70% during the monitoring period. The resolutions indicate that if the minimum percentage allowed is lower, complementary activities such as plant replacement must be carried out.

Our model seeks to increase the survival rate and reduce the costs of replacing plants that die by minimizing competition in the plantation.

The steps to carry out reforestation are as follows.

1. Choose the site to be reforested
2. Identify the type of soil
3. Select the species to be used.
4. Determine the time of year for planting.
5. Site preparation.
6. Planting.
7. Maintenance

The plantation design is determined once the species and quantity to be planted in a hectare have been determined . Figure 2 shows the two most common types of planting [8], which are described below.

Real frame: In this design, the plants are arranged in squares or rectangles. This design is recommended for flat lands or slopes of less than 20

Three bolillo: The design involves placing plants in equilateral triangles. The distance between each plant depends on the spacing that the species requires as an adult, regardless of the terrain.

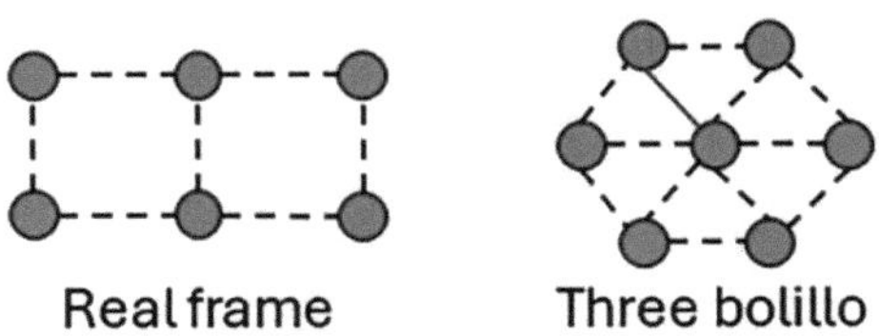

Fig. 2. Plantation design.

Currently, reforestation practices involve planting more trees than necessary in the reforestation area, anticipating natural mortality caused by inter-species and intra-species competition [7].

Competition indices and spatial parameters have been refined to better model growth dynamics in uneven-aged forests [4].

This research focuses on minimizing interspecific competition in reforestation areas by optimizing the spatial distribution of tree species. An initial approach using an exact mathematical model was implemented to identify optimal planting configurations based on species compatibility and competition factors. However, due to the model's computational limitations when addressing large-scale instances, a Genetic Algorithm (GA) was developed as an alternative metaheuristic solution capable of efficiently exploring complex solution spaces and generating feasible planting layouts for large reforestation areas.

2 Problem Description

Reforestation projects require careful planning to ensure the long-term survival and co-existence of planted species. One of the critical challenges during the planting stage is determining not only which species to plant, but also how to spatially distribute them to minimize competition for limited resources.

This behavior has been studied through individual-based models that show species with greater internal variability may have a competitive advantage [1]. Recent studies emphasize that local intraspecific competition is essential to explain spatial co-existence in vegetation models [2].

When forest species are in close proximity they tend to compete for various resources such as:

- Sunlight
- Water
- Space
- Nutrients.
- Aboveground and belowground space
- Pollinators
- Space for natural regeneration
- Mycorrhizal associations and beneficial microorganisms

Excessive interspecific competition can reduce growth rates, increase mortality, and ultimately lower the overall survival rate of the plantation.

Figure 3 shows the competition between species based on the node's position. Therefore, if the level of competition is not minimal, the plant at that node will either die or fail to develop optimally.

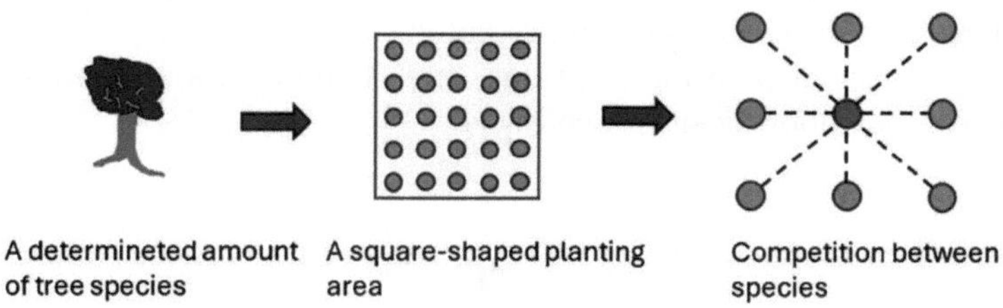

Fig. 3. Planting process.

Although operational planting manuals and field experience provide guidelines for species selection and general planting procedures [6], these guidelines often follow fixed patterns or traditional designs that do not fully account for complex interspecies interactions. As a result, the spatial arrangement of species may not be optimal, potentially leading to higher competition levels than necessary.

This work focuses on developing an optimization-based approach to design spatial planting layouts that minimize interspecific competition while fulfilling species-specific planting demands. The aim is to assign each planting site to a particular species in such a way that neighboring plants are compatible, reducing negative competitive effects and maximizing survival probabilities.

The problem is modeled as a spatial assignment problem, where the plantation area is represented as a grid of discrete planting sites. Each site must be assigned a single species, respecting the total planting demand for each species as well as the compatibility relationships between neighboring species. The level of competition between adjacent plants is quantified through species-specific competition coefficients, which capture the degree of interaction between any pair of species when located in adjacent positions.

Solving this problem requires finding a configuration that minimizes total competition across the plantation, ensuring that species coexist harmoniously and the survival rate is maximized. Recent models incorporating local intraspecific interactions have proven critical to understanding species coexistence [2].

In addition, it is important to note that the formulation of the problem and the experimental design follow the technical rules established by CONAFOR / USPAE for reforestation programs. These rules set minimum survival thresholds and define the proportion of species to be planted per hectare, as reflected in table 2. Therefore, the optimization approach proposed in this work is aligned with the official requirements for reforestation success in Mexico.

3 Problem Modeling and Solution Approach

The reforestation problem is modeled as a spatial optimization problem, where the objective is to minimize competition between different species while ensuring the planting demand for each species is satisfied. The plantation area is discretized into a set of seeding sites, represented as vertices in a graph $G = (V, A)$, where V is the set of planting positions, and A represents adjacency relationships between neighboring sites. See Fig. 4.

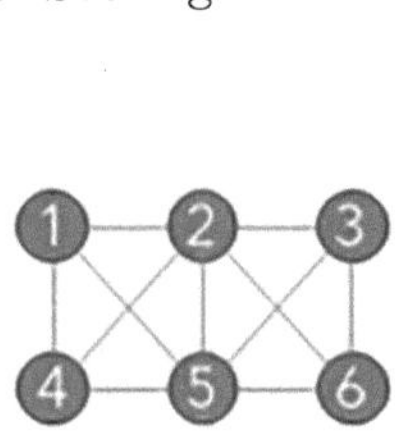

Fig. 4. Example of graph

Let P denote the set of species to be planted, with $o \in P$ and $p \in P$ representing species indices. Each vertex $i \in V$ can be assigned exactly one species p. The parameter DT indicates the total planting demand (number of plants per hectare), and d_o specifies the demand for each species o. The adjacency relationship between planting positions is captured by the parameter $w(i, j)$, which equals 1 if positions i and j are neighbors, and 0 otherwise. The parameter cop represents the competition factor between species o and p.

Binary decision variables x_{oi} are defined, where $x_{oi} = 1$ if species o is planted at position i, and 0 otherwise. The variable R_{ij} represents the competition level assigned to the arc (i, j), which depends on the combination of species planted at the adjacent positions.

Proficiency Level: Answers the question:

Is the plant o at position i and plant p at position j?

Table 1. Proficiency level.

X_{oi}	x_{pj}	Result
0	0	0
0	1	0
1	0	0
1	1	1

The mathematical model aims to minimize the total interspecies competition across the entire plantation (Eq. 1), formulated as:

$$\min z = \sum_{i=1}^{n} \sum_{j=1}^{n} R_{ij} \tag{1}$$

subject to:

$$(x_{oi} + x_{pj} - 1) \cdot w_{ij} \cdot c_{op} \leq R_{ij}, \quad i \in V, j \in V, o \in P, p \in P \tag{2}$$

$$\sum_{i=1}^{n} x_{oi} \geq d_o, \quad \forall o \in P \tag{3}$$

$$\sum_{o=1}^{m} x_{oi} = 1, \, \forall i \in V \tag{4}$$

$$\sum_{i=1}^{n} \sum_{o=1}^{n} x_{oi} = DT \tag{5}$$

$$x_{oi} = \{0, 1\} \tag{6}$$

$$R_{i,j} \geq 0 \tag{7}$$

The first constraint (Eq. 2) calculates the competition value R_{ij} between neighboring species according to their compatibility levels, to this end, the adjacency matrix $w_{i,j}$ is used together with Table 1, which serves as a truth table. The second constraint (Eq. 3) ensures that the demand for each species is satisfied. The third (Eq. 4) and fourth constraints (Eq. 5) ensure that exactly one species is assigned to each planting position, and that the total planting demand is fulfilled, respectively. Binary restrictions (Eq. 6 and 7) are applied to the assignment variables x_{oi}, while competition variables R_{ij} are non-negative.

4 Results

The work is carried out according to the needs of USPAE-CONAFOR, which sets technical requirements for reforestation success [9] within a reforestation area where 625 individuals from ten different species must be planted per hectare. The Table 2 shows the percentage of each species that will be planted in relation to the total required.

Table 2. Percentage of each species that will be planted

Species	Percentage of plants per hectare
1	13.17
2	6.3
3	29.96
4	7.44
5	4
6	6.3
7	6.3
8	5.73
9	9.73
10	11.07
Total	**100**

The experiment was conducted on a computer with the following specifications:

- Model: Latitude 5410
- Processor: Intel(R) Core(TM) i5-10310U CPU @ 1.70GHz 2.21GHz
- RAM: 16.0 GB (15.6 GB usable)
- System type: 64-bit operating system, x64 processor
- Operating system: Windows 10 Enterprise Version 22H2
- CBC Solver in PULP 2.9.0 in Python

A set of instances of different sizes was created to test the performance of the mathematical model. The instances were designed as square sections of planting areas, with the goal of representing one hectare, since this is the unit of measurement used by CONAFOR in plantation design [6,8]. The idea behind using smaller square sections is that, when combined, they reproduce the full hectare; for example, 25 sections of 25 plants each. The computing time was limited to three hours per instance.

The Table 3 shows the results of the experiment.

Table 3. Results of the experiment

Nodes	Objective	Time	GAP
25	72.3	10800	9.92
49	169.6	10800	40.71
64	223.8	10800	62.12
100	377.7	10800	174.22
144	555.2	10800	1331.56
169	669.8	10800	inf
225	899.9	10800	inf
289	1175.1	10800	inf
324	1355.7	10800	inf
361	-	10800	-
400	-	10800	-
625	-	10800	-

The initial attempt to solve the problem relied on a mathematical optimization model designed to minimize inter-species competition by determining the optimal spatial arrangement of tree species within the plantation site. However, as the results table shows, the obtained solution was limited in scalability and flexibility. The model struggled to provide feasible solutions as the number of species and spatial constraints increased, causing computational bottlenecks and suboptimal configurations.

Due to these limitations, a genetic algorithm (GA) was adopted as an alternative solution method. GA is well-suited for complex, multi-variable, nonlinear optimization problems like this one because it explores a broader solution space and is less likely to become trapped in a local optimum.

The choice of Genetic Algorithm is justified by its proven suitability for large-scale combinatorial and forestry planning problems, as reported in previous studies [3]. Although other metaheuristics could be considered, the GA offers a balance between solution quality and computational efficiency, making it an ideal starting point for the development of scalable reforestation planning tools.

4.1 Genetic Algorithm Configuration

To address the complexity of species allocation in the reforestation grid and to minimize inter-species competition in adjacent planting spaces, a Genetic Algorithm (GA) was implemented with the following configuration:

- **Chromosome type:** numérico entero, donde cada número representa una especie y cada gen es un nodo que representa un punto de siembra.
- **Chromosome length:** Depends on the total number of plants to be assigned, denoted as L
- **Initialization criterion:** Random initialization, respecting the occurrence probability of each species
- **Stopping criterion:** $15 \times L$ generations
- **Fitness function:** Maximize $\max(R_{ij})$, es decir, se basa en la función objetivo del modelo matemático.
- **Selection method:** Roulette wheel selection
- **Population size:** $20 \times \sqrt{L}$
- **Crossover probability:** 1.0
- **Number of crossover points:** 3
- **Crossover location:** Random
- **Mutation probability:** 0.1 per gene replacement
- **Replacement criterion:** The best individual is preserved (elitism)
- **Stopping criterion:** 1000 iterations.

The initial solutions and the offspring generated after the mutation process satisfy the problem constraints, ensuring that all solutions are feasible. Figure 5 illustrates how the set of nodes is represented as a chromosome and shows an example solution for the given case. It can be observed that each gene represents a planting node in the reforestation area.

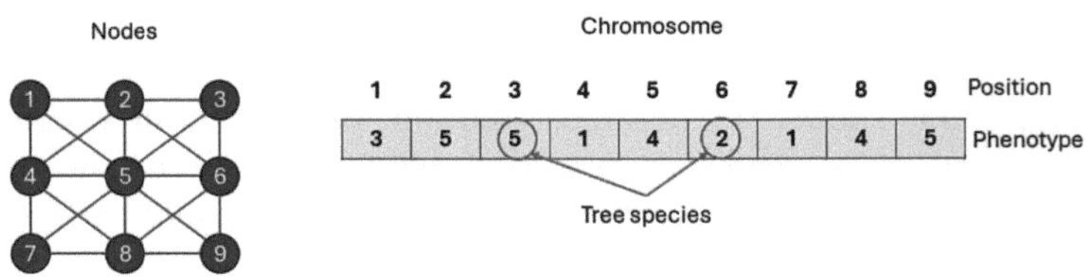

Fig. 5. Chromosome representation proposed for the problem.

The test instances were created based on the species distribution percentages defined by CONAFOR (see Table 2) and using grids of various sizes, from 25 to 625 nodes. Each experiment was executed ten times with independent random seeds, and the reported values correspond to the average across the best results obtained from the independent runs. The GA was implemented in Python, and the random initialisation respected the official proportions of each species. These

Table 4. Comparative results between Pulp solver and Genetic Algorithm

Nodes	Pulp Objective	Gap	GA Objective	Time (s)	Difference %
25	72.3	9.92	70.03	2.44	−9.405255878
49	169.6	40.71	163.17	5.21	−3.793238994
64	223.8	62.12	221.62	6.03	−0.975573429
100	377.7	174.22	368.40	10.59	−2.462271644
144	555.2	1331.56	551.55	19.30	−0.657420749
169	669.8	inf	657.32	24.40	−1.86374042
225	899.9	inf	900.23	38.76	0.037041153
289	1175.1	inf	1128.90	61.58	−3.931580291
324	1355.7	inf	1336.20	83.10	−1.438371321
361			1498.35	117.85	
400			1670.15	131.05	
625			2676.20	349.44	

details ensure reproducibility and enable replication of the results by following the same configuration.

An experimental design was performed with 10 independent runs for each problem size to evaluate the robustness and consistency of the algorithm.

Table 4 presents the comparative results between the exact mathematical model (solved with Pulp) and the Genetic Algorithm. The "objective" columns represent the best solution found by each method. The "Gap" column reflects the deviation of the Pulp solver from the optimal solution or reports "inf" when only a feasible solution was obtained within the established stopping time. The "Difference" column indicates the absolute difference between the objective value obtained by the Genetic Algorithm and the one obtained by Pulp for each instance size. The average computational time used by the GA ranges from 0.654% to 3.236% of the total time required by Pulp. Overall, the Genetic Algorithm outperforms the mathematical model in both the number of solved cases and the quality of the solutions, providing better results in almost all instances, as reflected in the negative difference values.

The results show that while the exact solver experiences significant difficulties in solving larger instances (with several cases reporting infinite gaps), the Genetic Algorithm is able to consistently provide feasible solutions within reasonable computation times, even for large problem sizes,

4.2 Analysis and Discussion of Results

The results presented in Table 4 allow for a comprehensive comparison between the exact mathematical approach (Pulp solver) and the Genetic Algorithm (GA). Several important observations can be drawn:

First, as problem size increases (i.e., number of nodes), the Pulp solver begins to face significant computational challenges. For smaller instances (up to 100 nodes), Pulp is capable of finding solutions, although the reported gaps suggest that even for these instances, optimality is not always guaranteed. As the number of nodes increases beyond 144, the solver is unable to compute feasible solutions within the allowed computational limits, leading to infinite gap values.

In contrast, the Genetic Algorithm demonstrates strong robustness and scalability. For all problem sizes, including large instances with 400 and 625 nodes, the GA consistently provides feasible solutions within reasonable computation times. While some deviations from the Pulp objective values are observed, the differences remain within acceptable ranges for heuristic methods, particularly considering the scale of the problem and the computational effort required.

The "Difference" column illustrates that the GA often finds solutions close to or even better than those obtained by the Pulp solver in some cases, especially where the Pulp solver struggles or fails to converge. This behavior highlights the GA's capability to effectively explore the solution space and escape local optima that may trap exact methods under strict time limits.

Overall, the Genetic Algorithm proves to be a suitable and scalable alternative for solving large-scale instances of this species allocation problem in reforestation scenarios, where exact methods become impractical due to computational intractability.

5 Conclusions

This work addressed the problem of optimizing species allocation in reforestation areas with the goal of minimizing inter-species competition and improving plantation survival rates. An exact mathematical programming model was first formulated to represent species compatibility and spatial interactions; however, it demonstrated computational infeasibility as problem size increased. The Pulp solver was unable to generate feasible solutions for large instances within the allocated time limits.

To overcome these limitations, a Genetic Algorithm was implemented. The GA consistently produced feasible and competitive solutions across all problem sizes, including large-scale reforestation scenarios involving hundreds of planting positions and multiple species. The evolutionary approach allowed the algorithm to explore diverse solution configurations, handle multiple constraints simultaneously, and avoid local optima that typically challenge exact methods.

The results demonstrate that Genetic Algorithms are a practical, scalable, and effective alternative for real-world reforestation planning problems where exact optimization models become computationally intractable. Future research may focus on hybridizing metaheuristics with exact methods, incorporating additional ecological objectives, or extending the model to address multi-period planning and dynamic environmental factors.

In summary, this work contributes both a rigorous mathematical model that formally defines the reforestation allocation problem and a Genetic Algorithm that ensures scalability in large instances. The mathematical model itself provides a systematic way to reduce the competition among plants allocated within a reforestation area. This combination provides theoretical soundness and practical efficiency, offering robust solutions for real-world reforestation planning. Furthermore, the Genetic Algorithm offers a good balance between solution quality and runtime efficiency, making it a suitable first approach, while leaving the door open to the exploration of other metaheuristics in future research.

References

1. Uchmański, J.: Can a more variable species win interspecific competition? Acta. Biotheor. **69**(4), 591–628 (2021). https://doi.org/10.1007/s10441-021-09408-0
2. Eigentler, L.: Intraspecific competition in models for vegetation patterns: decrease in resilience to aridity and facilitation of species coexistence. arXiv preprint arXiv:2002.05677v2 (2020). https://arxiv.org/abs/2002.05677v2
3. Castro, I., Salas-González, R., Fidalgo, B., Farinha, J.T., Mendes, M.: Optimising forest management using multi-objective genetic algorithms. Sustainability **16**(23), 10655 (2024). https://doi.org/10.3390/su162310655
4. Kobal, M., Levanič, T.: Optimizing competitor definitions for the sustainable management of dominant silver fir trees in uneven-aged mixed forests. For. Ecosyst. **14**, 100346 (2025). https://doi.org/10.1016/j.fecs.2025.100346
5. FAO: Global forest resources assessment 2020 – key findings. Food and Agriculture Organization of the United Nations (2020)
6. CONAFOR: Manual para el establecimiento y mantenimiento de plantaciones forestales comerciales. Comisión Nacional Forestal (2020). https://www.gob.mx/conafor
7. Rodríguez, J.A., López, M.: Principios de silvicultura aplicada. Ediciones Forestales, México (2018)
8. Comisión Nacional Forestal (CONAFOR): Prácticas de reforestación. Manual básico. Primera edición. Gerencia de Reforestación, Coordinación General de Conservación y Restauración. CONAFOR, Zapopan, Jalisco, México (2010)
9. CONAFOR: Ficha técnica CD003110. Criterios técnicos de reforestación 2010. Comisión Nacional Forestal, Dirección General Adjunta de Producción y Productividad Forestal, México (2010)
10. Diario Oficial de la Federación: Reglas de operación del programa apoyos para el desarrollo forestal sustentable. México (2024)

Tracking a Small Oil Pan with xArm Using RGB-D Data and Deep Pose Estimation

Rubén de Jesús Hilario Cruz(✉), Juan José Jaúregui Barba, Gustavo De los Ríos Alatorre, and Luis Alberto Muñoz Ubando

Facultad de Ingeniería y Ciencias, Robótica y Sistemas Digitales, Instituto Tecnológico y de Estudios Superiores de Monterrey, Monterrey, Nuevo León, Mexico
{A00835860,A00836722,A01410922,amunoz}@tec.mx

Abstract. This paper presents a real-time system for object tracking and pose estimation of an industrial part—a small oil pan—using an xArm robotic manipulator. The system integrates an RGB-D sensor (Azure Kinect) within the Robot Operating System 2 (ROS2) Humble framework to acquire synchronized color and depth data. A You Only Look Once (YOLOv8) model performs semantic segmentation, enabling point cloud extraction and filtering. Coarse pose estimation is achieved using RANSAC, followed by refinement through Wunsch registration. The resulting transformation informs the robot's inverse kinematics to align its end-effector with the target. Experimental results in controlled settings validate the system's robustness and its potential for industrial automation.

Keywords: Object tracking · Pose estimation · RGB-D camera · xArm · ROS2 · YOLO · Point cloud registration · Inverse kinematics

1 Introduction

Industrial robotic arms are increasingly used for automation tasks involving object manipulation, part inspection, and assembly. These tasks demand precise perception and control strategies to enable robots to detect, localize, and interact with objects in dynamic environments. In this work, we present a prototype system that allows an xArm robot to track and follow an industrial part—a small oil pan—in real time using computer vision and point cloud processing.

Our approach relies on an RGB-D sensor (Azure Kinect) that provides synchronized color and depth data. The system is implemented using ROS2 Humble, allowing for modular and scalable development. The target object is localized and segmented in the RGB stream using a YOLO-based deep learning model, this segmentation mask is applied to the corresponding depth image to extract a clean 3D point cloud representing only the object.

To estimate the object's pose, we align the observed point cloud with a scaled CAD model of the oil pan. A coarse alignment is first performed using

L. Martínez-Villaseñor et al. (Eds.): MICAI 2025, CCIS 2712, pp. 28–36, 2025.
https://doi.org/10.1007/978-3-032-08704-1_3

RANSAC, followed by fine pose correction using the Wunsch algorithm. This yields a transformation matrix defining the object's pose relative to the camera frame.

Finally, this transformation is used to compute the required joint angles for the xArm using inverse kinematics, enabling the robot to align its end-effector with the object. The system continuously adjusts the robot's configuration to keep the object both centered in the camera view and within a predefined operational range, ensuring optimal visibility for accurate pose estimation.

This paper is organized as follows: Sect. 2 describes the materials and methods used, including the hardware setup and software architecture. Section 3 details the pose estimation and registration process. Section 4 explains the control and tracking strategy. Section 5 presents preliminary experimental results. Section 6 outlines future work, and Sect. 7 concludes the paper.

2 Related Work

Pose estimation and object tracking using RGB-D data have been widely explored in recent years due to their importance in robotics, augmented reality, and automation. Classical methods for pose estimation include Iterative Closest Point (ICP) and its robust variants such as Random Sample Consensus (RANSAC)-based alignment [1]. These techniques enable coarse alignment between a scene point cloud and a known object model. However, for accurate and reliable registration, finer methods such as the Wunsch algorithm [2] are often used to refine the alignment after initial pose estimation.

Deep learning approaches such as YOLO have shown remarkable performance in real-time object detection and segmentation [3]. These models are particularly useful when the target objects vary in lighting or orientation, as is common in industrial environments. The combination of segmentation with depth information enables the extraction of clean object point clouds for accurate pose matching.

In robotic manipulation, the integration of perception with control is essential for interactive tasks. Systems that leverage inverse kinematics to compute motion based on observed pose estimation, such as MoveIt-based planners [4], have been used in dynamic scenarios to allow robots to follow or reach moving objects. In this work, we build upon these foundations and integrate RGB-D perception, deep learning segmentation, point cloud registration, and inverse kinematics to track and follow an industrial part using an xArm robotic arm.

3 Materials and Methods

The system was developed using an xArm robotic manipulator and an Azure Kinect sensor, integrated through ROS2 Humble middleware. The following subsections describe the hardware configuration, software architecture, and the data processing pipeline.

3.1 Hardware Setup

- **xArm 6 DOF Robot:** Used to follow and align with the detected object based on pose estimation results. It is controlled via ROS2 interfaces.
- **Azure Kinect RGB-D Camera:** Provides synchronized RGB and depth frames at approximately 30 FPS. Positioned statically to capture the workspace from above.
- **Computer:** Equipped with an NVIDIA GPU for running YOLO inference and point cloud processing.

3.2 Software Framework

All system components were implemented as modular ROS2 Humble nodes, each responsible for a specific stage of the processing pipeline.

- **YOLOv8 Segmentation Node:** A pretrained custom YOLOv8 model was used to detect and segment the small oil pan in RGB frames. The model was trained on a labeled dataset specific to the target object.
- **Depth Masking Node:** Using the binary mask from YOLO, the depth frame is masked to isolate the object in 3D.
- **Point Cloud Generation Node:** The masked depth is converted to a 3D point cloud using camera intrinsics and Open3D tools. Points outside a predefined depth threshold are discarded.
- **Model Matching Node:** "A scaled CAD-based mesh model of the oil pan is loaded and scaled. First, a rough alignment is computed using RANSAC. Then, the pose is refined using the Wunsch algorithm to minimize residual errors.
- **Pose-to-Transform Node:** The result of the registration is a 4 × 4 transformation matrix (rotation and translation) that aligns the model with the observed point cloud.
- **IK Controller Node:** This transformation is translated into joint angles using inverse kinematics. The arm is commanded to move to a position aligned with the object, maintaining a predefined safe distance.
- **Tracking Feedback Node:** Continuously checks if the object remains in the center region of the camera view. If drift is detected, pose estimation and re-alignment are triggered.

3.3 Object-Centered Tracking Strategy

To ensure optimal pose estimation, the object is kept centered in the field of view. The camera's image is divided into three horizontal zones. If the detected object moves out of the central zone, the robot readjusts its position via small corrections to return the object to the optimal visual zone. This strategy improves pose estimation accuracy by maximizing object visibility and minimizing occlusion.

4 Pose Estimation and Registration

Accurate pose estimation of the tracked object is essential for enabling the xArm to follow and interact with it. In our system, the pose estimation pipeline consists of five main stages: RGB-D segmentation, point cloud filtering, coarse alignment via RANSAC, fine alignment with Wunsch registration, and final pose transformation computation.

In the context of this work, the term *pose estimation pipeline* refers to the entire process, from image segmentation to the final extraction of the object's transformation matrix. Within this pipeline, the *registration stage* specifically refers to the geometric alignment of point clouds using RANSAC and Wunsch algorithms.

4.1 Object Segmentation and Depth Filtering

The pipeline begins by processing the RGB image using a custom YOLOv8 model trained to detect the target object—a small oil pan. Upon detection, a segmentation mask is produced and applied to both the RGB and depth images. Using the depth image and the corresponding mask, a filtered depth map is extracted containing only the pixels corresponding to the segmented object.

This filtered depth data is then transformed into a 3D point cloud by projecting the valid depth pixels using the known camera intrinsic matrix. Points that fall outside a predefined valid depth range (typically 0.3 to 1.2 m) are discarded to remove noise and background clutter (Figs. 1 and 3).

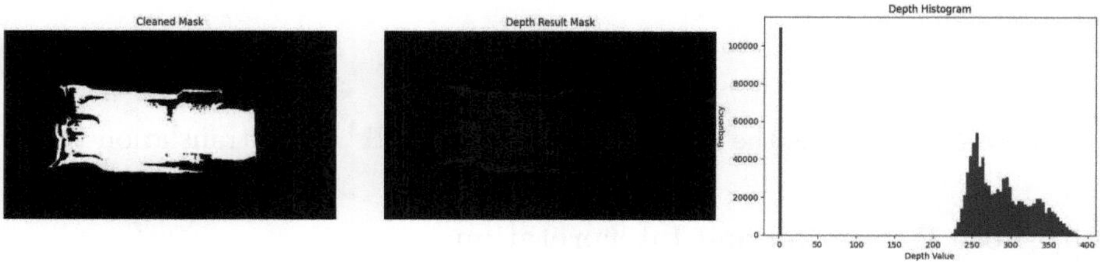

Fig. 1. Segmentation Pipeline in Depth Camera.

4.2 Point Cloud Preprocessing

The segmented point cloud is downsampled using a voxel grid filter to reduce computational cost and mitigate redundancy. Normals are estimated for the point cloud, and a centroid is computed to center the data. This preprocessed point cloud represents the observed view of the oil pan.

Concurrently, a 3D mesh model of the oil pan is loaded from a CAD file and converted into a point cloud. The CAD model undergoes identical preprocessing and is appropriately scaled to match real-world dimensions.

4.3 Coarse Alignment with RANSAC

The initial alignment between the observed and model point clouds is performed using a RANSAC-based registration algorithm [1]. This method samples random point correspondences between the two clouds and selects the transformation that yields the highest number of inliers under a given threshold. The result is a rough estimate of the object's pose relative to the camera.

RANSAC is particularly useful for handling noise and partial views of the object, especially when the point cloud from the depth sensor includes missing or corrupted regions.

4.4 Fine Alignment Using Wunsch Registration

To refine the initial transformation and achieve a more accurate pose estimation, the Wunsch algorithm [?] is applied. This algorithm minimizes the alignment error between corresponding points using a combination of geometric and iterative optimization techniques.

Unlike standard Iterative Closest Point (ICP), which may converge to local minima, the Wunsch method incorporates confidence weighting and a more robust correspondence association strategy. The output is a refined 4×4 transformation matrix $T_{cam \rightarrow obj}$ that defines the pose of the object in the camera frame, as shown in Eq. 1:

$$T_{cam \rightarrow obj} = \begin{bmatrix} R & t \\ 0 & 1 \end{bmatrix} \tag{1}$$

where $R \in SO(3)$ is the rotation matrix and $t \in \mathbb{R}^3$ is the translation vector.

4.5 Pose Extraction and Interpretation

The final pose is extracted from the transformation matrix by decomposing it into its rotational and translational components. Specifically, the rotation matrix $R \in SO(3)$ and the translation vector $t \in \mathbb{R}^3$ are obtained as expressed in Eq. 2:

$$T_{cam \rightarrow obj} = \begin{bmatrix} R & t \end{bmatrix} \tag{2}$$

This pose information is published as a Robot Operating System 2 (ROS2) transform, allowing downstream nodes to use it for control and visualization.

An example of the aligned point clouds and the overlaid transformed model is shown in Fig. 2. In most cases, the average alignment error after refinement was below 5 mm, which is sufficient for manipulation tasks that require relative positioning rather than precision grasping.

To ensure temporal consistency, pose estimation is periodically triggered (every three frames), with a validation module assessing continuity against the last known pose. If a large discontinuity is detected, typically due to misdetection or occlusion the system reverts to the last known good pose and re-initiates the detection-tracking cycle.

This hybrid approach, combining segmentation with geometric registration and temporal filtering, ensures both robustness and accuracy in real-time operation.

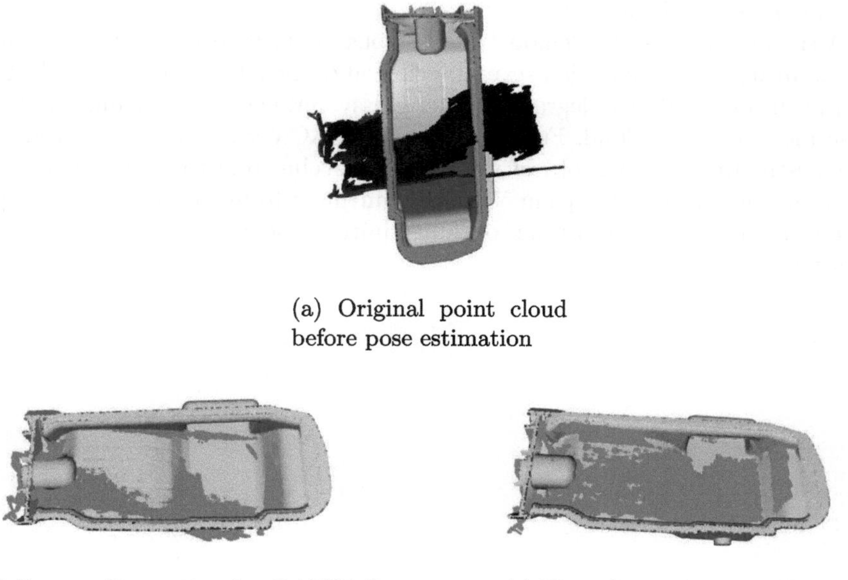

(a) Original point cloud before pose estimation

(b) Coarse alignment using RANSAC

(c) Fine alignment using Wunsch

Fig. 2. Visualization of the pose estimation process. (a) shows the original segmented point cloud before alignment; (b) is the result of RANSAC-based coarse pose estimation; (c) shows the refined pose after applying Wunsch registration.

5 Results and Discussion

The proposed system was implemented as a ROS2-based prototype and tested in controlled indoor environments. Given the early development stage, most evaluations were performed in simulation and within limited physical setups involving a static table. The primary goal was to validate the feasibility and integration of the full tracking and control pipeline.

5.1 Preliminary Performance Evaluation

The object detection model (YOLOv8) achieved an average inference time of approximately 18 ms per frame on a NVIDIA QUADRO P620 GPU, allowing for real-time operation. Detection accuracy on the small oil pan exceeded 95% under controlled conditions. Depth segmentation and point cloud extraction took approximately 50 ms, and the RANSAC + Wunsch registration pipeline required about 120–150 ms per cycle depending on scene complexity.

The entire perception pipeline operated at approximately 5 Hz, which was sufficient to track a slowly moving object in real-time. The xArm was able to respond to the estimated pose updates and adjust its joints accordingly to maintain alignment with the object.

Although the system demonstrated strong performance under ideal conditions, during experimentation several technical challenges emerged. Notably, the depth sensing reliability degraded under glossy surfaces, introducing significant noise into the point cloud. Furthermore, RANSAC occasionally produced poor initial estimates when the object was partially occluded or tilted at steep angles, which prevented the subsequent Wunsch refinement from converging. These limitations highlight the importance of robust initial pose priors and adaptive depth filtering.

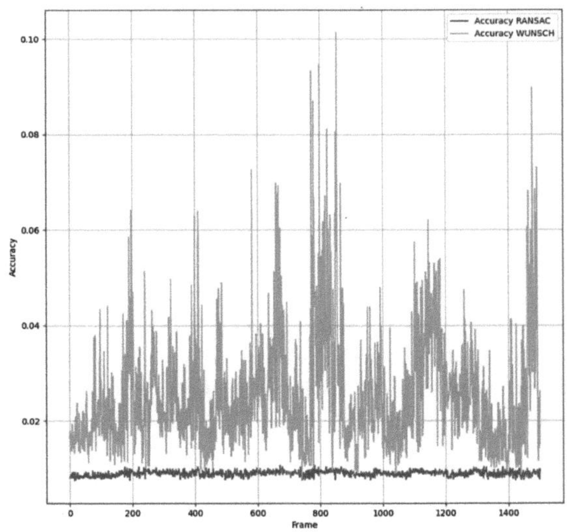

Fig. 3. Comparison between RANSAC and Wunsch alignment.

Additionally, the lack of end-to-end real-world testing in complex environments (e.g., a cluttered industrial workspace) limits the generalizability of these results. Nonetheless, the system serves as a functional prototype that demonstrates the viability of integrating RGB-D sensing, segmentation, pose registration, and robotic control in ROS2.

6 Future Work

Several improvements and extensions are considered as a future development phase of this project:

- **Multi-Object Tracking:** Include the capability to track multiple object instances and distinguish between different parts in a scene.
- **Improved Depth Filtering:** Enhanced denoising techniques and multi-view fusion will be explored to improve the quality of the point cloud, especially in reflective or low-light settings.
- **Simultaneous Localization and Mapping (SLAM) Integration:** Integration of RTAB-Map or ORB-SLAM3 is planned to enable dynamic scene understanding and mobile manipulation. These SLAM systems will be used to maintain a global map and localize both the camera and the object within it, enabling tracking beyond static viewpoints.
- **Feedback-Controlled Grasping:** While the current implementation only aligns the end-effector with the object, future work will include autonomous grasp planning and manipulation using pose feedback.
- **Benchmarking and Evaluation:** A standardized set of benchmarks will be defined to evaluate tracking accuracy, pose estimation error, and control responsiveness across a variety of scenarios.
- **Learning-Based Registration:** Future iterations may incorporate deep learning approaches such as PoseCNN or DenseFusion to improve robustness under occlusions and enable end-to-end learning of the registration process.

These directions aim to transition the system from a lab-scale demonstration to a deployable robotic solution for dynamic object tracking in industrial or academic settings.

7 Conclusion

In this paper, we presented a real-time object tracking system that enables an xArm robotic manipulator to follow a small industrial part using RGB-D data and pose estimation. The system integrates deep learning-based segmentation (YOLO), 3D point cloud filtering, RANSAC and Wunsch-based registration, and inverse kinematics control within a ROS2 framework.

Despite being in a prototype stage, the system demonstrated robust detection and tracking capabilities in structured environments. Preliminary results show the feasibility of using the proposed pipeline to align a robotic arm with a moving or repositioned object in real time.

While the system currently operates under controlled conditions, future work will address generalization, scalability, and the integration of autonomous mobility and grasping capabilities. This research serves as a foundation for more complex perception-guided manipulation systems applicable in industrial automation and intelligent robotics.

References

1. Rusu, R.B., Cousins, S.: 3D is here: Point Cloud Library (PCL). In: Proceedings of the IEEE International Conference on Robotics and Automation (ICRA), pp. 1–4. IEEE (2011). https://doi.org/10.1109/ICRA.2011.5980567
2. Wunsch, P., Hirzinger, G.: Registration of CAD-models to images by iterative inverse perspective matching. In: Proceedings of the 13th International Conference on Pattern Recognition (ICPR), pp. 78–83. IEEE Computer Society (1996). https://doi.org/10.1109/ICPR.1996.545995
3. Liu, C., Tao, Y., Liang, J., Li, K., Chen, Y.: Object detection based on YOLO network. In: Proceedings of the 2018 IEEE 4th Information Technology and Mechatronics Engineering Conference (ITOEC), Chongqing, China, pp. 799–803. IEEE (2018). https://doi.org/10.1109/ITOEC.2018.8740604
4. Sucan, I.A., Chitta, S.: MoveIt! motion planning framework. In: ICRA Workshop on Open Source Software. IEEE (2013). http://moveit.ros.org

Human-Friendly Explanation Model Based on the Aristotelian Practical Syllogism for Reinforcement Learning Agents in Urban Intelligent Design

Daniel Adrián Contreras Olivas(✉), Lourdes Martinez-Villaseñor, and Alan Crespo Murillo

Universidad Panamericana, Augusto Rodin 498, Insurgentes Mixcoac, Benito Juárez, 03920 Ciudad de México, CDMX, Mexico
dcontreraso@up.edu.mx

Abstract. This paper introduces a novel explanation model for reinforcement learning agents, grounded in Aristotle's practical syllogism, with the goal of enhancing human-friendly explanations (HFEs) in urban intelligent design. By aligning the internal processes of a Q-learning agent with Aristotelian categories such as *telos*, *phronēsis*, and *boulesis*, the model enables the interpretation of agent behavior as a form of ethically structured practical reasoning. The selected case study focuses on an urban planning agent designed to optimize service accessibility and spatial coherence in real city environments. Through this alignment, the agent's policy learning, state-action evaluation, and reward optimization are made intelligible to human users in terms of goals, normative principles, perception, deliberation, and action. Evaluated using the Human-Friendly Explanations (HFE) checklist, the model exhibits strengths in interpretability, comprehensibility, and ethical relevance, while identifying areas for improvement such as contrastive reasoning, personalization, and regulatory compliance. This work offers a conceptual and methodological foundation for integrating philosophical models into Explainable Reinforcement Learning (XRL), facilitating transparent, ethical, and user-aligned AI systems. Future directions include empirical validation, interactive implementation, and domain-specific adaptation across sociotechnical contexts.

Keywords: Reinforcement Learning · Explainable AI · Q-learning · Human-Friendly Explanations · Aristotle · Practical Syllogism · Urban Planning · Explainable Reinforcement Learning

1 Introduction

1.1 Reinforcement Learning

Reinforcement learning is a computational methodology in which an agent interacts with an environment, learns by evaluating its actions accordingly to a reward

L. Martínez-Villaseñor et al. (Eds.): MICAI 2025, CCIS 2712, pp. 37–54, 2025.
https://doi.org/10.1007/978-3-032-08704-1_4

function, updates its knowledge in a learning model, and converges to strategy [11,12]. The agent's goal is to achieve an optimal policy that maximizes its reward; To achieve this, the agent is trained in two phases: the exploration phase and the exploration phase [13,26,28].

The exploration-explotation paradigm involves a trade-off between exploring new actions with the aim of discovering strategies that maximize reward or exploting the best policy gotten at the moment [2,26,27].

Q-learning is a model-free reinforcement learning algorithm that enables an agent to learn how to act optimally by using a Q table (a learning model in which the future expected reward for each states and actions is saved [2,27]. Thanks to the Q-table, this model offers interpretability and escalation [13,26].

A Q-learning agent trains by trial and error, each step the agent updates the future expected reward by using the Bellman equation given by [26]:

$$Q(S_t, A_t) \leftarrow Q(S_t, A_t) + \alpha\big[R_{t+1} + \gamma \max_a Q(S_{t+1}, a) - Q(S_t, A_t)\big] \tag{1}$$

The Bellman equation uses three parameters: γ, (discount factor) which controls the relative importance of future rewards; α, (learning rate) which determines the extent to which new information overrides previous estimates; and ϵ, which regulates the exploration rate in the ϵ-greedy policy [26].

1.2 RL Applied to Urbanism

Urbanism involves numerous interdependent factors and there are no known optimal solutions [5,6,9]. For this reason, RL offers promising opportunities to address complex urban challenges such as city planning and traffic management, as demonstrated in the literature [15,17,22,27]. For example, H'sain and Crespo et al. have developed reinforcement learning agents capable of designing urban layouts based on different objectives. The agents of H'sain aim to maximize the number of buildings regardless of geographical constraints, while the agents of Crespo are designed to ensure that all essential services are accessible within a walking distance of n minutes [15,22].

In this paper, Aristotle's practical syllogism is used to explain the decision-making process of the Q learning agent developed by Crespo et al. [22]. This agent was selected due to its applicability to real-world urban layouts and its interpretability. Specifically, it was chosen because it was applied to improve the layout of the city of Rome and because its pseudocode offers a transparent representation of its internal logic.

The agent's environment receives a predefined city layout (containing elements such as roads, streets, and buildings that cannot be removed). Then, the agent starts exploring the city layout; first, the agent visits all the empty states (each cell in the grid is a state) and chooses an action (an action is to place a building such as streets, residences or services). After visiting all empty states, the agent evaluates the final reward of the city; this steps are called as an *episode*.

The city's reward is calculated by summing up the individual reward of each residence. The reward of each residence is calculated by summing the reward of each service multiplied by a bonus for attaining a proper amount of services. The reward of each service is calculated by the compatibility that service with its neighbooring buidlings.

After calculating the city's reward, the agent updates its Q table by using the Eq. 1. Every time the agent builds a city, its epsilon decreases and tends to explote the best obtained policy. Retraining is necessary to explore better policies, this retraining process is managed by *series*, which *pauses* and increases epsilon. Further explanation in [22].

Implementing an explanation model into an urbanism agent opens the door not only to real-world applications but also to making its decisions understandable to users. This creates opportunities to improve the availability of services, proximity and walkability in cities; these factors are essential to achieve livability [9,16,25].

1.3 Explainable AI, Explainable Reinforcement Learning and Explanations Models

Explainable AI (XAI) consists of a set of methods to explain the behavior decision making process of complex models to humans; as a consequence, opaque systems turn into understandable systems for users [14,20]. The goal of XAI is to provide transparent and trustworthy explanations of their actions to users; XAI considers that AI models should not only have high accuracy and well-predictions, but also a comprehensive and communicative explanation to stakeholders. As a consequence, XAI improves and facilitates the usability of the model in solving real-world problems [4].

XAI frameworks commonly differentiate between two main approaches: models that are inherently interpretable, such as decision trees and linear regressions, and post hoc explanation methods designed for opaque black-box models, such as convolutional neural networks or ensemble algorithms [10]. Post hoc techniques include feature attribution methods (e.g. SHAP [19], LIME [23]), counterfactual explanations, example-based reasoning, and saliency maps. These approaches seek to address critical questions such as 'Why did the model produce this output?' or 'What changes in input would alter the prediction?' [3,8,21].

Explainable Reinforcement Learning (XRL) is a subfield of XAI that contains its own challenges. This field focuses on explaining the policies, behavior, and decision making process of the RL agents. RL agents tend to use complex learning models such as neuronal networks, which is why XRL uses specific questions to explain the behavior of the agents. Some of these questions include: "Why the agent chose a specific action in a given state?", "What long-term strategy or policy the agent has learned?", "How a particular sequence of actions led to an observed outcome?", and "What would happen under alternative scenarios (counterfactuals)?" [1,3].

An explanation model is a structured system that addresses explaining the behavior of an agent and its decision-making process. Create human-friendly explanations that answer questions such as *why?* and *why not?* and allow users to trace decision rationales [3,18].

AI integration into decision-making environments has increased recently; this brings up new problems about its transparency and users trust. Its important to develop an explanation model that ensure interpretability, especially in domains such as health, laws, and urbanism. This study develops and proposes an explanation model that, by using Aristotle's practical syllogism, explains deeply the decision rationales of reinforcement learning agents. The aim is to improve the applicability of RL agents and to improve the user comprehension of the agent decision [24].

2 Methodology

2.1 Aristotle's Practical Syllogism

The practical syllogism constitutes a rational structure proper to the active life of the human being, in which a universal normative principle (**καθόλου**), formulated as an expression of the good or of the desired end, converges with a particular perception (**καθ' ἕκαστον**) that pertains to the concrete circumstances in which the agent finds himself. This conjunction results in an inference whose conclusion is not a theoretical or propositional judgment, but rather an action effectively carried out (**πρᾶξις**). The practical syllogism thus manifests as an operational synthesis between deliberative judgment and desiderative tendency, not as a purely abstract or detached piece of reasoning, but as a living articulation of thought in action.

The function of the practical syllogism is made possible by the mediation of rationally shaped desire (**βούλησις**) and by the guidance of **φρόνησις** , the intellectual virtue of praxis. Far from being reducible to a formal logical structure, this reasoning process belongs to the domain of practical rationality (**λογισμὸς πρακτικός**), whose truth does not reside in propositional correctness but in the congruence between moral judgment and enacted behavior. Through this framework, Aristotelian ethics affirms that rational agency is not exhausted by theoretical contemplation, but is realized in moral conduct responsive to particular contexts and ordered toward the good.

As Aristotle succinctly puts it: "the practical syllogism has one premise affirming the universal good [...] the other concerns a particular; the conclusion is not that one ought or chooses to do this, but that one does it" (*Nicomachean Ethics*, VI, 1147a2530, trans. mod.). The conclusion, in this sense, is not a linguistic proposition but an embodied act, arising when deliberation and desire converge within the agent's moral constitution. This account underscores that human action, in its fully rational form, is neither impulsive nor mechanistic, but the fruit of a structured ethical intelligence attuned to both universality and singularity.

2.2 APS as an Explanation Model

The Aristotelian Practical Syllogism (APS) serves as a foundational explanatory model for rational action in Aristotle's practical philosophy. Rather than being a merely descriptive account of behavior, APS offers a formal structure that elucidates how agents endowed with reason and desire transition from ethical judgment to concrete conduct. The model operates by articulating a syllogistic structure composed of a universal normative principle (καθόλου) as major premise, a particular perceptual or situational judgment (καθ' ἕκαστον) as minor premise, and a conclusion that is not a proposition but an action (πρᾶξις) itself. In this framework, explanation is not aimed at epistemic justification in the theoretical mode, but at the intelligibility of action as rationally structured and ethically grounded.

2.3 Human Friendly Explanations

Human-friendly explanations (HFEs) aim to bridge the gap between complex algorithmic processes and human understanding by providing insights that are accessible, meaningful, and actionable to non-technical users. Unlike purely technical explanations that focus on internal model states or mathematical formulations, HFEs prioritize the interpretability of system behavior in ways that align with human cognitive and communicative capacities. This involves tailoring the explanation's format, content, and complexity to the user's background knowledge, goals, and situational context, often incorporating narrative, analogical, or teleological reasoning to support intuitive comprehension and engagement.

A key characteristic of HFEs is their *pragmatic orientation*: they are not just about transparency but about usefulness in real-world decision-making. This means that effective HFEs are often *contrastive* (explaining why one outcome occurred instead of another), *selective* (focusing on the most relevant causes), and *interactive* (allowing users to ask questions or test scenarios). They are also ideally *context-sensitive*, adapting to user profiles and situational stakes. This personalization increases the likelihood that users will trust, accept, and responsibly use AI outputs, especially in domains like healthcare, education, or public policy, where moral, legal, and social consequences are significant.

Moreover, HFEs play a critical role in fostering *accountability* and *ethical alignment* in AI systems. By articulating the reasoning behind an agent's decisions in a form that reflects human deliberative patterns—such as intentions, values, or normative rules—they allow stakeholders to evaluate whether those decisions are justifiable and fair. This is particularly relevant in reinforcement learning systems, where behavior emerges through interaction with the environment rather than from explicit programming. Embedding HFEs into such agents supports both user empowerment and institutional oversight, ensuring that autonomous systems act not only intelligently but also intelligibly and responsibly.

Principles, Values and Criteria. The Human-Friendly Explanations (HFE) checklist is grounded in a coherent set of principles, values, and evaluative criteria that shape its structure and intended impact. At its core, the checklist is built on the principle of *human-centricity*, ensuring that explanation mechanisms are not only technically accurate but also meaningfully aligned with users' cognitive, ethical, and contextual needs. This includes a commitment to *practical intelligibility*, whereby explanations should facilitate informed decision-making and responsible interaction with AI agents. Other foundational principles include epistemic humility, participatory relevance, and normative accountability—each of which ensures that explanations remain sensitive to human capacities and limitations, while promoting agency, dignity, and transparency.

The values embedded in the HFE checklist operationalize these principles into concrete desiderata for explanation design. These include *clarity*, *contextualization*, *contrastiveness*, and *actionability*, which together ensure that explanations are tailored to user goals and adaptable across use cases. Further values such as *fairness*, *non-manipulability*, and *trustworthiness* orient the checklist toward socially responsible AI by promoting justifications that users can scrutinize, contest, and understand without being misled or overwhelmed. The HFE framework thus reframes explanation not merely as a matter of opening the black box, but as a dialogical process that facilitates sense-making, negotiation of meaning, and ethical transparency.

Finally, the evaluative criteria derived from these values provide a systematic approach for assessing whether a given explanation satisfies the requirements of human-friendliness. These criteria distinguish between the structural, functional, and normative dimensions of explanation: structurally, explanations must be comprehensible and relevant; functionally, they must support learning, trust, and decision-making; normatively, they must be aligned with moral and institutional standards of justification. This tripartite framework enables both qualitative and quantitative assessments, inviting empirical validation while preserving conceptual rigor. By integrating principles, values, and criteria into a unified tool, the HFE checklist offers a robust methodology for fostering explainability that is not only technically sound but also ethically meaningful.

XRL H-F-E Checklist. The *Human-friendly Explanations Checklist for Reinforcement Learning* (XRL H-F-E Checklist) [7], offers a comprehensive evaluative framework for explainable reinforcement learning (XRL) with a strong emphasis on human-centered design. Unlike generic or purely technical explanations, this checklist organizes explanation quality along four key axes: foundational principles, question-driven content structure, qualitative explanation traits, and human-centric delivery. The first section, *Principles*, focuses on essential evaluation criteria such as correctness, robustness, bias awareness, scalability, and legal compliance—ensuring that XRL explanations are not only valid, but ethically and technically sound. These criteria respond to the increasing demand for accountability and traceability in machine learning systems operating in sensitive or high-stakes environments. Complementing this, the *Why and Why Not Explanation* section introduces intuitive explanatory categories aligned with user inquiry logic, such as justification, contrastive reasoning, and counterfactual analysis. This structuring reinforces the cognitive alignment between agent outputs and human interpretive frameworks, encouraging clarity, interaction, and practical understanding.

Further enriching the checklist, the *"Good" Explanations* section identifies qualities like selectiveness, causality, adaptability to user expertise, and context sensitivity—ensuring explanations remain meaningful and actionable rather than overwhelming or abstract. Finally, the *Human-Friendly Characteristics* section consolidates principles from cognitive science and user experience research to ensure delivery is intuitive, consistent, and tailored. Notably, features such as interactivity, personalization, and visualization facilitate a more participatory and perceptible user experience, transforming otherwise opaque agent behavior into transparent decision pathways.

3 Results

Explanation Model. This model proposes a philosophical-conceptual bridge between Aristotelian practical reasoning and the internal mechanisms of a reinforcement learning (RL) agent, particularly a Q-learning agent applied in urban planning. The aim is to enhance human-friendly explanations by aligning technical agent behaviors with recognizable structures of ethical and deliberative action.

As an explanatory scheme, APS integrates cognitive, desiderative, and dispositional elements into a coherent model that avoids reduction to either causal mechanism or subjective intention. What is at stake is not only what the agent does, but why the agent does it in light of a certain conception of the good and under particular circumstances. The practical syllogism thus explains action by referencing both the agent's orientation toward ends (τέλος) and the agent's evaluative perception of means and context, mediated by the intellectual virtue of φρόνησις . In this sense, APS functions not merely as a predictive or deductive device, but as a hermeneutic structure that renders moral agency intelligible by showing the internal rationality of action. It tells us not simply that something occurred, but how an act emerged from deliberative and ethical reasoning.

Moreover, APS possesses a unique explanatory power in that it illuminates the normative dimension of action without severing it from embodiment and singularity. Unlike theoretical models that aim at necessary conclusions from fixed premises, the practical syllogism explains contingent action in light of practical truth (ἀλήθεια πρακτική), which arises from the alignment of right desire (ὀρθή ὄρεξις) and correct reasoning. This alignment is not static but dynamic, conditioned by the agent's habituation (ἕξις), moral disposition, and situational awareness. Hence, APS not only explains why actions follow from deliberation, but also highlights the ethical preconditions for such deliberation to be successful. In doing so, it embodies Aristotle's commitment to a teleological and integrative account of human praxis, where explanation entails not only logical coherence but existential justification.

Table 1. Mapping between Practical Syllogism and RL Implementation

Element of the Practical Syllogism	Technical Aristotelian Meaning	Parallel in RL	RL Implementation of Q-Learning Urbanism	Technical Aspect of the Agent
Telos	Rational ultimate end toward which ethical action tends, identified with the good. It may serve as the final principle and ultimate cause that constitutively guides both thought and action toward a good desired for its own sake	Policy the agent seeks to optimize through training	Policy assigns high values to ideal urban configurations in Q-table	Compatibility and distance matrices weight Q-values according to desirable layout attributes
Major premise	Universal statement expressing a general normative principle, guiding practical deliberation	Reward function programmed by the designer	Reward based on urban accessibility and compatibility	Formulas weight services and urban states
Minor premise	Particular judgment by which the agent perceives or interprets a concrete situation as relevant for realizing a universal practical principle, which, when aligned with a normative major premise, triggers action	Informa-tion the agent receives from the environment	The state St encodes location, adjacencies, cell type, and history	The agent receives its location and the adjacent buildings
Practical conclusion	Operational outcome of practical reasoning, which does not culminate in a proposition but in a performed action, the result of deliberate choice	Action selected by the agent in a given state	Selection and execution of action At with highest value Q(St, At)	The action consists in building a structure if feasibility conditions are met
Phronesis	Intellectual virtue of the deliberative soul, enabling sound judgment about appropriate means toward human good in particular situations. It integrates rational desire with the ethical perception of contingencies and constitutes the regulative principle of the practical syllogism	Q-table update, neural network weight adjustment, or another learning method	Update of Q(s,a) through TD learning and adaptive epsilon decay	Use of episodes (series), pausing successful states, and TD(Q)-based updates

Table 2. Mapping of Aristotelian Concepts to RL Implementation

Element	Technical Aristotelian Meaning	Parallel in RL	RL Implementation	Technical Aspect of the Agent
Orexis	Motivational faculty of the soul that drives movement toward an end represented as good. In the practical syllogism, it serves as a moving principle by integrating rational desire with practical judgment	Exploration phase in which the agent explores new policies to find the optimal one	Trade-off between exploration (epsilon) and exploitation of higher-Q actions	Epsilon decay using the Gompertz function.
Temporal perception	Specifically human cognitive capacity that enables the agent to project beyond the immediate present, evaluating the future consequences of actions and ordering desires according to long-term ends	Agents divide their training into phases; retraining may occur after each phase	Learning divided into episodes (short-term) and series (long-term)	The agent trains in series of 100 episodes, evaluates habitability, and adjusts learning
Hexis	Stable state of the soul by which the agent acquires a firm disposition to act according to reason necessary condition for the proper execution of the practical syllogism	Exploitation phase where the agent chooses higher-reward actions	Convergence of Q-table after prolonged training	Use of paused states and alpha to reinforce and correct Q-values
To prakton	Proper object of rational desire and final term of the practical syllogism, defined as that which can be performed by an agent under concrete conditions	Rules that limit the possible actions	Filtering based on environmental constraints: connectivity, compatibility, etc	Condition: cell must be connected to a road or be a valid extension
To deon	Normative determination of action that expresses, in the context of the practical syllogism, the practical form of the good applied to a specific situation what, according to deliberative judgment guided must be done here and now in light of the ethical end	Agents contain neural networks or Q-tables to learn and store the best action under certain circumstances	Penalization of actions that overbuild or unbalance service distribution	Penalization when service totals exceed thresholds or zones are saturated. Also penalizes lack of services

Table 3. Cognitive and Motivational Components in the Practical Syllogism and RL

Element	Technical Aristotelian Meaning	Parallel in RL	RL Implementation	Technical Aspect of the Agent
Rational desire or volition	Appetite for the good as recognized by reason as an end desirable in itself. In the practical syllogism, it constitutes the deliberative motor principle that orients choice toward the functioning as a motivational premise in the teleological structure of action	Agents are designed to seek the strategy that leads to the highest reward	The agent is designed to choose the best actions in each state.	The agent uses the Bellman equation, seeking the greatest reward both short- and long-term
Delibe-ration	Rational process by which the agent examines possible means to achieve an end previously desired. It constitutes a central phase of the practical syllogism, allowing prudent determination of what can be done here and now in view of the good. It seeks to adapt action to contingencies through practical judgment informed by experience and guided	Evaluation of the best action via Q-table or neural network output	Selection of best available action by *max Q-table* in observed state	Policy, evaluated in each state the agent finds itself in
Ethical perception	Sensory and evaluative faculty that enables the agent to grasp what is relevant in a concrete situation. In the practical syllogism, it serves as a condition for the correct formation of the minor premise, since without a fine apprehension of the singular it is not possible to apply the universal principle justly to the case	Agents perceive their current state, available actions, and possible rewards	The agent, through the reward function and Q-table, knows the possible reward of each action	The Q-table stores past rewards, allowing the agent to estimate the value of each action

Table 4. Cognitive and Motivational Components in the Practical Syllogism and RL

Element	Technical Aristotelian Meaning	Parallel in RL	RL Implementation	Technical Aspect of the Agent
Discursi-ve thought	Rational mediating faculty enabling the soul to deliberate, infer, and calculate about what could be otherwise. In the practical syllogism, it is the structural principle connecting the desired end with the available means	Equation, neural networks, or other learning method linking the reward function and the state to the action	The agent uses Q-table and Bellman equation that stores the state (minor premise) and action rewards to seek the best outcome (major premise)	The agent evaluates possible action rewards using Bellman's equation (populated through learning), and then selects an action
Appetite	Basic form of that drives the subject toward immediate pleasures tied to bodily sensation. In the practical syllogism, it represents a lower motivational tendency that may conflict with reason	Agents include gamma (discount factor), which, when close to zero, encourages short-term high-reward actions	When gamma is low, the value of future rewards decreases in Bellman's equation	Gamma multiplies the best action's reward in the next state; thus, a low gamma leads the agent to favor short-term rewards

This model presents a comprehensive mapping between the components of the Aristotelian practical syllogism and their counterparts in reinforcement learning (RL), specifically within the context of Q-learning applied to urban environments. Each row aligns a classical philosophical element—such as *Telos*, *Major premise*, *Minor premise*, and *Practical conclusion*—with its technical Aristotelian meaning, a corresponding citation from Aristotle's works, and modern interpretations in RL. The table further extends this mapping by detailing the RL implementation in urban design scenarios and identifying the technical mechanisms used in agent-based simulations. This interdisciplinary alignment illustrates how ethical reasoning structures can inform the modeling of intelligent agents, supporting more transparent, interpretable, and value-aligned behaviors in applied AI systems.

Table 2 extends the conceptual mapping introduced in Table 1 by shifting the focus from the structural components of the Aristotelian practical syllogism to the dynamic cognitive and ethical processes that inform agent behavior in reinforcement learning (RL). While Table 1 emphasizes the logical sequence of reasoning—such as premises and conclusions—Table 2 highlights essential psychological and deliberative faculties, including temporal perception, rational desire, hexis, and deliberation. These elements provide a richer understanding of how an agent evaluates long-term goals, ethical constraints, and adaptive strategies during learning. Notably, the table demonstrates how concepts like *to deon* and *deliberation* manifest through neural networks, Q-tables, and environmental filtering in RL. It also illustrates how these Aristotelian principles contribute to sophisticated mechanisms such as the Bellman equation, epsilon decay, and episodic learning, thereby integrating ethical reasoning into both the temporal structure and motivational architecture of agent behavior.

Table 3 deepens the Aristotelian-RL alignment by shifting focus from structural reasoning elements (as in Table 4) and cognitive-ethical processes (as in Table 2) to the motivational and computational underpinnings of intelligent agent behavior. This table introduces critical faculties such as *ethical perception*, *discursive thought*, and *appetite*, linking them to concrete implementations within reinforcement learning mechanisms. While Table 1 outlined the logical skeleton of the practical syllogism and Table 2 highlighted deliberative functions like temporal reasoning and volition, Table 3 emphasizes the internal evaluation and motivational dynamics that guide action selection. It shows how sensory evaluation (ethical perception), cognitive inference (discursive thought), and baseline drives (appetite) are operationalized through mechanisms like Q-tables, Bellman's equation, and the discount factor γ. This allows for a more nuanced understanding of how agents balance immediate rewards against long-term outcomes, ultimately reinforcing the ethical depth and complexity required for AI systems to act in value-aligned, context-sensitive ways.

Checklist Evaluation of the APS XRL Model. In order to assess the explanatory strength and potential limitations of the Aristotelian Practical Syllogism (APS) as an eXplainable Reinforcement Learning (XRL) framework, the Human-Friendly Explanations (H-F-E) checklist was applied. This evaluation allows for a systematic examination of the model across multiple dimensions, including correctness, robustness, bias, human comprehensibility, transferability, and scalability, among others. By aligning philosophical principles with technical requirements, the checklist highlights both the advantages of the APS-based approach—particularly its conceptual clarity and ethical grounding—and its current shortcomings, such as the lack of empirical validation or interactive mechanisms. The results of this evaluation are presented in Table 5, 6, 7 and 8.

4 Discussion

The proposed explanation model, grounded in Aristotle's practical syllogism, presents a novel bridge between classical ethical reasoning and the technical decision processes of reinforcement learning agents. By mapping Q-learning elements to Aristotelian categories—such as *telos*, *phronēsis*, and *boulesis*—the model achieves a high level of conceptual alignment and interpretability. This philosophical scaffolding enriches the explanatory capacity of the RL system, especially for interdisciplinary users seeking to understand the ethical and deliberative structure behind agent actions. The HFE checklist evaluation confirms the model's strength in dimensions such as comprehensibility, causal transparency, justification, and relevance, which are crucial for fostering meaningful interactions with AI in critical domains such as urban planning.

However, the evaluation also reveals clear limitations, particularly in terms of empirical robustness, user interaction, and practical applicability. The model does not currently offer quantitative or visual tools to test its robustness or scalability in real-time deployments. Additionally, it lacks contrastive and counterfactual capabilities, limiting its explanatory depth in scenarios where users must compare actions or evaluate alternative strategies. The absence of interactivity and personalization mechanisms further constrains its usability across different stakeholder profiles. These shortcomings suggest the need for future enhancements that integrate computational tools such as scenario simulators, visual state trajectories, and adaptive interfaces. Despite these gaps, the model provides a strong foundation for the development of normatively aligned and human-comprehensible XRL systems. Its interpretive lens is particularly valuable in high-stakes applications, where AI decisions must be not only effective but also ethically justifiable and intelligible. The next steps should include empirical validation in applied settings, iterative user studies to assess explanation effectiveness, and the formalization of supplementary metrics that extend the checklist into quantifiable dimensions. In this way, the model could evolve from a conceptual contribution into a fully operational framework for explainable and responsible reinforcement learning in real-world environments.

The pertinence of this study lies in its interdisciplinary contribution to both artificial intelligence and practical philosophy by proposing an explanation model that renders reinforcement learning behavior intelligible through Aristotelian reasoning. In high-stakes domains such as urban planning—where agent decisions impact societal wellbeing, resource distribution, and livability—understanding

Table 5. Evaluation of the APS XRL Model about the *Principles* of the H-F-E Checklist.

Principles	Evaluation
Correctness	**Yes**. The model aligns each component of the RL mechanism with its Aristotelian equivalent in a consistent and non-misleading way. For example, the reward function (major premise) and state observation (minor premise) logically lead to action (practical conclusion), matching the Q-learning architecture
Robustness	**No**. The model does not empirically verify robustness across varying input conditions or environments. It lacks stress-testing for stability under perturbation
Bias	**Partial**. While normative ethical alignment is discussed (e.g., penalization functions as *to deon*), there is no explicit mention of detecting or mitigating statistical or systemic bias
Improvement	**Yes**. The mapping to phronēsis and deliberation suggests that the model can be introspectively useful for refining policy behaviors and training strategies
Transferability	**Yes**. The conceptual framework is generalizable to other RL domains where ethical or goal-aligned behavior is relevant, not limited to urbanism
Human Comprehensibility	**Yes**. By grounding in well-known philosophical constructs, the model enhances accessibility for interdisciplinary audiences (e.g., ethicists, policymakers)
Transparency and Robustness	**Partial**. The model promotes conceptual transparency but lacks formal verification procedures or quantitative traceability for robustness
Adaptability and Tamper-resistance	**No**. There is no mechanism proposed to adapt the explanation to diverse users or protect it from manipulation
Scalability	**Partial**. The model is philosophically scalable but may become technically complex or ambiguous in high-dimensional environments without formalization
Regulatory and Legal Aspects	**No**. The framework lacks references to compliance with AI regulations (e.g., GDPR, AI Act), fairness audits, or explainability rights

Table 6. Evaluation of the APS XRL Model about the *Why and Why Not Explanation* of the H-F-E Checklist.

Why and Why Not Explanation	
Comprehensi-ve	**Yes**. It explains how the agent reasons, acts, learns, and adapts through a comprehensive ethical lens
Descriptive	**Yes**. Each step is described in detail (e.g., state input, Q-value update, action execution), making the agent's behavior traceable
Justification	**Yes**. Every action is justified by corresponding ethical principles and technical mechanics (e.g., Bellman equation = deliberation)
Contrastive	**No**. The model does not explain why a given action was chosen over an alternative. No counter-decision pathways are illustrated
Counterfac-tual	**No**. The model does not address how the agent would behave if environmental or state variables were different
Goal-oriented Counterfactual	**No**. There is no operational guidance on how a user could modify the state to elicit a desired action

Table 7. Evaluation of the APS XRL Model about the *"Good" Explanations* of the H-F-E Checklist.

"Good" Explanations	
Contrastive	**No**. As above, the model does not provide comparison with alternative actions not chosen
Selective	**Yes**. The explanation focuses on key features like reward function, state encoding, and convergence. Redundant elements are omitted
Causal	**Yes**. Clear causal links are made between reward function, state-action values, and output behavior
Adaptable to the User's Knowledge	**Partial**. While well-suited to a philosophically trained audience, the model may be too abstract for non-expert users in RL or ethics
Contextuali-zed	**Yes**. The urbanism domain provides strong grounding for context-sensitive explanation
Facilitating Actions	**No**. It does not explicitly guide users to adjust parameters or influence the agent's decision-making in practice

Table 8. Evaluation of the APS XRL Model about the *Human-Friendly Characteristics* of the H-F-E Checklist.

Human-Friendly Characteristics	
Comprehensi-bility	**Yes.** Clear, readable narrative anchored in Aristotelian theory facilitates interdisciplinary comprehension
Relevance	**Yes.** The mapping to ethical concepts enhances relevance for societal and value-driven applications of RL
Consistency	**Yes.** Explanations are internally consistent and conceptually coherent across all steps
Visualization	**No.** The model lacks graphical or visual tools (e.g., decision trees, state maps) to enhance understanding
Interactivity	**No.** The explanation is static and does not support user queries, parameter tweaking, or what-if analysis
Personaliza-tion	**No.** There is no mechanism to adapt content depth or focus to different types of users
Focus on Causality	**Yes.** The explanation model foregrounds cause-effect structures between input, policy, reasoning, and action

the rationale behind autonomous actions is crucial. The integration of the practical syllogism offers a philosophically grounded framework that aligns technical mechanisms with human ethical intuition, enhancing both the transparency and trustworthiness of AI systems. This alignment not only supports explainability in abstract terms but also addresses real-world concerns about fairness, accountability, and moral coherence in automated decision-making.

The proposed explanation model opens multiple avenues for future development and application across domains that require interpretable and ethically aligned artificial intelligence. By formalizing the connection between Aristotelian practical reasoning and reinforcement learning, this framework can be adapted to design explainable agents in contexts such as healthcare, education, law, and public policy, where moral justification and user comprehension are critical. Moreover, its modular structure allows for integration with visualization tools, natural language interfaces, and adaptive user profiling systems, potentially enabling interactive and personalized human-AI dialogue. The model also invites further empirical research on its cognitive effectiveness and usability, offering a rich foundation for building AI systems that are not only intelligent but also philosophically transparent and socially responsible.

5 Further Directions

One of the most immediate directions for future work involves validating the explanation model through empirical user studies. This requires engaging participants with varying levels of expertise—ranging from urban planners and policymakers to AI practitioners and ethics scholars—to evaluate the model's comprehensibility, relevance, and utility. Both quantitative metrics (e.g., comprehension scores, task performance) and qualitative feedback (e.g., interpretability perceptions, ethical resonance) should be collected to assess the model's impact across cognitive profiles and disciplinary backgrounds. Such validation would offer critical insights into the model's practical intelligibility and its capacity to foster trust and responsible use of AI outputs.

Another promising direction involves the design and development of a fully implemented explanation module embedded within an RL agent's architecture. This would entail encoding the Aristotelian components—such as telos, phronēsis, and orexis—as traceable elements within the learning process, and mapping them onto real-time explanatory outputs interpretable by users. Tools such as decision visualizations, natural language generation, and interactive dashboards could help render this abstract structure into operational systems. This implementation phase would bridge the conceptual model with applied AI engineering, turning philosophical insights into usable, agent-level components.

Finally, a critical frontier lies in understanding how such explanation models can be adopted and adapted to diverse domains and cultural contexts. Each domain—healthcare, urban governance, education—carries its own normative standards and user expectations, requiring the explanation system to be sensitive to domain-specific constraints and values. Additionally, adaptation may involve aligning explanations with different ethical frameworks or user interfaces tailored to sociotechnical environments. Investigating these adoption pathways will ensure that the model's application is not only technically feasible but also contextually appropriate and ethically legitimate across varied real-world settings.

References

1. Adadi, A., Berrada, M.: Peeking inside the black-box: a survey on explainable artificial intelligence (XAI). IEEE Access **6**, 52150 (2018)
2. Bacardit, J., et al.: The Intersection of Evolutionary Computation and Explainable AI. In: GECCO'22 Companion: Proceedings of the 2022 Genetic and Evolutionary Computation Conference Companion. Ed. by Fieldsend, J. ACM, 2022, pp. 1757–1762. https://doi.org/10.1145/3520304.3533974
3. Bekkemoen, Y.: Explainable Reinforcement Learning (XRL): a systematic literature review and taxonomy. Mach. Learn. **113**(1), 355–441 (2024). https://doi.org/10.1007/s10994-023-06479-7
4. Belle, V., Papantonis, I.: Principles and practice of explainable machine learning. Front. Big Data **4**, 688969 (2021). https://doi.org/10.3389/fdata.2021.688969
5. Canese, L., et al.: Multi-Agent reinforcement learning: a review of challenges and applications. Appl. Sci. **11**(11), 4948 (2021). https://doi.org/10.3390/app11114948
6. Castrellon, J.P., et al.: Smart loading zones. A data analytics approach for loading zones network design. Transp. Res. Interdisc. Perspect. **4** (2024). https://doi.org/10.1016/j.trip.2024.101034
7. Contreras Olivas, D., Martinez-Villaseñor, L.: Human-friendly explanations checklist for reinforcement learning: XRL H-F-E Checklist. In: Proceedings del Congreso Mexicano de Inteligencia Artificial (COMIA 2025), Part II. Ed. by García, A. and Ruiz, C, vol. 2553, pp. 123–135. Communications in Computer and Information Science. Heidelberg: Springer (2025)

8. Dieber, J., Kirrane, S.: Why model why? Assessing the strengths and limitations of LIME. In: arXiv preprint arXiv:2012.00093 (2020)
9. Doğan, M.: Urban vision a strategic planning. Eur. J. Econ. Finance Adm. Sci. **29** (2011) ISSN: 1450–2275
10. Doshi-Velez, F. et al.: Accountability of AI under the law: the role of explanation. In: CoRR abs/1711.01134 (2017). https://doi.org/10.48550/ARXIV.1711.01134
11. Ernst, D., Loutte, A.: An introduction to reinforcement learning. Université de Liège, Bélgica (2024)
12. François-Lavet, V. et al.: An introduction to deep reinforcement learning. Found. Trends Mach. Learn. **11**(3-4), 219–354 (2018)
13. Geron, A.: Hands-On Machine Learning with Scikit-Learn, Keras, and TensorFlow: Concepts, Tools, and Techniques to Build Intelligent Systems. 2nd. O'Reilly Media, Inc. (2019)
14. Gunning, D. et al.: XAI—Explainable artificial intelligence. Sci. Robot. **4**(37) (2019)eaay7120
15. H'sain, H.: Deep reinforcement learning for urban modeling: morphogenesis simulation of self-organized settlements. PhD thesis, The Graduate School of Engineering and Science, Bilkent University (2023). URL: https://repository.bilkent.edu.tr/server/api/core/bitstreams/2547447e-f783-4415-a31b-578592cb5bec/content
16. Khavarian-Garmsir, A., et al.: From garden city to 15-minute city: a historical perspective and critical assessment. Land **12** (2023). https://doi.org/10.3390/land12020512
17. Li, Z., et al.: A survey of collaborative reinforcement learning: interactive methods and design patterns. In: Designing Interactive Systems Conference 2021 (DIS '21). Virtual Event, USA: ACM, p. 19 (2021). https://doi.org/10.1145/3461778.3462135
18. Lim, B.Y., et al.: Why and Why Not Explanations Improve the Intelligibility of Context-Aware Intelligent Systems. In: Carnegie Mellon University, Intel Research Seattle (2009). https://doi.org/10.1145/1518701.1519023
19. Lundberg, S., Lee, S.I.A: Unified Approach to Interpreting Model Predictions (2017). arXiv:1705.07874 [cs.AI]. URL: https://arxiv.org/abs/1705.07874
20. Molnar, C.: Interpretable Machine Learning: A Guide for Making Black Box Models Explainable. 2nd edn. (2023). URL: https://christophm.github.io/interpretable-ml-book/
21. Mosca, E. et al.: SHAP-based explanation methods: a review for NLP interpretability. In: Proceedings of the 29th international conference on computational linguistics, pp. 4593–4603 (2022)
22. Murillo, A.C., et al.: Reinforcement learning in urbanism: building the cities of the future with AI. In: Proceedings of the XVII Congreso Mexicano de Inteligencia Artificial (COMIA) (2025)
23. Ribeiro, M., et al.: Why Should I Trust You? Explaining the Predictions of Any Classifier. In: Proceedings of the 22nd ACM SIGKDD International Conference on Knowledge Discovery and Data Mining (KDD), pp. 1135–1144 (2016)
24. Seth, P., Sankarapu, V.K.: Bridging the Gap in XAI-Why Reliable Metrics Matter for Explainability and Compliance (2025). URL: http://arxiv.org/abs/2502.04695
25. Singh, S., Kumar, V.: Modeling the determinants for sustainable smart city through interpretive structure modeling and analytic hierarchy process. Comput. Urban Sci. (2024). https://doi.org/10.1007/s43762-024-00125-1
26. Sutton, R.S., Barto, A.G.: Reinforcement Learning: An Introduction. 2nd ed. MIT Press (2018)

27. Wang, Z, Hong, T.: Reinforcement learning for building controls: the opportunities and challenges. Appl. Energy **269**, 115036 (2020). https://doi.org/10.1016/j.apenergy.2020.115036
28. Yarats, D., et al.: Reinforcement learning with prototypical representations. In: Meila, M. Zhang, T. (eds.) Proceedings of the 38th International Conference on Machine Learning, vol. 139, pp. 11920–11931. PMLR (2021) URL: https://proceedings.mlr.press/v139/yarats21a.html

Preliminary Investigation into the Use of Artificial Intelligence for Enhancing the Estimation of Concrete Compressive Strength via Non-Destructive Testing

Jesús Antonio Torres-Palacios[1], Luis Martín Torres-Treviño[2](✉), Alejandro Durán-Herrera[1], and Lucio Guillermo López Yépez[1]

[1] Facultad de Ingeniería Civil, Universidad Autónoma de Nuevo León, San Nicolás de los Garza, Nuevo León, México

[2] Facultad de Ingeniería Mecánica y Eléctrica, Universidad Autónoma de Nuevo León, San Nicolás de los Garza, Nuevo León, México

luis.torres.ciidit@gmail.com

Abstract. The need to reduce time and costs in the construction industry, specifically in the field of concrete, has turned its attention to non-destructive testing as an opportunity to estimate the compressive strength of concrete. However, the interpretation models for these results have shown some issues with reliability and accuracy. This is why this research proposes developing a compressive strength estimation model using artificial intelligence tools like neural networks and maximum sensitivity. This is for concretes of 20, 25, 30, and 40 MPa at ages of 3, 7, 14, 28, 56, and 90 days. For these, rebound hammer, ultrasonic pulse velocity, and the corresponding response, compressive strength, were measured. With these results, a linear regression reference model, an artificial neural network model, and a maximum sensitivity model were developed to reduce the error between actual and predicted values. The results help us form better expectations of AI tools and consider using them as complexity increases (more variables, more responses).

Keywords: Concreto · Inteligencia Artificial · Pruebas No Destructivas

1 Introduction

Within the construction industry, concrete is often the most used material in infrastructure projects. This makes evaluating its performance properties significant. Among these, the compressive strength of concrete is defined as the most important parameter for controlling the material's quality [1, 2]. To monitor compressive strength in in-situ structures, destructive tests are often employed. These tests demand a high economic cost, can sometimes reduce the load-bearing capacity of existing structures if not performed properly, and may present considerable time periods to obtain value for the studied parameter [3]. However, this property can also be evaluated using non-destructive tests (NDT) When combined with compressive strength, NDTs allow for the estimation of

L. Martínez-Villaseñor et al. (Eds.): MICAI 2025, CCIS 2712, pp. 55–66, 2025.
https://doi.org/10.1007/978-3-032-08704-1_5

concrete's strength value based on empirical relationships [4, 5]. On the other hand, the construction industry's need to predict concrete strength has increased nowadays. This is because obtaining these values directly influences decision-making regarding factors such as: the time to remove formwork, the completion of curing, the necessary strength for post-tensioning application, and/or the opening of the construction site [6]. For many years, researchers have proposed various models for predicting concrete strength, as well as for estimating strength based on non-destructive tests [6]. However, the accuracy of mathematical models shows relatively low precision due to the complexity of concrete and the fact that the models are based on limited datasets [7].

Based on the foregoing, this project seeks to innovate the concrete quality control sector by employing Artificial Intelligence (AI) techniques, which are used to interpret complex information and increase productivity [8]. Refining the analysis to determine the relationship between the mechanical behavior of concrete and microstructural properties measured through non-destructive tests, with the aim of generating new knowledge for the development of estimation models. Solving a current problem through a methodological framework and developing models for estimating the compressive strength of concrete using non-destructive tests such as rebound hammer and ultrasonic pulse velocity on concretes of 20, 25, 30, and 40 MPa, for ages of 3, 7, 14, 28, 56, and 90 days. The aim is for these models to show smaller errors than typical models developed by simple or multiple linear regressions.

2 Theoretical Framework

2.1 Rebound Hammer (RH)

One of the most well-known techniques is the rebound hammer, developed in 1948 by Swedish engineer Ernst Schmidt. This test is based on the rebound of an elastic mass that strikes a concrete surface. The impact causes an absorption of energy, which is then associated with the hardness of the concrete's surface [9]. This portable equipment is used to test the quality of hardened concrete by performing rebound analyses at different points on an element made from this material. It can also estimate compressive strength by correlating its readings with measured values of this property obtained through destructive tests.

2.2 Ultrasonic Pulse Velocity (VPU)

Another non-destructive test with high application in the construction industry is the ultrasonic pulse velocity (UPV). This test generally involves a transducer emitting an ultrasonic wave that travels through a concrete element and is then captured by a receiver. The transit time from one transducer to another is directly related to the density of the material studied and the elastic properties of the analyzed material (elastic modulus and Poisson's ratio) [10].

2.3 SonReb

When properties or conditions of concrete affect the results obtained from non-destructive tests, applying NDTs separately is not sufficient to reliably estimate the compressive strength of concrete [11]. In these types of cases, combining methods can be useful [12] to provide a solution for the compressive strength estimation requirements of the construction industry. In this context, the SonReb method emerged (the application of both rebound hammer and ultrasonic pulse velocity), which was developed by RILEM Technical Committees 7 NDT and TC-43 CND [13, 14] which is based on the increased reliability provided by combining concrete hardness data with ultrasonic wave velocity results, which are related to the material's physical and elastic properties [12].

2.4 Artificial Intelligence Tools

There are several approaches than can be used to establish a relationship between non-destructive tests and destructive tests. A multivariable linear regression, a multilayer Perceptron and a maximum sensibility neural network are considered for this modeling processes.

2.4.1 Linear Regression

A multivariable linear regression model (often more accurately called multiple linear regression) is a statistical model that estimates the linear relationship between a quantitative dependent variable and two or more independent variables (also known as explanatory variables, predictor variables, or regressors). The general mathematical form of a multiple linear regression model is: $Y = \beta 0 + \beta 1\, X1 + \beta 2\, X2 + \cdots + \beta p\, Xp + \epsilon$ Where: Y is the dependent variable (the outcome we are trying to predict or explain). X1, X2,…,Xp are the p independent variables (regressors). These can be continuous, discrete, or categorical. β0 is the y-intercept or expected value of Y when all Xi are zero. β1, β2,…,βp are the regression coefficients. Each βj represents the change in the expected value of Y for a one-unit increase in Xj, while holding all other independent variables constant. ϵ is the error term (or residual), representing the unobserved factors that influence Y and the random noise in the relationship. It's assumed to be normally distributed with a mean of zero and constant variance. The most common method for computing these regressors is Ordinary Least Squares (OLS) where β = inverse(transposed(X)*(X))*transposed(X)*Y where $\beta = [\beta 0\ \beta 1\ \beta 2 \cdots + \beta p]$.

2.4.2 Multilayer Perceptron Linear Regression

This approach is one of the simplest and most pioneering models of artificial neural networks. It consists of two layers of artificial neurons and simplifies the function of a natural neuron. The behavior of a single neuron is given by: y = fa(x1w1 + x2w2+…+xn * wn + bias) In this equation, each weight regulates the contribution of its corresponding input to the neuron's output. The function fa(.) serves as an activation function that approximates the behavior of an ideal biological neuron. A simplified architecture with several I inputs, one hidden layer, and a single output can be described as:

yn = fa(wo(1) * n(1) + wo(2) * n(2)+...+wo(i)n(i)+...+wo(n)n(n)) Here, n(i) represents the output of the i-th neuron in the hidden layer, which is connected to the input layer of the network. The output of each hidden neuron is computed as: n(i) = fa(x(1) * wn(n,1) + x(2) * wn(n,2)+...+x(I) * wn(n,I)) The process of computing weights that minimize the difference between the actual output and the desired output yd is referred to as the learning mechanism. Several methods exist for this purpose; however, in this case, we use classical backpropagation to compute gradients for both the output and hidden layers.

The gradient at the output layer is: δo = (yd − yn) * fa'(wo(1) * n(1) + wo(2) * n(2)+...+wo(i) * n(i)+...+wo(n) * n(n)) The gradient at the hidden layer for the i-th neuron is: δmi = fa'(x(1) * wn(n,1) + x(2) * wn(n,2)+...+x(I) * wn(n,I)) * δo * woi These gradients are computed using the derivative of the activation function fa'(.). The weights are then updated using the momentum method (alpha), which helps stabilize convergence regulating learning factor (eta). The weight update rules are: wn(k+1) = wn(k) + alpha * wn(k−1) + eta * w(k) * δm * n, and wo(k+1) = wo(k) + alpha * wo(k−1) + eta * wo(k) * δo * yn. These updates apply to the inner and outer layers, respectively in k iterations.

2.4.3 Maximum Sensibility Neural Network

Maximum Sensitivity Neural Network (MSNN) is a learning architecture related to artificial neural networks and is based on two fundamental principles: (i) the winner takes all, and (ii) use it or lose it. It is designed so that similar stimuli produce similar responses. The structure consists of a Total Number of Neurons (TN) that store information about stimulus clusters, a Total Number of Inputs (TI), and a Total Number of Outputs (TO). Typically, an input vector X(TI) – which represents a set of stimuli or sensor signals – is compared to a set of weight vectors W(TN×TI), where each row of W represents a cluster of similar stimuli. These clusters are linked to specific output responses stored in the matrix AC(TN, TO). In the case of a single output (TO = 1), the response matrix AC can be treated as a vector. Each cluster also maintains a use weight (UW), which tracks how often a cluster is used. This use weight decays over time by a forgiveness factor (fo): UW ← UW − fo. The maximum sensitivity is computed as a value inversely related to the distance between the input X and each cluster's weight vector. This is typically done using a Gaussian or triangular function with a specific width parameter λ, which controls the network's sensitivity. If the sensitivity value exceeds a predefined margin of sensitivity (ms), the stimulus is considered known, and the corresponding cluster is declared the winner. If not, all clusters contribute proportionally to generate an approximate response. Evaluation Equations:

```
Sn = FG(X - W(nn), λ), wn = argmax(Sn)
if max(Sn) > ms then
    yn = AC(wn), maxsens = 1; UW(wn) = 1
else
    yn = sum(AC(n) * Sn(n)) / sum(Sn(n)), maxsens = 0
```

Learning Mechanism: If a desired output YD is available, learning is performed as follows:

```
if maxsens = 1 then
    W(wn) ← ip * X + (1 - ip) * W(wn)
    AC(wn) ← ip * YD + (1 - ip) * AC(wn)
else
    nn = argmin(UW)
    W(nn) ← X
    AC(nn) ← YD
```

Definitions: maxsens: Binary flag indicating whether maximum sensitivity was triggered (1) or not (0). wn: Winner neuron (cluster with highest sensitivity). nn: New neuron (least-used cluster selected when no match is found). ip: Importance parameter that controls how much new information influences the cluster. If $ip \approx 1$, the cluster retains most of its original information. If $ip \approx 0$, the current stimulus and response override existing data. A balance is typically set with $ip = 0.5$.

2.4.4 Metrics for Modeling Validation

The Mean Squared Error (MSE) is the average of the squared differences between the predicted values and the actual observed values. The result gives an overall measure of the average squared prediction error across the dataset. A near zero value is expected. PRESS is the sum of squared prediction errors. PRESS measures how well a model generalizes by evaluating its performance on unseen data. A low value of PRESS is expected. The R2 (R-squared) value represents the proportion of the total variance in the observed data that is explained by the model. R2 is close to 1, indicating a good model. If the model predicts no better than the mean of the data, R2 is 0. If it predicts worse than that, R2 becomes negative. It is expected an R2 near one to be considered a good model.

3 Experimental Methodology

See Figure 1

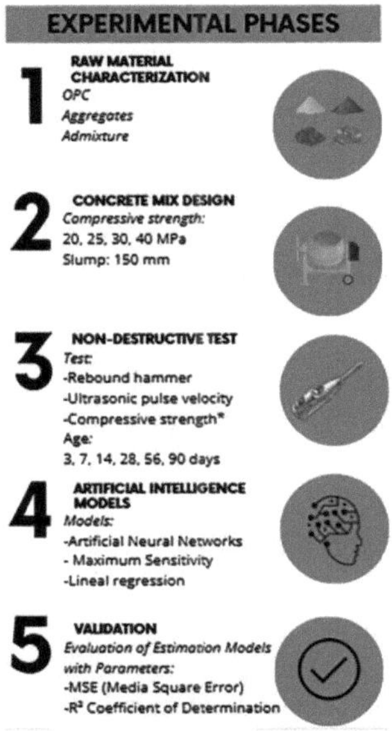

Fig. 1. Graphical Description of Experimental Methodology

3.1 Specimen Preparation

To measure rebound hammer and ultrasonic pulse velocity, concrete blocks measuring 60 × 30 × 30 cm were fabricated. Their faces were used to distribute the different measurement ages for the non-destructive tests.

Meanwhile, to monitor the compressive strength of the concrete, standard 10 × 20 cm cylinders were manufactured.

3.2 Rebound Hammer and Ultrasonic Pulse Velocity (UPV)

To measure the rebound hammer, three concrete prisms were selected. On one face of each prism, 15 rebound measurements were taken. A minimum distance of 5 cm from the edge and 2.5 cm between each measured point was maintained. Afterward, the first 10 values were selected and averaged. If discarding values was necessary, an additional 5 points were available. All these measurements were performed under ASTM C805 using a Silver Schmidt OS8200 device.

For UPV (Ultrasonic Pulse Velocity) measurements, three concrete prisms were also selected, with one face from each chosen for testing. The test is performed by pressing the transducer tips against the concrete; the equipment then measures the transit time of the wave from one tip to the other, dividing this by the distance between them to display the wave velocity. The equipment parameters were adjusted based on ASTM C 597, and a UK1401 Surfer ACS device was used. Figure 2 graphically illustrates the data collection process (the figure is not to scale).

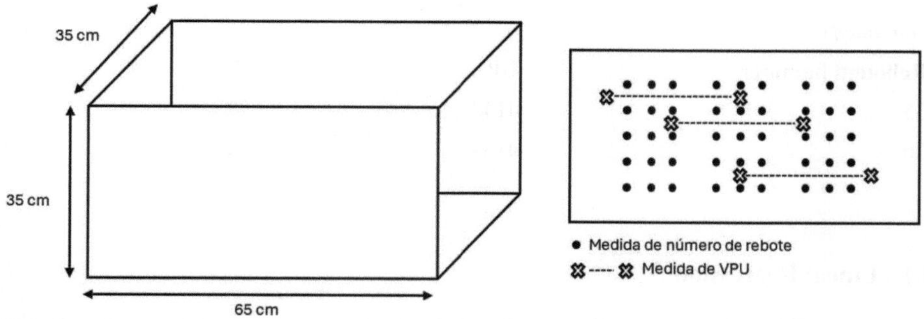

Fig. 2. Example of a concrete prism for non-destructive test measurements (left) and distribution of rebound hammer and ultrasonic pulse velocity measurements (right).

3.3 Compressive Strength

Regarding the compressive strength of concrete, three cylinders were tested for each age. Sulfur was used for capping the specimen faces, and the testing followed the guidelines described in ASTM C39 standard.

4 Results

Below is a table showing some results from the non-destructive tests and their corresponding compressive strength obtained from the tested cylinders.

Rebound hammer	UPV	f′c
52	4770	468
55	4717	464
56	4733	464
52	4843	466
52	4870	466
51	4830	466
33	4010	222
35	4100	242
37	4010	222
35	4240	242
37	4423	275
40	4433	282
43	4643	348
43	4607	344
49	4737	418

(continued)

(*continued*)

Rebound hammer	UPV	f′c
35	4143	223
36	4187	223

4.1 Lineal Regression

Below, you'll find the comparative graph of actual values versus values estimated by the linear regression model (Fig. 3).

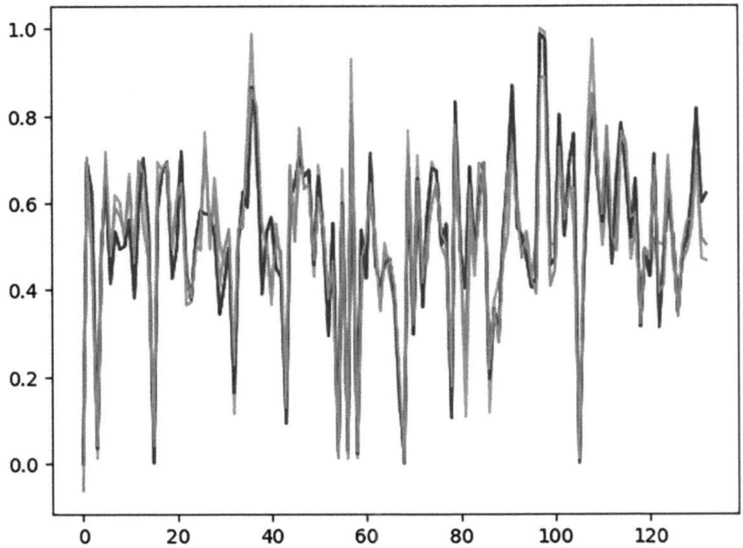

Fig. 3. Real (green) vs Lineal Regression Model (Red) (color figure online).

The following table presents the values obtained for MSE (Mean Squared Error), PRESS (Prediction Error Sum of Squares), and R2 (Coefficient of Determination), along with the respective regressors that form the equation (Table 1).

4.2 Artificial Neural Networks

Below, you'll find the comparative graph of actual values versus values estimated by Artificial Neural Networks (Fig. 4).

The following table presents the values obtained for MSE (Mean Squared Error), PRESS (Prediction Error Sum of Squares), and R2 (Coefficient of Determination), for Artificial Neural Networks (Table 2).

Table 1. Linear Regression Model Evaluation Results.

Lineal Regression	
MSE (Media Square Error)	0.003877
Press	0.515763
R2 (Coefficient of Determination)	0.905339
Equation	
F'c = −0.060996 + RH (0.546071) + UPV (0.426265)	

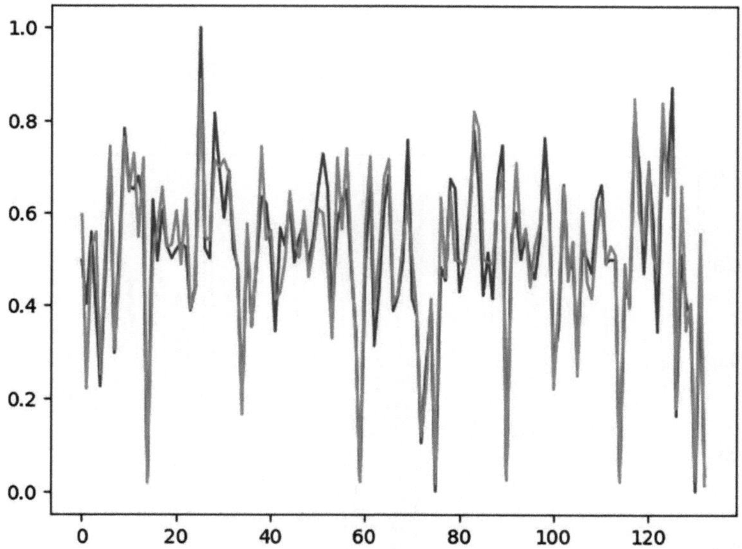

Fig. 4. Real (blue) vs Artificial Neural Networks Model (Orange) (color figure online).

4.3 Maximum Sensitivity

Below, you'll find the comparative graph of actual values versus values estimated by the Maximum sensitivity model (Fig. 5).

The following table presents the values obtained for MSE (Mean Squared Error), PRESS (Prediction Error Sum of Squares), and R2 (Coefficient of Determination), for Maximum Sensitivity (Table 3).

Table 2. Artificial Neural Networks Model Evaluation Results

Artificial Neural Networks	
MSE (Media Square Error)	0.004738
Press	0.630238
R2 (Coefficient of Determination)	0.858047
Architecture	
Neurons	5
Eta	0.8
Alpha	0.125
Epochs	3,000
Error	0.07571

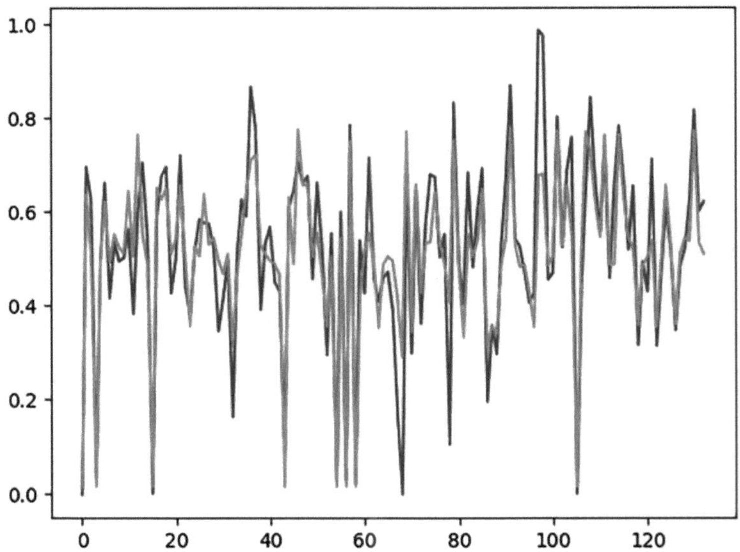

Fig. 5. Real (blue) vs Max Sens Model (Orange) (color figure online).

Table 3. Maximum Sensitivity Model Evaluation Results

Artificial Neural Networks	
MSE (Media Square Error)	0.007029
Press	0.934912
R2 (Coefficient of Determination)	0.822513

5 Conclusion

Of the three models developed, it was observed that under the analysis of the R2, MSE, and Press metrics, the one that showed the best results was linear regression, with an R2 of 0.90 and a low error of 0.0038, while the Press value corresponds to 0.51. Therefore, this model would be the one that best represents the behavior of these nondestructive tests and the compressive strength of the concrete. The reason that linear regression is the best model for this work is probably because it only has two inputs, which facilitates a description for a model of this origin; however, there are no guarantees that by using more inputs, the performance of linear regression will be maintained. Since it is necessary to include new inputs, future work will focus on testing performance with other paradigms proposed in the literature, such as support vector machines or decision trees.

References

1. Poorarbabi, A., Ghasemi, M., Azhdary Moghaddam, M.: Concrete compressive strength prediction using neural networks based on non-destructive tests and a self-calibrated response surface methodology. J. Nondestr. Eval. **39**(4) (2020). https://doi.org/10.1007/s10921-020-00718-w
2. Neville, A.M.: Properties of Concrete (1968). https://api.semanticscholar.org/CorpusID:136389082
3. Karahan, Ş, Buyuksarac, A., Işık, E.: The relationship between concrete strengths obtained by destructive and non-destructive methods. Iran. J. Sci. Technol. Trans. Civ. Eng. **44**, 1–15 (2020). https://doi.org/10.1007/s40996-019-00334-3
4. Hoła, J., Schabowicz, K.: New technique of nondestructive assessment of concrete strength using artificial intelligence. NDT E Int. **38**(4), 251–259 (2005). https://doi.org/10.1016/j.ndteint.2004.08.002
5. BS 1881. Testing Concrete Part 207. Recommendations for the Assessment of Concrete Strength by Near-to-Surface Tests, United Kingdom (1992)
6. Lee, S.C.: Prediction of concrete strength using artificial neural networks. Eng. Struct. **25**(7), 849–857 (2003). https://doi.org/10.1016/S0141-0296(03)00004-X
7. Arora, H.C., et al.: Ensemble learning based compressive strength prediction of concrete structures through real-time non-destructive testing. Sci. Rep. **14**(1) (2024). https://doi.org/10.1038/s41598-024-52046-y
8. Laysi, H., Farid, M.: Can Artificial Intelligence Improve Nondestructive Evaluation of Concrete Strength. Concreto Latinoamérica, pp. 9–15 (2024)
9. Qasrawi, H.Y.: Concrete Strength by Combined Nondestructive Methods Simply and Reliably Predicted
10. Breysse, D.: Nondestructive evaluation of concrete strength: an historical review and a new perspective by combining NDT methods. Constr. Build. Mater. **33**, 139–163 (2012). https://doi.org/10.1016/j.conbuildmat.2011.12.103
11. Alavi, S.A., Noel, M., Moradi, F., Layssi, H.: Development of a machine learning model for on-site evaluation of concrete compressive strength by SonReb. J. Build. Eng. **82**, 108328 (2024). https://doi.org/10.1016/j.jobe.2023.108328
12. Bonagura, M., Nobile, L.: Artificial neural network (ANN) approach for predicting concrete compressive strength by SonReb. SDHM Struct. Durabil. Health Monit. **15**(2), 125–137 (2021). https://doi.org/10.32604/sdhm.2021.015644

13. Rilem Report TC43-CND. Draft Recommendations for in situ Concrete Strength Determination by Combined Non-Destructive Methods (1983)
14. Merzoug, W., Chergui, S., Cheikh Zouaoui, M.: The impact of reinforced concrete on the modern-day architectural heritage of Algeria. J. Build. Eng. (2020)

Interpretable Machine Learning for Engineering Admission Trends at the University of Guadalajara

Anyer Jacobo, Yuritzi Mondragón, Juan Carlos Kelly, Jose A. Morales, and German Preciat(✉)

Departamento de Bioingeniería Traslacional, CUCEI, Universidad de Guadalajara, Guadalajara, México
german.preciat@academicos.udg.mx

Abstract. This study investigates long-term trends in admissions to science, technology, engineering, and mathematics programs at the Universidad de Guadalajara (2010–2025), with a particular focus on engineering. Using institutional data, we analyzed key indicators—including applicant volume, admission thresholds, and selectivity ratios—through artificial intelligence-based techniques. Principal Component Analysis revealed structural differences in program competitiveness, while anomaly detection algorithms identified careers with irregular behavior. Segmented regression models captured the impact of the COVID-19 pandemic, showing post-2020 volatility and declining interest in engineering despite growing demand in health-related fields. A seasonal autoregressive integrated moving average forecast further predicts a downward trend in applicant numbers over the next three years. These results provide insight into vocational misalignment and highlight the need for strategic intervention in career orientation and capacity planning. All data and code are publicly available to support reproducibility and future applications.

Keywords: Engineering Programs · Principal Component Analysis · Anomaly Detection · Data-driven Forecasting · Educational Planning · Time Series Forecasting · Mexico

1 Introduction

Engineering and other STEM (Science, Technology, Engineering, and Mathematics) disciplines are foundational to the sustainable development and technological sovereignty of nations [1]. Yet, despite global efforts to promote STEM careers, numerous countries—including Mexico—face a stagnation or even decline in student enrollment in engineering fields [2]. While certain sectors such as health sciences and business administration have shown consistent growth in university applications, engineering programs at many public institutions, including the Universidad de Guadalajara (UdeG), appear to be plateauing in demand despite growing national needs for professionals in this area.

L. Martínez-Villaseñor et al. (Eds.): MICAI 2025, CCIS 2712, pp. 67–78, 2025.
https://doi.org/10.1007/978-3-032-08704-1_6

A comprehensive review of admission data at UdeG over nearly two decades reveals that while the number of applicants to engineering programs has not drastically declined, it has not shown proportional growth when compared to other academic areas. Moreover, as universities expand admission capacity, the relative demand per available seat (demand intensity) in engineering is decreasing. This raises an important and complex question: Why is interest in engineering careers not increasing, even as society becomes more technologically dependent?

Previous research suggests that career choices are shaped by a combination of social context, perceived employability, gender expectations, prior academic exposure, and personal identification with the professional role [3, 4]. Studies show that STEM disciplines, particularly engineering, suffer from persistent stereotypes—often perceived as difficult, male-dominated, and disconnected from social impact [5]. At the same time, new technologies such as Artificial Intelligence (AI) are reshaping the landscape of engineering education and professional opportunity [6], yet students' awareness or interest in these transformations remains underexplored. However, the institutional datasets used in this study do not include demographic or perceptual variables such as gender, socioeconomic status, or student attitudes. To address this limitation, our future survey-based analysis will incorporate these dimensions to better explain the social and motivational factors shaping STEM career choices.

Several recent studies have explored similar challenges in STEM education across diverse geographical and institutional settings. For example, González-Pérez et al. [7] analyzed vocational interest trends among high school students in Colombia using longitudinal enrollment data, identifying critical gender gaps and regional disparities. In Europe, the Horizon 2020 *SESTEM* project used survey-based cluster analysis to segment students by motivational and perceptual variables, revealing how personal identity and institutional messaging influence STEM trajectories [8]. More recently, studies such as that by Gao et al. [9] have demonstrated the effectiveness of machine learning models in predicting students' program selection based on early academic records, socioeconomic status, and self-reported interest. These works provide both conceptual grounding and methodological guidance for integrating artificial intelligence with educational policy research—an approach we adopt and adapt in the present study.

In Mexico, regional disparities, socioeconomic barriers, and insufficient vocational guidance further complicate the transition from secondary to higher education in STEM. Addressing this issue is not only critical for aligning educational output with national economic priorities, but also for promoting equity and informed decision-making in young students. This study aims to fill that gap by combining longitudinal institutional admission data (spanning from 2010 to 2025), leveraging AI-driven models to gain deeper insight into behavioral and motivational patterns.

We hypothesize that the stagnation in engineering career interest is not merely a consequence of academic difficulty or availability, but the result of a more complex interplay of perceived relevance, and lack of exposure to emerging STEM applications such as AI. Furthermore, we propose that by using machine learning models to analyze historical and perceptual data, we can uncover latent variables and predictive patterns that are not visible through traditional statistical methods.

This work positions itself at the intersection of data science, educational policy, and behavioral analysis. The integration of AI techniques—not just as subject matter, but as methodological tools—allows for a novel understanding of STEM vocational trends that may inform institutional strategies, curricular design, and policy interventions.

2 Methodology

This study analyzes longitudinal admission data from the UdeG, covering the period from 2010 to 2025. The dataset includes over 70 academic programs across six major university centers. For each program and semester, we collected the number of applicants, admitted students, and the minimum admission score.

Our analytical framework consisted of three core stages:

2.1 Univariate Statistical Modeling

We applied simple linear regression models to each program and university center to assess trends over time in applicants, admission rates, and minimum scores. To capture the structural impact of COVID-19, the timeline was segmented into three distinct phases: pre-pandemic (until 2019), during the pandemic (2020–2021), and post-pandemic (from 2022 onward). This segmentation reflects both institutional transitions and national health policy shifts.

2.2 Multivariate AI Modeling

To uncover hidden structures and shifts across programs, we employed unsupervised machine learning techniques. Principal Component Analysis (PCA) was used for dimensionality reduction, as it provides a stable and interpretable low-dimensional representation directly linked to applicants, admission rates, minimum scores, and demand ratios—an essential feature for transparency in institutional planning. In addition, anomaly detection with Isolation Forest and Local Outlier Factor (LOF) was applied to identify programs with irregular admission patterns, especially during the pandemic.

2.3 Predictive Forecasting Using SARIMA

To complement the descriptive and clustering analyses, we implemented a short-term forecasting model aimed at predicting future applicant volume in CUCEI engineering programs. We used the SARIMA (Seasonal Autoregressive Integrated Moving Average) model, specified as SARIMA(1,1,1)(1,1,1,2), which captures both linear trends and semester-based seasonality. The model was trained on historical semester-level applicant data from 2010 to 2025. Forecasts were generated for six future semesters (2026–2028), providing a 3-year projection of admission demand. SARIMA was selected over other approaches such as Prophet or XGBoost due to its interpretability, avoidance of implausible negative values, and natural handling of periodic fluctuations.

2.4 Validation and Scope

We performed cross-center consistency checks and tested the stability of clustering results across time intervals. Limitations related to censored programs, missing data, and the lack of perceptual or demographic variables are addressed in the supplementary material, which also includes full code, preprocessing scripts, and analysis notebooks for reproducibility.

3 Results

This section presents the main findings derived from the application of statistical analysis and AI-driven modeling to institutional admission data. The results are organized into three thematic blocks: general trends, clustering patterns, and pandemic effects.

3.1 General Trends and Temporal Dynamics

Although the focus of this study is on STEM-related programs, the longitudinal analysis includes data from all academic areas at the University of Guadalajara (Figs. 1 and 2):

- The **growth phase** (2010–2015) was characterized by a steady increase in applicant volume across most university centers, reflecting an expanding interest in science and engineering disciplines (red in Figs. 1 and 2).
- The **plateau phase** (2016–2019) saw stabilization of demand, particularly in engineering programs. Applicant numbers leveled off, suggesting a saturation point in some centers or a redistribution of student preferences toward other academic fields.
- The **disruption phase** (2020–2021), coinciding with the COVID-19 pandemic, brought marked declines in applicant numbers across most centers. These drops were likely influenced by broader socioeconomic uncertainty, remote learning limitations, and shifting career priorities. Some recovery is observed from 2022 onward, although not uniformly across programs.

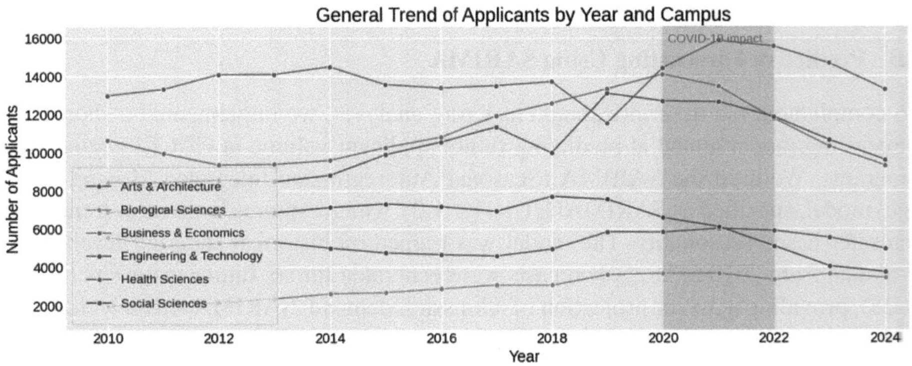

Fig. 1. Applicant Trends by University Center (2010–2025). This figure illustrates applicant volume across university centers at UdeG. Engineering & Technology, Health Sciences, and Business & Economics grew until 2019 but declined sharply after 2020. Arts & Architecture and Biological Sciences rose gradually, while Social Sciences declined since 2018. These shifts highlight structural changes in demand and inform forecasting for academic planning.

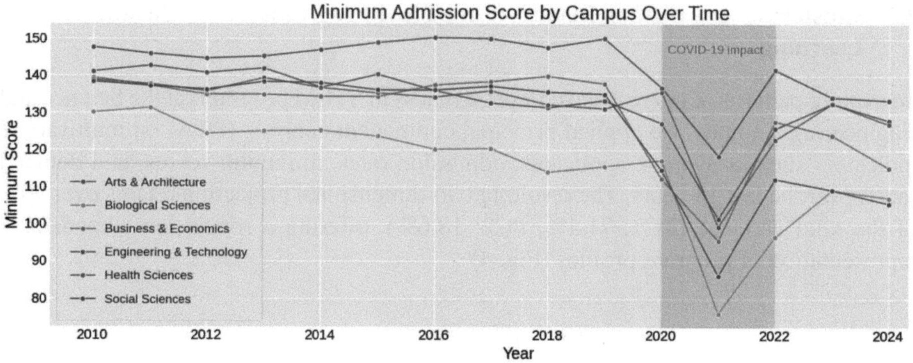

Fig. 2. Trends in Minimum Admission Scores by University Center (2010–2025). Minimum scores remained stable until 2019, then dropped sharply across all centers, reaching historic lows in 2021 during the COVID-19 peak. Engineering & Technology and Health Sciences show partial recovery, while other areas continue declining. These shifts underscore the need to consider PM variability in predictive and anomaly detection models.

3.2 Admission Capacity and Demand Gap

Understanding the balance between applicant demand and institutional capacity in STEM programs is essential for evaluating the performance and equity of the admission system. By comparing the total number of applicants and admitted students over time, we can assess whether these high-demand programs are expanding access or facing structural limitations (Fig. 3).

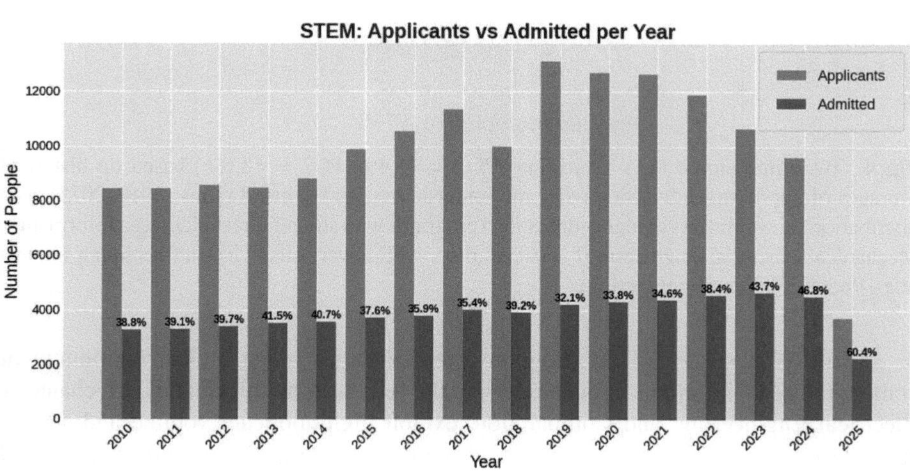

Fig. 3. The evolution of applicants and admissions in Engineering & Technology from 2010 to 2025. Applicant demand grew until 2019 but admissions remained stable, revealing a structural bottleneck. After 2022, applicants declined while admissions stayed nearly constant—until a sharp drop in 2025. This gap highlights tensions between student interest and institutional capacity, underscoring the need for predictive planning and policy evaluation.

3.3 Clustering and Outlier Detection in STEM Programs Using Unsupervised Learning

To explore patterns of interest and competitiveness in STEM programs at the Science and Engineering Campus, we applied principal component analysis (PCA) on multivariate indicators such as average applicants, admission rates, minimum scores, and demand ratios over the last 15 years. The resulting two-dimensional projection retains over 90% of the total variance (PC1: 71.4%, PC2: 18.6%), offering a robust low-dimensional representation of program profiles (Fig. 4).

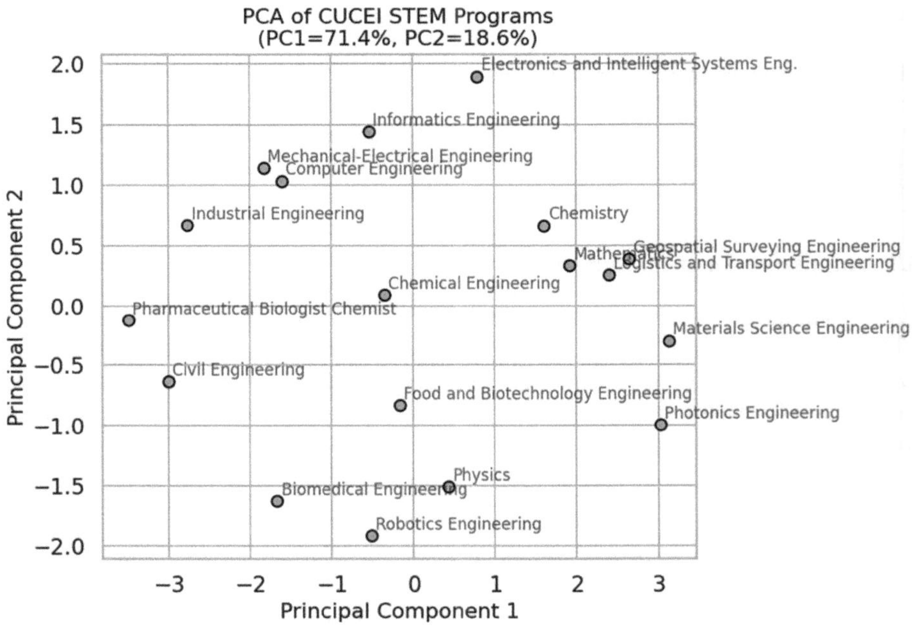

Fig. 4. Two-dimensional PCA projection (PC1 = 71.4%, PC2 = 18.6%) based on historical averages of applicants, admission rates, minimum scores, and demand ratios (2010–2025). The distribution shows clusters of highly demanded programs with stricter thresholds (e.g., Informatics, Mechanical-Electrical Engineering) versus outliers with lower selectivity and declining interest (e.g., Photonics, Food Engineering).

In this PCA space, STEM programs are distributed along a clear continuum of competitiveness. Programs concentrated on the left, such as Informatics, Mechanical-Electrical Engineering, and Computation, exhibit high applicant volume and stricter selection criteria—signaling sustained student interest and institutional prestige. Toward the center, programs like Chemical Engineering and Industrial Engineering reflect intermediate selectivity and more variable demand. In contrast, outlying positions on the right or lower quadrants correspond to less demanded programs such as Photonics or Food Engineering, characterized by high admission rates and lower application pressure. This spatial separation reflects structural differences in attractiveness and provides a visual foundation for strategic profiling.

To identify exceptional behaviors beyond group trends, we implemented an ensemble anomaly detection approach using two unsupervised algorithms: **Isolation Forest** and **Local Outlier Factor (LOF)**. Programs were flagged as anomalous if detected by either method. This allowed us to capture both global and local deviations without relying on labeled data or predefined thresholds (Fig. 5).

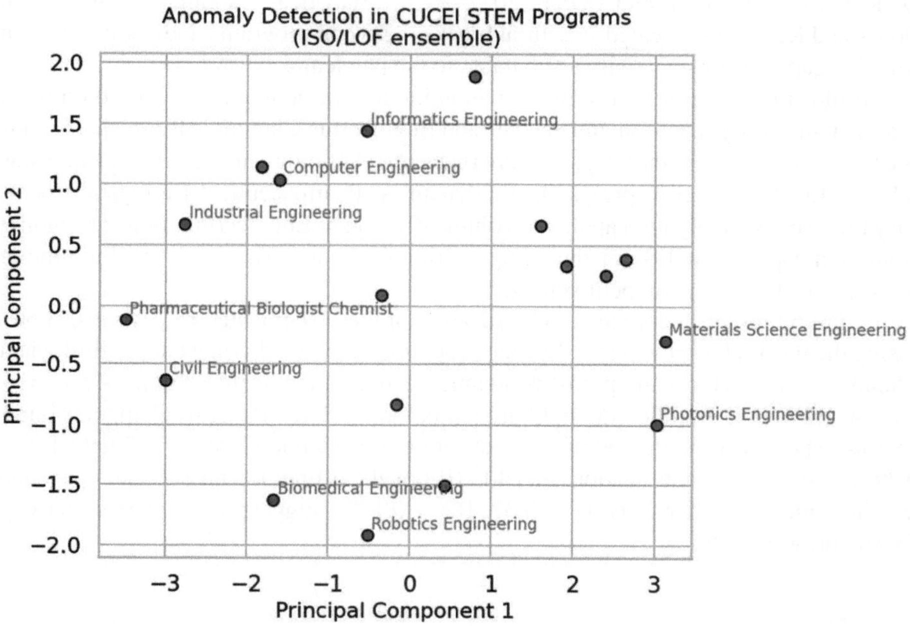

Fig. 5. Anomaly detection using Isolation Forest and LOF. Red points mark programs with atypical behavior in scores, applicants, or selectivity. Biomedical Engineering and Informatics stand out as outliers, highlighting systemic imbalances and guiding early interventions in STEM education.

The model flagged 11 programs with statistically atypical behavior. Among them, **Biomedical Engineering** stands out within the STEM cluster. Despite being considered a competitive program in prior metrics, it diverges sharply from expected trends in recent years—suggesting emerging enrollment or structural inconsistencies. Other outliers include Civil Engineering, Informatics, Industrial Engineering, and Photonics, each of which exhibits deviations in score variability, demand ratio, or applicant trends. These findings align with regression-based evidence and confirm that traditional metrics (e.g., minimum score) alone are insufficient to capture program health.

By combining PCA with anomaly detection, we gain a richer understanding of how STEM programs evolve in response to systemic pressures. This AI-driven profiling enables early identification of vulnerable or underperforming programs, and offers actionable insight for increasing enrollment interest. Institutions can use this approach to redesign outreach, reallocate resources, or adapt curricular offerings in ways that are responsive to real-world behavioral patterns—laying the groundwork for data-informed educational policy.

3.4 Regression Models and COVID-19 Effects

To evaluate how the COVID-19 pandemic influenced university admission dynamics, we applied segmented linear regression models to three key indicators—number of applicants, number of admitted students, and minimum admission scores—across all programs. These regressions were structured around three periods: PRE (2010–2019), DURING (2020–2021), and POST (2022–2025). Statistically significant changes in slopes and R2 values revealed structural breaks in several programs, indicating shifts in demand, capacity, or selectivity attributable to the pandemic.

To illustrate differentiated impacts within the STEM domain, we focused on three representative programs from the Science and Engineering Campus—Biomedical Engineering, Computer Engineering, and Pharmaceutical Biological Chemistry. Each was selected for its distinctive pre-pandemic dynamics: Pharmaceutical Biological Chemistry for its consistently high applicant volume, Computer Engineering for its expanding admission capacity, and Biomedical Engineering for its historically elevated minimum scores, reflecting high competitiveness.

Figure 6 presents a composite visualization of these segmented regressions, showcasing the most relevant variable for each program. Panel A (Pharmaceutical Biological Chemistry) illustrates a sharp post-pandemic decline in applicant volume (slope = −130.14; R2 = 0.559), following mild growth before COVID. Panel B (Computer Engineering) shows accelerated admissions during the pandemic (slope = +29.50; R2 = 0.791), followed by stabilization. Panel C (Biomedical Engineering) reveals a decline in minimum score after COVID (−3.32; R2 = 0.189), suggesting reduced selectivity despite prior growth.

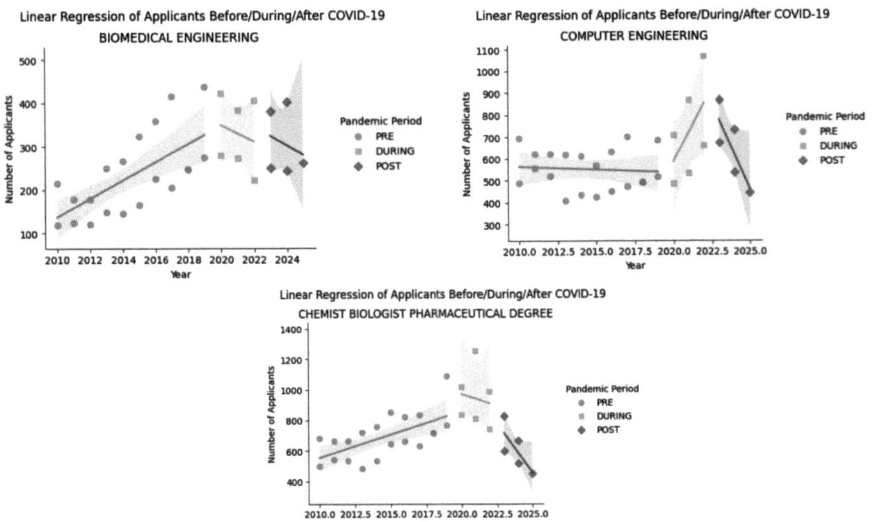

Fig. 6. Segmented linear regressions of applicants across three COVID-19 periods (PRE, DURING, POST) for Biomedical Engineering, Computer Engineering, and Pharmaceutical Biological Chemistry at the Science and Engineering Campus.

Biomedical Engineering exhibited steady pre-pandemic growth, followed by a marked decline in selectivity during the post-COVID period. Computer Engineering showed an unusual spike in admissions during the pandemic, likely reflecting the increased relevance of the tech sector, but stabilized afterward. Pharmaceutical Biological Chemistry, traditionally one of the most demanded programs, experienced a sharp post-pandemic decline in applicants. These differentiated trajectories illustrate how systemic disruptions reshaped demand across STEM fields.

Together, these segmented regressions reveal that pandemic-related disruptions Full regression models for all programs and centers are available in the supplementary material. These findings support the integration of AI-informed monitoring systems that detect early structural shifts and guide data-driven policy in higher education.

3.5 Forecasting Applicant Volume in CUCEI Engineering Programs

Figure 7 shows the SARIMA-based forecast of total applicants to engineering programs at CUCEI for the period 2026 to 2028. The historical data exhibit semester-specific fluctuations—typically with lower applicant counts in semester B—but an overall decline beginning after the pandemic period.

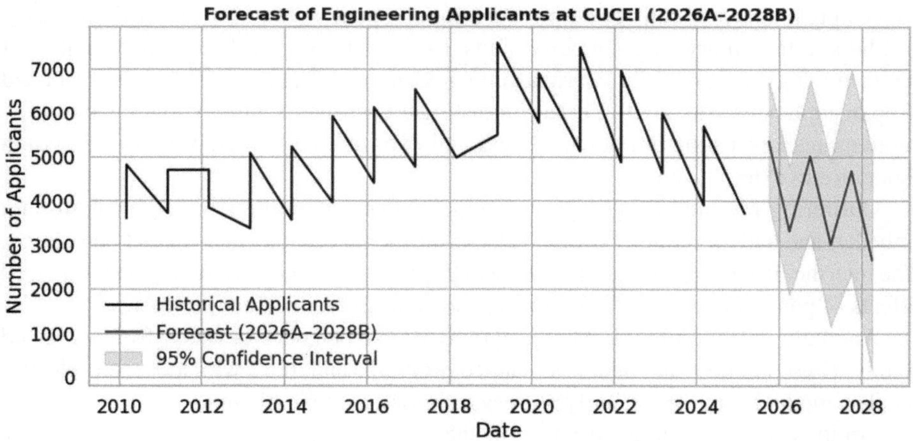

Fig. 7. Forecast of Engineering Applicants at CUCEI (2026–2028). Time-series forecast using SARIMA(1,1,1)(1,1,1,2) based on historical applicant volume per semester. The forecast predicts a steady decline with seasonal fluctuations and increasing uncertainty, underscoring the urgency of proactive institutional planning. Error metrics for SARIMA forecasts are reported in the supplementary notebook.

The model projects a continued downward trend in applicant volume, with clear seasonal variation between semesters A and B. The 95% confidence intervals suggest the decline is statistically robust, and unless offset by intervention, CUCEI engineering programs may experience historically low applicant numbers within three years. This forecast aligns with previous findings on stagnation and post-pandemic volatility in STEM interest.

Additional validation analyses and extended model comparisons are available in the supplementary Jupyter Notebook provided with this article. These include sensitivity tests for anomaly detection, alternative regression specifications, and extended SARIMA forecast evaluations. The supplementary material complements the main results presented here and ensures that the robustness of the methodology can be independently verified and reproduced.

4 Discussion

This section interprets the findings and reflects on their institutional and social implications. Rather than revisiting technical details, we focus on how the discovered patterns inform equity, planning, and educational policy.

The differentiated impact of the COVID-19 period was evident across STEM programs, and to illustrate this we selected three representative careers based on their long-term performance across all admission cycles. Biomedical Engineering consistently registered the highest average minimum score ($\approx$166.20), Computer Engineering showed the highest average number of admitted students ($\approx$237.65), and Pharmaceutical Biological Chemistry recorded the highest average number of applicants ($\approx$725.52). During the pandemic, Biomedical Engineering experienced a decline in minimum admission scores, suggesting reduced selectivity despite its prior competitiveness. Computer Engineering exhibited a temporary surge in admissions, likely reflecting the increased visibility of the technology sector, while Pharmaceutical Biological Chemistry showed a sustained drop in applicants after 2020. These contrasting trajectories highlight how systemic disruptions reshaped program attractiveness and exposed the vulnerability of admission dynamics to external shocks.

Clustering revealed that program competitiveness is multifactorial, involving not only demand and minimum scores but also institutional capacity and student perception. The intermediate positioning of Biomedical Engineering, for example, suggests nuanced effects of pandemic-related disruption and societal shifts in career preference.

Anomaly detection highlighted programs whose behavior deviated from expected trends. These include both under-demanded programs and those with loosened selectivity. The method provides an early alert system for academic planning.

Equity concerns emerge strongly in the distribution of competitiveness clusters. Programs serving students from under-resourced regions were less resilient during the pandemic. This echoes recent findings on fairness-aware clustering approaches, such as those proposed by Quy et al. [11]. Without incorporating demographic and protected attributes, current models risk reinforcing systemic disparities.

Our segmented regression models revealed diverging post-pandemic trends, especially between STEM and non-STEM programs. STEM careers showed a stronger recovery ($R2 > 0.85$, $p < 0.01$), while humanities remained flat or declined. These results are consistent with Gao et al. [9], who demonstrated predictive differences based on program characteristics. We extended this by validating cluster profiles with regression slopes and anomaly markers.

Unlike deep learning approaches, our interpretable AI pipeline supports real-time institutional monitoring. This aligns with the methodological recommendations of Zhang et al. [10], who advocate for transparent clustering and predictive models in educational planning.

While technically robust, our models lack perceptual or behavioral inputs. Including data such as student interest in AI, socioeconomic background, or gender identity would enhance explanatory power and policy relevance in future iterations.

The forecasted decline in applicant numbers—if realized—would reinforce the need for targeted interventions to revitalize interest in engineering. Based on our findings, we propose a multi-pronged strategy:

1. **STEM outreach campaigns** highlighting the societal impact of engineering, particularly Biomedical and Computing disciplines, which showed prior competitiveness but recent volatility.
2. **Integration of AI and emerging technologies** in the curriculum to enhance program attractiveness and align with student interests in innovation.
3. **Vocational orientation in high schools**, informed by data on gender disparities, regional gaps, and program misperceptions.
4. **Capacity expansion and diversification** within high-demand programs, such as Computer Engineering, to absorb latent interest and reduce barriers.

The data-driven forecasting pipeline introduced here can serve as a diagnostic and planning tool for other university centers, enabling responsive policy design in the face of changing vocational landscapes.

5 Conclusion and Future Work

This study applied artificial intelligence techniques to uncover long-term patterns in STEM admissions at the University of Guadalajara, with a particular focus on engineering programs. Using clustering (PCA + K-Means), segmented linear regression, and anomaly detection, we identified that while general demand remains stable, certain engineering careers face stagnation, regional disparities, and declining competitiveness. These results suggest that program attractiveness depends not only on academic thresholds but also on institutional perception, geographic context, and post-pandemic social dynamics.

The results also shows that the COVID-19 pandemic marked a turning point in admission dynamics. Biomedical Engineering, for instance, experienced a decline in minimum admission scores despite its prior competitiveness, while Computer Engineering showed a temporary surge in admissions that coincided with increased visibility of the tech sector. In contrast, Pharmaceutical Biological Chemistry, traditionally one of the most demanded programs, exhibited a sustained drop in applicants after 2020. These contrasting patterns demonstrate how systemic shocks reshaped demand and selectivity, leaving long-term effects that must be considered in institutional planning.

AI modeling uncovered subtle patterns—such as hidden competitiveness and unexpected drops in demand—that traditional methods may miss. These findings are valuable for vocational guidance, capacity planning, and curriculum adaptation. Future work will expand the dataset to include student-level and perceptual variables (e.g., socioeconomic background, gender, perceptions of AI) and apply predictive modeling techniques to forecast enrollment trends.

While the findings of this work are restricted to the University of Guadalajara, the reproducible methodology developed here is scalable to other institutions in Western Mexico. By integrating clustering, anomaly detection, segmented regression, and SARIMA forecasting into a transparent pipeline, the study provides a practical tool that can be adapted to monitor vocational trends and guide evidence-based policy in diverse educational contexts..

Reproducibility and Code Availability

All supplementary materials—including the full dataset, Jupyter notebooks, and code used for preprocessing, modeling, and visualization—are available at: https://github.com/Gpreciat/dataTRICKS/tree/main/projects/stemUdeG, ensuring full reproducibility and enabling future extensions or applications. The notebooks also include additional exploratory analyses and figures not included in the main manuscript.

Acknowledgments. We thank Dr. Alicia Garcia Arreola from the Science and Engineering Campus, Universidad de Guadalajara, whose vision for inclusive and strategic STEM education inspired the core ideas of this project.

Disclosure of Interests. The authors declare no competing interests relevant to this study.

References

1. UNESCO. Engineering for Sustainable Development: Delivering on the Sustainable Development Goals. UNESCO Publishing, Paris (2021)
2. OECD. Education at a Glance 2022: OECD Indicators. OECD Publishing, Paris (2022)
3. Lent, R.W., Brown, S.D., Hackett, G.: Social cognitive career theory. In: Brown, S.D., Lent, R.W. (eds.) Career Development and Counseling, pp. 101–127. John Wiley & Sons (2005)
4. Eccles, J.S.: Understanding women's achievement choices: looking back and looking forward. Psychol. Women Q. **25**(1) (2001)
5. UNESCO. Cracking the Code: Girls' and Women's Education in STEM. Paris (2017)
6. Skliar, A., Morales-Menendez, R.: Artificial intelligence in engineering education: current challenges and future opportunities. IEEE Access **8** (2020)
7. González-Pérez, M.A., Maldonado, A., Arbeláez-Campillo, D.F.: Gender and regional inequalities in STEM higher education access in Colombia. Int. J. Educ. Dev. **84**, 102406 (2021)
8. SESTEM Project Consortium. Understanding Student Engagement with STEM Subjects: Final Report. European Commission Horizon 2020 (2019)
9. Gao, C., Zhang, H., Yu, S.: Predicting college major choice using machine learning: a multi-institutional study. IEEE Trans. Learn. Technol. **15**(1), 44–55 (2022)
10. Zhang, Y., et al.: Predicting STEM major choice: a machine learning classification approach. J. STEM Educ. Res. **6**, 358–374 (2023)
11. Quy, T.L., Friege, G., Ntoutsi, E.: A review of clustering models in educational data science towards fairness-aware learning (2023)
12. Trujillo, F., Pozo, M., Suntaxi, G.: Artificial intelligence in education: a systematic literature review of machine learning approaches in student career prediction. J. Technol. Sci. Educ. **15**(1), 162–185 (2025)
13. Yang, S.J.H., et al.: AI and Big Data in education: learning patterns identification and intervention leads to performance enhancement. Inf. Technol. Educ. Learn. **3**(1) (2023)

Machine Learning

Modeling the International Mobility of Tec Graduates: Predicting Emigration with Machine Learning

Bella Perales Melendez(✉), Andrea Badillo, Alexa Ramirez, Scarlet Soto, and Neil Hernandez-Gress

Tecnológico de Monterrey, Monterrey, Mexico
{A01625514,A00833511,A00833943,A00833423,ngress}@tec.mx

Abstract. This study aims to develop and validate a data-driven predictive model that estimate the probability of Tecnológico de Monterrey graduates emigrating abroad within five to ten years after graduation, thereby generating actionable insights to strengthen the university's internationalization strategy and alumni follow-up programs. The dataset consists of demographic, academic, and institutional variables, including socio-family background, professional trajectory, and well-being. A calibrated CatBoost model was developed to estimate the probability of student emigration, highlighting its balanced performance. The CatBoost model achieved balanced performance (77 % accuracy), while highlighting nine high-leverage characteristics (campus, program, age, parental education, scholarships, and postgraduate status). This calibrated pipeline can shift graduate mobility management from reactive tracking to proactive, evidence-based engagement, preserving alumni ties while maximizing Tec's global impact.

Keywords: international mobility · Tecnológico de Monterrey · emigration prediction · machine learning

1 Introduction

Tecnológico de Monterrey (Tec) has documented the impact of its alumni through studies conducted for its 75th (2018) and 80th anniversaries (2023), revealing key contributions in entrepreneurship (43% founded businesses), innovation (8,588 Scopus publications), and social responsibility ('32,000 NGOs established) [12] [13]. As part of Tec's internationalization strategy, the institution maintains relationships with more than 100 universities around the world. The institution currently has more than 746 agreements with foreign universities and institutions in more than 50 countries [11].

Despite Mexico's growing rate of highly educated professionals, significant structural barriers continue to drive a considerable outflow of talent. It is important to identify and point to the elements that not only contribute to graduates deciding to migrate, but also lead to the so-called "brain drain" [1].

L. Martínez-Villaseñor et al. (Eds.): MICAI 2025, CCIS 2712, pp. 81–92, 2025.
https://doi.org/10.1007/978-3-032-08704-1_7

With the purpose of further researching about these elements, this study utilizes a detailed database, containing variables such as socio-family background, professional trajectory, and well-being, to develop a predictive model that complements the internationalization strategy, adding the post graduation follow up, focused on emigration abroad. The main approach is to develop and validate a data-driven predictive model that estimate the probability of Tecnológico de Monterrey graduates emigrating abroad based on year of graduation, thereby generating actionable insights to strengthen the university's internationalization strategy and alumni follow-up programs.

Research Question: can a graduate's demographic, academic, and institutional characteristics predict whether they will emigrate based on the year of completing their studies at Tecnológico de Monterrey?

Hypothesis: The demographic, academic, and institutional characteristics of Tecnológico de Monterrey graduates–considered jointly–have a statistically significant effect on (and therefore can be used to predict) the likelihood that a graduate will emigrate abroad after finishing their studies

This study relies solely on the alumni dataset released by Tecnológico de Monterrey for its 80th anniversary. Using the demographic, academic, and institutional variables provided, it develops and calibrates a CatBoost model trained on alumni data to predict whether graduates emigrate abroad within five to ten years after graduation. The findings are descriptive, limited to the Tec cohorts represented in the dataset, and do not claim causal inference to other institutions.

This paper is organized as follow: Sect. 2 explains the State of the Art, Sect. 3 describes the methodology followed to develop the model with Python and Sect. 4 explains all the results that were obtained. Section 5 concentrates on the analysis of the results and finally, Sect. 6 concludes and makes recommendations.

2 State of Art

2.1 Key Factor Categories in Graduate Migration

Most graduate migration flows are driven by the pursuit of study opportunities abroad [4], with the decision to migrate shaped by an evolving mix of economic, social, and psychological factors. First, many potential graduates face limited opportunities at home: in Mexico, there is often no adequate infrastructure to support high-skilled work, which causes even those who are employed locally to consider emigrating [9] .

Second, the desire for international experience and academic prestige motivates many students to leave. Graduates perceive that Mexico's knowledge economy has not advanced sufficiently, Mexican institutions do little research and development, then going abroad becomes the best way to access cutting-edge facilities and build a global curriculum [4]. As a result, highly skilled students respond more strongly to opportunities abroad: their probability of migrating increases significantly, especially if they secure a full scholarship. Female students are particularly likely to take up this option, whereas male students may be less influenced by work-based alternatives at home [2].

Third, socio-demographic background plays a crucial role. Even in systems that aim to be meritocratic, factors such as family income, parental education, and existing social networks strongly affect who can afford to study abroad and who ultimately chooses to do so. These differences in access mean that, in practice, not all graduates have the same probability of leaving [8].

Finally, psychological costs also matter: migration decisions are not driven solely by financial or professional considerations. Non-monetary costs–such as homesickness, cultural adjustment, and perceived well-being–can sway a graduate's choice even when economic incentives are strong. In other words, the expected emotional and social satisfaction associated with a given destination can tip the balance for those on the fence [9]. Together, these four categories: limited local opportunities, the appeal of international experience, socio-demographic influences, and psychological costs give an image of why Tecnológico de Monterrey graduates might remain in Mexico or choose to pursue their careers abroad.

2.2 Predictive Modeling Methodologies

Understanding the factors that influence why graduates choose to leave or stay in their home country has been a topic of interest for researchers around the world. To determine the methodologies that have been employed, several studies have been reviewed that apply AI, algorithmic, and quantitative techniques in their methodology. This analysis aims to identify common findings and gaps, defining the methodology and predictive framework that will be employed in this research approach.

2.2.1 Macro-Level Regression and Time-Series Analysis

Researchers often begin with regression or time-series models to find spatial and temporal trends in migration, but these approaches typically rely on aggregate data (regional exam scores or population flows) and cannot directly incorporate factor predictors. To overcome this limitation, a common strategy is to employ hierarchical regressions that order individual survey data (e.g., parental occupation, study program) within regional indicators [10]. Researchers also use penalized or regularized regression (e.g., LASSO) to select the most relevant factors from large administrative datasets, reducing overfitting while retaining interpretability. Finally, integrating time-series components (e.g., ARIMA terms) so the model can track how things change over different years.*2.2.2 Machine-Learning Classifiers*

Researchers frequently employ supervised learning algorithms to predict individual outcomes when detailed person-level and institution-level data are available. For instance, [7] developed an enhanced Random Forest model (BORF) to predict graduate turnover. Similarly, Alvarado et al. [3] compare four classifiers–Decision Tree, Support Vector Machine (SVM), Neural Network, and Random

Forest–on a Tec de Monterrey dataset of 500 students. [6] Use XGBoost to forecast first-year student mobility. *2.2.3 Decision Trees and Rule Based Insights*

Decision-tree methods produce clear "if–then" rules that support early intervention by identifying high-risk groups. [5] Suresh et al. plotted standalone Decision Trees (using both "party" and "rpart" in R) on a 500-student Tec de Monterrey sample, getting 90% accuracy and yielding rules. To prevent overfitting and address class imbalance, these studies reduce trees based on validation performance or use cost-sensitive splitting to emphasize minority cases. When single trees become unstable, researchers define rules from ensemble models (e.g., Random Forest) and modify them into a simpler, interpretable rule set. Validating extracted rules ensures robustness across different graduation years and evolving policy environments.

3 Experimental Development

The first step of the experimentation was the analysis of the database, corresponding to the information on graduates of Tec. Columns that could be relevant to the hypothesis were identified. The data preparation process included the elimination of variables that were not directly related to the hypothesis, normalization, filling in missing values, conversion of categorical variables to binary format, creation of a new binary variable to indicate whether the graduate went abroad, comparing the living country and if they left the country before studies.

Initially, the code for implementing Random Forest Classifier was created, with which the variables with the highest predictive weight for the hypothesis were identified, in relation to the target variable "went_to_abroad" (see Fig. 1).

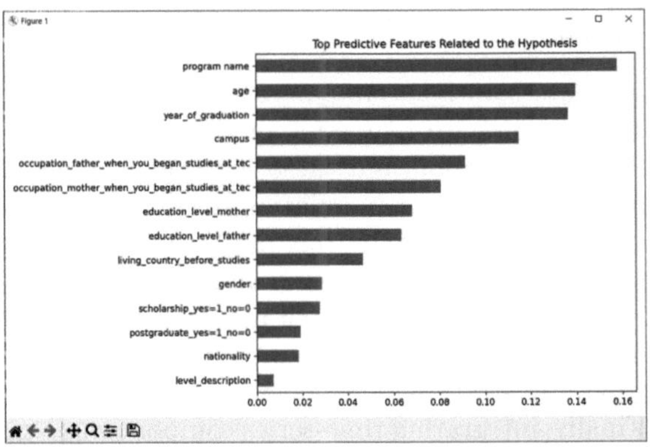

Fig. 1. Impact of variables on prediction.

The most influential variables were taken to use CatBoost model code, in order to have a prediction and to verify, or not, the hypothesis.

Catboost Model.

Train and Test data were divided from the general database, considering (80 % training, 20 % test). The feature set comprised nine socio-economic and academic variables, and the binary target variable was if they went abroad. The workflow used the libraries pandas, scikit-learn, imbalanced-learn and CatBoost. For the pre-processing and encoding a ColumnTransformer with two branches: Z-score scaling (StandardScaler) and One-Hot Encoding for the eight categorical features, eliminating perfect multicollinearity and handling unseen levels at inference time. The transformer sits at the head of the pipeline, ensuring transformations are learned only on training data and consistently applied to all CV folds and the test set. The outcome exhibits marked class imbalance. SMOTE (Synthetic Minority Over-sampling Technique) was applied within each CV fold, and CatBoost's parameter was enabled to further penalize misclassification of the minority class.

A random search was run with 3-fold CV, 20 parameter combinations and Average Precision (PR-AUC) as the optimization metric–more informative than ROC-AUC under imbalance. After selecting the best estimator, a Precision–Recall curve was built on the test set. The threshold that maximizes the F1-score–balancing precision and recall–was chosen to replace the default 0.5 cut-off, reducing false negatives without excessively inflating false positives.

Refined CatBoost Model.

CatBoost model was refined with additional calibration. The complete dataset was used for training, then partitioned into 80% training and 20% validation subsets, via stratified sampling to preserve the original class distribution. Custom class weights $0 : 1.0$, $1 : 1.5$ were specified–softening the penalty on the majority class to reduce the surge of false positives observed during exploratory runs. SMOTE remained in the pipeline to synthetically increase the minority class within each CV fold, yielding a hybrid oversample-plus-reweight approach. A CatBoostClassifier was wrapped in an ImbPipeline along with the preprocessing and SMOTE steps(Table 1). A randomized search with 3-fold cross-validation explored the same hyperparameter grid as before, optimizing Average Precision (PR-AUC):

Table 1. Hyperparameters space evaluated for Catboost

Left-aligned	Centered
iterations	200, 500, 1000
depth	4, 6, 8
learning_rate	0.01, 0.05, 0.1
l2_leaf_reg	1, 3, 5
bagging_temperature	0.0, 0.5, 1.0

All stages used random_state = 42 for reproducibility. Unlike the F1-maximisation of the first pipeline, this variant aligns the predicted positive rate with the empirical prevalence in the validation set.

4 Results

4.1 Model Training and Selection

Refined CatBoost Model. The CatBoost classifier was evaluated on a test set of 5072 graduate students(Table 3). The confusion matrix (Fig. 2) shows:

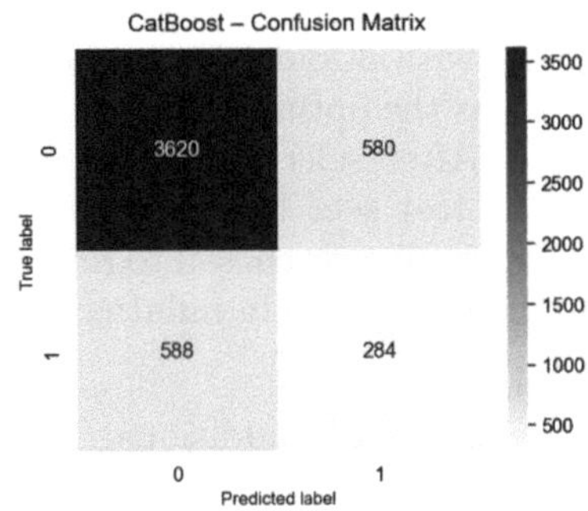

Fig. 2. Confusion matrix of CatBoost model.

From these results, the following diagnosis metrics were obtained (see Table 2):

Table 2. Diagnosis metrics on the test set

Metric	Value
Accuracy	77.0%
Specificity (True-Negative Rate)	86.2%
Sensitivity/Recall (True-Positive Rate)	32.6%
Precision (PPV)	32.9%
F1-score	0.33
Balanced accuracy	59.4%

The model is conservative: it avoids false positives by not labeling non-emigrants as emigrants, even at the cost of missing some true cases. This is due to the fact that the data set does not have the sufficient information to make the model more accurate when predicting for real emigrants, therefore, it correctly filters the majority of non-emigrants while identifying one-third of the actual emigrants, nevertheless is impactful given the class imbalance. The selected threshold yields a predicted emigration prevalence that mirrors the true test-set rate with nearly 100% fidelity (see Fig. 3). This alignment is valuable because it helps Tec in knowing overall the number of emigrants in a graduating range almost exactly right; although the model is not perfectly accurate at predicting every person correctly, it does a great job matching the real percentage of emigrants. That makes it especially useful for forecasting how many students will leave in a given year because planners care more about getting the total count correct than about catching every single case.

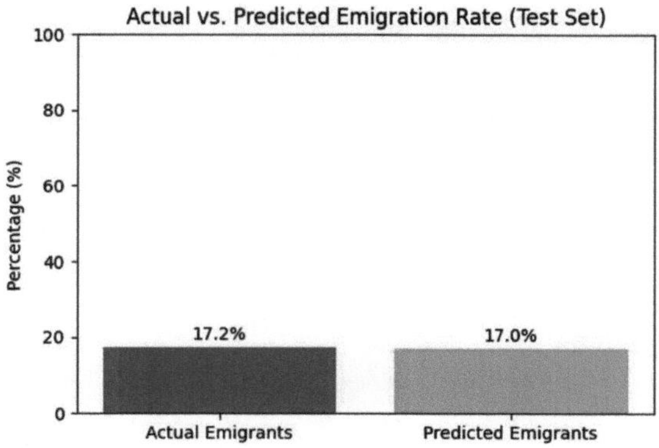

Fig. 3. Actual vs. Predicted Emigration Rate on the Test Set (17.2% observed versus 17.0% predicted).

Temporal Distribution in the Test Set.
Figure 4 breaks down all 864 predicted emigrants by graduation year. Two patterns were identified:

1. Minimal emigration prior 1990: Predicted emigrant counts are effectively zero for older registers, in line with historical records.
2. Gradual acceleration from 1990 s onward: Beginning around 1997, predicted counts change significantly, peaking with 61–68 predicted emigrants between 2015 and 2017.

These year-by-year patterns mirror the actual emigration count across the full data set (Fig. 5). While the numbers slightly differ from the predicted numbers (Fig. 4), the pattern of "minimal emigration prior to 1990 to gradual acceleration from 1990 s onward" is preserved. With this it can be confirmed the CatBoost ability to predict, even though it is in a subset of data, the year-by-year trend it produces follows the same pattern seen in the real, full dataset.

Short-Term Projections (2023–2030). To explore near-future scenarios, the trained CatBoost model was applied to the new prediction range of 2023 to 2030, holding last 2022s features to match the new distribution.

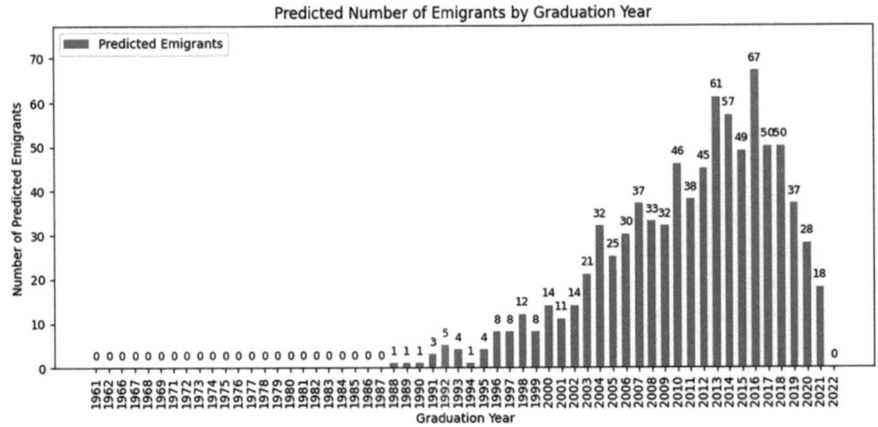

Fig. 4. Actual vs. Predicted Emigration Rate on the Test Set (17.2% observed versus 17.0% predicted).

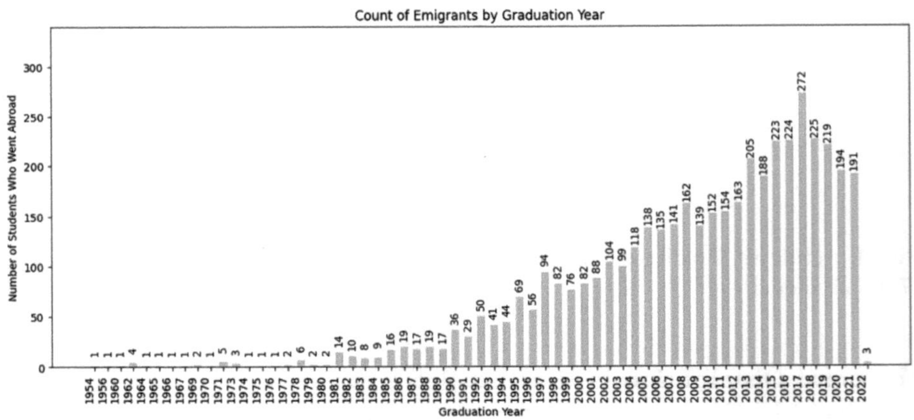

Fig. 5. Count of Emigrants by Graduation Year of real full data set.

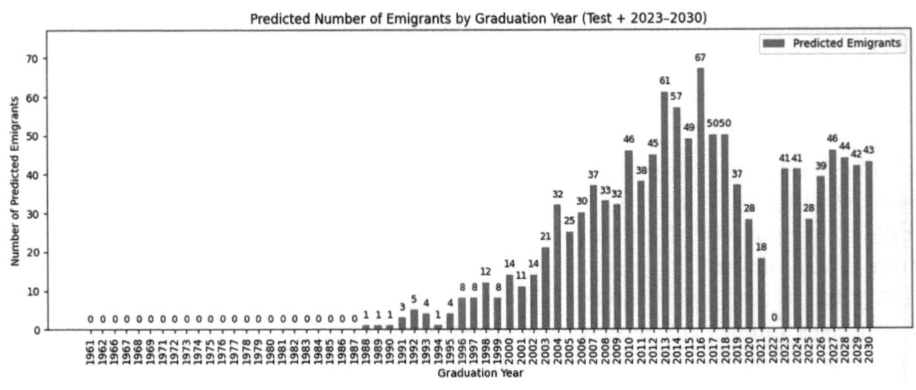

Fig. 6. Predicted Number of Emigrants by Graduation Year on test dataset.

Figure 6 shows that the predicted emigrant count remains high (between 45 and 68 per year) from 2024 through 2029, before settling to around 56 for the last year of prediction, 2030. During the eight new years of prediction added, the model forecasts approximately 480 additional emigrants, an average of 17%, which it consistent with recent historical results using the full dataset.

By maintaining these calibrated results, the CatBoost model provides a great proposal to anticipate student flows. Educational planners can leverage these predictions to allocate resources, such as alumni outreach, talent retention programs, or strategic partnerships in order to be able to benefit from it.

4.2 Model Refinement

In order to further address class imbalance and optimize generalization, two refinement experiments were conducted: adjusting the positive-class weight and varying the train-test split ratio.

1. **Class-Weight Tuning**

a. **Original setting:** The baseline CatBoost model was trained with class weights {0: 1.0, 1: 1.5} to mildly penalize misclassification of the minority "emigrant" class.
b. **Increased positive weight:** Try increasing the weight for class "1" (emigrant) to {0: 1.0, 1: 4.0}, thereby making false negatives four times more costly than false positives during gradient-boosted tree construction.
c. **Observed effect:** Although this approach was expected to make a more aggressive weighting, the accuracy fell to 77% and against the model's predicted emigration rate also fell to 16.8% (Fig. 7).

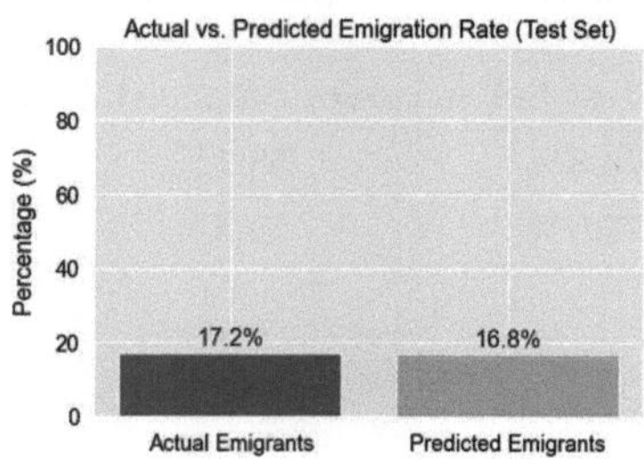

Fig. 7. Actual vs Predicted Emigration Rate with weight class of 4.0.

Making the predicted number of emigrants with that class weight to start predicting from 1988 (Fig. 7)

2. **Train-Test Split Comparison**

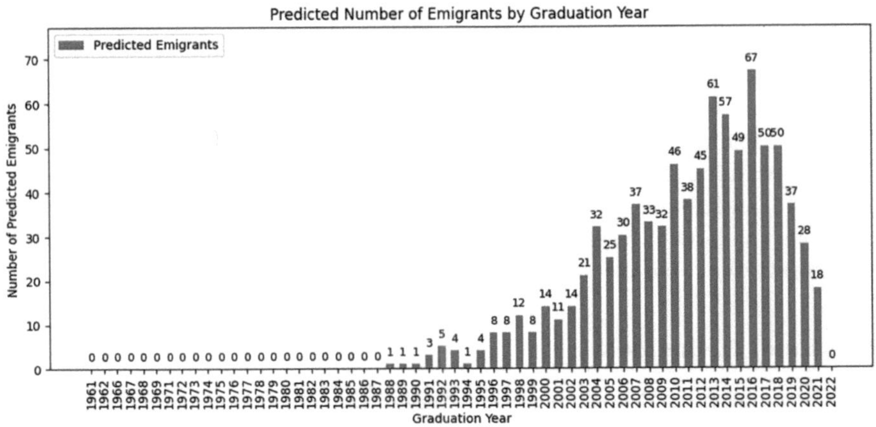

Fig. 8. Actual vs Predicted Emigration Rate with weight class of 4.0.

a. **70%–30% split:** The CatBoost pipeline was retrained on a 70 %–30 % training/test partition to explore whether a larger held-out set would improve evaluation stability.
b. **80 %–20 % split (baseline):** The original experiments used an 80 %–20 % split.
c. **Comparison results:** The 80 %–20 % split achieves higher accuracy (77.0 % vs. 75.8 %), better balanced accuracy (59.4 % vs. 58.1 %), and lower variability (SD 1.2 % vs. 1.8 %) than the 70 %–30 % split, justifying its use as the default.

Table 3. Performance Comparison by Train–Test Split

Train–Test Split	Test-Set Accuracy	Balanced Accuracy	Variability
70 %–30 %	75.8 %	58.1 %	1.8 %
80 %–20 %	77.0 %	59.4 %	1.2 %

4.3 Model Re-Training

After analyzing the performance metrics, a different training and testing proportions were used to improve predictive accuracy and generalization. As a result of this iterative tuning process, it was decided to split the dataset: one split for training and one for testing. This approach allowed for clearer control over the evaluation process and helped ensure that the model were assessed fairly on unseen data.

5 Analysis

CatBoost successfully captures both individual and level patterns of graduate emigration. On the held-out test set (5072 students), the model achieved 77 % overall accuracy, with a high specificity of 86 % meaning it correctly identifies the vast majority of non-emigrants–while identifying roughly one-third of true emigrants (sensitivity 33 %). Crucially, by calibrating the decision threshold so that the model's predicted emigration rate (17.0 %) nearly matches the observed rate (17.2 %), Cat Boost produces level forecasts that faithfully mirror real-world prevalence. These findings demonstrate that a calibrated CatBoost approach not only identifies which graduates are most likely to emigrate but also generates accurate, year-by-year forecasts.

6 Conclusion and Future Work

From a policy point of view, Tec can rely on these calibrated projections to plan alumni outreach, international programs or strategic partnerships with other foreign universities, focusing resources on the most feasible years of prediction; while acknowledging that individual recall remains up to changes and could be improved by incorporating additional data in order to train the model to be more accurate in the emigrant classification. The CatBoost model enables Tec to anticipate cohort-level outflows and prioritize data-quality investments around the most influential variables. The conclusions are tempered by class imbalance, single-institution scope, and missing macro-economic covariates, yet they underline a clear path forward: enrich the dataset, validate the model on newer cohorts, and embed explainable-AI tools so program directors can act on individual risk flags.

7 Recommendations

It is a priority to expand the dataset with more recent records and ensure the consistency of key variables; this will increase the accuracy of predictive models that support decision-making. To inform both these campaigns and the data model, it is recommended to implement a periodic survey targeting graduates that directly investigates their interest and willingness to work or study abroad, including career goals and perceived limitations. The results would provide quantifiable feedback to adjust mobility initiatives and refine emigration prediction algorithms. To strengthen the internationalization strategy, it is proposed to launch information campaigns targeting the alumni community. These initiatives, which may include explanatory sessions on recruitment processes abroad and networking opportunities, will allow them to learn about job opportunities abroad and build strategic contacts.

Acknowledgment. Sincere gratitude to Tecnologico de Monterrey for the academic support provided throughout this research. We are deeply indebted to our family and friends for their unwavering encouragement and understanding.

References

1. Aragonés, A. M.: Uberto Salgado: migration of mexican talent: myths and realities. ACM Int. Conf. Proc. Series (2022). https://doi.org/10.19052/eq.vol1.iss38.1
2. Batista, C., Costa, D.M., Freitas, P., Lima, G., Reis, A.B.: What matters for the decision to study abroad? a lab-in-the-field experiment in cape verde. J. Develop. Econ. **173** (2025). https://doi.org/10.1016/j.jdeveco.2024.103401
3. Alvarado-Uribe, J., et al.: Student dataset from tecnologico de monterrey in mexico to predict dropout in higher education. Data **7**(9) (2024). https://doi.org/10.3390/data7090119
4. Villalobos, L., Maggio, M.L.: Motivaciones para migrar: las clases medias mexicanas profesionistas en los estados unidos. NORTEAMÉRICA **14**(1) (2019). https://doi.org/10.22201/cisan.24487228e.2019.1.364
5. Litmeyer, M.-L., Hennemann, S.: Graduates' prediction system using artificial intelligence. ACM Int. Conf. Proc. Series (2021). https://doi.org/10.1145/3484824.3484873
6. Litmeyer, M.-L., Hennemann, S.: Forecasting first-year student mobility using explainable machine learning techniques. Rev. Reg. Res. **44**(1), 119–140 (2024). https://doi.org/10.3390/data7090119
7. Liu, M., Yang, B., Song, Y.: Research on predicting the turnover of graduates using an enhanced random forest model. Behav. Sci. **14**(7) (2024). https://doi.org/10.3390/bs14070562
8. Netz, N., Cordua, F.: Why do women more often intend to study abroad than men? High. Educ. (2022). https://doi.org/10.1016/j.jdeveco.2024.103401
9. Rashid,N.K.A., Dalam, A.M., Husain, Z., Mohamad, Z.: Big five personality traits on migration intention among terengganu graduates. Malays. J. Consum. Fam. Econ. **31**, 724–756 (2023). https://doi.org/10.22201/cisan.24487228e.2019.1.364
10. Yang, S., Ye, X., He, D.: Global pathways: new evidence on the international graduate school choice of chinese outbound students. High. Educ. **86**(6), 1415–1454 (2022). https://doi.org/10.1007/s10734-022-00979-6
11. Tecnológico de monterrey: internacionalizacón (2025). https://tec.mx/es/internacionalizacion, Accessed 6 Jun 2025
12. Tecnológico de Monterrey, Unidad de Inteligencia QS: Impacto económico y social de los egresados del tec de monterrey en el mundo. Tech. rep., Tecnológico de Monterrey, Unidad de Inteligencia QS (2019). https://impacto75.tec.mx
13. Tecnológico de Monterrey, Unidad de Inteligencia QS: Estudio de impacto económico y social global de las y los egresados del tecnológico de monterrey: Resumen ejecutivo. Tech. rep., Tecnológico de Monterrey, Unidad de Inteligencia QS (2023). https://impacto75.tec.mx

Comparison of Neural Network Models for Predicting Rhetorical Roles in Legal Documents

Hansel Lázaro Valdés Pérez(✉), Gabriela Giovana Pérez López, Darnes Vilariño Ayala, Beatriz Beltrán Martínez, David Pinto Avendaño, and Carmen Cerón Garnica

Facultad de Ciencias de la Computación, Benemérita Universidad Autónoma de Puebla, Puebla, Mexico
{vp224470264,pl224470262}@alm.buap.mx
{darnes.vilarino,beatriz.beltran,david.pinto,carmen.ceron}@correo.buap.mx

Abstract. The analysis of legal documents, specifically Indian ones, which are characterized by their length and terminological complexity, poses significant challenges, as traditional approaches are not adequate for drawing conclusions efficiently. This article presents an evaluation of neural network models for predicting rhetorical roles in Indian court judgments, as part of Subtask A of Task 6 of SemEval-2023, dedicated to the understanding of legal texts. Experiments were conducted with models such as BERT, LegalBERT and RoBERTa to classify Rhetorical Roles (RR) in Indian legal texts. The results show that the LegalBERT model performed best, with an F1 score of 0.6318 (63.18%) compared to the other models tested.

Keywords: legal documents · texts · SemEval · neural networks

1 Introduction

Countries such as India have traditionally followed a common law system, in which jurisprudence is based on the doctrine of judicial precedent. In this context, any task involving the retrieval of information from case documents, such as document summarization, can be complex to automate and, to a large extent, has continued to be performed manually over the years. However, as cases accumulate, the manual management of legal documents becomes more difficult [1–3].

Nowadays, legal case documents usually consist of several pages detailing all aspects of the case, with each sentence or paragraph serving a specific purpose in providing information about the case, the arguments presented by both parties, the rulings of the lower courts, etc. [4]. While this helps create comprehensive narratives for individual cases, these voluminous documents require greater effort to read, analyze, and understand. To that end, tagging sections or phrases in a legal document can help streamline the search, summary, and classification

L. Martínez-Villaseñor et al. (Eds.): MICAI 2025, CCIS 2712, pp. 93–103, 2025.
https://doi.org/10.1007/978-3-032-08704-1_8

of these documents. Rhetorical functions are tags assigned to phrases based on their semantic function in a legal case document. In a judicial setting, tasks such as automated prediction [5,6], the summary of documents [7,8] or the recovery of precedents [9] can benefit greatly from rhetorical roles (RR), focusing only on specific sentences or paragraphs rather than having to process the entire document [3].

There is growing interest in using advances in natural language processing (NLP) and machine learning to benefit the legal community. In particular, tasks such as summarization, RR tagging, and precedent retrieval are in high demand among lawyers and paralegals [10].

The complexity of legal documents requires the use of advanced NLP techniques to facilitate their understanding and analysis. Semantic segmentation of legal texts in RR is essential to improve the efficiency of legal research, improve access to justice, and support automated legal decision-making systems. It also facilitates various subsequent tasks, such as legal research, case synthesis, and analysis [11]. Automatic detection of RR in the sentences of a court ruling can help with numerous tasks, such as summarizing legal decisions, conducting legal searches, etc. Therefore, this problem has become a field of interest for various research projects [12].

The objective of this article is to compare neural network models in predicting RR in legal documents; associated with the SemEval-2023 competition, in Task 6: LegalEval, specifically Subtask A: RR Prediction, which focuses on understanding legal texts.

The remaining sections of the article are organized as follows: Sect. 2 presents a brief summary of related work on RR prediction. Section 2 explains the methodology used. Section 2 is devoted to the analysis of the data used for RR prediction. Section 2 presents the results obtained from the experiments carried out with the different models. The final conclusions of the article are found in Sect. 2.

2 Related Works

The processing of legal documents using NLP techniques has evolved favorably in recent years, stimulating multiple research projects dedicated to automating key tasks such as verdict prediction, legal text summarization, RR prediction, among others.

In a legal context, the expression "rhetorical labeling" or RR of a sentence refers to understanding the semantic function associated with it. Legal case documents have a standard structure, such as the facts of the case, the lower court's ruling, the issues under debate, the parties' arguments, the current court's final ruling, etc. Distinguishing these rhetorical functions of sentences in a legal case document can help improve the readability of the document and support various subsequent tasks, such as semantic similarity, text summarization, case law analysis, etc. [12].

The ability to automatically recognize the RR of words in a court ruling is an essential area to work on, because it is potentially useful for a wide range of subsequent activities, such as summarizing court rulings and conducting legal searches. [13,14]. Next, we will review works that address this topic from different perspectives.

The use of NLP techniques in the legal field has become an important area of research. In particular, research [4,5,12,15–19] have focused on addressing specific legal issues, such as anticipating rulings, analyzing legal texts, predicting RR, among others.

Research related to RR prediction associated with Subtask A of Task 6 in the SemEval-2023 competition highlights the use of different models, including ERNIE 2.0 and RoBERTa [12], learning-based model multitasking (MTL) [20], LEGAL-TransformerOverBERT (LEGAL-ToBERT) [21,22] proposes HiCuLR, a hierarchical curriculum learning framework for RR, [23] used LegalBERT, BiLSTM and Conditional Random Fields (CRF), [3] used multitask learning-based models for RR labeling, called MARRO, which uses multitask attention inspired by transformers, BERT model [24], LegalBERT [25,26], RoBERTa [27,28] used BERT with two layers of BiLSTM and [25] implemented Legal-BERT-HSLN. In the specific case of the results of Subtask A, the average F1 Score achieved was 0.7216 (72.16%); the best result recorded was 0.8593 (85.93%) from [23], while the lowest value was 0.2609 (26.09%).

3 Methodology

In this paper, experiments were conducted with neural network models, specifically models such as LegalBERT, BERT and RoBERTa. These models are capable of capturing complex semantic relationships and understanding the context of a sentence beyond individual words, with the goal of improving predictive performance. The methodology used for RR prediction is described below.

Initially, a data cleaning process was performed, normalizing the text by converting it to lowercase, removing numbers, leading or trailing blanks, and any extraneous characters or symbols present in the content. In this research, closed-ended words were retained because they contribute to maintaining syntactic structure and semantic context, particularly in legal texts. This allowed for the ability to give meaning to technical expressions and ensure that the model captures the relationships between terms, improving its capacity and achieving greater accuracy in predicting outcomes.

Each sentence was extracted from the provided corpus [5] along with its respective start and end indices, as well as its annotated RR. Finally, the corpus was divided into 80% for training and 20% for testing. Once the above process was completed, the neural network-based models were applied; the process described above is represented in the form of pseudocode 1 with the aim of providing a comprehensible algorithmic representation of the methodology used in the research.

Algorithm 1. Corpus Processing for RR Prediction

Read Corpus
    Data Cleaning (corpus):
        Convert to lowercase, remove numbers, spaces and strange characters
Split corpus into training (80%) and testing (20%)
Return processed corpus, training and test corpus

Once the text was processed, the aforementioned neural network-based models were applied. The process described is represented in pseudocode 2, providing a structured description of the steps performed.

Algorithm 2. Model Application Pseudocode

Read corpus
for each Neural Network Model **do**
    Train model with data_training
    Evaluate model with test_data
    Record metrics
end for
Return accuracy results (Precision, F1, Recall)

The experiments conducted in this research for the transformer-based models BERT, RoBERTa, and Legal-BERT were fine-tuned with homogeneous hyperparameter settings to ensure a fair and reproducible comparison. All models were trained for 8 epochs, which allows for adequate tuning of the task without compromising generalization through overfitting, especially relevant in resource-constrained domains such as the legal one. The maximum sequence length was set at 512 tokens, matching the native context limit of these models, ensuring that their ability to model long-term dependencies in legal documents is leveraged, with truncation and padding applied as needed. Training used the AdamW optimizer, an improved variant of Adam that decouples weight regularization, with a learning rate of 2e-5, a value for fine-tuning pre-trained models, as it balances learning stability without destroying the linguistic knowledge acquired during training. A weight decay of 0.01 was applied to mitigate overfitting by penalizing excessive magnitudes in the model parameters. The batch size was set to 8 due to memory limitations in the testing environment. By standardizing all these parameters, differences in performance can be more confidently attributed to the specific capabilities of each model, rather than to variations in the training setup. A summary of the parameters used is shown in the Table 1).

Table 1. Common parameters of the evaluated transformer models

Parameter	BERT	RoBERTa	Legal-BERT
Base model	`bert-base-uncased`	`roberta-base`	`nlpaueb/legal-bert-base-uncased`
Max length	512	512	512
Batch size	8	8	16
Epochs	8	8	8
Learning rate	2e-5	2e-5	2e-5
Optimizer	AdamW	AdamW	AdamW
Weight decay	0.01	0.01	0.01

In Fig. 1 the process detailed above is outlined to offer a clear and organized view of the methodology followed, facilitating the understanding of each of the stages.

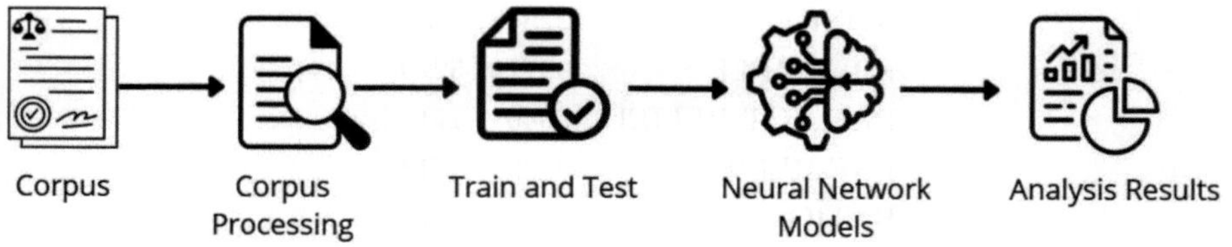

Fig. 1. Graphic representation of the methodology.

4 Data Analysis

The corpus analyzed comes from [5], is composed of legal documents related to rulings issued by the Supreme Court of India. These texts were collected from the official portals of Indian courts and are separated into training, validation, and test sets. The training section contains annotations corresponding to 247 rulings, while the validation set includes 30 additional rulings. The test set, meanwhile, consists of 50 unannotated rulings. The initial and final positions of each sentence within the documents are specified, thus accurately identifying each instance and classifying them with one of the 13 labels described below.

The corpus includes a total of 12 RR categories, plus an additional category called "none" (NONE), used when none of the other tags are relevant. The tags defined by the authors are: Preamble (PREAMBLE), Facts (FAC), Decision of the Lower Court (RLC), Issues (ISSUE), Argument of the Petitioner (ARG PETITIONER), Argument of the Respondent (ARG RESPONDENT), Analysis (ANALYSIS), Statutes (STA), Precedent Cited (PRE RELIED), Precedent Not Cited (PRE NOT RELIED), Basis for the Decision (RATIO), and Current Court

Ruling (RPC). These labels allow us to identify the RR that each sentence fulfills within the argumentative and legal context of the document: from the introduction of the case and the relevant facts, through the arguments of the parties and the analysis of the court, to the final resolution and the legal grounds that support it. The training and validation sets were integrated into a single corpus, thus obtaining 35 868 labeled instances and a vocabulary of 30 760 unique terms, which are shown in Table 2):

Table 2. Token and Sentence Data by Tag

Description	Tokens	Senteces
ANALYSIS	379105	12934
ARG_PETITIONER	55008	1638
ARG_RESPONDENT	26359	818
FAC	189441	7257
ISSUE	17195	461
NONE	22646	1839
PREAMBLE	99710	5270
PRE_NOT_RELIED	6646	171
PRE_RELIED	63399	1712
RATIO	28212	877
RLC	30665	955
RPC	27586	1370
STA	31609	566

Once corpus preprocessing was completed, 34 805 instances and a vocabulary composed of 16 796 distinct terms were obtained. A statistical summary of the results is shown in Table 2 below (Tabla 3):

It should be noted that both the original and resulting corpus are not balanced in terms of the representativeness of each class, and the number of tokens and sentences corresponding to each class.

Table 3. Token and Sentence Data by Tag

Description	Tokens	Sentences
ANALYSIS	304067	12798
ARG_PETITIONER	43589	1611
ARG_RESPONDENT	21324	813
FAC	149788	7179
ISSUE	13305	449
NONE	14491	1649
PREAMBLE	71960	4743
PRE_NOT_RELIED	5103	170
PRE_RELIED	48976	1699
RATIO	22995	873
RLC	24332	936
RPC	21449	1340
STA	25381	545

5 Analysis of Results

In this section, we analyze the final performance of the aforementioned models used in the research. For the evaluation, the F1 score, Recall, Precision AUC-ROC metrics were used, using the F1 score as a reference for the corresponding analyses. The following section (Table 4) shows the results for the models applied to both the training and test data.

Table 4. Precision, Recall, F1-score, and AUC-ROC Results for Different Models

Train				
	Precision	Recall	F1	AUC-ROC
Roberta	0.9168	0.9185	0.9162	0.9932
Bert	0.9747	0.9742	0.973	0.9992
LegalBert	0.9501	0.9495	0.9484	0.999
Test				
	Precision	Recall	F1	AUC-ROC
Roberta	0.6312	0.6317	0.6300	0.8990
Bert	0.622	0.6288	0.6243	0.8715
LegalBert	0.6315	0.6399	**0.6318**	0.8926

The difference between the AUC-ROC and F1-Score values is related to the significant imbalance between classes in the corpus, where the model successfully distinguishes between classes but fails to classify instances of minority classes. This behavior aligns with the proposals made in [29,30], where the AUC-ROC remains robust to imbalance, while metrics such as F1 reflect operational biases. Future work can implement resampling techniques to balance label distribution during training.

In the following graph (Fig. 2) The following graph shows a summary considering the average F1; It is noteworthy that in the case of the LegalBert model, better results were obtained with 0.6318 (63.18%) F1-Score by a small margin with respect to the RoBERTa model; it is relevant to highlight that the results obtained are low compared to the F1 scores achieved by participants in Subtask A of Task 6 of SemEval 2023; however, it is higher than the lowest result obtained in the competition.

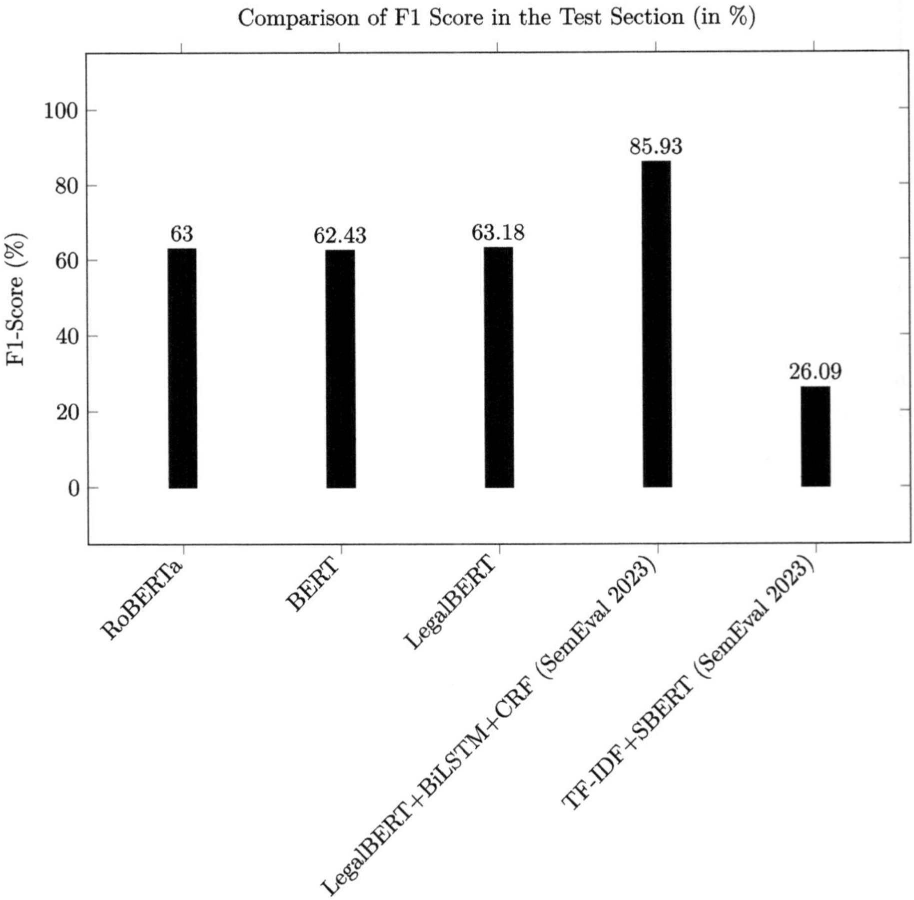

Fig. 2. Graph with the F1 Score values obtained in different models.

As part of SemEval-2023 Task 6, [23] proposed system won first place in Subtask A: RR Prediction. The approach employed is based on a hierarchical HSLN architecture that combines a pre-trained LegalBERT model with Bi-LSTM layers at the word and sentence levels, followed by a CRF layer to model sequential dependencies. LegalBertzlucia was used as the base model, which was further pre-trained with 200,000 sentences from Indian legal cases, achieving a significant performance improvement (F1: 83.65). To address the small size and imbalance of the training set, data augmentation strategies at the document (BLOCK) and sentence (TreeMix, back-translation) levels, as well as the incorporation of external data with partially overlapping labels (O2T), were implemented. In addition, auxiliary tasks such as BIOE labeling, supervised contrastive learning (SCL), and prototypic contrastive learning (PCL) were integrated to improve discrimination between confusing labels. Finally, an ensemble of five models trained using cross-validation was used, selecting the best model per partition and applying majority voting. This comprehensive approach achieved an F1 score of 85.93 on the test set. Future work proposes using some of these techniques to improve the F1 score results of this research.

6 Conclusions and Future Work

In this article, we present a methodology for the RR prediction task in Task 6 of the Legal Assessment "Understanding Hindi Legal Texts" of SemEval 2023, using BERT-based models and comparing their results using F1-Score as a reference. The experimental results reveal that the LegalBert model, with an F1-Score of 0.6318 (63.18%), obtained the best result of the tests performed; however, it is still below the best result obtained in SemEval 2023, which is 0.8593 (85.93%). It is worth noting that the number of instances and tokens of each class shows that the 13 classes are unbalanced, which affects the results. Therefore, it is proposed to explore techniques to manage class imbalance, such as advanced sampling strategies (SMOTE), among others.

References

1. Hazra, A.K., Micevska, M.B.: The problem of court congestion:evidence from indian lower courts. Technical report,ZEF Discussion Papers on Development Policy (2004)
2. Katju, J.M.: Backlog of cases crippling judiciary (2019)
3. Bambroo, P., Adhikary, S., Bhattacharya, P., Chakraborty, A., Ghosh, S., Ghosh, K.: Marro: multi-headed attention for rhetorical role labeling in legal documents. Artificial Intelligence and Law, 1–30(2025)
4. Malik, V.,et al.: ILDC for CIPE : indian legal documents corpus for court judgment prediction and explanation.arXiv preprint arXiv:2105.13562 (2021)
5. Kalamkar, P., et al.: Corpus for automatic structuring of legal documents. arXiv preprint arXiv:2201.13125 (2022)

6. Lyu, Y.,et al.: Improving legal judgment prediction through reinforced criminal element extraction. Inf. Proc. Manag. **59**(1), 102780 (2022)
7. Jain, D., Borah, M.D., Biswas, A.: Summarization of legal documents: where are we now and the way forward. Comput. Sci. Rev. 40, 100388 (2021)
8. Anand, D., Wagh, R.: Effective deep learning approaches for summarization of legal texts. J. King Saud Univ. Comput. Inf. Sci. **34**(5),2141–2150 (2022)
9. Thenmozhi, D., Kannan, K., Aravindan, C.: A text similarity approach for precedence retrieval from legal documents. In: FIRE (Working Notes),pp. 90–91 (2017)
10. Parikh, V., Mathur, V.,Mehta, P., Mittal, N., Majumder, P.: Lawsum: a weakly supervised approach for indian legal document summarization.arXiv preprint arXiv:2110.01188 (2021)
11. Nigam, S.K., Dubey, T., Sharma, G., Shallum, N., Ghosh, K., Bhattacharya, A.: Legalseg: unlocking the structure of indian legal judgments through rhetorical role classification.arXiv preprint arXiv:2502.05836(2025)
12. Kohli, G.S., Kaur, P., Bedi, J.: Automatic detection of rhetorical role labels using ernie2. 0 and roberta. In: FIRE (Working Notes),pp. 581–588(2021)
13. Mehta, P.: From extractive to abstractive summarization: a journey. In: ACL (student Research Workshop),pp. 100–106(2016).Springer
14. Tas, O., Kiyani, F.: A survey automatic text summarization. PressAcademia Procedia 5, 1, 205–213.Crossref (2017)
15. Das, A., Goyal, V.: Indian legal case judgment document mining: semantic segmentation and information extraction. PhD thesis, IIIT-Delhi (2024)
16. Ghosh, T., Kumar, S.: A survey of legal text analysis techniques for indian legal documents. In: 2024 International Conference on Circuit, Systems and Communication (ICCSC),pp. 1–6(2024). IEEE
17. Singh, D.: Legal documents text analysis using natural language processing(NLP). In: 2024 2nd International Conference on Self Sustainable Artificial Intelligence Systems (ICSSAS),pp. 1302–1307(2024). IEEE
18. Tekade, P., Jadhav, N., Chawda, S., Bhosale, V., Akashe, Y.: Legal lens: exploring NLP for document analysis in law. In:2024 IEEE International Conference on Blockchain and Distributed Systems Security (ICBDS),pp. 1–5(2024). IEEE
19. Deshpande, A., Deshmukh, P.: Legalai across languages: a comprehensive survey on tasks,methodologies and challenges. In: 2025 1st International Conference on AIML-Applications for Engineering and Technology (ICAET),pp. 1–6(2025).IEEE
20. Kapoor, A.,et al.: HLDC: hindi legal documents corpus.arXiv preprint arXiv:2204.00806(2022)
21. Marino, G., Licari, D., Bushipaka, P., Comandé, G., Cucinotta, T.: Automatic rhetorical roles classification for legal documents using legal-transformeroverbert. In: CEUR WORKSHOP PROCEEDINGS,vol.3441,pp. 28–36(2023). CEUR-WS
22. Santosh, T.,Isaia, A.,Hong, S.,Grabmair, M.: Hiculr: hierarchical curriculum learning for rhetorical role labeling of legal documents.arXiv preprint arXiv:2409.18647(2024)
23. Huo, J., et al.: Antcontenttech at semeval-2023 task 6: domain-adaptive pretraining and auxiliary-task learning for understanding indian legal texts. In: Proceedings of the 17th International Workshop on Semantic Evaluation (SemEval-2023),pp. 402–408 (2023)
24. Devlin, J.,Chang, M.-W.,Lee, K.,Toutanova, K.: Bert:pre-training of deep bidirectional transformers for language understanding. In: Proceedings of the 2019 Conference of the North American Chapter of the Association for Computational Linguistics:Human Language Technologies, Volume 1 (long and Short Papers),pp. 4171–4186(2019)

25. Jin, X., Wang, Y.: Understand legal documents with ontextualized large language models.arXiv preprint arXiv:2303.12135(2023)
26. Tasneem, F., Hossain, T.,Naim, J.,Chy, A.N.: Csecu-dsg at semeval-2023 task 6: segmenting legal documents into rhetorical roles via fine-tuned transformer architecture. In: Proceedings of the 17th International Workshop on Semantic Evaluation (SemEval-2023),pp. 2112–2117(2023)
27. Liu, Y., et al.: Roberta: a robustly optimized BERT pretraining approach.arXiv preprint arXiv:1907.11692(2019)
28. Noviello, Y.,Pallotta, E.,Pinzarrone, F.,Tanzi, G.:Teamunibo at semeval-2023 task 6: a transformer based approach to rhetorical roles prediction and NER in legal texts. In: Proceedings of the 17th International Workshop on Semantic Evaluation (SemEval-2023),pp. 275–284 (2023)
29. Saito, T., Rehmsmeier, M.: The precision-recall plot is more informative than the roc plot when evaluating binary classifiers on imbalanced datasets. PloS one**10**(3),0118432 (2015)D
30. Davis, J.,Goadrich, M.:The relationship between precision-recall and roc curves. In: Proceedings of the 23rd International Conference on Machine Learning ,pp. 233–240 (2006)

Semi-Supervised Learning Ensemble Model for Water Quality Classification in Mexican Municipalities

Raquel Cossío-Ramírez, Hortencia A. Ramírez-Vázquez, Amanda Valdez-Calderon(✉), Miguel González-Mendoza, and Enrique Garcia-Ceja

Tecnológico de Monterrey, Ave. Eugenio Garza Sada 2501, 64849 Monterrey, NL, Mexico

amvc62@outlook.com

Abstract. Water quality in Mexico has been largely affected by pollutants, which have had a negative impact on the health of the country's water resources. Although monitoring stations are located within 1046 municipalities of Mexico, 1432 remain unaccounted. We developed a Semi-Supervised Learning Ensemble Model (SSLEM) using an integrated dataset containing water quality information, demographics, and industry metrics for each municipality. The SSLEM integrates predictions from three distinct supervised algorithms: XGBoost, CatBoost, and Random Forest. It employs an averaged-confidence-based selection strategy that retrains itself with labeled data and pseudo-labels from predictions with at least 75% confidence. This confidence threshold was chosen by evaluating SSLEM under different confidence thresholds (70%, 75%, 80%, and 85%). After at most 40 iterations, the SSLEM predicted 80% of the missing data, achieving 54% accuracy using three-level labels (good, medium, and bad). The predicted labels of these 1,136 municipalities translate to an estimated population of 20 million by the year 2020. The SSLEM was compared to an ensemble model (EM) without self-learning, which produced predictions for only 53% of the missing data with at least 75% confidence and a 52% accuracy. Additionally, the SSLEM could be best suited for proposing to the respective authorities which municipalities could benefit most from placing measuring stations in vulnerable areas.

Keywords: Water Quality · Semi-Supervised Learning · Mexico

1 Introduction

According to the 2023 water quality data from the National Network of Water Quality Measurements (RENAMECA), a monitoring system of the National Water Commission (CONAGUA), water quality in Mexico is facing significant water contamination challenges due to various factors, including natural contaminants, industrial pollution, agricultural runoff, urbanization, and overexploitation, leaving only a few water bodies unaffected [1]. In the context of public

L. Martínez-Villaseñor et al. (Eds.): MICAI 2025, CCIS 2712, pp. 104–116, 2025.
https://doi.org/10.1007/978-3-032-08704-1_9

health, access to information is of critical importance. An integrated analysis using the RENAMECA data quality at the municipal level revealed that, among the 2,478 existing municipalities in Mexico [2], information is available for only 1,046 of them. Lack of comprehensive data hinders the implementation of targeted interventions, the enhancement of public awareness, and the accountability of responsible parties. To address this gap, this study proposes the development of a Semi-Supervised Learning Ensemble Model (SSLEM) capable of accurately predicting water quality classifications (color labels) for unlabeled data by using patterns learned from labeled instances.

Several studies have been conducted recently to assess and predict water quality in Mexico. For instance, L. Díaz-González et al. [3] present a water quality classification model with hyperparameter tuning and cross-validation to analyze data from four water body types:groundwater, lotic, lentic, and coastal waters. This study provided a Python-based tool that integrates certain models to identify hybrid water quality types. Similarly, [4] studies water quality in Mexico by predicting contaminant presence in Mexican water bodies using machine learning algorithms.

To implement a novel approach for water quality prediction, a SSLEM is proposed. The following are the specific contributions of the present paper:

- Integration of dataset that combines municipalities features and water quality indicators in Mexico.
- Architecture of a Semi-Supervised Learning (SSL) model that integrates three supervised classifiers (XGBoost, CatBoost, and Random Forest) to predict water quality classification for municipalities lacking labeled data from Mexico.
- Evaluation of the proposed SSLEM against an Ensemble Model (EM) to assess its effectiveness in handling missing labels.
- Prediction of the water quality classification for municipalities of Mexico lacking a water quality label.

The paper is organized as follows:Sect. 2 provides more in-depth explanations of work related and background to our problem. Section 3 describes the proposed work in detail. Section 4 explains the datasets and methodology implemented for this study. Section 5 describes the results obtained and the comparisons made with traditional approaches. Conclusions are provided in the last section.

2 Related Work and Background

CONAGUA operates monitoring sites across Mexico, tracking surface and groundwater quality according to information reported by RENAMECA. In 2023, 27.3% of observed surface waters were reported as good quality, 21.8% as medium quality, and 50.9% as poor quality. Observed groundwater was reported as 55.4% good quality, 12.9% medium quality, and 31.7% poor quality [1]. This means that, for measured surface waters, only a quarter contains little to no contamination, while measured underground water is only half of it.

Despite CONAGUA's attempt to offer public datasets [5] containing information about water quality across the country, their monitoring stations are not sufficiently distributed to offer information about every municipality in the country. This lack of access can cause public health issues and hinder the government's ability to make informed decisions about water-related policies.

Several studies have explored the challenge of predicting water quality using machine learning approaches around the world. For instance, previous work on Water Quality Index (WQI) prediction has demonstrated the effectiveness of Supervised Learning (SL) methods in reducing the cost and complexity of water quality assessments. Regression and classification models have been applied to predict WQI in the Santiago-Guadalajara river, optimizing the number of parameters required for accurate estimation from 17 to 12 features [6]. Similarly, a study [7] integrated the principal regression method for WQI prediction and utilized the gradient boosting classifier to predict water quality status. This model is evaluated on a Gulshan Lake-related dataset and achieves an overall accuracy of more than 90%.

Furthermore, Artificial Neural Networks (ANNs) have been widely used in environmental modeling, particularly in water quality prediction. Rustam et al. [8] employed ANNs with seven layers in the framework to predict water quality and water consumption, achieving an accuracy of 96% in the proposed model.

Finally, a comparison has been made using different models to predict WQI, including Random Forest, Neural Networks, multiple Linear Regression, Support Vector Machines, and Boosting Tree Models [9]. These models have demonstrated varying degrees of accuracy and efficiency in water quality assessment. These models present similar accuracy values, ranging between 98% and 100%.

These studies illustrate the effectiveness of various machine learning models in predicting water quality. However, many of these approaches rely on obtaining water quality parameters that can be expensive and time-consuming to measure. This challenge motivated our approach to develop a SSL framework that integrates three different models and after a selection strategy makes the final prediction of water quality.

2.1 Machine Learning Models

For the proposed work, two main categories of machine learning approaches are considered:**Supervised Learning** (SL) and **Semi-Supervised Learning** (SSL).

A. Supervised Learning (SL). SL is one of the most applied machine learning methods. For SL approach, models are trained with annotated data and these models can be used to classify other unlabeled data. The methods (XGBoost, CatBoost and Random Forest) utilized for the SSLEM are described following.

Gradient Boosting (GB). [10] is an ensemble predictive model that is used for regression and classification tasks. It combines multiple weak models (decision trees) sequentially to create a strong predictive model. In each new model, GB reduces the residual errors of the previous one, improving the performance and accuracy in predictions [11]. Some of the algorithms that are based on GB that will be implemented as part of our proposed work are XGBoost and CatBoost.

Random Forest (RF). [12] combines the output of multiple decision trees to reach a prediction. It utilizes the bagging method and feature randomness, only selecting a subset of all possible features, to create an uncorrelated forest of decision trees.

B. Semi-Supervised Learning. SSL [13] trains a classifier using both labeled and unlabeled instances in a given dataset. Furthermore, it aims to predict more accurately with unlabeled data than SL that uses only labeled data. SSL generates output labels from input data by uncovering relationships between different elements within the dataset.

3 Proposed Work

Following an initial exploration of the water quality situation in Mexico, this study addresses the limited availability of municipal-level water quality data. Proposed methodology involves data collection and preparation, dataset merging, model development using a self-training model, validation of the model and analysis of results.

The general objective of this study is to develop and evaluate a SSLEM capable of accurately predicting water quality by municipality based on environmental factors such as population, inundability, and industrial activity.

Specific objectives are to preprocess and prepare the dataset by separating labeled and unlabeled records suitable for SSL classification. Design and implement a SSL framework that integrates labeled and unlabeled data for imputation. Evaluate the effectiveness of the proposed classification approach in comparison to a baseline model that does not implement SSL.

4 Methodology

This section contains in-detail information about the data and methodology developed for water quality classification.

4.1 Datasets

In order to predict water quality for municipalities that were not covered by measuring stations, we opt to build a dataset with features that could be indirectly related to water quality. Features per municipality such as population [14], altitude [14], area (Fig. 1) [15], flood-ability threshold [16], number of water treatment facilities and wastewater discharge points [17], and number of people working in industries (Fig. 2) [18] were included. For the total 2478 municipalities and boroughs present in Mexico, nine of them were excluded because they lacked enough available data, so the final municipalities count considered in this study is 2469. From this total only 1046 (42.4%) contained water quality measurements and the remaining 1423 (57.6%) were left for prediction.

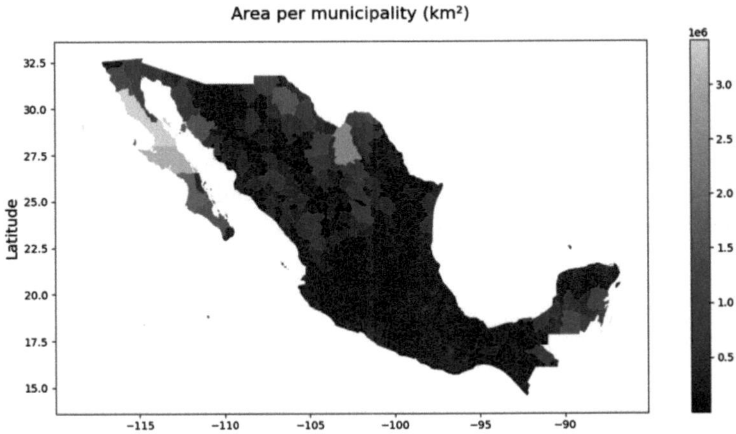

Fig. 1. Input dataset: Area per municipality [15]

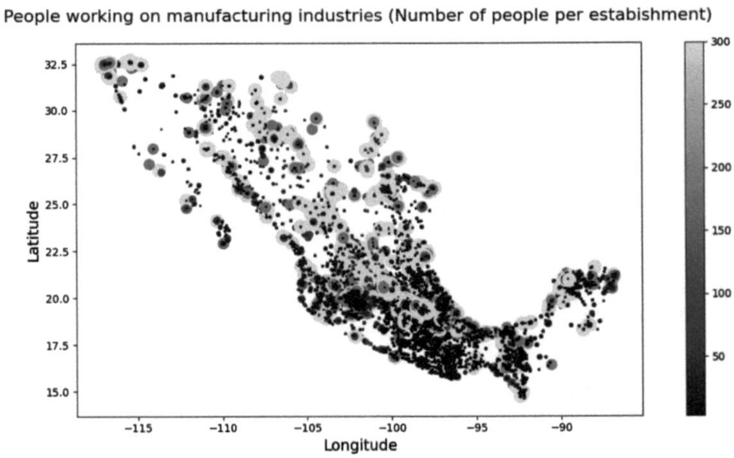

Fig. 2. Input dataset: Economic activity. Manufacturing industries [18]

4.2 Preprocessing

The first step of preprocessing included filling in missing values according to the dataset, correcting typos and recordings with different formats or characters.

To be able to merge all databases, general organization was adjusted. Because records could be found to be made in different time periods (monthly, yearly, for a period that comprised several years), data were averaged for the years from 2019 to 2023.

Four water quality datasets were found, each for a different type of water body:lotic, lentic, coastal and underground water. The main column was the traffic light color, which summarized water quality with a color (green for good quality, yellow for average quality and red for bad quality). When averaging these bases and merging them together, target column was assigned based on the mode of the recordings.

Finally, all datasets mentioned above were merged together based on their geographical key, which is a numerical value of four or five digits, where the first two represented the state and the last two or three the number of municipality. Once a final dataset was obtained, the good/medium/bad label was hot encoded and no scaling was necessary due to the chosen models' nature.

4.3 Preliminary Model

An initial exploratory analysis was performed to gain better understanding of the dataset's structure and behavior. This was done through a baseline EM (without self-learning) using only labeled data for training. This model combined XGBoost, CatBoost and Random Forest models, and achieved an accuracy of 52% and a total of assigned 1318 labels, which denoted a reasonable starting point, but also highlighted the limitations of relying solely on labeled data. These preliminary results revealed the need for a more robust approach capable of leveraging the available unlabeled data. Consequently, a semi-supervised learning strategy was adopted to enhance model performance by incorporating the full dataset.

Table 1. Ensemble Model Metrics

Metric	Precision	Recall	F1-Score	Support
Good	0.37	0.25	0.30	56
Medium	0.54	0.64	0.58	89
Bad	0.59	0.60	0.60	65
Overall accuracy	-	-	-	0.52

4.4 Semi-Supervised Model

In this study, SSL approach was employed to make use of both labeled and unlabeled data. This method is suitable for this case where more than half the data did not possess classification and it is of public importance to know said label. The SSLEM was developed using Python's libraries SciKit Learn [19], XGBoost [20] and CatBoost [21].

The model followed a self-training paradigm, which is a SSL approach. The process began with an initial classifier trained only on the available labeled data. Once training was done, this classifier was used to generate predictions for the unlabeled data. To assess the certainty of each prediction, the model's probability outputs, obtained through the predict_proba() function from the respective model's library, were examined, considering that they are normalized with values between 0 and 1 and sum up to 1 in total. Predictions with a probability score that exceeded the predefined 75% confidence threshold were considered high-confidence predictions.

These high-confidence predictions were then assigned as pseudo-labels and added to the original training set. The model was retrained on the expanded dataset. This cycle was repeated until no more high-confidence predictions were obtained. Over these iterations, the training set gradually grew in size and diversity, enabling the model to incorporate new patterns and information. The result was that the number of unlabeled samples decreased significantly.

The selection strategy for assigning a pseudo-label (Fig. 3) begins by retrieving the normalized class probabilities output by each of the three models. For each class, probabilities are summed across models, producing an aggregated probability per class. The class with the highest probability is selected and divided by the amount of models (three, in this case), which returns the average probability for that class. If that averaged probability exceeds the chosen confidence threshold of 0.75, the corresponding label is assigned to the municipality as a pseudo-label. In case it does not meet the threshold, the predictions are discarded and that instance remains unlabeled.

Proposed SSLEM Architecture is presented in Fig. 4. To perform the model training process, the following steps were executed:

1. Dataset was divided into two groups:labeled (1046 records) and unlabeled (1423 records) municipalities.
2. The labeled records were then split into the training set for the model, which accounts for 80% of those data, and the other 20% was saved for validation once the model was fully trained.
3. This training set was input into the three mentioned models (XGBoost, CatBoost and Random Forest) to train them individually. Once this was done, unlabeled data was used as input for each of the models in the ensemble, and their prediction probabilities were calculated and passed to the selection strategy.
4. Confidence threshold was set to 75%, so predictions that surpassed that threshold were labeled with said quality and added to the training set made up of labeled data. Predictions that did not meet the confidence requirements were discarded and the records were sent back to the unlabeled set to be predicted in the next iteration.
5. Steps 3 and 4 are repeated on a loop until there are no unlabeled records or no more predictions exceed the threshold, therefore no more learning can be

done. While this repetition of steps happen, the training set keeps growing with the newly labeled data, while the test set remains the same size since the split.

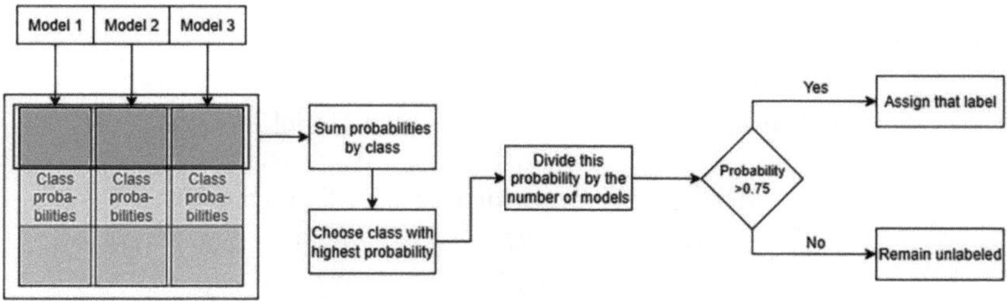

Fig. 3. Selection Strategy Diagram

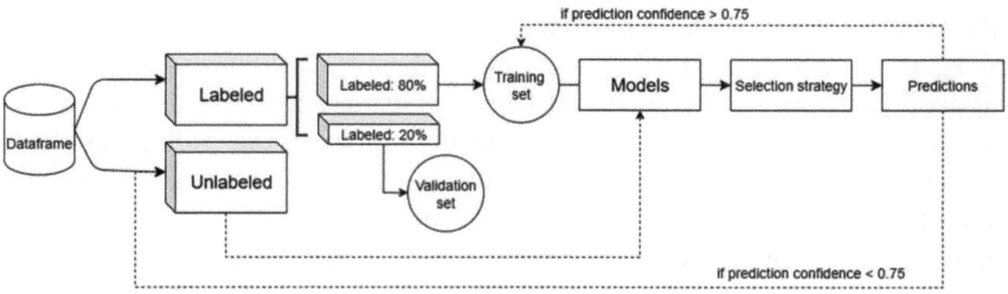

Fig. 4. Proposed SSLEM Architecture

5 Results

This section presents the results obtained after training the SSLEM, and its evaluation metrics.

The SSLEM model was evaluated under different confidence thresholds (70%, 75%, 80%, and 85%) to analyze how the choice of threshold affects performance. As shown in Table 2, the threshold directly influences accuracy, Fleiss Kappa, the number of iterations, and the amount of predicted labels. A lower threshold (70%) increases label coverage but at the cost of accuracy, while higher thresholds (80âĂŞ85%) reduce the number of predicted labels and accuracy levels. Considering this trade-off, the 75% threshold provided the best balance between accuracy and prediction coverage.

A threshold of 75% was selected to evaluate the performance of the SSLEM. Using this threshold the model achieved an overall accuracy of 54%, reflecting

Table 2. SSLEM Behavior with Different Thresholds

Threshold	Accuracy	Fleiss Kappa	Max Iterations	Total Labels
70%	52%	83%	24	2075
75%	54%	80%	35	1966
80%	51%	78%	36	1845
85%	51%	75%	33	1614

Table 3. Semi-Supervised Ensemble Model Metrics

Metric	Precision	Recall	F1-Score	Support
Good	0.37	0.23	0.29	56
Medium	0.58	0.66	0.62	89
Bad	0.56	0.63	0.59	65
Overall accuracy	-	-	-	0.54

the difficulty of the classification task. Despite this, certain classes were more consistently predicted such as bad (with 63% of recall) and medium (with 58% of precision), as shown in Table 3.

Figure 5 presents the evolution of the evaluation across iterations. Accuracy and Macro F1 remain relatively stable throughout training, reflecting the difficulty of achieving balanced performance across classes. In contrast, Fleiss Kappa and Label's Coverage steadily increase and level off above 0.80, indicating that the model's predictions become more consistent and that it assigns labels to a larger portion of the data.

Results are also visualized in a confusion matrix (Fig. 6). This matrix shows that the model performed well for assigning bad quality and medium quality categories. Furthermore, many true good labels are misclassified as bad or medium, which could be false alarming.

Real labels of water quality are shown in Fig. 7 while resulting predictions are shown in Fig. 8. We can observe that territories between same-color municipalities are usually predicted with that same water quality.

In total our model predicts 561 new labels, given a total of 1966 water quality labels from which 325 are predictions for bad quality, 441 for medium and 280 for good. Using this model we increased the number of municipalities with water quality labels from only 42% to 80%, considering 2478 municipalities and boroughs present in Mexico in 2025. From 57% missing label data around Mexico's municipalities, our model predicts 52% of all missing data under a 75% of confidence threshold. For more details in data collection and processing, the https://github.com/raqcoss/ML-water Github Repository is included.

Additionally, the SSLEM is compared to the ensemble model without using the semi supervised learning approach. The last one achieved an accuracy of

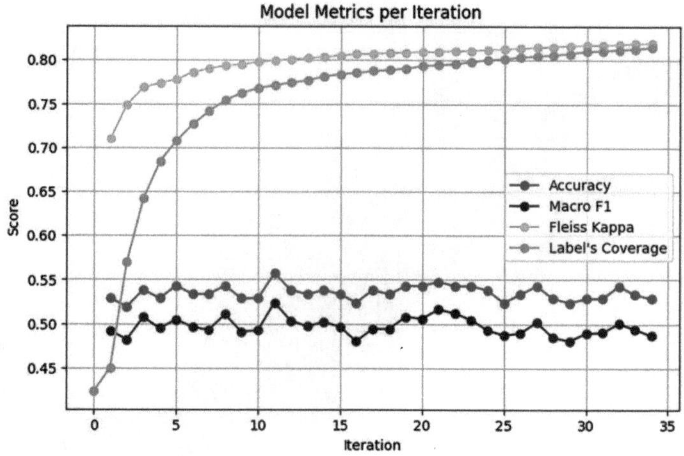

Fig. 5. SSLEM performance metrics (Accuracy, Macro F1, Fleiss Kappa and Label's Coverage) per iteration using 75% of threshold

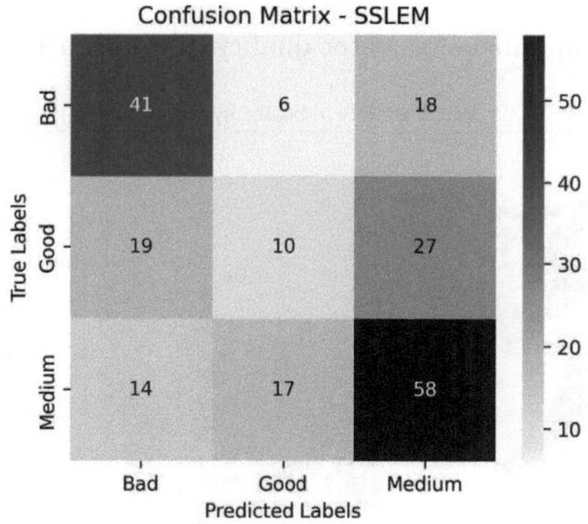

Fig. 6. Confusion Matrix of the SSLEM.

52%. Despite achieving higher precision, recall, and F1-score for some labels (Table 1), the ensemble model predicted only 274 new labeled data points.

6 Conclusions

Although some classes were classified more accurately than others, the overall accuracy of 54% at a 75% confidence threshold reflects the challenges posed by the dataset. Even the SSLEM trained only on labeled data performed poorly, suggesting that the main limitation lies in data quality and labeling rather than in the model itself.

The dataset provided by CONAGUA included chemical indicators of water quality along with a summarized 3-level classification (Bad, Medium, Good),

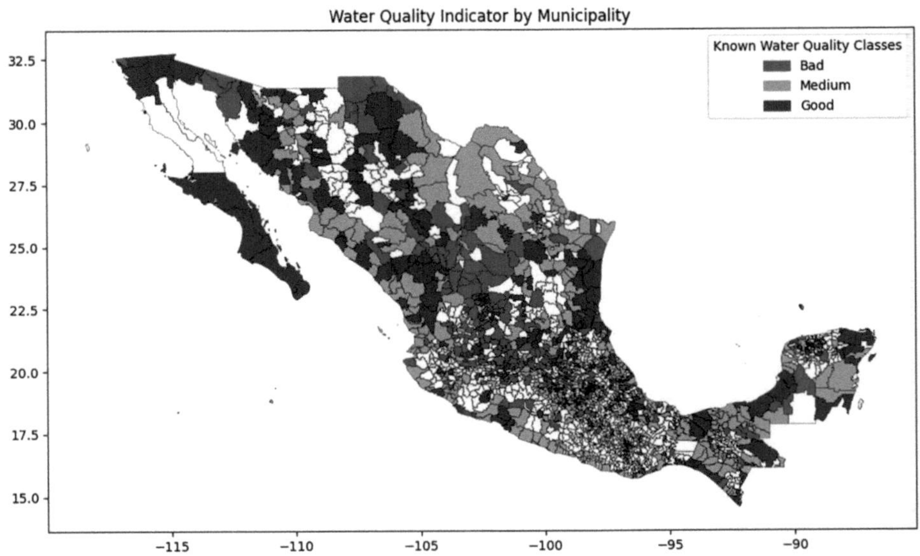

Fig. 7. Original labels for water quality on Mexico's municipalities

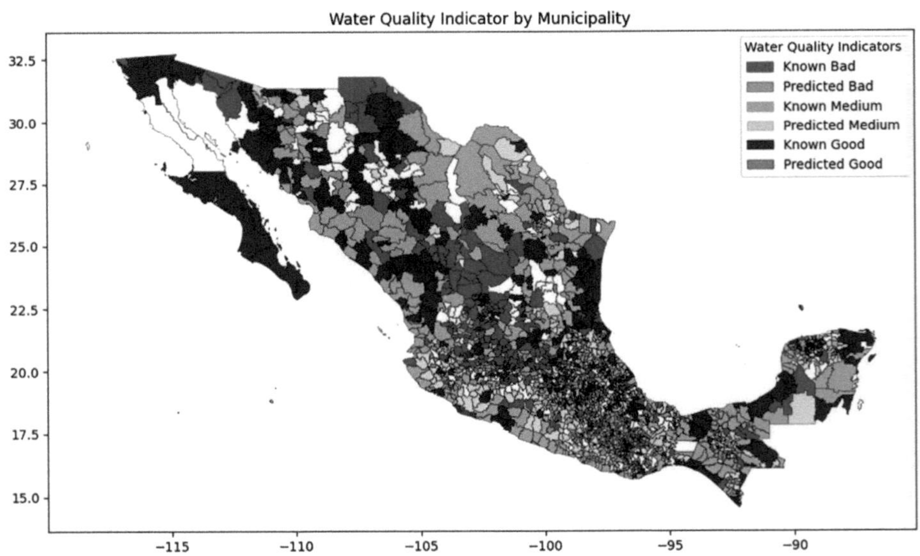

Fig. 8. "Original (solid color) and predicted (transparent colors) labels for water quality(Color figure online)

whose subjective nature likely contributed to systematic misclassifications, reducing both interpretability and performance.

Despite these limitations, the results highlight the potential of the approach. We increased the coverage label from 1,046 to 2,182 labeled municipalities.

Furthermore land coverage increased from 71% to 87% of Mexico's total area, impacting around 20 million people censed to live in these municipalities by 2020 [22]. With more reliable and consistently labeled data, models could achieve stronger performance and provide valuable insights for decision-making on monitoring and interventions. This could directly support policies addressing water quality issues in critical areas.

Future work will explore alternative labeling strategies, such as clustering-based methods, and greater integration of domain knowledge. Collaboration with environmental authorities to improve data collection protocols and labeling transparency will be essential for developing more robust and actionable models for water quality monitoring in Mexico.

Acknowledgements. The authors would like to thank the financial support from Tecnológico de Monterrey through the School of Engineering and Sciences. Amanda Valdez, Raquel Cossío and Hortencia A. Ramírez gratefully acknowledge the scholarship from SECIHTI to pursue their postgraduate studies in Computer Science.

References

1. Conagua, Renamecaf - red nacional de monitoreo de la calidad del agua (2025)
2. Inegi, Catálogo Único de claves de Ãreas geoestadísticas estatales, municipales y localidades, (2025)
3. Díaz, J.M., Pérez, L., Ramírez, A., González, M.: Machine learning for predicting water quality: an application in mexico. Environ. Model. Softw. vol. 170, p. 105839 (2025)
4. Molina-Garay, L., Treviño-Garza, N., Longoria-RodríÂŋguez, F.E., González-RamíÂŋrez, R., Gonzlez-FaráÂŋas, F.: Predicting water quality parameters using machine learning: a case study in northeastern mexico. In: 2024 International Conference on Computational Science and Computational Intelligence (CSCI), pp. 238–242, 2024
5. Conagua, Bancos de información de calidad del agua, (2025)
6. Fernández del Castillo, A., Yebra-Montes, C., Verduzco Garibay, M., de Anda, J., Garcia-Gonzalez, A., Gradilla-Hernández, M.S.: Simple prediction of an ecosystem-specific water quality index and the water quality classification of a reservoir, Water, vol. 14, no. 20, p. 3163 (2022)
7. Khan, Z., Ghani, I., Aslam, M., Hameed, I.A., Yasin, A., Mahmood, H.: Gradient boosting for groundwater quality prediction. Appl. Sci. **12**(9), 4697 (2022)
8. Rustam, F., Ashraf, I., Tanveer, M., Bin Ijaz, M.F., Vergara, P.P.L.: A performance comparison of supervised machine learning models for the prediction of soil fertility. Front. Environ. Sci. vol. 10, p. 949610, 2022
9. Hassan, Y., Elbeltagi, A., Morsy, S., Hagras, M., El Baroudy, A.: Developing a water quality index using machine learning algorithms: a case study of the nile river in egypt. J. Environ. Manage. **290**, 112594 (2021)
10. Friedman, J.H.: Greedy function approximation: a gradient boosting machine. Ann. Stat. **29**(5), 1189–1232 (2001)
11. Shahid, O., Nawaz, M., Iqbal, A., Ghani, I.: Comparative analysis of machine learning algorithms for groundwater quality prediction: a case study of pakistan. Environ. Monit. Assess. **196**, 25 (2024)

12. Biau, G., Scornet, E.: A random forest guided tour. TEST **25**(2), 197–227 (2016). https://doi.org/10.1007/s11749-016-0481-7
13. Yang, Z., Qiu, P., Pan, L.: Multi-task self-supervised learning framework for water quality prediction. In: 2023 IEEE 11th International Conference on Information, Communication and Networks (ICICN), pp. 109–114 (2023)
14. Inegi, Encuesta intercensal, población por municipio, (2020)
15. Inegi, Marco geoestadístico, división municipal, (2022)
16. Cenapred, Atlas nacional de riesgos, inundabilidad, (2017)
17. Conagua, Sistema de información de saneamiento de aguas residuales, (2025)
18. Inegi, Anuario estadíÂŋstico y geográfico de los estados unidos mexicanos , (2022)
19. Pedregosa, F., et al.: Scikit-learn: machine learning in python. J. Mach. Learn. Res. **12**, 2825–2830 (2011)
20. Chen, T., Guestrin, C.: Xgboost: a scalable tree boosting system. In Proceedings of the 22nd ACM SIGKDD International Conference on Knowledge Discovery and Data Mining, pp. 785–794, 2016
21. Dorogush, A.V., Ershov, V., Gulin, A.:Catboost: gradient boosting with categorical features support. In: Conference on Neural Information Processing Systems (NIPS), (2017)
22. Instituto Nacional de Estadística y GeografíÂŋa (INEGI),Censo de población y vivienda 2020: Resultados por municipio (2020). https://www.inegi.org.mx/programas/ccpv/2020/

Intelligent Classification of Three Floral Classes (*Bellis perennis*, *Lavandula angustifolia*, and *Helianthus annuus*) Utilizing Convolutional Neural Networks

Marilyn Juárez-Flores[1(✉)], Juan Carlos Olguín-Rojas[1,2], Jorge Víctor Prado-Hernández[1], and Juan Loaeza-Joachin[3]

[1] Posgrado en Ingeniería Agrícola y Uso Integral del Agua, Universidad Autónoma Chapingo, Texcoco, Estado de México, Mexico
floreslyn343@gmail.com, JOLGUINR@chapingo.mx, JPRADOH@chapingo.mx

[2] Departamento de Ingeniería Mecánica Agrícola, Universidad Autónoma Chapingo, Texcoco, Estado de México, Mexico

[3] Posgrado en Socioeconomía, Estadística e Informática-Cómputo Aplicado, Colegio de Postgraduados Campus Montecillo, Montecillo, Texcoco, Estado de México, Mexico

Abstract. This study presents the development and evaluation of an intelligent flower classification system using convolutional neural networks (CNNs) for three species: *Bellis perennis* (Daisy), *Lavandula angustifolia* (Lavender), and *Helianthus annuus* (Sunflower). Given the morphological similarity among floral species and the need for non-invasive and precise methods, four widely documented CNN architectures were employed: VGG16, VGG19, InceptionV3, and Xception. The training was structured through three strategies: Data Augmentation (DA), Feature Extraction (FE), and Fine Tuning (FT). Each model was evaluated with different optimizers (Adam, RMSprop, and SGD), selected based on their performance reported in previous studies on flower classification. A customized dataset, balanced across classes, totaling 3,000 images was used. The results demonstrate that CNN-based models are highly effective, exceeding 94% accuracy in the test set in several cases. InceptionV3 and VGG19 optimized with Adam showed the best overall performance, highlighting the consistency and robustness of this optimizer. The Xception model also presented competitive results, achieving accuracies above 93% in testing, with stable behavior across different training strategies and optimizers evaluated. In contrast, the SGD optimizer showed good performance only with InceptionV3. The Feature Extraction technique achieved the highest validation accuracy (97.50%), indicating that fine tuning is not always essential. Overall, it is concluded that the combination of architecture and optimizer has a more significant impact on performance than the applied training strategy.

L. Martínez-Villaseñor et al. (Eds.): MICAI 2025, CCIS 2712, pp. 117–140, 2025.
https://doi.org/10.1007/978-3-032-08704-1_10

Keywords: Floral classification · convolutional neural networks · InceptionV3 · VGG19

1 Introduccion

Convolutional neural networks (CNNs) have multiple applications across various fields of knowledge, including agriculture [11]. In particular, they have proven to be effective tools for visual recognition tasks, due to their ability to automatically learn discriminative features.

The automatic classification of floral species has gained importance in fields such as botany, floriculture, and precision agriculture. However, the high visual similarity between many species and the variability in environmental conditions make their identification difficult using traditional methods. In fact, classifying different types of flowers poses a significant challenge due to the wide range of colors within the same class and the notable similarity across different species [8,12,17]. Even expert botanists and gardeners may struggle to identify them accurately, as flowers are not rigid objects; their appearance can be affected by external factors such as temperature, sunlight, nutrition, or humidity. This highlights the need for a competent automated system capable of reliably identifying and recognizing floral species [9]. Notably, Tian et al. [21] developed a CNN-based method for flower identification under real-world conditions, demonstrating that deep learning can effectively manage visual variability and class similarity, achieving robust performance in diverse scenarios.

Deep learning, particularly transfer learning, has enabled the use of pretrained architectures such as VGG16, VGG19, InceptionV3, and Xception, achieving remarkable results even with moderately sized datasets. Recent studies support their applicability in flower classification, emphasizing the need for comparative evaluations of their performance under different training and optimization strategies [1,2,13].

This work clarifies its novel contribution along four axes. First, it adopts an integrated, factorial experimental design that jointly ablates architecture (VGG16, VGG19, InceptionV3, Xception), training strategy (Data Augmentation, Feature Extraction, Fine Tuning), and optimizer (Adam, RMSprop, SGD), enabling a systematic attribution of performance drivers. Second, the study targets three floral species with high morphological similarity, a setting that is less common in the literature and that stress-tests inter-class discrimination beyond broad, generic datasets. Third, we provide an explicit analysis of the architectureâĂŞoptimizer coupling, showing it exerts greater influence on performance than the training strategy itself. Finally, we include an exploratory scalability experiment extending the label space to 13 classes under a fixed protocol (Xception + Feature Extraction), offering initial evidence on generalization when the number of species increases.

This study develops an intelligent system for the classification of three floral species by combining various architectures, training techniques, and optimizers. The aim is to identify efficient configurations that enable accurate, robust, and generalizable classification, thereby contributing to the advancement of automated solutions for plant species recognition.

2 Related Work

Automatic Automatic flower classification has gained significant relevance in recent years due to its usefulness in various fields such as botany, agriculture, medicine, floriculture, and biodiversity conservation. This task poses a major challenge, as many floral species exhibit high similarity in color, shape, and texture, which complicates their identification using traditional methods [4,15]. Moreover, manual species recognition is costly and impractical given the existence of more than 350,000 flower species worldwide [1,8].

Traditional image processing methods, such as the use of black backgrounds, multilevel thresholds, co-occurrence matrices, or simple classifiers like k-NN and SVM, have proven to be unfeasible or insufficient to achieve robust and generalizable classification, especially when one requires distinguishing between very similar species [4,7,16]. Added to this is the difficulty of manually designing filters or rules that optimally capture the natural variations in flowers.

In contrast, modern deep learning techniques—especially convolutional neural networks (CNNs)—have demonstrated high effectiveness in image classification tasks, enabling the automatic extraction of discriminative features [8]. These architectures, composed of convolutional, pooling, and dense layers, have been complemented with mechanisms such as prior segmentation, visual attention, data augmentation, or feature selection using methods like mRMR or CMI [2,17].

Several studies have shown that the use of transfer learning—leveraging pretrained models such as VGG16, VGG19, DenseNet121, InceptionV3, AlexNet, GoogLeNet, and ResNet50—significantly improves model performance, even with limited datasets. For example, Kumar and Bhatia achieved an accuracy of 98.6% using DenseNet121 on the Oxford-102 dataset [12], while other studies have reported accuracies above 90% with VGG16, VGG19, and InceptionV3 [1,4,6].

In more localized applications, such as flower identification in Bangladesh, a CNN model with data augmentation techniques has been used to achieve an accuracy of 85%, highlighting the potential of these technologies in specific contexts and with limited resources [8]. Likewise, the implementation of the InceptionV3 model has demonstrated not only adequate accuracy (88.9%) but also remarkable inference efficiency (0.0736 s per image), making it a viable alternative for real-time applications [1,16].

The automation of floral species recognition not only optimizes collection and classification processes but also supports both experts and non-experts in identifying rare or new species, contributing to the development of digital catalogs and ecological preservation [13]. Moreover, these systems have the potential to be integrated into mobile tools or robotic systems, with applications in precision agriculture, image retrieval, environmental monitoring, and science education.

The review of related work revealed a variety of studies using convolutional neural networks (CNNs) for flower classification, some focused on a few classes and others on multiple species. However, most of these studies target general or popular datasets and do not specifically address the comparison between CNN architectures applied to particular floral categories. For this reason, the objective of this work was to develop and evaluate an intelligent floral image classification system based on convolutional neural networks (CNNs), comparing the performance of four architectures (VGG16, VGG19, InceptionV3, and Xception), three training strategies (Data Augmentation, Feature Extraction, and Fine Tuning), as well as widely used optimizers (Adam, RMSprop, and SGD), in order to identify the most effective configuration for the accurate classification of three selected species: *Bellis perennis* (Daisy), *Lavandula angustifolia* (Lavender), and *Helianthus annuus* (Sunflower). These species were chosen for their relevance in floriculture and because they exhibit distinct visual patterns while also sharing characteristics that can make them difficult to distinguish. To achieve this objective, well-known CNN architectures recognized for their effectiveness in computer vision were evaluated, experimenting with different hyperparameters for each in order to identify the configuration that offers the best results for this specific task.

Beyond CNN-based methods, earlier approaches relied on traditional classifiers such as k-Nearest Neighbors (k-NN) and Support Vector Machines (SVM), typically combined with handcrafted texture and shape descriptors. For instance, Guru et al. [7] employed k-NN using texture features for flower classification, reporting limited generalization capabilities in complex scenarios. Similarly, other studies [8,15] discuss the transition from these classical methods to deep learning models, highlighting how CNNs overcome the limitations of manual feature design by automatically extracting discriminative patterns.

While numerous studies have applied CNNs and transfer learning for flower classification [1,4,6,8,12,15], most of them either focus on a specific model or report results on generic datasets such as Oxford-102. In contrast, this work contributes by conducting a systematic factorial comparison across multiple CNN architectures, training strategies, and optimizers, applied to floral species with high morphological similarity. Although the models evaluated are well-established, the study provides a rigorous experimental design that clarifies the relative strengths of different approaches, thus complementing prior reports centered on isolated methods or dataset-specific benchmarks.

More recently, novel architectures have been proposed that go beyond conventional CNNs, such as EfficientNet [20], Vision Transformers (ViT) [5], and ConvNeXt [14]. These models have demonstrated state-of-the-art results in large-scale image classification by improving parameter efficiency, incorporating attention mechanisms, or redesigning convolutional blocks. Although this study focused on established CNN architectures to ensure comparability and reproducibility, future research could explore these newer approaches to assess their scalability and potential benefits in floral classification tasks involving larger or more complex datasets.

3 Materials and Methods

3.1 CNN Architectures Analyzed

To achieve accurate and non-invasive classification of three floral species, a vision system based on convolutional neural networks (CNNs) was developed. The selected architectures were VGG16, VGG19, InceptionV3, and Xception, known for their effectiveness in computer vision tasks and widely used in scientific literature. Additionally, different optimizers (Adam, RMSprop, and SGD) were evaluated with the aim of identifying the optimal combination of architecture, training strategy, and optimizer to maximize performance in the automatic classification of flowers. It is important to note that the models were primarily trained using transfer learning, freezing the pre-trained convolutional layers and adapting the top layers to the specific multiclass classification problem.

3.2 Dataset Description

The images used in this study were obtained from the online platform Kaggle [10], from which a total of 3,000 images were extracted, evenly distributed across three classes: 1,000 images of *Bellis perennis* (Daisy)(Figure 1A), 1,000 of *Lavandula angustifolia* (Lavender) (Fig. 1B), and 1,000 of *Helianthus annuus* (Sunflower) (Fig. 1C).

The images used in this study are characterized by a high diversity in lighting conditions, color variations, and different phenological stages of the flowers, accurately reflecting the natural conditions in which these species may appear. The dataset includes flowers in various colors, ranging from floral buds to full bloom, as well as in different contexts: single flowers, clusters in open fields, potted plants, and floral arrangements. Additionally, the backgrounds of the images vary in tone and texture, representing heterogeneous visual scenarios.

Since the images came from different datasets, their original dimensions were heterogeneous. For this reason, preprocessing was applied to standardize the dimensions using the parameters target_size and input_shape, setting a standard size of 200 × 200 pixels. This dimension was selected based on the approximate average size of the images and after conducting comparative tests with resolutions of 100 × 100, 150 × 150, 180 × 180, 210 × 210, 224 × 224, and 250 × 250 pixels. The results showed that the 200 × 200 size offered better performance in terms of test accuracy, suggesting the existence of an optimal image size for this specific problem.

The dataset (comprising the three classes) was divided as follows: 70% of the images were allocated for training, 15% for validation, and the remaining 15% for testing the model.

Although Kaggle provides accessible and well-organized image repositories, these datasets may present certain biases. For instance, images are often curated, visually homogeneous, or pre-processed, which reduces the presence of noise, background variability, or inconsistencies typical of real-world conditions. This limitation may lead to an overestimation of the model's generalization capacity when deployed in uncontrolled environments, such as open fields or natural habitats. Future work should consider the collection of images directly in the field, under diverse environmental conditions, to validate the robustness of the models in realistic scenarios. For transparency, the dataset used in this study corresponds to "Kaggle – Classification Datasets" (ID: 13302-Classification), available at: https://www.kaggle.com/datasets?tags=13302-Classification.

Fig. 1. Examples of the *Bellis perennis*, *Lavandula angustifolia*, and *Helianthus annuus* classes.

To provide a transparent overview of the datasets used in this study, including both the initial 3-class experiment and the extended 13-class scenario, we summarize in Table 1 the number of classes, images per class, total samples, and their partition into training, validation, and test sets. This structured summary facilitates reproducibility and highlights the balanced nature of the datasets employed.

Table 1. Datasets employed and their distribution across training, validation, and test sets.

Dataset	Classes	Images per class	Total images	Training	Validation	Test
3 Class (Kaggle)	3	1,000	3,000	2,100	450	450
3 Class (Kaggle)	13	1,000	13,000	9,100	1,950	1,950

The partitioning followed a standard 70%–15%–15% split (training/validation/test) to ensure balance across all classes. All images were obtained from Kaggle [10], and the same preprocessing pipeline was applied in both the initial and extended experiments.

3.3 VGG16, VGG19, InceptionV3, and Xception Architectures

In this study, four convolutional neural network (CNN) architectures were used with the aim of comparing their performance in floral image classification: VGG16, VGG19, InceptionV3, and Xception. The VGG16 and VGG19 architectures, proposed by Simonyan and Zisserman [18], achieved high accuracy levels on ImageNet thanks to their deep design structured in sequential convolutional blocks. InceptionV3, introduced by Szegedy et al. [19] as part of the GoogLeNet family, stands out for its computational efficiency by using Inception modules that combine convolutions of multiple sizes in parallel. Meanwhile, Xception, proposed by Chollet [3], is an architecture that improves the efficiency of convolutions through the use of depthwise separable convolutions, achieving an optimal balance between accuracy and speed.

For all architectures, the pre-trained weights were reused and the original dense layers were removed (include_top=False) to perform transfer learning. The convolutional layers were frozen, and new fully connected layers were added, tailored to the three-class flower classification problem. The custom configuration consisted of a Flatten layer, a dense layer with 512 neurons and ReLU activation function, a Dropout layer with a rate of 0.5 to prevent overfitting, and an-output layer with three neurons and Softmax activation.

To evaluate the impact of the optimizer on performance, two or three versions were implemented for each architecture: Adam and RMSprop for VGG16; Adam and SGD for VGG19; and Adam, SGD, and RMSprop for InceptionV3 and Xception using Feature Extraction and Fine Tuning. Each model was trained under the same conditions, using data augmentation (ImageDataGenerator) and overfitting control through EarlyStopping and ModelCheckpoint. Subsequently, the models were evaluated using an independent test set.

This comparison allowed for the analysis of each architecture's behavior with different optimization strategies, observing accuracy and loss curves, confusion matrices, and classification reports, in order to identify the most effective combination for the multiclass classification of the floral species studied.

3.4 Experimental Desing

A set of treatments was established, defined as combinations of convolutional neural network architecture and training configuration, with the purpose of evaluating their effectiveness in the classification of three floral species: *Bellis perennis* (Daisy), *Lavandula angustifolia* (Lavender), and *Helianthus annuus* (Sunflower). Each treatment corresponded to a specific combination of the following factors: base architecture (VGG16, VGG19, InceptionV3, and Xception), training technique (Data Augmentation, Feature Extraction or Fine Tuning), optimizer used (Adam, RMSprop, or SGD with momentum), and learning rate.

The factorial nature of the design involved a high number of possible combinations. To make the computational execution of the experiment feasible, it was divided into two stages. In the first stage, multiple configurations were explored with a limited number of epochs (30), with the aim of identifying the combinations with the greatest potential in terms of accuracy and validation stability. This phase helped to narrow down the most promising learning rates and the most effective optimizers for each architecture.

In the second stage, the selected combinations were refined through extended training, up to a maximum of 100 epochs, using early stopping techniques to prevent overfitting and model checkpointing to save the model weights with the best validation performance. Additionally, this phase included a systematic evaluation of performance on the test set, the generation of confusion matrices, detailed classification reports, and graphs showing the evolution of accuracy and loss over the epochs.

With this experimental design, it was possible to analyze not only the individual impact of each factor (architecture, training strategy, and optimizer) but also their interactions, allowing the identification of the most effective configurations for automatic flower classification, evaluated based on validation and test set accuracy.

3.5 Guided Exploration

The present work follows a guided exploration approach for optimizing performance in automatic floral image classification using convolutional neural networks (CNNs). This method involves an iterative and staged testing of hyperparameter combinations, prioritizing configurations with greater potential based on preliminary results, in order to maximize computational efficiency and the effectiveness of the training process.

Therefore, the approach adopted in this study represents a compromise between thoroughness and practical feasibility, ensuring a balance between computational resources and the achievement of reliable and representative results for the specific task of multiclass classification of floral species.

3.6 Tools and Execution Environment

The implementation of the models and experiments was carried out using free and open-source software, ensuring transparency and reproducibility. Python 3.6 was used as the main programming language, supported by specialized libraries for processing and machine learning, including Keras for the design and training of convolutional neural networks.

The execution environment was the Google Colaboratory platform, which provides cloud-based computational resources, including access to GPUs. Most experiments were executed on Tesla T4 GPUs with 16 GB of VRAM, while in some cases Colab Pro was used, which allowed access to more powerful hardware such as NVIDIA A100 and L4 GPUs. This significantly reduced training time: while on the free tier a complete training (100 epochs) required 30âĂŞ40 min per model, on Colab Pro the same process took 10âĂŞ15 min on average.

Memory limitations inherent to Colab were managed by using mini-batches of size 32, as well as data generators (ImageDataGenerator) to avoid loading the entire dataset into memory. Additionally, EarlyStopping and ModelCheckpoint were applied to optimize training efficiency and prevent unnecessary computation. These strategies ensured that experiments could be carried out feasibly even within the restricted environment of a cloud-based GPU service.

3.7 Evaluation Metrics

To evaluate the performance of the models in classifying *Bellis perennis* (Daisy), *Lavandula angustifolia* (Lavender), and *Helianthus annuus* (Sunflower), standard metrics for multiclass classification were used: accuracy, precision, recall, F1-score, and confusion matrix. These metrics allow for the analysis of both overall performance and class-specific behavior.

In addition to overall accuracy, we report per-class metrics (precision, recall, and F1-score) together with macro, micro, and weighted averages, to capture both global and class-specific performance while mitigating potential effects of class balance. Metrics were computed with Scikit-learn, using the standard classification report (per class) and macro/micro/weighted averages.

Furthermore, as a complementary metric recommended in the literature for multiclass classification, we acknowledge the value of Cohen's Kappa coefficient because it accounts for chance agreement; although not included in this study, we plan to incorporate it in future work to enable a more robust assessment in settings with high visual similarity between classes.

3.8 Extension to 13 Classes

Based on the promising results obtained with the initial three species, an exploratory extension was conducted to evaluate the scalability of the proposed methodology to a broader floral classification scenario. For this purpose, images of ten additional floral classes were collected from the Kaggle platform [10], following the same data collection strategy applied to the initial dataset. Each of the new classes contained 1,000 images, resulting in a balanced dataset of 13,000 images distributed across 13 classes.

The same preprocessing pipeline described in Sect. 3.2 was applied, including image resizing to 200 $\times$ 200 pixels, normalization, and data partitioning into training (70%), validation (15%), and test (15%) subsets. This ensured consistency with the experimental conditions of the three-class scenario.

For this extended evaluation, the Xception architecture with the Feature Extraction strategy was selected, as it achieved the best performance in the initial experiments. The training and validation procedures, as well as the use of optimizers and regularization mechanisms (early stopping, dropout, and model checkpointing), followed the methodology previously described.

4 Results

The results obtained confirm the effectiveness of an intelligent classification system based on convolutional neural networks for identifying three floral species: *Bellis perennis* (Daisy), *Lavandula angustifolia* (Lavender), and *Helianthus annuus* (Sunflower). Four CNN architectures (VGG16, VGG19, InceptionV3, and Xception) were compared under different training strategies and optimizers, with the goal of identifying the most effective combination.

As shown in Table 1, the InceptionV3 and VGG19 models optimized with Adam achieved test accuracies above 94%, demonstrating a high capacity to distinguish species with similar morphological patterns.

The Xception model also showed competitive results, with accuracies above 93% and stable performance across the different configurations evaluated.

It can also be observed that the Feature Extraction strategy applied to the Xception model achieved the highest validation accuracy (97.50%), while the VGG19 and InceptionV3 architectures optimized with Adam obtained the best results on the test set, exceeding 94% accuracy.

In contrast, the VGG19 model trained with the SGD optimizer showed the lowest performance, with a test accuracy below 88%, suggesting that this combination is not recommended for this specific task. These findings reinforce the importance of selecting the appropriate architecture and optimizer to maximize performance in floral classification tasks.

Besides overall accuracy, we computed per-class precision, recall, F1-scores, and macro, micro, and weighted averages using the Scikit-learn classification report. These metrics offered a clearer view of model performance and revealed classification challenges, particularly between *Bellis perennis* and *Helianthus annuus*, which share high morphological similarity.

Table 2. Summary of the highest validation and test accuracy values obtained for each evaluated configuration.

Model	Best val_accuracy	Test Accuracy
Xception (Feature Extraction)	*97.50%*	93.56%
InceptionV3 (Adam)	*96.36%*	94.00%
InceptionV3 (SGD)	*95.91%*	93.78%
InceptionV3 (RMSprop)	*95.68%*	92.67%
VGG19 (Adam)	*94.32%*	94.22%
Xception (Fine Tuning)	*94.55%*	93.56%
VGG16 (RMSprop)	*91.36%*	91.56%
VGG16 (Adam)	*93.18%*	92.89%
Data Augmentation (Xception)	*93.18%*	89.56%
VGG19 (SGD)	*87.05%*	87.78%

4.1 Confusion Matrix

The confusion matrices obtained for each model allowed a detailed analysis of performance in the classification of the three floral species, showing that most models achieved overall accuracies above 90%. Some of them are as follows:

Figure 2 shows the confusion matrix of the Xception model with Feature Extraction, reflecting the performance of the model with an overall accuracy above 93%. It can be observed that correct classifications dominate across all three floral classes. Misclassifications are minimal and dispersed, with a small number of confusions between Daisy and Lavender, as well as between Daisy and Sunflower. This highlights the model's ability to effectively distinguish species with similar visual patterns, demonstrating stability and consistency across the different configurations evaluated.

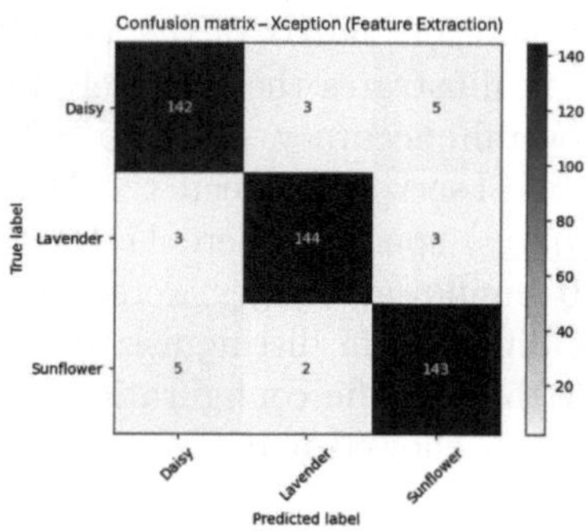

Fig. 2. Confusion matrix of the Xception model using the Feature Extraction technique.

Figure 3 shows the confusion matrix of the VGG19 model with the Adam optimizer; it can be observed that it achieves high accuracy in classifying the three floral species. Few misclassifications are noted, mainly between Daisy and Sunflower (where some images were incorrectly classified). The Lavender class showed the fewest errors, with most images correctly identified. This pattern indicates that, although the model is highly accurate, certain morphological similarities between Daisy and Sunflower may cause slight difficulties in classification. Overall, the model maintains excellent discriminative capability among the evaluated classes.

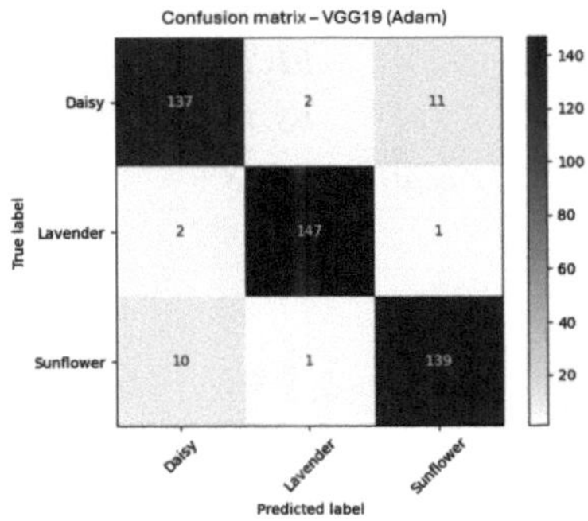

Fig. 3. Confusion matrix of the VGG19 model optimized with Adam.

Figure 4 shows the confusion matrix of the InceptionV3 model with the Adam optimizer; it demonstrates excellent performance by the InceptionV3 model, with a high number of correct classifications across the three floral species. Only minimal errors are observed, with slight confusions between Daisy and Lavender, and some misclassifications of Sunflower, mainly confused with Daisy. The Lavender class shows the highest accuracy. These results reflect the model's strong discriminative capacity and its stability in handling similar morphological patterns among the species.

Figure 5 presents the confusion matrix of the VGG19 model optimized with SGD; this confusion matrix illustrates the relatively lower performance of this configuration, with an overall accuracy close to 87%. A higher number of classification errors can be observed between the Daisy (*Bellis perennis*) and Sunflower (*Helianthus annuus*) species, where 11 Daisy images were misclassified as Sunflower and 10 Sunflower images were confused with Daisy. These errors reflect the model's difficulty in distinguishing between species with similar visual patterns under this specific configuration. In contrast, the Lavender (*Lavandula angustifolia*) class showed a better correct classification rate with few confusion errors.

These findings highlight that the choice of architecture and optimizer has a more significant impact on performance than the training strategy applied, thus laying the foundation for reliable and accurate automated systems in floral classification, in line with the objective of the study.

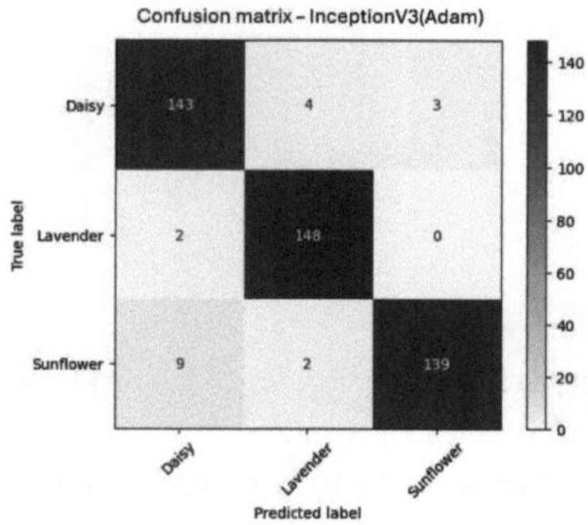

Fig. 4. Confusion matrix of the InceptionV3 model with the Adam optimizer.

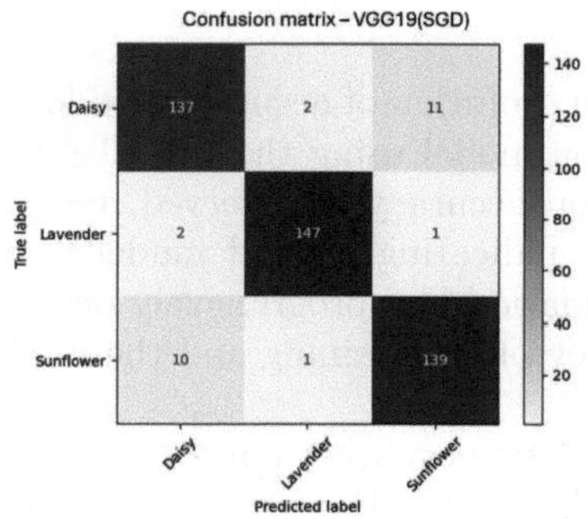

Fig. 5. Confusion matrix of the VGG19 model optimized with SGD.

4.2 Accuracy and Loss in the Data Augmentation Strategy

Accuracy Fig. 6A and loss chart 6B during training with the Data Augmentation strategy show favorable model behavior. The loss in both training and validation consistently decreases over the course of 35 epochs, indicating that the model is learning progressively without overfitting. Additionally, accuracy in both sets increases and remains close, reflecting good generalization ability and robust performance in classifying the floral species.

These curves confirm the effectiveness of the augmentation strategy in preventing overfitting, as training and validation metrics remain closely aligned. Notably, validation accuracy stabilizes near 90%, while the validation loss decreases smoothly without major oscillations, reinforcing the robustness of the model under augmented conditions.

A) Accuracy during training **B)** Loss during training

Fig. 6. Accuracy and loss during training and validation using data augmentation.

4.3 Accuracy and Loss in the Xception Model with Fine Tuning Strategy

Figs. 7A and 7B show the evolution of accuracy and loss during the training and validation of the Xception model using the Fine Tuning strategy. A consistent improvement in validation accuracy is observed, reaching values close to 94% toward the final epochs, indicating a good model fit without evident overfitting. In parallel, the validation loss progressively decreases and remains stable, reinforcing the consistency of the training and the model's ability to generalize effectively.

In particular, the validation accuracy curve rises steadily with minor fluctuations, converging faster than in the Data Augmentation strategy and stabilizing near 94%, while the validation loss shows a smooth decline without abrupt spikes, further confirming the model's stable convergence.

A) Accuracy during training. **B)** Loss during training.

Fig. 7. Training and Validation Accuracy and Loss – Fine Tuning with Xception.

4.4 Comparison of the VGG16 Model with Adam and RMSprop in the Xception Model with Fine Tuning Strategy Optimizers: Accuracy and Loss

Figs. 8A and 8B present the evolution of accuracy and loss during training and validation for the VGG16 architecture using the Adam and RMSprop optimizers.

Both optimizers surpass 90% training accuracy by the midpoint of the epochs, with Adam consistently achieving higher validation accuracy across most of the process. This behavior highlights Adam's superior ability to generalize and its resilience against early overfitting.

In terms of loss, both optimizers display a steady decrease in the initial epochs followed by stabilization. However, RMSprop exhibits larger oscillations and slightly higher validation loss compared to Adam, indicating less stable convergence. In contrast, Adam demonstrates smoother and more consistent learning dynamics, maintaining validation accuracy close to 93% with reduced variance.

Overall, these results confirm that Adam is the more robust and effective optimizer for the VGG16 architecture in this classification task, providing stronger generalization capacity and reinforcing its selection as one of the best optimization strategies for multiclass flower classification.

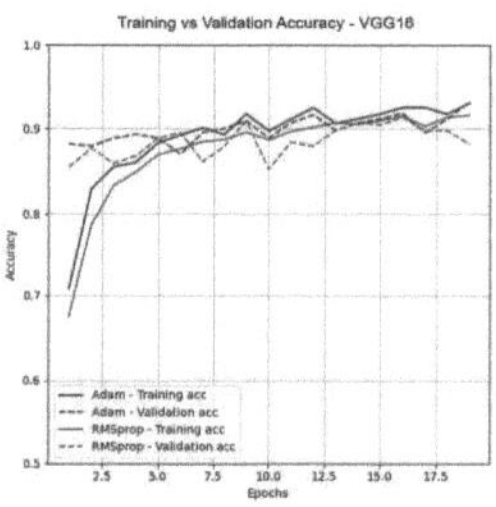

A) Training Accuracy in VGG16.

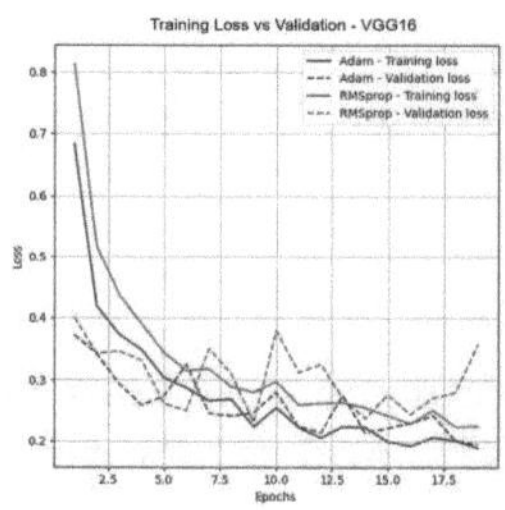

B) Validation during training in VGG16.

Fig. 8. Training and Validation Accuracy in VGG16 with Adam and RMSprop Optimizers.

4.5 Accuracy and Validation for VGG19 with Adam vs. SGD Optimizers

Figs. 9A and 9B illustrate the training and validation behavior of the VGG19 model using Adam and SGD optimizers. Adam consistently outperformed SGD, achieving validation accuracy above 90% throughout most epochs, while SGD stabilized at lower values around 80âĂŞ85%. This performance gap demonstrates Adam's superior capacity for generalization in this architecture.

Regarding loss dynamics, Adam exhibited a faster reduction and smoother stabilization of both training and validation loss. In contrast, SGD showed larger oscillations and slower convergence, with higher final loss values, suggesting less efficient optimization.

In particular, the validation accuracy with Adam remained stable above 90% with minimal fluctuations, while SGD fluctuated considerably and plateaued near 85%. Likewise, Adam's validation loss decreased progressively and stabilized, whereas SGD's curve showed noise and irregularities. These results confirm that Adam ensures faster and more stable convergence for VGG19, making it the more reliable optimizer for the classification of the three floral species evaluated.

A) Training Accuracy in VGG19.

B) Validation during training in VGG19.

Fig. 9. Accuracy and Validation Curves for VGG19 with Adam vs. SGD Optimizers.

4.6 Accuracy and Loss During Training for InceptionV3 with Adam, SGD, and RMSprop Optimizers

Figs. 10A and 10B compare the accuracy and loss curves of the InceptionV3 model trained with Adam, SGD, and RMSprop optimizers. Among the three, Adam demonstrated the most stable and consistent performance, achieving validation accuracies above 90% early in training and maintaining smooth convergence with stable loss values.

SGD also reached competitive results but with slower convergence and more pronounced oscillations in both accuracy and loss, suggesting the need for further

A) Training Accuracy in InceptionV3.

B) Loss during training in InceptionV3.

Fig. 10. Accuracy and Loss during Training and Validation for InceptionV3 with Adam, SGD, and RMSprop Optimizers.

tuning of hyperparameters such as learning rate or regularization. RMSprop achieved validation accuracies comparable to Adam; however, its validation loss presented noticeable fluctuations, indicating reduced stability during training.

Overall, these results highlight the importance of optimizer selection in deep learning models. Adam stands out as the most reliable and robust option for InceptionV3 in the floral classification task, while SGD and RMSprop may require additional adjustments to reach comparable stability and generalization.

4.7 Results for the 13 Class Extension

Building on the promising outcomes of the three-class classification scenario, an exploratory evaluation was conducted to assess the scalability of the proposed methodology to a larger dataset comprising 13 floral species (Aster, Daisy, Dandelion, Iris, Lavender, Lily, Lotus, Marigold, Orchid, Poppy, Rose, Sunflower, and Tulip), each represented by 1,000 images. The Xception model with the Feature Extraction strategy was selected based on its superior performance in the initial experiments.

The results revealed that the model maintained adequate training performance, with accuracy values approaching 90% and a consistent decrease in training loss. However, validation accuracy plateaued around 75âĂ§78%, with validation loss exhibiting moderate fluctuations. This indicates the presence of overfitting, suggesting that the model's generalization ability decreases as the number of classes increases.

The confusion matrix (Fig. 11) reflected this trend, with higher misclassification rates among morphologically similar species. This behavior aligns with prior findings in large-scale floral classification tasks, where visual similarity and increased class diversity amplify classification difficulty.

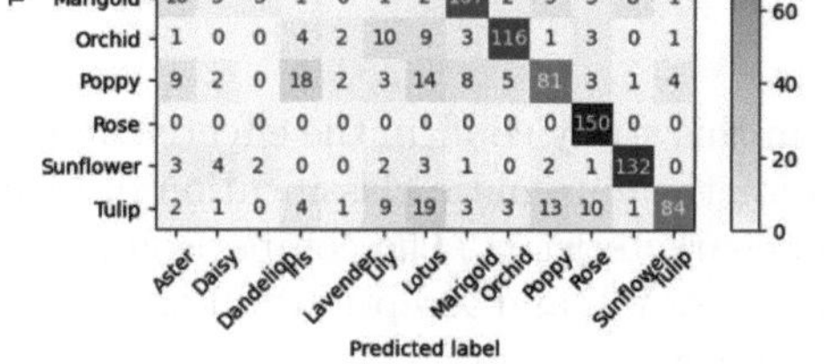

Fig. 11. Confusion Matrix for 13 Class Floral Classification with the Xception Model Using the Feature Extraction Strategy.

The accuracy graph (Fig. 12A) reveals a rising trend in training accuracy, reaching nearly 90%, while validation accuracy remains stable around 75âĂŞ78%, indicating a significant gap between the two curves and suggesting a possible slight overfitting.

On the other hand, the loss graph (Fig. 12B) shows a consistent reduction in training loss, while validation loss remains relatively high and fluctuates somewhat, further supporting the hypothesis of moderate overfitting.

Figures 12A and 12B further illustrate the training dynamics, showing a widening gap between training and validation accuracy and a corresponding divergence in loss curves. These findings suggest that, although the proposed methodology scales reasonably well to more complex datasets, further improvements are needed to enhance generalization. Potential strategies include stronger regularization, more aggressive data augmentation, hyperparameter tuning, and exploration of alternative architectures such as EfficientNet, Vision Transformers, or ConvNeXt.

A) Accuracy during training in InceptionV3.

B) Loss during training in InceptionV3.

Fig. 12. Accuracy and Loss during Training and Validation of the Xception Model with Feature Extraction.

Overall, the 13-class extension highlights both the strengths and limitations of the current approach, confirming its feasibility for broader floral classification while also identifying key areas for future refinement.

5 Discussion

The results obtained in this study confirm the effectiveness of convolutional neural networks (CNNs) for the automatic classification of three floral species with similar morphological characteristics. The comparison among four architectures (VGG16, VGG19, InceptionV3, and Xception) allowed the identification of significant differences in terms of accuracy, stability, and behavior depending on the training strategies and optimizers applied.

Beyond reusing pretrained CNNs, our contribution differs from prior flower-classification studies (e.g., [8,12,15]) in three ways: (i) a factorial comparison that crosses architectures, training strategies, and optimizers, allowing a principled attribution of gains; (ii) a focus on visually similar species to probe failure modes that are under-represented in evaluations on broad, generic datasets; and (iii) an exploratory 13 class extension under a fixed protocol to examine scalability, whose detailed results are reported in Sect. 4.7. Taken together, these elements delineate the study's originality and practical relevance, complementing existing reports centered on single architectures or dataset-specific benchmarks.

Despite the variations (in texture, lighting conditions, color variations, and different phenological stages of the flowers), the developed models demonstrated a remarkable ability to correctly identify and classify the species. This highlights the robustness and generalization capability of the system for application in real and diverse environments, and it also underscores that having a high-quality and adequately representative image dataset is essential to obtain an effective model.

In particular, the InceptionV3 and VGG19 models optimized with Adam achieved the highest overall accuracies, consistently exceeding 94% on the test set, highlighting the robustness of this optimizer for such tasks. Recent studies confirm that the Adam optimizer improves training stability and facilitates convergence in image classification tasks: Yi, Ahn, and Ji (2020) report that Adam provides robust performance across various machine learning problems, due to its adaptive estimation of first and second-order moments. On the other hand, the Xception model showed competitive results, with accuracies above 93%, and stable performance under different training strategies. This is consistent with Chollet (2017), who demonstrated that depthwise separable convolutions can maintain or improve accuracy while offering considerable computational efficiency.

The Feature Extraction technique stood out as the most effective strategy, achieving the highest validation accuracy (97.50%) and producing confusion matrices with minimal errors. This suggests that, for the specific problem of multiclass floral classification, full fine-tuning is not always necessary to achieve optimal performance, allowing for faster and less computationally expensive training. Similar findings were reported by Kumar and Bhatia (2021), who demonstrated that using pre-trained models with feature extraction significantly improves accuracy in floral datasets without requiring extensive computational resources. Likewise, Narvekar and Rao (2020) highlighted that feature extraction from deep CNN architectures enables efficient model adaptation, especially in domains with limited training data. These studies support the idea that transfer learning through feature extraction offers a practical balance between model performance and computational efficiency in high-precision visual classification tasks.

While classical approaches such as k-NN and SVM [7] achieved moderate success in controlled conditions, their performance tends to degrade when facing datasets with higher variability in morphology, background, and lighting. This explains why recent works [8,15], and the present study, demonstrate that CNNs are substantially more effective for complex multiclass problems, as they automatically learn robust hierarchical features instead of relying on handcrafted descriptors.

In contrast, the combination that showed the lowest performance was VGG19 with the SGD optimizer, with a test accuracy of around 87.8%, along with a confusion matrix showing a relatively higher number of misclassifications. This finding underscores the importance of selecting the appropriate optimizer according to the architecture and dataset, as SGD was less effective in this scenario, although it performed well with InceptionV3. Similar results were reported by Chollet (2017), who emphasized that deeper architectures like VGG19 may require more adaptive optimization strategies, such as Adam, to effectively handle vanishing gradients and ensure faster convergence. Additionally, Cıbuk et al. (2019) noted that model performance in flower classification tasks is highly sensitive to the choice of optimizer, especially when dealing with subtle interclass similarities. The differing results obtained with SGD across models in this study reinforce the idea that optimizer selection should be carefully tuned to the architecture's characteristics and the complexity of the data.

The accuracy and loss curves per epoch also revealed differences in training convergence and stability. Models trained with Adam generally reached convergence more quickly and exhibited less overfitting compared to those trained with RMSprop and SGD. For example, Yi, Ahn, and Ji (2020) demonstrated that Adam provides faster and more stable convergence in various machine learning tasks, due to its adaptive learning rate adjustment mechanism.

It is important to note that, although widely accepted metrics such as precision, recall, F1-score, and confusion matrices were employed, Cohen's Kappa coefficient was not included. Its incorporation in future work could provide a more comprehensive view of performance, as it better reflects the agreement between predictions and labels beyond chance, particularly in classes with high morphological similarity.

Overall, these results emphasize that the choice of architecture and optimizer has a more significant impact on final performance than the training strategy used, as long as techniques such as data augmentation and regularization mechanisms (e.g., dropout, early stopping) are applied. This conclusion is consistent with the findings of Kamilaris and Prenafeta-Boldú (2018), who highlight the critical influence of architecture and optimizer on the performance of deep learning models in agricultural applications. Similarly, Kumar and Bhatia (2021) point out that these decisions have a greater effect on the outcome than the fine-tuning strategy itself.

Finally, the confusion matrices and class-specific classification reports revealed that, although most models performed well overall, greater confusion was observed between the Bellis perennis and Helianthus annuus classes, likely due to their morphological similarities. This finding highlights a clear opportunity for improvement in future work, where efforts should focus on enhancing discrimination between visually similar species. This type of challenge has been documented by Narvekar and Rao (2020), who emphasize the difficulties involved in classifying species with closely related visual characteristics. To address this limitation, advanced image preprocessing techniques—such as color-based normalization, contour-guided segmentation, or the enhancement of distinctive morphological features—could be explored. These techniques have been recommended by Desai et al. (2022) to optimize the extraction of relevant patterns and improve the model's ability to distinguish between similar species.

Beyond the architectures tested in this work, recent state-of-the-art models such as EfficientNet [20], Vision Transformers (ViT) [5], and ConvNeXt [14] have shown superior results in large-scale image classification benchmarks. These architectures incorporate advances in parameter efficiency, attention mechanisms, or convolutional block design, offering promising alternatives for more complex or large-scale floral datasets. Although not included in the present study, future research could integrate and compare these newer models to assess their scalability and potential for improving generalization in challenging agricultural classification scenarios.

Compared to previous contributions, which often highlight single architectures such as DenseNet [12] or focus on generic benchmarks like Oxford-102 [16], the present study offers complementary insights by systematically analyzing how different architectures, training strategies, and optimizers behave in a controlled, application-oriented setting. Although it does not introduce a new architecture, the factorial comparison and the focus on visually similar floral species provide practical knowledge that can inform both applied deployments and future research on model scalability.

6 Conclusion

This study demonstrated that convolutional neural networks (CNNs) are an effective tool for the automatic classification of three floral species with high morphological similarity: *Bellis perennis* (Daisy), *Lavandula angustifolia* (Lavender), and *Helianthus annuus* (Sunflower). The comparison of four architectures (VGG16, VGG19, InceptionV3, and Xception) under different training strategies and optimizers allowed the identification of optimal configurations that maximize classification accuracy.

Models based on InceptionV3 and VGG19 with the Adam optimizer stood out for their high performance, achieving test accuracies above 94%, while Xception showed competitive results and stability across multiple configurations. The Feature Extraction technique proved to be the most effective strategy for this task, reaching a maximum validation accuracy of 97.50%, indicating that full fine-tuning is not always necessary to obtain robust results.

The appropriate choice of architecture and optimizer was found to be more decisive for performance than the training strategy applied, which has important implications for the design of automatic floral classification systems that must optimize accuracy, efficiency, and computational resources.

These findings support the development of reliable and accurate systems for the automatic identification of floral species, with potential applications in fields such as botany, precision agriculture, and environmental conservation. As future work, it is recommended to explore advanced preprocessing techniques and hybrid models to enhance the discrimination between species with very similar visual characteristics. Along these lines, a promising development is the creation of a mobile application that integrates the trained convolutional neural network (CNN) models, enabling their deployment in real-world scenarios for real-time floral species identification. This application would allow users—such as farmers, botanists, students, and nature enthusiasts—to capture images using their mobile device cameras and receive immediate classification of the detected species. To achieve this, a system architecture is envisioned consisting of an intuitive interface, a backend capable of executing inferences through optimized CNN models, and a geolocation module to spatially contextualize the observations. Additionally, features such as historical identification logs, access to detailed botanical information for each species, and the ability to contribute to collaborative databases could be incorporated. This proposal would not only facilitate accessible and in-field identification but also promote the digitalization of plant monitoring with practical applications in precision agriculture, biodiversity conservation, and environmental education.

Additionally, the proposed system could be integrated with broader digital agriculture platforms, such as drones equipped with imaging systems, IoT-based field monitoring tools, or autonomous robotic platforms. These integrations would allow large-scale, real-time monitoring of plant health and biodiversity, strengthening the role of artificial intelligence in sustainable agriculture and environmental conservation.

Acknowledgments. The support and collaboration received for the completion of this study are gratefully acknowledged.

Disclosure of Interests. The authors have no competing interests to declare in relation to the content of this article.

References

1. Anggara, F., Ximenes, J.D.A.D., Sulistiyo, M.D., Saputra, M.F., Hadiyoso, S.: Efficient flower classification using CNN with InceptionV3 transfer learning. In: 2024 International Conference on Information and Communication Technology (ICoICT), IEEE (2024). https://doi.org/10.1109/ICoICT61617.2024.10698064
2. Cıbuk, M., Budak, U., Guo, Y., Ince, M.C., Sengur, A.: Efficient deep feature selections and classification for flower species recognition. Measurement **137**, 7–13 (2019). https://doi.org/10.1016/j.measurement.2019.01.041
3. Chollet, F.: Xception: deep learning with depthwise separable convolutions. In: Proceedings IEEE Conference on Computer Vision Pattern Recognition (CVPR), pp. 1251–1258 (2017). https://doi.org/10.1109/CVPR.2017.195
4. Desai, S., Gode, C., Fulzele, P.: Flower image classification using convolutional neural network. In: 2022 International Conference on Electrical, Electronics, Information and Communication Technology (ICEEICT), IEEE (2022). https://doi.org/10.1109/ICEEICT53079.2022.9768635
5. Dosovitskiy, A., et al.: An image is worth 16×16 words: transformers for image recognition at scale. In: International Conference on Learning Representations (ICLR) (2021). https://doi.org/10.48550/arXiv.2010.11929

6. Giraddi, S., Seeri, S., Hiremath, P.S., Jayalaxmi, G.N.: Flower classification using deep learning models. In: 2020 International Conference on Smart Technologies in Computing, Electrical and Electronics (ICSTCEE), IEEE (2021). https://doi.org/10.1109/ICSTCEE49637.2020.9277041
7. Guru, D.S., Sharath, Y.H., Manjunath, S.: Texture features and KNN in classification of flower images. Int. J. Comput. Appl. (IJCA) **1**, 21–29 (2010). http://citeseerx.ist.psu.edu/viewdoc/download?doi=10.1.1.206.5702. Special Issue on RTIPPR
8. Islam, S., Ahmed Foysal, M.F., Jahan, N.: A computer vision approach to classify local flower using convolutional neural network. In: 2020 International Conference on Intelligent Computing and Control Systems (ICICCS), IEEE (2020). https://doi.org/10.1109/ICICCS48265.2020.9121143
9. Jayalaxmi, G.N., Giraddi, S., Seeri, S., Hiremath, P.S.: Flower classification using deep learning models. In: Proceedings 2020 International Conference on Software Test, Engineering, and Knowledge (ICSTCEE), IEEE (2020). https://doi.org/10.1109/ICSTCEE49637.2020.9277041
10. Kaggle: Classification datasets. (2025). https://www.kaggle.com/datasets?tags=13302-Classification
11. Kamilaris, A., Prenafeta-Boldú, F.X.: Deep learning in agriculture: a survey. Comput. Electron. Agric. **147**, 70–90 (2018). https://doi.org/10.1016/j.compag.2018.02.016
12. Kumar, S., Bhatia, P.K.: Flower classification using deep learning and transfer learning. In: 2021 11th International Conference on Cloud Computing, Data Science & Engineering (Confluence), pp. 472–477. IEEE (2021). https://doi.org/10.1109/Confluence51648.2021.9443129
13. Lin, K., Yang, H.-F., Chen, C.-S.: Flower classification with few training examples via recalling visual patterns from deep CNN. In: Processing IPPR Processing on Computer Vision, Graphics, and Image Processing (CVGIP) (2015). https://www.iis.sinica.edu.tw/papers/song/19840-F.pdf
14. Liu, Z., Mao, H., Wu, C.-Y., Feichtenhofer, C., Darrell, T., Xie, S.: A ConvNet for the 2020s. In: Proceedings of the IEEE Conference on Computer Vision and Pattern Recognition (CVPR), pp. 11976–11986 (2022). https://doi.org/10.48550/arXiv.2201.03545
15. Narvekar, C., Rao, M.: Flower classification using CNN and transfer learning in CNN-agriculture perspective. In: 2020 3rd International Conference on Intelligent Sustainable Systems (ICISS), pp. 660–664. IEEE (2020). https://doi.org/10.1109/ICISS49785.2020.9316030
16. Nilsback, M.-E., Zisserman, A.: Automated flower classification over a large number of classes. In: 2008 Sixth Indian Conference on Computer Vision, Graphics & Image Processing (ICVGIP), pp. 722–729. IEEE (2008). https://doi.org/10.1109/ICVGIP.2008.47
17. Qin, W., et al.: Flower species recognition system combining object detection and attention mechanism. In: Huang, D.-S., Hussain, A., Chang, K.-H. (eds.) Intelligent Computing Methodologies. ICIC 2019. Lecture Notes in Computer Science, vol. 11645, pp. 1–8. Springer, Cham (2019). https://doi.org/10.1007/978-3-030-26766-7_1
18. Simonyan, K., Zisserman, A.: Very deep convolutional networks for large-scale image recognition. arXiv preprint arXiv:1409.1556 (2014). https://doi.org/10.48550/arXiv.1409.1556

19. Szegedy, C., Vanhoucke, V., Ioffe, S., Shlens, J., Wojna, Z.: Rethinking the inception architecture for computer vision. In: Proceedings of the IEEE Conference on Computer Vision and Pattern Recognition (CVPR), pp. 2818–2826 (2016). https://doi.org/10.1109/CVPR.2016.308
20. Tan, M., Le, Q.V.: EfficientNet: rethinking model scaling for convolutional neural networks. In: Proceedings of the 36th International Conference on Machine Learning (ICML), pp. 6105–6114. PMLR (2019). https://doi.org/10.48550/arXiv.1905.11946
21. Tian, M., Chen, H., Wang, Q.: Flower identification based on deep learning. J. Phys.: Conf. Ser. **1237**, 022060 (2019). https://doi.org/10.1088/1742-6596/1237/2/022060
22. Yi, D., Ahn, J., Ji, S.: An effective optimization method for machine learning based on ADAM. Appl. Sci. **10**(3), 1073 (2020). https://doi.org/10.3390/app10031073

Optimizing Urban Layouts Using Reinforcement Learning (Q-Learning Agent and Deep Q Network Agents)

Alan Crespo Murillo(✉), Alejandro Villafaña Anaya, Bruno Galli Hambleton, Daniel Adrián Contreras Olivas, Humberto Ángel Plata Durán, Oscar Cueto Farley Rivas, and Rodrigo Naranjo Hernández

Faculty of Engineering, Universidad Panamericana, Mexico City, Mexico
rlurbanism@gmail.com

Abstract. This paper explores the use of reinforcement learning (RL) to optimize urban layouts under the n-minute city model, a planning paradigm that aims to ensure that all essential services are accessible within a short walk distance. The paper presents two RL agents: **Qtopia**, a Q-learning agent that builds cities from scratch through episodic reward maximization, and **city_planner**, a Deep Q-Network (DQN) agent capable of classifying and redesigning preexisting city grids. Both agents aim to generate livable, modular and accessible urban environments by balancing proximity, diversity, and spatial compatibility. Both agents were tested and validated on artificial grids and a real-world layout of Rome, integrating natural constraints such as the Tiber River. A new metric for urban efficiency—*residential service reachability rate*—was introduced to measure how many residences are within the target service radius. The results demonstrate the potential of RL as a scalable tool for intelligent urbanism.

Keywords: Reinforcement Learning · Q-Learning · Deep Q-Network · Urban Planning · N-Minute City · City Design · Artificial Intelligence · Livability · Spatial Optimization

1 Introduction

Urban planning faces increasing challenges in scalability, livability, and service accessibility. Traditional planning methods often lack the adaptability required to address these challenges dynamically. Reinforcement Learning (RL) offers a promising solution, enabling agents to learn and optimize city layouts by interacting with urban environments.

This paper presents the development and implementation of two RL agents to design cities under the n-minute city framework:

- **Qtopia:** A Q-Learning agent that places buildings based on state-action values and a custom reward function.

L. Martínez-Villaseñor et al. (Eds.): MICAI 2025, CCIS 2712, pp. 141–155, 2025.
https://doi.org/10.1007/978-3-032-08704-1_11

- **City_planner:** A dual Deep Q-Network agent composed of a grid generator and a building classifier.

Both agents are applied to the layout of Rome. Their decision-making processes are evaluated based on a newly introduced metric: the *residential service reachability rate*, which quantifies the proportion of residences with access to all essential services. This new metric highlights the practicality of the n-minute city concept and enables a clearer evaluation of agent performance.

AI has previously been applied to urban planning [14,22,24]. For example H'sain, employed reinforcement learning to develop agents capable of designing city layouts while maximizing the number of buildings that adhere to specific constraints [14]. Their work demonstrates that RL presents opportunities for improving urban design processes [14].

In this paper, the agents developed a step further by optimizing livability within the n-minute city paradigm, incorporating accessibility, spatial compatibility, and modularity. The following sections detail the theoretical foundation, agent architecture, and evaluation of urbanism through reinforcement learning.

1.1 Urbanism: Livability and the N-Minute City

The planning of a city is a very complex task and can be influenced by a set of different factors, such as demographic, environmental conditions, and social conditions [4]. However, they are primarily guided by a set of objectives [8]. Among all the different objectives, livability stands out as one of the most important [2,10,13,14,17].

Livability is essential and unavoidable while building the cities of tomorrow, and therefore needs to be considered for the urbanist models [8]. Livability is centered around the inhabitants of a city, especially focusing on the quality of life and well-being of the inhabitants which are affected by the city environment. There are eight key principles to living. These principles are equity, safety, comfort, transit, participation, accessibility, walkability, and available services [5,16,18]. The agents presented in this study address all key principles; however, it will primarily focus on available services, walkability, and accessibility.

As mentioned before, every city is built around different objectives and goals; in order to achieve the particular goals and objectives, an appropriate urbanist model needs to be adopted. There are many different urbanist models, such as smart cities, zone models, mixed-use models, compact cities and n-minute cities [5,8,16,18,20]. The best fitting model for livability is the n-minute city model.

The n-minute city model refers to a model in which every important building is within n minutes of distance from residential buildings. This particular model is built around 3 core pillars; proximity, density and diversity [2,15]. However, the model also incorporates an additional 4 pillars; connectivity, modularity, mixed-use and human-scale urban design. All of the pillars ensure that most livability principles are addressed, to ensure that the other principles are incorporated with the different buildings [2,15,18,19].

Although an appropriate model is used to promote livability, certain key pillars are not fully addressed by the model alone. To compensate, specific buildings are constructed: residential buildings (yellow), retail/entertainment (pink), green areas (green), health institutions (blue), offices (brown), roads (white), supermarkets (purple), educational institutions (light blue) and government institutions (red). Additionally, for the particular agents discussed in the paper, an important factor to consider is the compatibility between buildings. To better capture this aspect, a compatibility matrix was developed to represent the relationships and interactions among different building types [6,7] (Fig. 1).

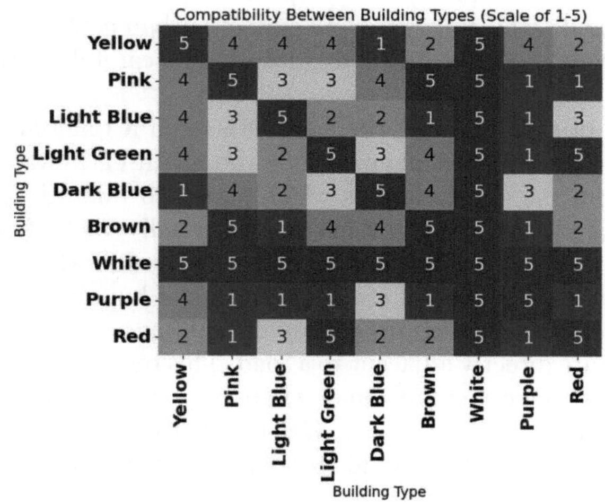

Fig. 1. The compatibility matrix used for the different buildings, classifying their relationship between one and five [6].

1.2 Reinforcement Learning

Reinforcement learning defines the interaction between an agent and its environment as a Markovian decision process (MDP), the agent's goal is to learn a policy that maximizes its cumulative long-term reward [9,10]. Q-learning is a model-free reinforcement learning algorithm, this means that the programmer does not have to have the p functions of the environment. This agent requires parameters such as γ (discount factor), α (learning rate), and ϵ (exploration rate), which respectively control how future rewards are valued, how quickly the agent learns, and how often it explores new actions in order to solve the *Exploration and Exploitation* dilemma [1,3,23].

γ, α and ϵ are parameters used in the Bellman equation for updating the reward of a state in the Q-table [21]. The equation is given by:

$$Q(S_t, A_t) \leftarrow Q(S_t, A_t) + \alpha\big[R_{t+1} + \gamma \max_a Q(S_{t+1}, a) - Q(S_t, A_t)\big] \quad (1)$$

Another method of reinforcement learning, Deep Q-Networks, was also employed. It is a neural network-based RL model for handling high-dimensional inputs. Neural networks are used because methods like Q-learning are limited in the sense that they do not scale very well to medium-large MDPs. These models were selected for their interpretability (QL) and scalability (DQN) [11].

2 Methodology

2.1 Qtopia: Q-Learning Agent

Qtopia, the first agent developed, is capable of generating city layouts either from an empty grid or by enhancing pre-existing urban configurations. Its capabilities are based on a well-designed algorithm and a carefully structured reward function.

At the start of each episode, the agent starts on a random road and visits all null states in its von Neumann neighborhood. In each state, by using the Bellman equation, the agent chooses which action to take. If **Qtopia** places a road, the agent adds this road to a list and eventually visits its null neighbors. When there are no more null neighbors adjacent to a road, the agent visits other null states and has the option of creating clusters of buildings [6].

A cluster of buildings refers to a group of buildings of the same type, where not all buildings are directly adjacent to a road. This reflects real-world scenarios, such as large parks or residential zones, where not every building is immediately connected to a street. *clusterSize* is a variable that defines how many buildings can be indirectly connected to a road through a single building directly adjacent to it [6,7].

Once all states have been visited, the episode ends. An episode represents a sequence of state-action steps carried out to design a city layout. At the end of each episode, the Q-table is updated, the epsilon decays, the environment is reset and the reward is calculated.

The reward function incentivizes **Qtopia** to place all essential services near each residence while maintaining a spatially compatible layout according to the compatibility matrix. The steps for calculating the reward of a city are:

1. **Compute building compatibility:** For each building, calculate its compatibility score by summing the compatibility values with all neighboring buildings within a Manhattan distance of 2.
2. **Calculate residential reward:**
   (a) Iterate over all services accessible to the residence (starting with the nearest). Multiply the compatibility score for each service by **maxAmount** before summing. maxAmount represents the ideal number of services of that type accessible to a residence and decreases progressively as more services of the same type are found. Once the limit is reached, it drops to zero; the value is reset to its default for each new residence.

(b) Sum the resulting values, multiply by the number of different services available to the residence, and divide by the total number of services the agent can place to compute the total reward for the residence.
3. **Compute total reward:** Sum the reward of all residential units to obtain the overall reward for the city layout.

$$R_a = \left(\left[\sum_{i=0}^{\text{Services available}} (maxAmount_i \cdot P_i) + P_a \right] \cdot \frac{\text{numberServicesaccessible}}{\text{totalServices}} \right)$$

$$R = \sum_{i=0}^{n} R_a^i \tag{2}$$

When the epsilon is low, **Qtopia** often converges to suboptimal policies. However, these policies can be improved through continued training. Incorporating retraining without resetting the Q-table allows the agent to address the explorationâĂŞexploitation trade-off more effectively, discovering better policies without significantly altering previously learned knowledge.

Epsilon decay follows the Gompertz function (Formula 3). This function was chosen because it includes parameters b and c, which allow smooth and flexible control over the explorationâĂŞexploitation balance during training [6,7].

$$\epsilon(x) = e^{e^{-c \cdot x + b}} \tag{3}$$

Qtopia retraining process is organized into *series*; each series is a sequence of 100 episodes. At the end of each series, **Qtopia** checks which states have the highest reward in the Q table and **pauses** them. When a state is paused, its epsilon value decays to zero, and the Q-table is no longer updated for that state [6].

2.2 City_planner: Double-Agent Force

A Deep Q-Network (DQN)-based RL model programmed to build urban environments by strategically placing streets and houses on a two-dimensional grid. The environment is built on the Gymnasium interface, where the agent operates within a discrete action space (placing a street or a house) and an observation space (the agent's current position and the value of its Moore neighborhood), allowing spatial awareness of the local urban context [6,7]. The reward function incentivizes efficient land use: small rewards are granted for placing buildings, while large penalties are issued if the agent halts with remaining unfilled cells, promoting complete and logical urban layouts [6,7].

Each episode begins next to a randomly placed initial street and progressively builds outwards, selecting neighboring empty cells next to existing streets for further development. Its movement is governed by a von Neumann neighborhood check, allowing movement only to valid neighboring tiles. The learning process follows an epsilon-greedy policy, where exploration is initially favored and gradually reduced to encourage exploitation [6,7]. At the end of training, **city_designer** produces visually structured and functionally complete cities. The final output is rendered graphically and exported as a JSON-formatted matrix. Figure 4 shows a resulting 20 × 20 grid developed by the agent, ready to be classified by **City_architect**.

Once **city_designer** has finished building its grid, it is passed to the second agent, called **City_architect**. This agent is built to receive two-dimensional matrices filled with numerical values that represent streets (zero), buildings (one), and unbuildable cells such as rivers, forests, or mountain slopes (negative numbers). It also has two types of hyperparameters, meant to give the user as much flexibility as possible. The behavior hyperparameters, shown in Fig. 3-(a), establish the neural network structure and other variables related to the training steps, such as epsilon decay. Just like **city_designer**, **City_architect** receives rewards for each action, instead of complete episodes, making its learning process a lot swifter than that of **Qtopia** (Fig. 2).

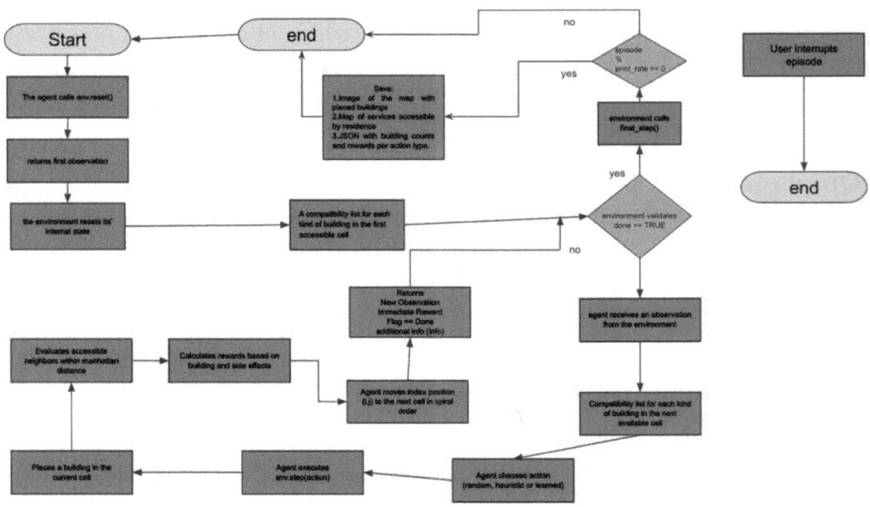

Fig. 2. The flow diagram shows the **City_architect** process for each episode of the DQN-learning.

The second type of hyperparameters (Fig. 3-(b)) allow **City_architect** to work with variable building types, allowing services to be added or removed with ease. They include the compatibility matrix, the grid size, the building types and their colors, among other variables. These allow the user to easily add, change, and remove buildings, making the grid as complex as possible. This version used the buildings listed in Sect. 1.1, as well as a Manhattan distance of fifteen.

Parameter	Description
policy	Custom policy with MLP and dropout layers
net_arch	Neural network architecture: **(128, 64, 128)**
dropout_rate	Dropout probability **(0.22)**
learning_rate	Learning rate of the optimizer
exploration_initial_eps	Initial exploration probability **(ε-greedy)**
exploration_fraction	Training steps over which ε decays linearly
exploration_final_eps	Minimum exploration probability **(0.05)**
total_timesteps	Total number of training steps
verbose	Agent logging level

(a) Behavior hyperparameters: neural network, epsilon decay, dropout, and related variables.

Parameter	Description
rows, columns	Size of the environment grid
buildings	Types of buildings the agent can place
building_colors	Colors associated with each building type
compatibility_matrix	Compatibility between building types
manhattan_distance	Maximum distance for accessible neighbors
print_rate	Frequency of visualizations
matrix	Binary matrix to be classified

(b) Environment hyperparameters: city grid, building types, and compatibility matrix.

Fig. 3. Hyperparameters used by **City_architect**: (a) behavior hyperparameters controlling the neural network and training dynamics; (b) environment hyperparameters defining the grid, building types, and compatibility rules.

Once the agent has received the grid, it begins to iterate over it in a spiral movement, starting at the center and slowly moving outwards. This keeps previously classified buildings close to the currently analyzed cell, giving the agent more information about what surrounds it. Whenever the agent falls on an unclassified cell, it counts each building type around it and calculates a compatibility list, based on the quantity it finds.

If average_compat ≥ 3:

$$\text{compatibility}_i = \frac{1}{1 + 0.5 \cdot \left(\frac{distance_i \cdot n_i}{\bar{compatibility_i}}\right)} \quad (4)$$

Otherwise:

$$\text{compatibility}_i = \frac{1}{1 + 0.5 \cdot \left(\frac{\bar{compatibility_i} \cdot n_i}{distance_i}\right)} \quad (5)$$

If it decides to place a residence, the reward equals the number of services provided by nearby buildings. If it decides to place a service instead, the reward equals the number of houses benefited by it (they did not have access to that service beforehand). This approach uses both the reward function and the compatibility index to focus on service accessibility without ignoring the compatibility matrix.

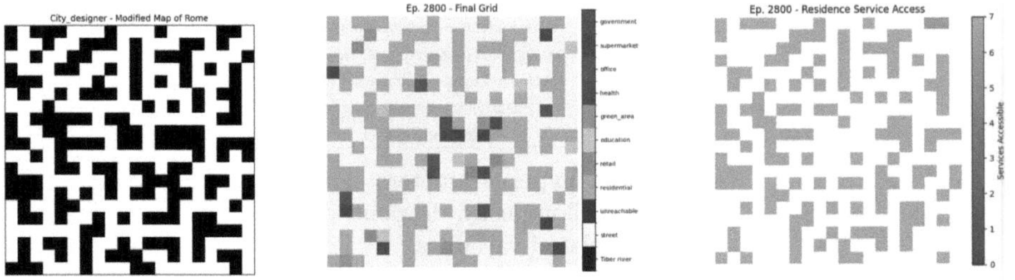

(a) 20×20 grid by **city_designer**.

(b) Classified grid by **City_architect**.

(c) Service availability (classified city).

Fig. 4. From initial city generation to classification and service coverage.

3 Implementation

3.1 Rome

One of the biggest challenges of a real city is their increased complexity due to economic, political, or geographic factors. Some of these challenges can be tackled little by little to make the agent more useful in real life situations. To start this process, a very interesting city was chosen: Rome. With the Tiber River flowing down the middle and multiple bridges crossing it at specific points, it gave **Qtopia** and **City_architect** an opportunity to test a new environment. Figure 5 shows the area of the city selected to train the agent.

3.2 Qtopia

The Rome layout was configured using a list of pairs with coordinates and building type. At the beginning of each episode, these buildings were placed on the grid, and the agent was not allowed to modify them. This setup enables scalability and flexibility, allowing **Qtopia** to receive predefined city layouts with existing residential and service buildings that users wish to preserve.

As explained in Section *Methodology. A.Qtopia: Q-Learning Agent*, Qtopia uses several parameters, including the learning rate, discount factor, maxAmount, cluster size, and Gompertz function parameters (b, c). These parameters were selected by several trial and error; the city designed with these parameters was shown to get more residences and converge faster than other combination of parameters.

Fig. 5. Image of Rome used to model the environment employed by the agents. The image shows the Tiber River flowing southeast of Vatican City. Coordinates: 41∘12’12” N, 12∘28’00’ E [12].

Table 1. Qtopia Parameter Configuration

Parameter	Value
Learning Rate (α)	0.5
Discount Factor (γ)	0.95
Series Length	100 episodes
Epsilon Parameter b	$-e$
Epsilon Parameter c	-0.03883259
maxAmount (per service)	2
Cluster Size	1

3.3 City_architect

Since the agent is only capable of modifying unclassified buildings (with a value of *one*), it received the grid at the beginning of each episode and began exploring from the center as it would in any other situation. It also used the same hyper-parameters shown in Fig. 3-(a), in order to test the performance of the neural network multi-layered perceptron structure (with **128**, **64**, and **128** neurons) against the one used in (with **128** and **256** neurons). It also received a small increase in the dropout rate, going from 20% to 22%, making an overfitting even less encouraged.

When testing the neural network with the grids shown in Fig. 4, the results showed great variability between episodes, some getting near-perfect accessibility while others struggled with multiple residences. However, the neural network was still tested in Rome, to see how it performed on a significantly larger grid made up of 100 × 81 cells with the added obstacle of the Tiber.

4 Results

Qtopia was trained on the layout of Rome's city using the parameters listed in Table 1. The agent successfully generated a city aligned with the principles of the n-minute city, such as proximity, walkability, and distribution of available services. As illustrated in Fig. 4, nearly all residential buildings have access to the seven essential services defined in this study. Despite these positive results, **Qtopia** has certain limitations. For example, some residences do not have access to all services, and the agent built significantly more services per residence than the ideal threshold defined by *maxAmount* (Fig. 6).

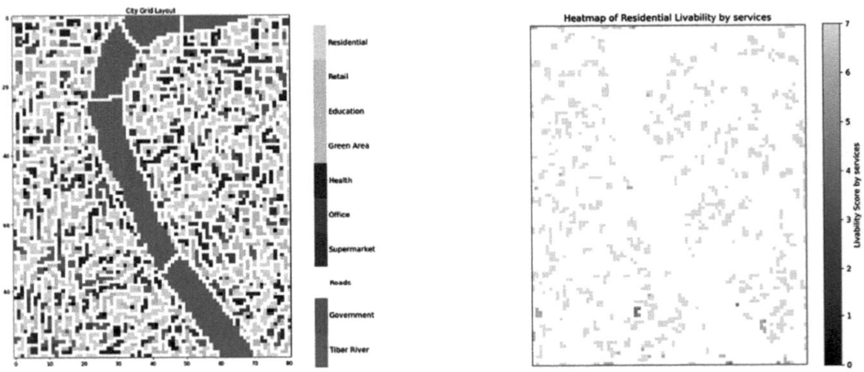

Fig. 6. Results at Episode 100 of Series 50. (Left) Final city grid layout generated by the agent. (Right) Heatmap of residential livability based on service access, where brighter colors indicate higher service availability.

The reason of these limitations is that **Qtopia** evaluates reward at the end of each episode, which makes it difficult to identify which states contribute more to city's reward and which do not. Incorporating rewards and penalties based on each state's contribution to the overall city reward would encourage the agent to avoid placing states that contribute little, allowing them to continue exploring alternative actions.

Meanwhile, the results of **City_architect** show a much larger number of residences, making them as common as possible. The results displayed in Fig. 7 also show that the agent preferred to use the buildings near the bridges to place residences, except for the top-most bridge. This probably occurred because the length of the bridges made them unreliable for service accessibility, leading the agent to prefer other locations here more residences could get easy access to the services.

As for the image shown in Fig. 7, it can be clearly seen that almost all residences received access to the seven services, with only one house, located on the left side of the grid, receiving access to four: hospitals, schools, government buildings, and supermarkets. Regardless, out of the 2803 residences built in this specific episode, a total of 2746, or 97.966% got a complete service availability, making its performance almost perfect.

It should be noted that the compatibility matrix is still struggling to influence the agent's overall performance, with incompatible buildings such as supermarkets, retail and government offices being frequently placed close together. **City_architect** is also incapable of dealing with different accessibility objectives. For example, there is no way for it to ensure every residence has access to two green areas instead of only one, making it less adaptable to varying user desires or situations.

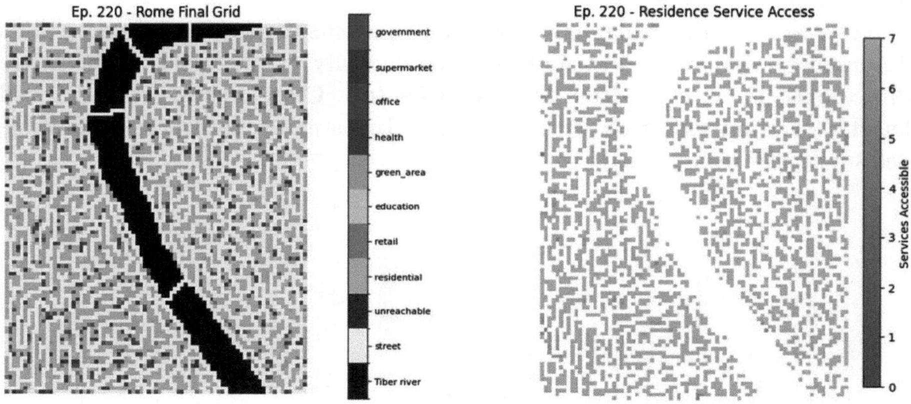

Fig. 7. Results of **City_architect** after 220 episodes on the Rome layout. (Left) Final grid output showing all buildings successfully classified, mainly using bridges to connect residences rather than services. (Right) Service availability, where most services received perfect coverage, with a few near the left corner struggling the most.

The implementation of the Tiber River did not affect in the least the agent's performance, making other obstacles such as forests or restricted areas easy to add. Nevertheless, like with the results of Fig. 4, the hyperparameters led the agent to produce unstable results: some episodes received a far lower accessibility rate. This shows that the smaller neural network worked better, leading us closer to the ideal set of parameters to use.

5 Discussion

Several metrics are needed in order to compare agents' performance; the reason is that both agents have different reward functions and different ways of using the compatibility matrix. As a consequence, both agents design cities with different scopes. Because of this, the metrics used to compare the agents are: total number of buildings per category, average distance from each residential unit to its nearest service, and average number of distinct services accessible per residential unit. Metrics such as accuracy or precision are not used because those imply that the best policy is known, which conflict with reinforcement-learning nature.

The first big difference found between them is related to the amount of each classified building type. Figures 4 and 7 show an incredible contrast in the number of residences particularly, with **City_architect** creating a city with short of 3000 residences, while **Qtopia** barely built a little over 900. The differences can be clearly seen in Fig. 8-(b), notably showing that both agents preferred residences a lot more than other building types. Another interesting similarity is that both agents chose an almost uniform amount for the services, with **City_architect** giving a little more to government buildings, while keeping the others largely the same.

The results in Fig. 8 highlight how the two agents emphasize different pillars of n-minute cities. While **Qtopia** focused on diversity, giving each residence more service options to choose from (see subfigure (c)), **City_architect** prioritized density, ensuring that each service was used by as many residences as possible (see subfigures (a) and (b)).

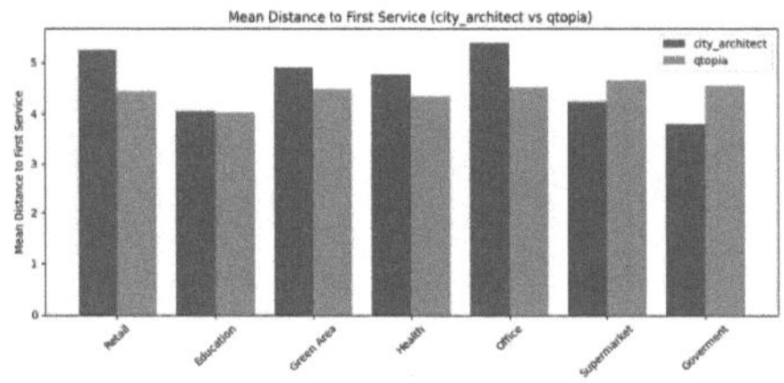

(a) Avg. distance to nearest service.

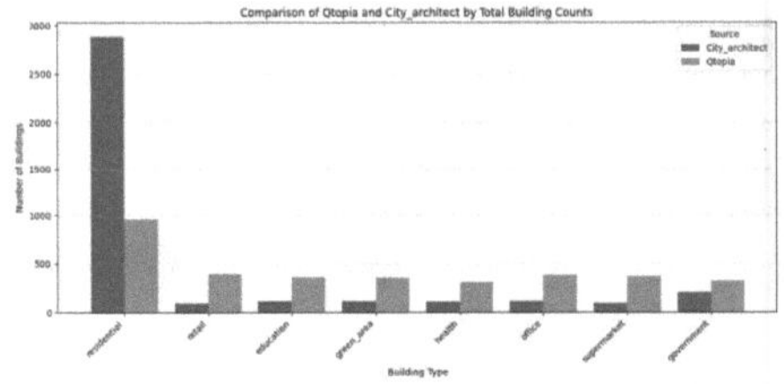

(b) Building counts: Qtopia vs City_architect.

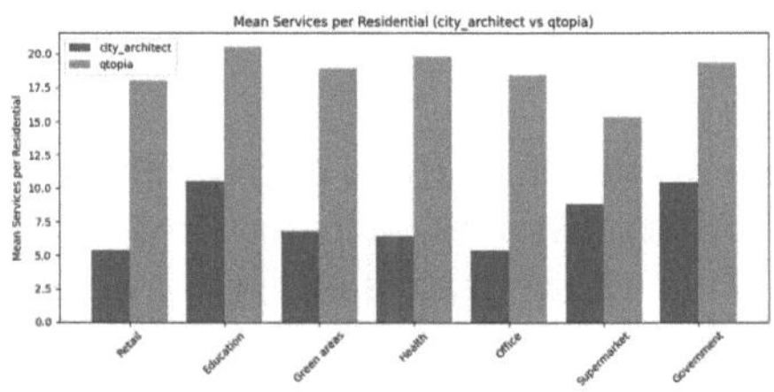

(c) Avg. number of distinct services accessible per residential unit.

Fig. 8. Comparative metrics between **Qtopia** and **City_architect**, including distances to services, building counts, and number of distinct services per residence.

This also made the resulting city of **City_architect** a lot less diverse in terms of services available within the n-minute distance, prioritizing space for a larger population. However, it is important to note that **Qtopia** has the capacity to merge neighboring cells of the same building type, so two hospital cells next to each other are likely a single larger hospital, not two distinct ones.

The biggest difference between the agents comes from scalability and training time. Even though **Qtopia's** approach is a lot easier to explain because of the nature of the Q-Table, it took a significantly larger amount of time to converge, while **City_architect** took less than an hour to find a satisfactory result. This is because of the latter's use of neural networks, which are a lot more efficient despite making the model a lot harder to explain. The metrics shown in the previous figures, though leading, also reflect a difference in the approach the agents take towards n-minute cities, their outcomes leaning more towards specific pillars.

6 Further Directions

This study demonstrated the applicability of reinforcement learning in urban planning through the development and comparative evaluation of two agents: **Qtopia** and **City_architect**. Each was tailored to address distinct challenges in the design of n-minute cities. **Qtopia**, based on Q-learning, excelled in generating service-diverse environments by prioritizing spatial compatibility and proximity. However, its episodic reward structure and reliance on static policies led to slower convergence and limited scalability. In contrast, **City_architect**, with its neural network-based DQN architecture, proved more effective in handling larger and more complex environments by using continuous, action-based feedback and adaptive exploration.

Despite their differences, both agents succeeded in generating livable and modular city layouts, with high levels of service accessibility and strategic land use. The integration of constraints from real urban contexts, such as the Tiber River in Rome, further validated the robustness of these systems in diverse geographical settings.

Nonetheless, challenges remain: **Qtopia** needs finer reward granularity to better attribute value to decisions, while **City_architect** requires stronger use of the compatibility matrix and more flexibility in service distribution. Future work will hybridize these approaches, add multi-agent coordination, and expand explainability layers to support human-in-the-loop planning. These advances could be a major step toward AI-driven, equitable, human-centered urbanism.

References

1. Bacardit, J., Brownlee, A.E.I., Cagnoni, S., Iacca, G., McCall, J., Walker, D.: The intersection of evolutionary computation and explainable AI. In: Fieldsend, J. (ed.) GECCO'22 Companion: Proceedings of the 2022 Genetic and Evolutionary Computation Conference Companion, Boston, USA, 9–13 July 2022, pp. 1757–1762. ACM (2022). https://doi.org/10.1145/3520304.3533974
2. Bocca, A.: Public space and 15-minute city. A conceptual exploration for the functional reconfiguration of proximity city. TeMA J. Land Use, Mobility Environ. (2021). https://doi.org/10.6092/1970-9870/8062

3. Botvinick, M., Wang, J.X., Dabney, W., Miller, K.J., Kurth-Nelson, Z.: Deep reinforcement learning and its neuroscientific implications. Neuron **107**(4), 603–616 (2020). https://doi.org/10.1016/j.neuron.2020.06.014
4. Canese, L., et al.: Multi-agent reinforcement learning: a review of challenges and applications. Appl. Sci. **11**(11), 4948 (2021). https://doi.org/10.3390/app11114948
5. Castrellon, J.P., Sanchez-Diaz, I., Gil, J.: Smart loading zones. A data analytics approach for loading zones network design. Transportation Research Interdisciplinary Perspectives (2024). https://doi.org/10.1016/j.trip.2024.101034
6. Crespo Murillo, A., et al.: Exploring AI Ethics and Urban Planning: A Deep Reinforcement Learning Approach to Intelligent Urbanism. In: 26th Annual Media Ecology Association Convention, Universidad Panamericana, Mexico City, Mexico (2025)
7. Crespo Murillo, A., et al.: Reinforcement learning in urbanism: building the cities of the future with AI. In: XVII Congreso Mexicano de Inteligencia Artificial, COMIA (2025)
8. Doğan, M.: Urban vision: a strategic planning. Eur. J. Econ. Financ. Admin. Sci. **29** (2011)
9. Figueiredo Prudencio, R., Maximo, M.R.O.A., Colombini, E.L.: A survey on offline reinforcement learning: taxonomy, review, and open problems. IEEE Trans. Neural Networks Learn. Syst. **35**(8), 10237–10257 (2024)
10. Gajcin, J., Dusparic, I.: ReCCoVER: detecting causal confusion for explainable reinforcement learning. In: Proc. of the Int. Conf. on Autonomous Agents and Multi-Agent Systems, pp. 1–12 (2022). https://doi.org/10.1007/978-3-031-15565-9_3
11. Geron, A.: Hands-On Machine Learning with Scikit-Learn, Keras, and TensorFlow, 2nd edn. O'Reilly Media Inc. (2019)
12. Google Earth 10.81.0.: North-Western Centro Storico near Vatican City. Coordinates: 41°12'12"N, 12°28'00'E. 3D Buildings data layer (2025). https://earth.google.com. Accessed 9 June 2025
13. Gutiérrez, A.: La ciudad y la modernidad en la obra de Eugenio Montejo. Concienciactiva, pp. 113–138 (2008)
14. H'sain, H.E.: Deep reinforcement learning for urban modeling: morphogenesis simulation of self-organized settlements. M.S. thesis, Bilkent University (2023). https://repository.bilkent.edu.tr/handle/11693/111111
15. Khavarian-Garmsir, A., et al.: From Garden City to 15-Minute City: a historical perspective and critical assessment. Land (2023). https://doi.org/10.3390/land12020512
16. Kusumastuti, D., Nicholson, A.J.: Mixed-Use Urban Planning and Development. Technical Report, BRANZ (2016). http://hdl.handle.net/10092/15417
17. Löw, M.: The city as experiential space: the production of shared meaning. Int. J. Urban Reg. Res. **37**(3), 894–908 (2013). https://doi.org/10.1111/1468-2427.12022
18. Martyka, A., Przesmycka, N.: Modelling and planning urban development: a case study of Lublin in the context of the challenges of 21st century urbanism. Sciendo (2024). https://doi.org/10.2478/he-2024-0007
19. Rodríguez, B., Benavidez, W.: Importancia de las áreas verdes para la salud en los hospitales. Arquitectura + (2018). https://www.lamjol.info/index.php/arquitectura/article/view/9214/10407
20. Singh, S., Kumar, V.: Modeling the determinants for sustainable smart city through interpretive structure modeling and analytic hierarchy process. Comput. Urban Sci. (2024). https://doi.org/10.1007/s43762-024-00125-1

21. Sutton, R.S., Barto, A.G.: Reinforcement Learning: An Introduction. 2nd edn. MIT Press (2018)
22. Li, Z., Shi, L., Cristea, A.I., Zhou, Y.: A survey of collaborative reinforcement learning: interactive methods and design patterns. In: Proc. of Designing Interactive Systems Conf. (DIS '21). ACM, pp. 1–19 (2021). https://doi.org/10.1145/3461778.3462135
23. Wang, Z., Yan, H., Wang, Y, Xu, Z., Wang, Z., Wu, Z.: Research on autonomous robots navigation based on reinforcement learning (2024)
24. Wang, Z., Hong, T.: Reinforcement learning for building controls: the opportunities and challenges. Appl. Energy **269**, 115036 (2020). https://doi.org/10.1016/j.apenergy.2020.115036

Driving Events Detection Using Short-Time Fourier Transform and Support Vector Machine with Soft Margin Optimization

Joel Aparicio(✉), Gamaliel Moreno, Efrén González, Daniel Alaniz, and Jesús Villa

Universidad Autónoma de Zacatecas, Maestría en Ciencias del Procesamiento de la Información, Zacatecas, México
{aparicio.joel,gamalielmch,gonzalezefren,dalaniz, jvillah}@uaz.edu.com

Abstract. Automated detection of abnormal driving events is crucial for improving road safety and emergency response. Current detection systems combine inertial sensors, cameras, and neural networks to identify risky driving behaviors. However, most approaches either require costly full-scale infrastructure or depend on visual systems and complex network architectures. This study presents a behavior-based event detection framework that combines short-time Fourier transform with support vector machine (SVM) classification. Using a scaled-vehicle that accurately replicates real driving conditions, we analyzed five characteristic events: deformable-object impact, progressive acceleration, constant velocity, sudden braking, and speed bump overpass. Our methodology extracts distinctive time-frequency patterns from triaxial acceleration data, which serve as input features for a soft-margin SVM classifier with radial basis function kernel. The system achieved a classification performance of 96.63% accuracy, which indicates the feasibility of this approach for identifying driver events. These results suggest potential applications in vehicle safety systems and driver assistance technologies, although further validation at full scale is required.

Keywords: Driving event detection · short-time Fourier transform · support vector machine · scale model car

1 Introduction

Road traffic accidents remain a critical global public health problem. According to the World Health Organization's 2023 Global Status Report on Road Safety, road crashes continue to be a critical public health issue worldwide. The report reveals a 5% decrease in annual traffic fatalities, dropping from 1.25 million in 2010 to 1.19 million in 2021 [1]. Although these figures reflect positive progress, the scale of the problem remains alarming, highlighting the need to continue developing effective systems for preventing, monitoring and responding to road incidents.

Automated detection of abnormal driving events, such as collisions or abrupt maneuvers, has gained increasing interest in the field of machine learning. Several strategies

L. Martínez-Villaseñor et al. (Eds.): MICAI 2025, CCIS 2712, pp. 156–169, 2025.
https://doi.org/10.1007/978-3-032-08704-1_12

have been explored, employing inertial sensors, cameras, mobile devices and neural networks, with the aim of predicting or detecting abnormal driving. However, many of these approaches focus on full-scale scenarios involving expensive infrastructure or rely on visual cues or complex networks.

This work proposes an accessible and reproducible alternative using inertial sensors (MPU6050) integrated to a scaled-vehicle. The methodology is based on the acquisition of dynamic acceleration and angular velocity signals, processed with the Short Time Fourier Transform (STFT), a powerful tool to analyze the time evolution of non-stationary signals. From these signals, spectral features are extracted and used to train a SVM model to automatically detect automotive events, particularly collisions, in a defined time window. Unlike other approaches, which attempt to predict behavioral anomalies prior to an accident occurring, this research focuses on identifying impact events after they have occurred. This is the first step towards designing real-time warning or assistance systems. The scaled experimental model allows replicating controlled physical conditions without compromising safety, which facilitates validation and iterative experimentation. It proposes a cost-effective approach for vehicle collision detection, based on the spectral analysis of inertial signals using STFT. The experiments carried out covered the detection of five events, achieving a high level of accuracy.

2 Related Works

Event, anomaly or driving pattern detection has been an active area of research in recent years, with applications ranging from improving automated driving systems [2], to optimizing practices for the insurance industry, as well as enhancing driver and passenger road safety.

Several studies have explored the acquisition of dynamic signals using mobile devices. In [3] and [4], smartphones are used to capture accelerometer and gyroscope data, allowing the detection of abnormal driver maneuvers and behaviors, including altered states such as drunk driving. The work of [5] incorporates a camera to classify driving styles as aggressive or passive. Meanwhile, [6] includes GPS (Global Positioning System) sensors to analyze acceleration and braking patterns, proposing a real-time monitoring system capable of detecting road irregularities such as potholes or speed bumps.

Other research has focused on computer vision. In [7], a near real-time accident detection system is proposed using YOLO-type convolutional neural networks for vehicle recognition, together with Violent Flow (ViF) motion descriptors and SVM classification.

Spectral analysis has also been used to detect anomalous behavior. In [8], power spectral density (PSD) features obtained using STFT are extracted and then processed using deep neural networks to identify unconventional driving. Also, in [9], six different types of driving behaviors are recognized through the analysis of unique acceleration and orientation patterns by training models with neural networks and SVM from data obtained with smartphones.

In another line of research, [10] implements an urban auditory monitoring system, classifying audio signals to infer vehicle type and driving conditions. Finally, in [11], the maneuverability in curves is evaluated using automotive simulations and machine learning techniques, achieving high accuracy with the use of SVM.

The aforementioned works constitute important advances in the characterization of driving behaviors by means of different sensory modalities, such as vision, sound, GPS or inertial sensors. Most of these approaches focus on the early detection of anomalies, abrupt maneuvers or risky behaviors.

In this context, our research proposes a complementary approach: collision detection in scale vehicular models, using exclusively inertial signals and time–frequency domain processing techniques. Unlike other works that focus on pre-accident behavior, this study seeks to establish a methodological basis to accurately identify collision events once they have occurred, with the goal of future integration into rapid response or road assistance systems. While the combination of Short-Time Fourier Transform (STFT) features with Support Vector Machines (SVM) is not algorithmically novel, this methodology offers a pragmatic balance between accuracy and computational efficiency. Prior reviews have highlighted that artificial intelligence algorithms, including SVM, generally achieve superior predictive performance compared to classical models such as ARIMA [12]. At the same time, data availability in sufficient quantity is crucial for the success of many machine learning approaches, with deep models like LSTM or ensemble methods such as Random Forests being particularly data-hungry [12].

In contrast, evidence from time-series forecasting tasks demonstrates that SVM can achieve comparable predictive precision to more complex models such as LSTM and Gradient Boosted Decision Trees (GBDT), while requiring fewer hyperparameters and significantly lower training overhead [13]. For resource-constrained platforms, such as embedded systems in small-scale vehicular models, this trade-off is decisive. By extracting compact time–frequency descriptors through STFT and leveraging the generalization capacity of SVM, our proposal emphasizes deployability and real-time applicability. Thus, although not introducing a novel algorithm, the contribution of this work lies in adapting a proven methodology to an underexplored domain—post-impact collision detection at scale model level—where literature remains scarce and where computational efficiency is critical for future implementation in rapid response systems.

3 Materials and Methods

This section will discuss the method of applying the short-time Fourier transform for signal analysis in scaled automotive events, the materials used for experimentation, and the application of the signals to train the classification model.

3.1 Materials

3.1.1 Inertial Measurement Units

An inertial measurement unit (IMU) sensor model MPU-6050 was used for this study. This device incorporates a microelectromechanical system (MEMS) that integrates a triaxial gyroscope and a triaxial accelerometer, each with 16-bit resolution, all on the same chip. It operates with a 3.3 V power supply and is capable of simultaneously capturing the x, y, and z channels of acceleration (a) and angular velocity (ω), thus providing six degrees of freedom (6DOF). The sensor communicates through SPI or I2C protocols depending on the configuration [14]; in this work, the I2C protocol was selected to ensure communication stability. For the experiments, the accelerometer was configured to ± 2 g at 16 bits, with a sampling rate of 1 kHz.

3.1.2 Embedded System

The Jetson Nano, developed by NVIDIA, was used for data collection due to its high performance and low power consumption. It features a quad-core ARM Cortex-A57 processor at 1.43 GHz, a 128-core NVIDIA GPU, 4 GB of RAM, microSD-based storage, and 40 Raspberry Pi-type I/O pins. A lightweight version of Linux-Ubuntu was installed to optimize resource usage, enabling higher sampling frequencies in combination with the IMU. The device was selected over other alternatives for its computational capacity, which prevents transmission overloads while allowing efficient data collection, processing, and storage through Python scripts. The embedded system requires a 5 V power supply ($\geq$4 A via barrel jack or 2.5 A via micro-USB) and was implemented in the scale model vehicle (see Fig. 1), to replicate specific driving conditions and capture representative samples of predefined automotive events. This setup allows controlled emulation of real scenarios while preserving the dynamic patterns characteristic of each event.

3.1.3 Test Vehicle Model

The MN-128 is an off-road 4x4 model, designed as a remote control (RC) vehicle, made of a rigid plastic structure, with independent spring suspension for each wheel, powered by a rechargeable Li-ion battery of 7.4 V, with dimensions of 35 cm (L) x 20 cm (W) x 18 cm (H), with a total weight of 1.945 k, and with it can reach a speed of up to 8 k/h (in optimal conditions). This model can be seen in Fig. 1, showing the embedded system within the vehicle (left) and the IMU sensor position with its orientation axes (right).

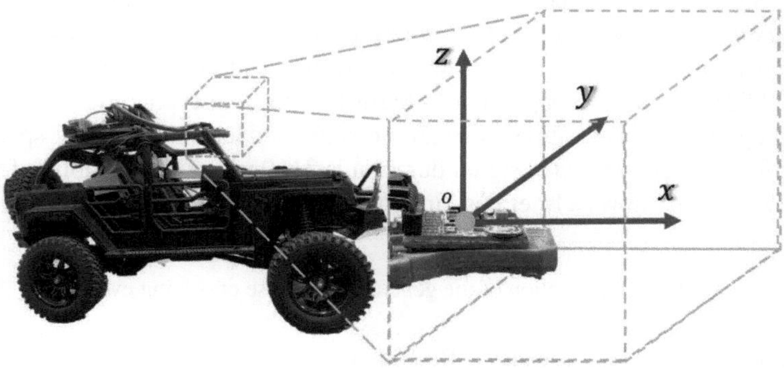

Fig. 1. Test vehicle model with the embedded system shown on the left and the IMU sensor's point of origin highlighted on the right.

Due to its compact size and sturdy design, the scale model was selected for its ability to controllably emulate realistic impact scenarios and vehicle dynamics in confined environments. This low-cost experimental platform allows repeatable recreation of automotive events without the need for full-scale testing, which is especially useful for training and validating algorithms that require large volumes of data under consistent and safe conditions.

3.2 Mining, Validation, and Labeling Samples

3.2.1 Sample Acquisition and Preprocessing

Data acquisition is performed using the MPU6050 sensor, which provides raw acceleration measurements for each axis (a_x, a_y, a_z) and angular velocity ($\omega_x, \omega_y, \omega_z$). Using Python, the sensor configuration was implemented, which included initialization of the I^2C protocol, calibration using offset correction and conversion of raw readings to physical units using the following scaling factors:

Acceleration $\left(m/s^2\right)$:

$$a_i(t) = \left(\frac{r_i(t) - o_i}{s_a}\right) \cdot g \tag{1}$$

Gyroscope $(\circ/s)$:

$$\omega_i(t) = \left(\frac{r_i(t)}{s_\omega}\right) \cdot \alpha \tag{2}$$

where $a_i(t)$ is the acceleration on the i-axis $(x, y, or\ z)$ at instant t, $r_i(t)$, raw sensor reading on the i-axis, o_i is the offset value of the i-axis, s_a is the accelerometer scale factor (e.g., 16384 for $\pm 2G$), g represents the gravitational acceleration $\cong 9.81$, $\omega_i(t)$ is the angular velocity on the i-axis in rad/s at instant t, s_ω is the gyroscope scale factor (e.g., 131 for $\pm 250°/s$), and α is the conversion factor from degrees to radians, $\alpha = \pi/180$.

3.2.2 Database Generation

As mentioned above, our experiments were conducted using a scale model car. For this preliminary database, variables such as vibration levels, surface noise, and sensor quality were disregarded in order to analyze the raw results and avoid information loss. We recorded 2,575 signals corresponding to the following five events: deformable-object impact, progressive acceleration, constant velocity, sudden braking, and speed bump overpass. The average recorded signal duration is 3110 ms, with a sampling frequency of ~1 kHz. Table 1 shows a brief description and the number of instances.

Table 1. Description of the generated database of driving events.

Event Name	Samples	Description
Deformable-object impact	508	Collision with a soft-deformable object.
Progressive acceleration	537	Gradual increase from standstill to maximum speed.
Constant velocity	506	Sustained driving at top speed.
Sudden braking	509	Rapid and abrupt deceleration.
Speed bump overpass	515	Fast traversal over a speed bump.

To validate the quality of the data, the maximum speed reached by the model was contrasted with that specified by the manufacturer of the MN128 scale vehicle, which establishes a speed of 8 km/h (equivalent to approximately 2.37 m/s). Only those samples that presented behavior compatible with this metric were retained.

Each of the 2575 samples was labeled according to the type of vehicle event to which it belongs: 5 classes in total. A balanced distribution of approximately 500 samples per class was maintained, which favors effective supervised learning without dominant class bias. In addition, a minimum analysis time of 0.65 s per event was defined, ensuring that each segment contained sufficient information to be processed by machine learning algorithms.

3.2.3 Window Configuration and STFT Overlapping

To analyze the time evolution of the non-stationary inertial signals captured by the MPU6050 sensor, the Short Time Fourier Transform (STFT) was applied on the acceleration vector magnitudes $m_a(t)$ and angular velocity $m_\omega(t)$, defined by the following Eq. (3):

$$\boldsymbol{m_a(t)} = \sqrt{\boldsymbol{a_x^2 + a_y^2 + a_z^2}}, \boldsymbol{m_\omega(t)} = \sqrt{\boldsymbol{\omega_x^2 + \omega_y^2 + \omega_z^2}} \tag{3}$$

The STFT allows decomposing these signals in temporal blocks, on which the spectral content is calculated as a function of time, allowing to analyze the temporal evolution of the frequencies in a non-stationary signal [15]. For this purpose, a sliding window of $\Delta t = 0.02$s with an overlap of 75% was used, i.e., if the window has N samples, the step between windows will be $N \cdot (1 - 0.75) = N \cdot 0.25$, generating windows that "scan" the signal to guarantee a high temporal and frequency resolution, expressed in (4). For each window centered at $t = mT$, the signal is multiplied by a window function $\gamma(t - mT)$ such as a Gaussian or Hamming, and the Fourier transform is applied:

$$\boldsymbol{STFT_x(m,f)} = \int_{-\infty}^{\infty} \boldsymbol{x(t) \cdot \gamma(t - mT) \cdot e^{-j2\pi ft} dt} \tag{4}$$

This results in a spectrogram, which can be interpreted as a matrix with time along the horizontal axis and frequency along the vertical axis, where each entry corresponds to the signal magnitude or energy at a given time and frequency. This case is shown in Fig. 2, applying the STFT to a signal of the Bumper class, represented on three axes: time, magnitude, and frequency (Hz).

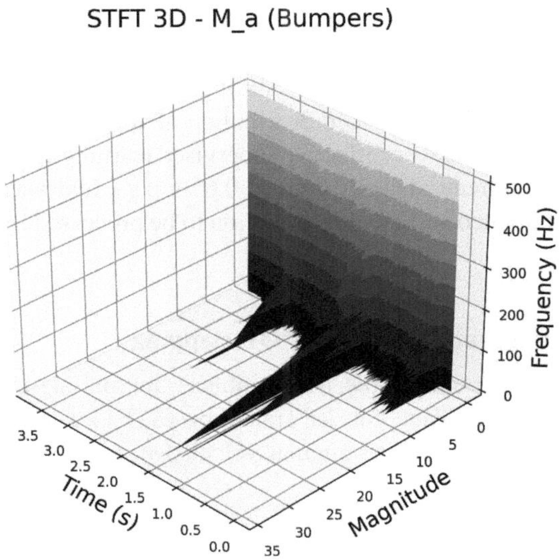

Fig. 2. Spectrogram matrix of a Bumper class signal using STFT.

3.2.4 Feature extraction with STFT

From the spectrogram generated with the STFT, three key features were extracted for each analysis window:

- Signal energy:

$$E_m = \sum |STFT_x(m,f)|^2 \tag{5}$$

- Total magnitude:

$$M_{Tot,m} = \sum |STFT_x(m,f)| \tag{6}$$

- Maximum magnitude:

$$M_{max,m} = max|STFT_x(m,f)| \tag{7}$$

These values describe the vibration behavior in that window, these metrics were calculated for the $m_a(t)$ and $m_\omega(t)$, signals, allowing to capture the spectral dynamics of the recorded vehicle events serving as input for the machine learning based classification models. In Table 2 shows the full set of features used to train the SVM model.

Table 2. Characteristics for model training.

Feature	Description
a_x, a_y, a_z	Signals from each axis emitted by the accelerometer sensor
$\omega_x, \omega_y, \omega_z$	Signals from each axis emitted by the gyroscope sensor
$STFT(a_i), STFT(\omega_i)$	(5), (6), (7) applied to each axis i of the signals
$STFT(m_a), STFT(m_\omega)$	(5), (6), (7) applied to each magnitude signal m_a y m_ω
$STFT(a_i), STFT(\omega_i)\forall E$	(5), (6), (7) applied to each axis i, of the signal applied during the event under analysis
$STFT(m_a), STFT(m_\omega)\forall E$	(5), (6), (7) applied to each vector magnitude (m_a and m_ω) during the analyzed event.
μ, σ, *kurtosis*, skewness, *min*, max, energy $\forall a_i, \omega_i$	Mean, standard deviation, kurtosis, skewness, minimum, and maximum of the signals for each sensor.
μ, σ, *kurtosis*, skewness, *min*, max, energy$\forall E(m_a), E(m_\omega)$	Mean, standard deviation, kurtosis, skewness, minimum, maximum and energy of the signals for each axis during the event (E)

4 Results and Discussion

4.1 Results

Our systematic evaluation of the parameters revealed significant performance variations during SVM training. Different combinations of signal data were tested, including raw and filtered signals, features derived from energy, maximum, and total magnitude per STFT window, as well as statistical descriptors and sensor response magnitudes. We also evaluated the same parameters restricted to the duration of each event. This latter configuration proved more representative for detecting specific events, since applying Principal Component Analysis (PCA), showed that classes exhibit less overlap when signals are limited to the event duration. This effect can be observed in Fig. 3 and Fig. 4, where the point clouds illustrate class separability for classification.

Figure 3 illustrates that the classes achieve a clearer grouping when signals are limited to the duration of the event, although complete separation is not attained. In contrast, Fig. 4 shows that when the full signal is considered, the class distributions overlap more closely, making multiclass classification more challenging.

The set of parameters considered included energy, total magnitude, and maximum magnitude derived from the *STFT* of each accelerometer and gyroscope axis, as well as aggregated signals m_a and m_ω. In addition, statistical descriptors such as mean (μ), standar derivation (σ), kurtosis, skewness, and minimum and maximum values were extracted for both m_a and m_ω. All these features were obtained during the duration of each event.

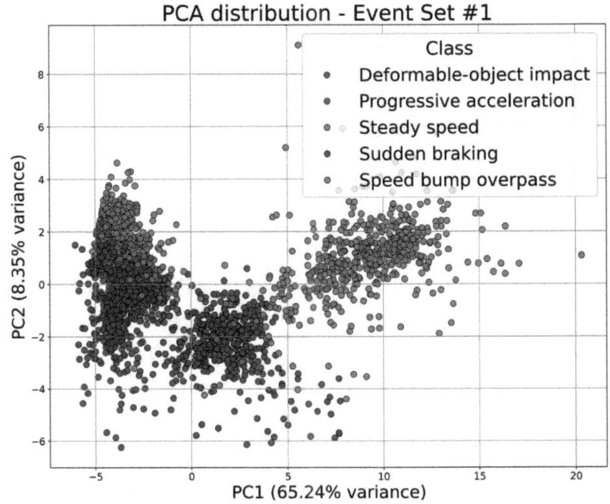

Fig. 3. PCA applied to the signal considering only the duration of the specific event.

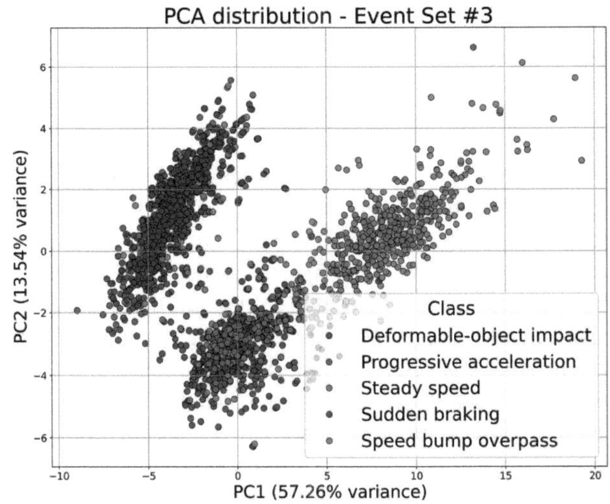

Fig. 4. PCA applied to the signal over the entire experimental duration.

This complete feature set was used to train the SVM model. However, preliminary evaluations revealed signs of overfitting when all parameters were considered. To address this, we applied the K-Best Features method, which evaluates each variable individually according to a statistical metric and selects the k most relevant ones. With $k = 9$, the following features were identified as the most discriminative: ax_stft_evn_max_mag, az_stft_evn_max_mag, az_stft_evn_energy, gy_stft_evn_total_mag, a_xyz_stft_evn_max_mag, g_xyz_stft_evn_total_mag, accel_event_std, accel_event_max, accel_event_energy. Their correlations are shown in Fig. 5, which highlights the relationships among the selected features.

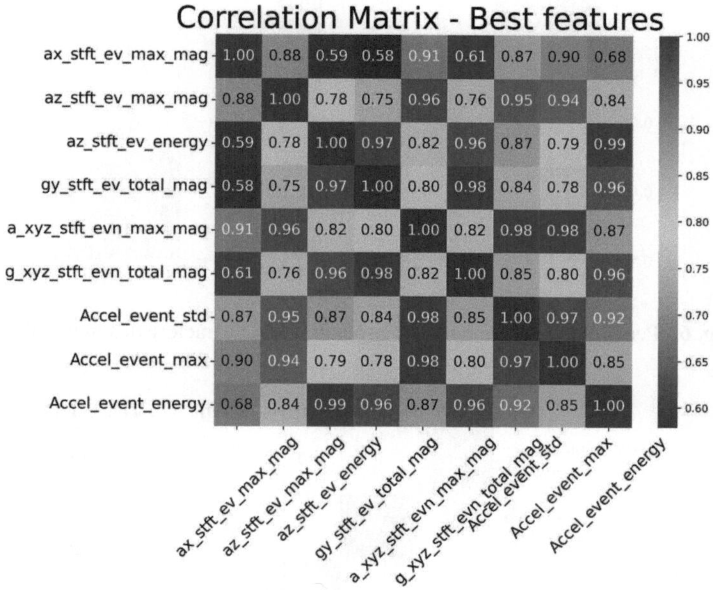

Fig. 5. Correlation matrix according to the best k characteristics.

The performance of the SVM model with these features is summarized in Fig. 6, where results across four kernels (linear, polynomial, radial basis, and sigmoid) are compared. The radial basis function (RBF) kernel achieved the best overall performance, followed by the linear kernel, while the polynomial and sigmoid kernels showed lower accuracy. Both RBF and linear kernels consistently provided high accuracy across the training, testing, and validation sets.

Based on the comparative results shown in Fig. 6, the RBF kernel achieved the highest performance across all datasets, which motivated its selection for the subsequent evaluations. Finally, model evaluation was completed using the confusion matrix (Fig. 7), a standard technique for supervised classification. The results confirm the robustness of the RBF kernel with minimal misclassifications across the five event classes.

$$Accuracy_k = \frac{TP_k}{TP_k + FP_k} \tag{8}$$

$$Recall_k = \frac{TP_k}{TP_k + FN_k} \tag{9}$$

$$F1_k = \frac{Precision_k \cdot Recall_k}{Precision_k + Recall_k} \tag{10}$$

$$Accuracy\,Total = \frac{\sum_k TP_k}{TotalSamples} \tag{11}$$

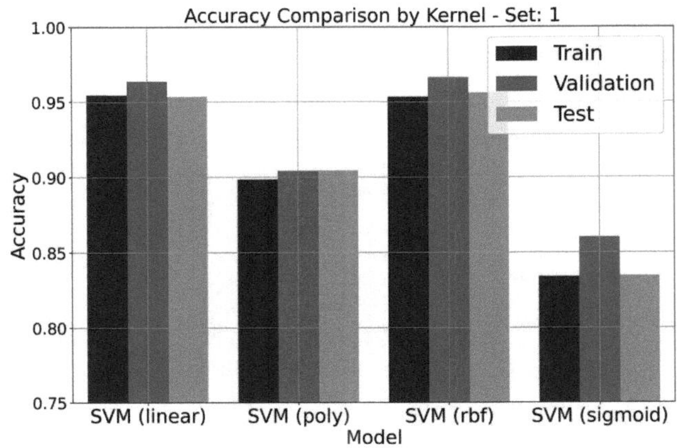

Fig. 6. Performance obtained when evaluating the characteristics in the SVM.

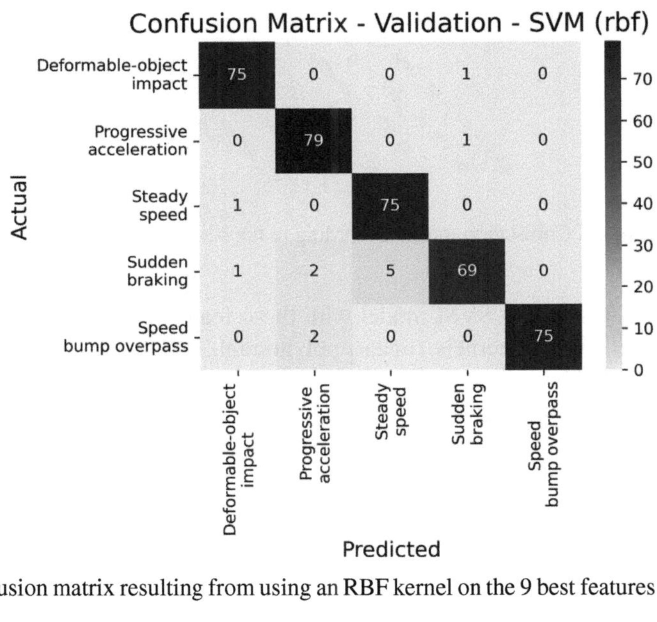

Fig. 7. Confusion matrix resulting from using an RBF kernel on the 9 best features and validation metrics.

Figure 7 presents the classification results for the validation dataset. In conjunction with the evaluation metrics defined above, these results allow for a detailed assessment of the SVM model, with the corresponding values summarized in Table 3.

Figure 8 shows the ROC (Receiver Operating Characteristic) curves obtained from the validation dataset, illustrating the model's ability to separate each driving event class. The curves represent the relationship between the true positive rate (TPR) and the false positive rate (FPR) for different decision thresholds. The high AUC values, close to 1 for all classes, indicate strong discriminative performance and high reliability in distinguishing among events, suggesting low risk of overfitting within the validation set.

Table 3. Accuracy of performance obtained by the RBF kernel in SVM.

Data Set	Accuracy	Precision	Recall	F1-Score	AUC- ROC
Train	0.95338	0.95703	0.95292	0.95231	0.99307
Test	0.95607	0.95933	0.95533	0.95491	0.98985
Validation	0.96632	0.96703	0.96626	0.96610	0.99390

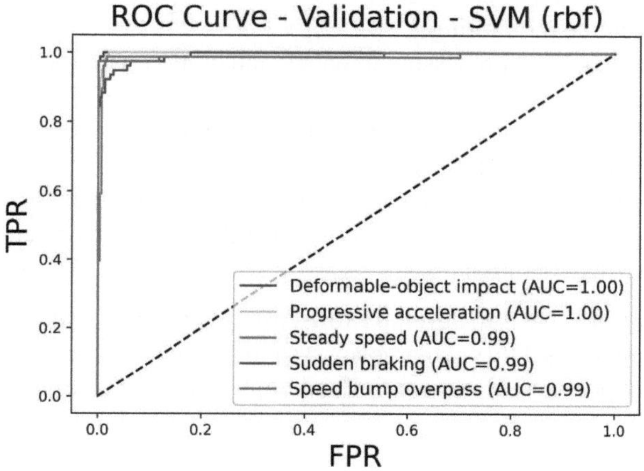

Fig. 8. ROC-AUC curve.

5 Conclusions and Future Work

5.1 Conclusion

In this preliminary study, we developed a driving event detection system that integrates Short-Time Fourier Transform (STFT) analysis with Support Vector Machine (SVM) classification. The STFT proved effective for representing the dynamic behavior of inertial signals (accelerometer and gyroscope), allowing the extraction of discriminative spectral features such as energy, total magnitude, and peak magnitude. These features, when used as input to an RBF-kernel SVM classifier, yielded an accuracy of 96.63% across five event classes: deformable-object impact, progressive acceleration, constant velocity, sudden braking, and speed bump traversal.

The results demonstrate the feasibility of combining STFT-derived features with SVM for event detection under controlled laboratory conditions using a scaled vehicle. Nonetheless, these findings should be considered preliminary, as further validation with larger datasets and full-scale testing is required before broad generalization can be achieved. Although this work centered on SVM classification with different kernel functions, future research will include comparative benchmarking with other machine learning techniques and feature optimization strategies to enhance performance and applicability.

5.2 Future Work

This study represents an initial step toward the development of an intelligent system for road monitoring and assistance based on low-cost sensors and spectral signal processing. Future work will focus on:

- Modeling a broader range of collision scenarios with varying levels of severity.
- Validating the proposed system in full-scale vehicles while maintaining the STFT-based detection framework.
- Incorporating additional sensing modalities (e.g., GPS, cameras) and communication modules for remote monitoring.
- Implementing real-time processing to enable integration with intelligent transportation systems.
- Evaluating the system under diverse traffic, terrain, and vibration conditions to strengthen robustness and reliability.
- Enhancing experimental scenarios by incorporating environmental elements such as lane markings, road irregularities, and surface damage to more closely reproduce real-world driving conditions.

The ultimate objective is to develop a low-cost, reliable, and scalable tool capable of integration into vehicle safety or emergency systems, ultimately contributing to reducing response times in post-accident scenarios and improving road safety.

References

1. OMS: Traumatismos causados por el tránsito. https://www.who.int/es/news-room/fact-sheets/detail/road-traffic-injuries. Accessed 6 June 2024
2. Ondruš, J., Kolla, E., Vertaľ, P., Šarić, Ž: How do autonomous cars work? Transport. Res. Procedia **44**, 226–233 (2020). https://doi.org/10.1016/J.TRPRO.2020.02.049
3. Dai, J., Teng, J., Bai, X., Shen, Z., Xuan, D.: Mobile phone based drunk driving detection (2010). https://doi.org/10.4108/ICST.PERVASIVEHEALTH2010.8901
4. Saiprasert, C., Pholprasit, T., Thajchayapong, S.: Detection of driving events using sensory data on smartphone. Int. J. Intell. Transp. Syst. Res. **15**(1), 17–28 (2017). https://doi.org/10.1007/S13177-015-0116-5
5. Johnson, D.A., Trivedi, M.M.: Driving style recognition using a smartphone as a sensor platform. In: IEEE Conference on Intelligent Transportation Systems, Proceedings, ITSC, pp. 1609–1615 (2011). https://doi.org/10.1109/ITSC.2011.6083078
6. Bose, B., Dutta, J., Ghosh, S., Pramanick, P., Roy, S.: Smartphone based system for real-time aggressive driving detection and marking rash driving-prone areas. In: ACM International Conference Proceeding Series (2018). https://doi.org/10.1145/3170521.3170549
7. Machaca Arceda, V., Riveros, E.L.: Fast car crash detection in video. In: XLIV Latin American Computer Conference (CLEI), pp. 632–637 (2018). https://doi.org/10.1109/CLEI.2018.00081
8. Nassuna, H., Eyobu, O.S., Kim, J.H., Lee, D.: Feature selection based on variance distribution of power spectral density for driving behavior recognition. In: Proceedings of the 14th IEEE Conference on Industrial Electronics and Applications, ICIEA 2019, pp. 335–338 (2019). https://doi.org/10.1109/ICIEA.2019.8834349

9. Yu, J., Chen, Z., Zhu, Y., Jennifer Chen, Y., Kong, L., Li, M.: Fine-grained abnormal driving behaviors detection and identification with smartphones. IEEE Trans. Mob. Comput. **16**(8), 2198–2212 (2017). https://doi.org/10.1109/TMC.2016.2618873
10. Asryullah Pratama, A., Sukaridhoto, S., Hery Purnomo, M., Lystianingrum, V., Putri, R., Budiarti, N.: Design of audio-based accident and crime detection and its optimization, pp. 214–220 (2023). www.joiv.org/index.php/joiv. Accessed 23 Oct 2024
11. Chandrasiri, N.P., Nawa, K., Ishii, A.: Driving skill classification in curve driving scenes using machine learning. J. Mod. Transport. **24**(3), 196–206 (2016). https://doi.org/10.1007/S40534-016-0098-2
12. Kontopoulou, V.I., Panagopoulos, A.D., Kakkos, I., Matsopoulos, G.K.: A review of ARIMA vs. machine learning approaches for time series forecasting in data driven networks. Multidisciplinary Digital Publishing Institute (MDPI) (2023). https://doi.org/10.3390/fi15080255
13. Gao, W., Li, Z., Chen, Q., Jiang, W., Feng, Y.: Modelling and prediction of GNSS time series using GBDT, LSTM and SVM machine learning approaches. J. Geod. **96**(10) (2022). https://doi.org/10.1007/s00190-022-01662-5
14. InvenSense Inc.: MPU-6000 and MPU-6050 register map and descriptions (2013). https://product.tdk.com/system/files/dam/doc/product/sensor/mortion-inertial/imu/data_sheet/mpu-6000-datasheet1.pdf?ref_disty=mouser. Accessed 4 May 2024
15. Qian, S., Chen, D.: Joint time-frequency analysis. IEEE Signal Process. Mag. **16**, 52–67 (1999)

Predictive Modeling of Child Mortality Rates from Diarrheal Diseases Based on Water Indicators in Mexico

Paola A. Castillo-Gutierrez[1(✉)], Daniela L. Macotela[1], Alejandro Gonzalez Saenz[1,2], Enrique Garcia-Ceja[1], and Miguel González-Mendoza[1]

[1] Tecnologico de Monterrey, Monterrey, Mexico
a00843399@tec.mx
[2] John Deere, San Pedro Garza García, Mexico

Abstract. In Mexico, the comparative effectiveness of budget allocation versus technical water treatment performance in reducing childhood diarrheal mortality remains unestablished. We conducted a nationwide predictive analysis of under-five diarrheal mortality across all 32 Mexican states from 2012 to 2022, integrating data from Mexican National Water Commission (CONAGUA) through their National Water Information System (SINA) on government budget allocation and chlorination efficiency. We employed Generalized Additive Models (GAM) with rolling-window cross-validation to quantify the relative importance of technical versus financial water management interventions. The analysis achieved robust predictive performance (mean $R^2 = 0.74$, MAE = 2.11 deaths per 100,000 children). Chlorination efficiency demonstrated superior predictive power (55.7% relative importance) compared to budget allocation (44.3% relative importance) in reducing child mortality. Southern states consistently showed both the highest mortality rates (Chiapas: 45.0 per 100,000 in 2022) and lowest chlorination efficiency (<80%), while northern states maintained low mortality with high technical performance (>95% efficiency). Technical water quality indicators outperform budget-based metrics in predicting child mortality outcomes. Our methodology provides a replicable framework for evidence-based water policy optimization in similar middle-income contexts.

Keywords: Child Mortality Prediction · Diarrheal Diseases · Water Quality · Generalized Additive Models · Public Health Informatics

1 Introduction

Diarrhea is a symptom of infections caused by a variety of bacterial, viral, and parasitic organisms, most of which are transmitted through water contaminated with feces. Infection is more common when there is a lack of hygiene and adequate sanitation services, and safe water for drinking, cooking, and washing. Among children under 5 years of age, the most common viral pathogens are rotaviruses, noroviruses, adenoviruses, and astroviruses [20]. Bacterial pathogens

L. Martínez-Villaseñor et al. (Eds.): MICAI 2025, CCIS 2712, pp. 170–185, 2025.
https://doi.org/10.1007/978-3-032-08704-1_13

include Escherichia coli, Salmonella spp., Shigella spp. and Campylobacter spp., while parasitic pathogens include Cryptosporidium, Giardia, and Entamoeba spp. Rotaviruses and E. coli bacteria are the most common pathogens among children of all age groups, while parasitic pathogens are common in children aged 3 to 5 years [20]. A significant proportion of these diarrheal diseases could be prevented through basic interventions: providing safe drinking water, ensuring adequate sanitation, and promoting proper hygiene practices [20].

Children under five years are disproportionately vulnerable to waterborne illnesses, particularly diarrheal diseases. Annually, more than 800,000 children die to preventable conditions stemming from inadequate water access, sanitation deficiencies, and poor hygiene practices [20]. Despite notable reductions in diarrhea-associated mortality, improvements in morbidity and incidence rates have been inconsistent across geographical regions and socioeconomic strata. The well-documented relationship between early pathogen exposure, diarrheal disease burden, and elevated stunting rates, collectively referred to as environmental enteropathy, underscores a critical public health concern. Water, sanitation, and hygiene (WASH) conditions and interventions have a multifaceted influence on pediatric growth and development, with scholarly consensus indicating that addressing undernutrition necessitates concurrent improvements in WASH infrastructure for disadvantaged pediatric populations globally [11]. Chlorination efficiency metrics directly address a key intervention point, as research indicates proper disinfection can reduce childhood diarrheal disease [5].

We used Generalized Additive Models (GAM) to capture non-linear relationships between water quality, budget allocation, and mortality rates that traditional methods might miss. GAM regression provides the flexibility to model smooth, non-parametric relationships between chlorination efficiency, budget allocation, and mortality rates while accounting for temporal trends. The predictive nature of these models offers a proactive tool for policy makers to forecast potential mortality outcomes under different budget allocation scenarios and water quality improvement strategies, moving beyond traditional descriptive epidemiological approaches to provide forward-looking decision support for water infrastructure investment prioritization across Mexico's diverse geographical and socioeconomic landscape.

This study has the following contributions:

1. **Integrated Water-Health Dataset**: Unified decade-long CONAGUA data (2012–2022) linking mortality rates, chlorination efficiency and budget allocation across all Mexican states. Curated data was made available via GitHub https://github.com/paolazcastillo/Child-Mortality-from-Diarrea-in-Mexico-2012-2022.
2. **Policy Effectiveness Quantification**: Empirically compared government budget investment versus chlorination efficiency impact on under-5 diarrheal mortality.
3. **Temporal Policy Impact Methodology**: Established a rolling-window validation framework to assess how water management interventions translate into measurable health outcomes over time.

Following this introduction, Sect. 2 examines related works, revealing a notable scarcity of contemporary research on the topic with only twelve studies identified in the last decade. Section 3 details the methodology employed, including data acquisition and curation from CONAGUA-SINA [1], GAM model specification, and rolling-window cross-validation strategy. Results and discussion are presented in Sect. 4, where model predictive performance is analyzed and the relative importance of chlorination efficiency versus budget investment in reducing child mortality is quantified. Section 5 addresses study limitations, acknowledging inherent constraints of available data and variables not included in the analysis. Finally, Sect. 6 synthesizes conclusions and their implications for water and sanitation public policy formulation in Mexico and similar middle-income country contexts.

2 Related Works

The related works represent a variety of approaches to childhood diarrheal mortality, examining it from perspectives that include epidemiological, microbiological, public health interventions, environmental exposures, microbiome analysis, socioeconomic policy, and vaccination coverage. Paternina-Caicedo et al. (2015, 2021) demonstrated the significant impact of the rotavirus vaccine, reporting a 30–50% reduction in mortality across Latin American countries, with an 18% decrease specifically in Mexico through interrupted time series analysis [14,15]. Sánchez-Uribe et al. (2016) and Richardson-López Collada et al. (2019) provided strong evidence of sustained mortality reductions of 53% and 52.6%, respectively, following the universalization of the rotavirus vaccine in Mexico, translating to approximately 959–970 deaths averted annually [16,17]. Bello-López et al. (2020) and Alcalá et al. (2023) focused on pathogen-specific analyses, revealing patterns of antibiotic resistance in Aeromonas spp. and the ongoing circulation of rotavirus (30.8%) and norovirus (8.6%) post-vaccination [4,6]. Cupul-Uicab et al. (2017) examined environmental determinants, highlighting an increased risk of diarrhea associated with prenatal DDT exposure in urban areas, while Toro-Monjaraz et al. (2021) investigated the restoration of the intestinal microbiome during acute episodes [10,19]. Cavalcanti et al. (2023) evaluated conditional cash transfer programs across 4,882 municipalities, demonstrating a 24% overall reduction in mortality, with stronger associations observed for poverty-related diseases, including diarrhea (RR = 0.41) [8]. Luna-Casas et al. (2019) compared vaccination schedules, indicating that a two-dose scheme yields superior coverage and compliance compared to a three-dose regimen [12]. The study by Chivardi et al. [26] represents a comprehensive longitudinal analysis examining the relationship between social determinants (income distribution, illiteracy rate, poverty rate, sewage access, access to piped water, healthcare infrastructure, and healthcare workforce) and child under-5 mortality rates across Latin America [26]. The research employed machine learning algorithms to analyze data from 4,894 municipalities spanning Brazil (3,669 municipalities), Ecuador (158 towns), and Mexico (1,067 municipalities) over a twenty-year period from

2000 to 2019 [26]. The data from Mexico was obtained from the National Institute of Statistics and Geography (INEGI) of Mexico [26]. The researchers utilized a municipal-level cohort design to investigate how various social determinants influence child mortality outcomes [26]. Their analytical approach primarily employed Random Forest models (with k-fold cross-validation technique with threefold), complemented by Gradient Boosting Machine (GBM) and Generalized Additive Model (GAM) for sensitivity analysis [26]. The study's findings revealed that poverty emerged as the most powerful predictor of child mortality across all three machine learning models of each nation, followed by illiteracy as the second most crucial factor, and the Gini inequality index as the third most significant predictor [26]. Their analysis had the Random Forest performing best with an R^2 of 0.16 and Root Mean Square Error (RMSE) of 241.08, followed by the Gradient Boosting Machine (GBM) with R^2 of 0.15 and RMSE of 242.36, and the Generalized Additive Model (GAM) with R^2 of 0.1 and RMSE of 249.74 [26].

In contrast to these traditional epidemiological and clinical approaches, our study employs a predictive framework specifically designed to assess the effectiveness of water infrastructure investments in Mexico, utilizing data from CONAGUA [1]. We employ GAM regression to quantify the relationship between chlorination efficiency and governmental budget allocation about child mortality outcomes, thereby providing an infrastructure-focused tool for policymakers to enhance the allocation of water management resources.

3 Methodology

The methodology section outlines our comprehensive approach to analyzing the relationship between water management interventions and child mortality outcomes in Mexico. Our analytical framework integrates three core components: systematic data acquisition from CONAGUA's National Water Information System (SINA) [1], data curation, and advanced predictive modeling using Generalized Additive Models (GAM). The variables chosen for analysis were based on publicly available data related to water indicators and child mortality rates due to diarrhea at the annual and state levels from 2012 to 2022, sourced from the SINA portal [1].

3.1 Data Collection

The dataset for this study was acquired from the Mexican National Water Commission (CONAGUA) through their National Water Information System (SINA) portal[1], providing comprehensive water quality and public health data across all 32 Mexican states for the period 2012–2022 [1]. It is essential to note that the data is not directly available; each variable that can be selected and visualized on the Mexican map at the portal must be exported as a .csv file to handle

[1] https://sinav30.conagua.gob.mx:8080/SINA/?opcion=salud.

the data directly. The data acquisition process involved systematic extraction of three primary datasets:

1. **Child Mortality Dataset**: Annual mortality rates for children under 5 years of age due to diarrheal diseases (`tasamortmenores5años`) per state
2. **Water Treatment Efficiency Dataset**: Annual chlorination efficiency percentages (`eficienciacloracion`) per state
3. **Budget Allocation Dataset**: Annual water management expenditure (`mdp`) in millions of Mexican pesos per state

3.2 Data Curation

We cleaned and standardized the CONAGUA data, merging mortality rates, chlorination efficiency, and budget allocation across states and years. We transformed the raw datasets from the portal into analysis formats for subsequent predictive modeling through three fundamental operations:

1. **Data cleaning** to remove inconsistencies, standardize naming conventions, and eliminate invalid entries
2. **Data integration** to merge heterogeneous datasets across different temporal granularities and variable types while preserving data integrity
3. **Data formatting (tidying)** following Wickham's principles [3] to ensure each variable forms a column, each observation forms a row, and each dataset maintains consistent structure and naming conventions.

3.3 Model Architecture and Specification

We employed Generalized Additive Models (GAM) as the primary analytical framework due to their superior capability to capture non-linear relationships between predictors and health outcomes.

The GAM framework models the expected mortality rate as an additive combination of smooth functions:

$$E[Y_{i,t}] = \beta_0 + f_1(\text{Chlorination}_{i,t}) + f_2(\text{Budget}_{i,t}) + f_3(\text{Year}_t) + \epsilon_{i,t}$$

where:

- $Y_{i,t}$ represents the child mortality rate from diarrheal diseases per 100,000 children under 5 years for state i in year t
- f_1, f_2, f_3 are smooth functions estimated using penalized regression splines
- β_0 is the intercept term
- $\epsilon_{i,t}$ represents the error term

Validation Strategy: Rolling-Window Cross-Validation. To ensure robust model performance assessment and temporal validity, we implemented a rolling-window cross-validation strategy with four distinct folds:

Fold 1: Train: 2012–2018 (7 years) → Test: 2019
Fold 2: Train: 2012–2019 (8 years) → Test: 2020
Fold 3: Train: 2012–2020 (9 years) → Test: 2021
Fold 4: Train: 2012–2021 (10 years) → Test: 2022

Feature Importance. We employed an approach to quantify predictor importance through partial dependence analysis:

Partial Dependence Range Calculation. For each predictor j, the partial dependence range is computed as:

$$\text{Range}_j = \max(f_j(x)) - \min(f_j(x))$$

This metric represents the total potential impact of optimizing variable j from its worst to best observed level while holding all other variables constant.

Relative Importance Estimation. The relative importance of predictor j is calculated as:

$$\text{Relative Importance}_j = \frac{\text{Range}_j}{\sum_{k=1}^{K} \text{Range}_k}$$

Statistical Significance Assessment. To establish confidence intervals for importance estimates, we implemented bootstrap resampling with 1,000 iterations across the 128 state×fold partial dependence range values, generating 95% confidence intervals for relative importance measures.

Evaluation Metrics. Model performance is assessed using complementary metrics:

- **R-squared** (R^2): Proportion of variance in mortality rates explained by the model, indicating overall predictive capacity
- **Mean Absolute Error (MAE)**: Average magnitude of prediction errors, providing interpretable accuracy measures in mortality rate units

4 Results and Discussion

With the application of a GAM and a Rolling-Window cross-validation strategy, we analyzed the relative influence of government budget investment in water management and water treatment effectiveness (chlorination efficiency) on under-5 diarrheal mortality rates across states throughout the years 2012 to 2022.

The reported average R^2 of 0.74 across all folds suggests that the GAM effectively captures a substantial portion of the variability in the target variable. The average MAE of 2.11 indicates the average deviation of the model's predictions from the actual mortality rates. In practical terms, this means our model predictions deviate by approximately 2.1 deaths per 100,000 children under 5 years from the observed mortality rates. To contextualize this error magnitude: in a state with 1 million children under 5, this translates to a prediction uncertainty of roughly 21 deaths annually. Given that mortality rates in our dataset range from near 0 to 45 per 100,000 live births, with a mean of approximately 8.5 per 100,000, this MAE represents a relatively modest 25% relative error, indicating good predictive accuracy for public health decision-making purposes. Our rolling-window cross-validation approach demonstrated consistent predictive performance across different time periods, with R^2 values ranging from 0.6544 to 0.8044 across folds as shown in Table 1.

Table 1. Metrics by Fold

Fold	Test Year	R^2	MAE
1	2019	0.7404	2.2954
2	2020	0.777	1.7638
3	2021	0.8044	1.8237
4	2022	0.6544	2.5629

The temporal analysis in Fig. 1 shows persistent regional disparities in under-5 mortality rates, with southern states (Chiapas, Oaxaca, Guerrero) consistently showing the highest mortality rates, while northern states (Nuevo León, Tamaulipas, Coahuila) maintain the lowest rates. Chiapas consistently shows the highest mortality rates throughout the study period, with a notable spike in 2022 (45.0 per 100,000 live births), while Oaxaca demonstrates considerable volatility, particularly during 2016–2019. Most other high-mortality states show relatively stable trends with gradual improvements over the decade, though Veracruz exhibits a consistent downward trend from 2016 to 2022, as observed in Fig. 2.

The analysis of CONAGUA budget allocation unveils significant disparities in federal water infrastructure investment across Mexican states. Mexico City (CDMX) and Estado de México consistently receive the largest allocations, reflecting population density and infrastructure needs, with budgets exceeding 20,000 million pesos annually. Notable patterns include budget reductions across most states during 2017–2018, followed by gradual recovery, as shown in Fig. 3.

Critically, southern states with high child mortality rates (Chiapas, Oaxaca, Guerrero) receive relatively modest budget allocations despite greater infrastructure needs. This inverse relationship between mortality burden and budget

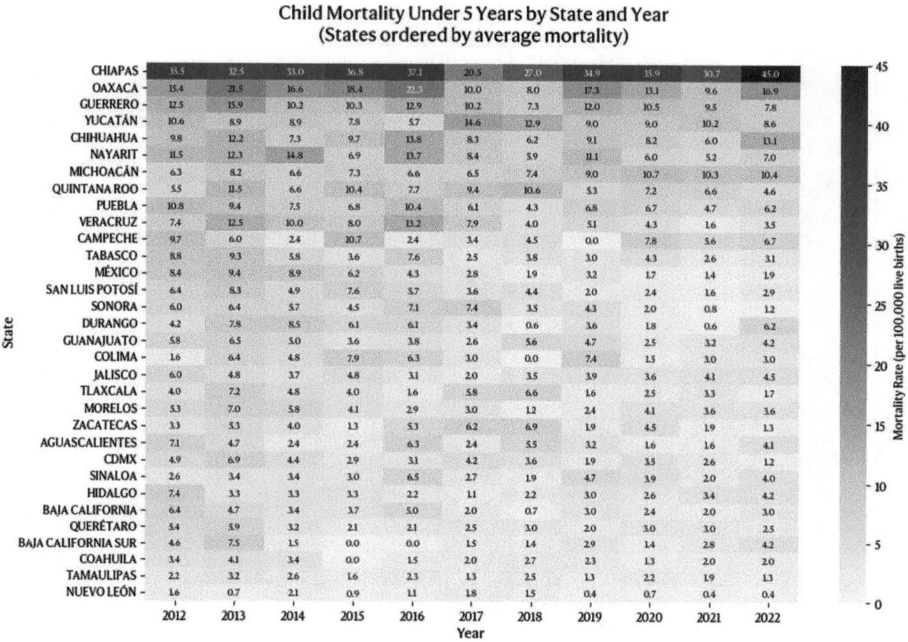

Fig. 1. Heatmap of under-5 mortality rates across Mexican states by year (2012–2022). States are ranked by average mortality rate over the study period, with darker red indicating higher mortality rates.

allocation suggests that financial resource distribution may not adequately reflect public health priorities or that budget allocation alone provides insufficient predictive power for health outcomes.

Data on water chlorination efficiency expose stark geographical disparities that closely mirror mortality patterns. Figure 4 helps understand this visually. The northern and central states consistently maintain high chlorination rates (>95%), while southern states with elevated child mortality rates show significantly lower and more variable chlorination efficiency. Chiapas demonstrates the poorest performance with efficiency rates below 80% throughout all years, directly correlating with its highest child mortality rates. The temporal analysis of the ten lowest-performing states in Fig. 5 shows considerable volatility in chlorination efficiency, with most states experiencing declining performance after 2017. Chiapas maintains consistently low efficiency (66.2–77%), while Guerrero demonstrates the most dramatic decline from 100% in 2017 to 62% by 2022. These erratic patterns suggest systemic challenges in maintaining consistent water quality standards in underperforming states, which notably overlap with regions experiencing elevated child mortality rates.

To understand the relative importance of budget investment and chlorination efficiency, we focused on the partial dependence ranges. The partial dependence plots show the isolated effect of each predictor on the predicted mortality rate,

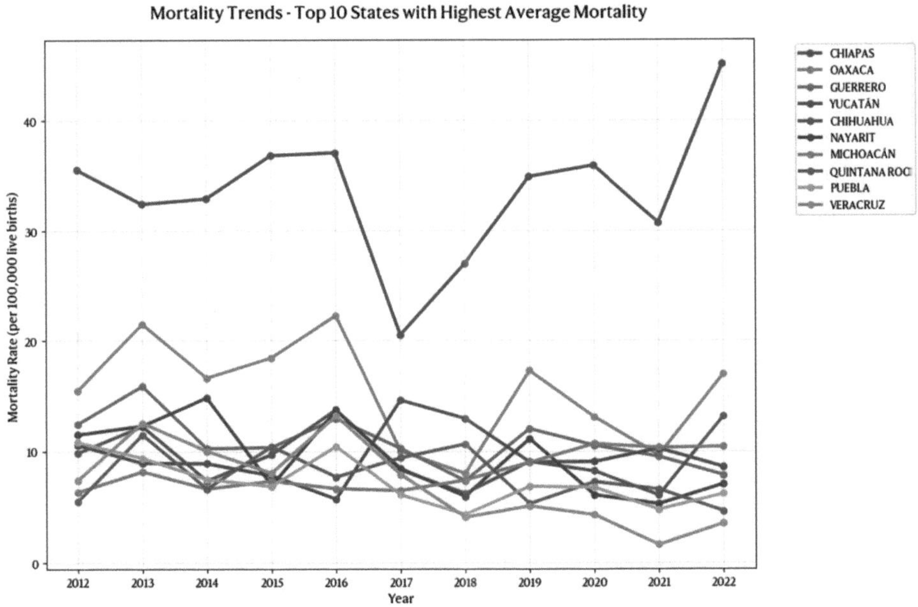

Fig. 2. Temporal trends in under-5 mortality rates across the ten Mexican states with the highest average mortality (2012–2022).

holding other variables constant. The analysis of the average relative importance (Fig. 6) reveals that chlorination efficiency (55.7%) has a considerably larger potential impact on reducing under-5 diarrheal mortality compared to budget investment (44.3%). This suggests that, on average, improvements in chlorination effectiveness across states could yield a greater reduction in child mortality from diarrheal diseases than similar proportional increases in the water management budget. The 95% confidence intervals for these relative importance estimates provide a measure of the uncertainty surrounding these findings.

The mean partial-dependence range by fold (Fig. 7) indicates some temporal variation in the potential impact of both factors. The magnitude of the difference between the chlorination efficiency and water budget varies slightly over time, suggesting that the relative influence of these factors on diarrheal mortality might not be static and could be influenced by other time-dependent factors or policy changes.

The scattered points in the Partial-Dependence Range analysis in Fig. 8 represent different state-year combinations across folds, with deviations from the diagonal indicating the influence of specific levels of chlorination and budget from certain periods. States with high chlorination efficiency but low budget allocation consistently show better health outcomes than states with high budget allocation but poor technical implementation, further supporting the primacy of technical competence in water management policy.

The study period encompasses several significant events that likely influenced the water-child mortality relationship, particularly during 2020–2022. The

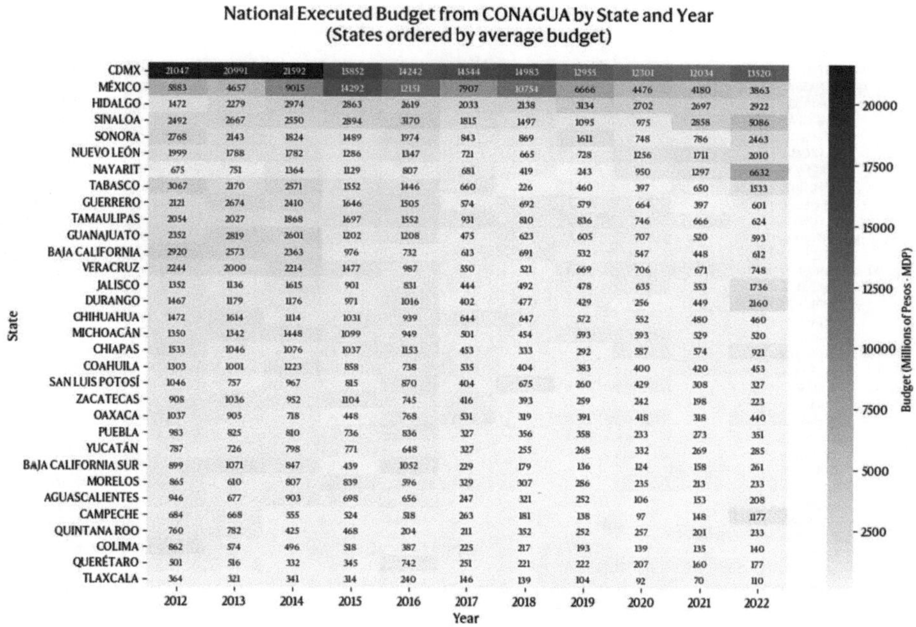

Fig. 3. National water infrastructure budget allocation by CONAGUA across Mexican states (2012–2022). Heatmap displays executed budget in millions of Mexican pesos (MDP), with states ordered by average budget allocation over the study period. Darker blue indicates higher budget allocations.

COVID-19 pandemic created unprecedented disruption to Mexico's health systems, with 325,415 excess deaths in 2020 alone, 34.4% of them not directly related to COVID-19, and massive reductions in access to essential health services affecting maternal and child health programs [23]. Simultaneously, the elimination of Seguro Popular (Mexico's flagship public health insurance program that operated from 2003 to 2020) and its replacement with INSABI in 2020 during the pandemic onset resulted in people lacking health service access increasing from 20.1 million (2018) to 35.7 million (2020), a 75% increase when health services were most needed [24]. The health system instability continued into 2022, when IMSS-Bienestar began operating by presidential decree, ultimately leading to INSABI's elimination in 2023 due to poor performance and substantial debt accumulation. Additionally, Mexico experienced its worst drought conditions since 2011, with 85% of the country experiencing drought in 2021 and 70% in 2022, including 20% under extreme drought conditions [25].

5 Limitations

This study presents several important limitations that should be considered when interpreting results. The current predictive models do not incorporate annual

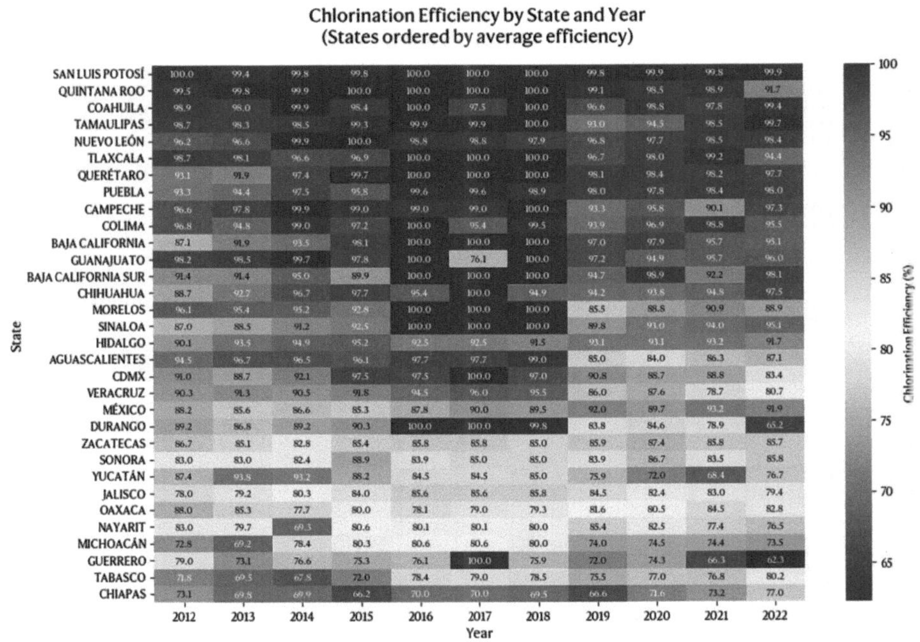

Fig. 4. Water chlorination efficiency across Mexican states by year (2012–2022). Heatmap displays the percentage of water supply systems with adequate chlorination levels, with states ordered by average efficiency over the study period. Green indicates higher efficiency (approaching 100 %), while red represents lower efficiency.

state-level rotavirus vaccination coverage, which represents a critical gap given that rotavirus accounts for approximately 40% of all diarrhea-related hospitalizations, with literature demonstrating 18–53% mortality reductions following vaccine implementation in Mexico [12]. Additionally, the analysis is constrained by the availability of CONAGUA SINA portal data [1], which limits the inclusion of key socioeconomic variables (poverty, marginalization, education), climatic factors (temperature, precipitation, seasonality), under five years population density, urbanization levels, and healthcare access indicators that have been shown to significantly influence childhood diarrheal disease outcomes. The study operates at state-level granularity rather than municipal or local levels, potentially masking important sub-regional variations in water quality and health outcomes. Furthermore, the models do not account for temporal lags between water quality improvements and health outcomes, nor do they incorporate spatial autocorrelation effects between neighboring states. The observational nature of the data limits causal inference capabilities compared to experimental or quasi-experimental designs employed in other epidemiological studies. While these limitations are inherent to the CONAGUA data framework and the study's specific focus on water infrastructure policy evaluation, they represent important considerations for interpreting model predictions and suggest areas for future research integra-

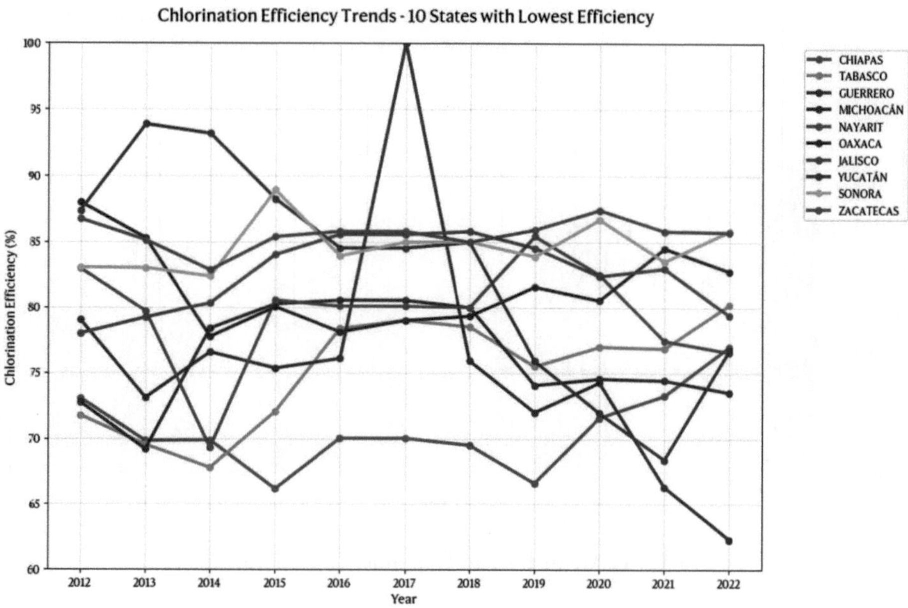

Fig. 5. Temporal trends in water chlorination efficiency for the ten Mexican states with lowest average performance (2012–2022).

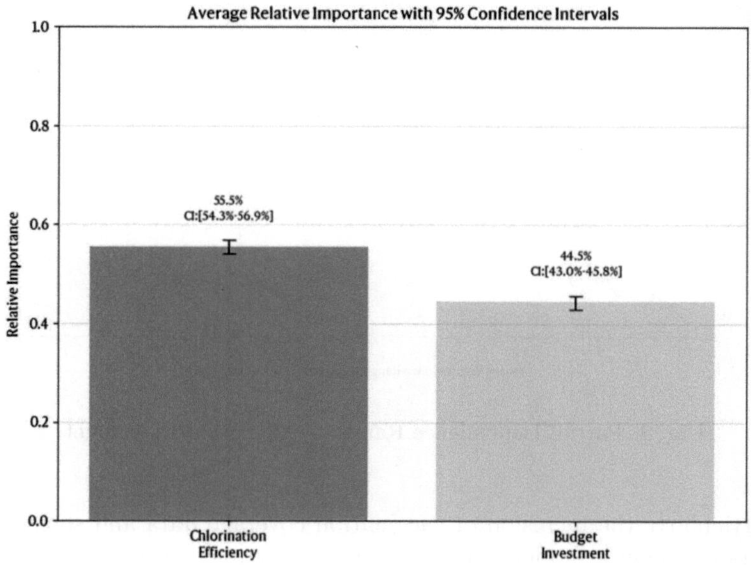

Fig. 6. Average Relative Importance.

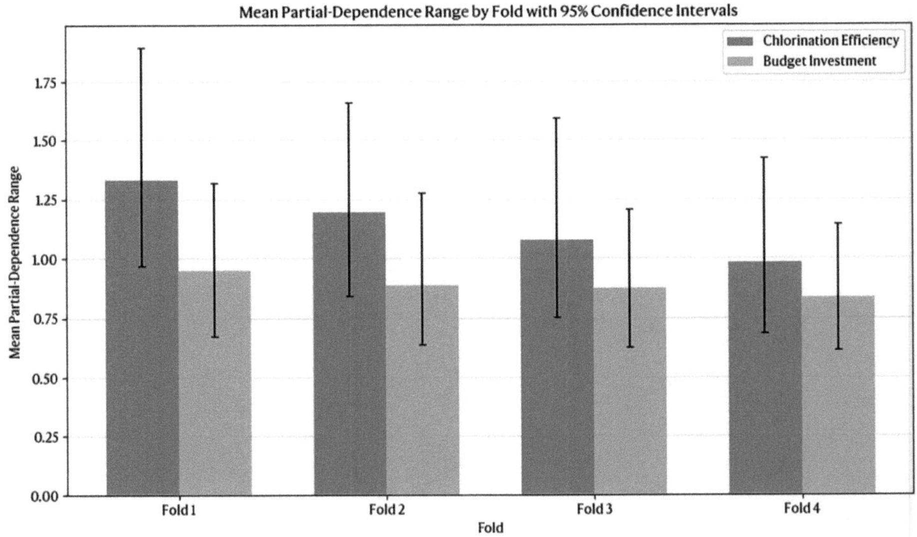

Fig. 7. Mean Partial-Dependence by fold.

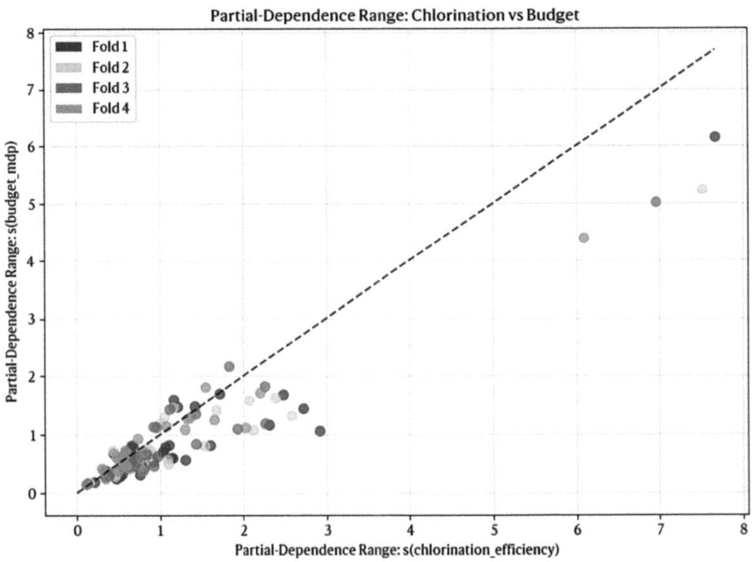

Fig. 8. Partial-Dependence Range: Chlorination vs. Budget.

tion, particularly the inclusion of vaccination coverage data and socioeconomic indicators to enhance model robustness and policy relevance.

6 Conclusion

The results from this comprehensive analysis of Mexico's water infrastructure and child mortality data (2012–2022) provide compelling evidence that technical water quality interventions are more effective than budget-based approaches in reducing diarrheal mortality among children under five. Our Generalized Additive Model (GAM) analysis indicates that chlorination efficiency (55.7% relative importance) is a significantly stronger predictor of reductions in child mortality compared to government budget allocation (44.3% relative importance), with robust statistical validation across multiple folds (mean $R^2 = 0.74$).

These findings carry profound implications for public health policy and resource allocation in Mexico, as well as in similar middle-income countries. Instead of primarily increasing financial investments in water infrastructure, policymakers should prioritize the quality of technical implementation, systematic monitoring of chlorination efficiency, and maintaining consistent water treatment standards across all states. The significant geographical disparities highlighted in our analysis, where southern states exhibit both the highest mortality rates and the lowest chlorination efficiency, underscore the urgent need for targeted technical assistance and quality assurance programs in underperforming regions. These predictive models consider a few variables and may not be sufficient to predict children's mortality rates from diarrhea accurately, but they represent a good starting point and demonstrate the capability of relying on chlorination efficiency.

Acknowledgments. P. Castillo-Gutierrez and D. Macotela would like to thank SECI-HTI (Secretaría de Ciencia, Humanidades, Tecnología e Innovación) and Tecnologico de Monterrey for the grant fund received.

Disclosure of Interests. The authors have no competing interests to declare that are relevant to the content of this article.

References

1. CONAGUA: SINA 3.0. Sistema Nacional de Información del Agua. https://sinav30.conagua.gob.mx:8080/SINA/?opcion=salud. Accessed 01 June 2025
2. Chivardi, C., et al.: Understanding the social determinants of child mortality in Latin America over the last two decades: a machine learning approach. Sci. Rep. **13**(1), 20839 (2023). https://doi.org/10.1038/s41598-023-47994-w
3. Wickham, H.: Tidy data. J. Stat. Softw. **59**(10), 1–23 (2014). https://doi.org/10.18637/jss.v059.i10 https://doi.org/10.18637/jss.v059.i10 https://doi.org/10.18637/jss.v059.i10
4. Alcalá, A.C., et al.: Detection of rotavirus and norovirus among children with acute gastroenteritis in Merida and Chihuahua cities. Mexico. J. Infect. Dev. Countries **17**(05), 707–712 (2023). https://doi.org/10.3855/jidc.16979
5. Arnold, B.F., Colford, J.M., Jr.: Treating water with chlorine at point-of-use to improve water quality and reduce child diarrhea in developing countries: a systematic review and meta-analysis. Am. J. Trop. Med. Hyg. **76**(2), 354–364 (2007)

6. Bello-López, J.M., et al.: Genetic and phenotypic determinants of resistance to antibiotics in Aeromonas spp., strains isolated from pediatric patients. J. Infect. Dev. Countries **14**(10), 1146–1154 (2020). https://doi.org/10.3855/jidc.12966
7. Savion, N., Guzner, N., Hashavya, S., Reif, S., Sarna Cahan, L.O.: Brucellosis in pediatric populations: an 11-year cohort study. IMAJ **25**, 542–546 (2023)
8. Cavalcanti, D.M., et al.: Evaluation and forecasting analysis of the association of conditional cash transfer with child mortality in Latin America, 2000–2030. JAMA Netw. Open **6**(7), e2323489 (2023). https://doi.org/10.1001/jamanetworkopen.2023.23489
9. Comisión Nacional del Agua [CONAGUA]: Sistema Nacional de Información del Agua: Salud. https://sinav30.conagua.gob.mx:8080/SINA/?opcion=salud
10. Cupul-Uicab, L.A., Terrazas-Medina, E.A., Hernández-Ávila, M., Longnecker, M.P.: In utero exposure to DDT and incidence of diarrhea among boys from tropical Mexico. Environ. Res. **159**, 331–337 (2017). https://doi.org/10.1016/j.envres.2017.08.027
11. Darvesh, N., Das, J.K., Vaivada, T., Gaffey, M.F., Rasanathan, K., Bhutta, Z.A.: Social determinants of health study team: water, sanitation and hygiene interventions for acute childhood diarrhea: a systematic review to provide estimates for the lives saved tool. BMC Public Health **17**(Suppl 4), 776 (2017). https://doi.org/10.1186/s12889-017-4746-1
12. Luna-Casas, G., et al.: Vaccine coverage and compliance in Mexico with the two-dose and three-dose rotavirus vaccines. Hum. Vaccines Immunother. **15**(6), 1251–1259 (2019). https://doi.org/10.1080/21645515.2018.1540827
13. Palacio-Mejía, L.S., et al.: Overview of acute diarrheal disease at the dawn of the 21st century: the case of Mexico. Salud Pública de México **62**(1), 14 (2019). https://doi.org/10.21149/9954 https://doi.org/10.21149/9954
14. Paternina-Caicedo, A., et al.: Effect of rotavirus vaccine on childhood diarrhea mortality in five Latin American countries. Vaccine **33**(32), 3923–3928 (2015). https://doi.org/10.1016/j.vaccine.2015.06.058
15. Paternina-Caicedo, A., Parashar, U., Garcia-Calavaro, C., de Oliveira, L.H., Alvis-Guzman, N., De la Hoz-Restrepo, F.: Diarrheal deaths after the introduction of rotavirus vaccination in 4 countries. Pediatrics **147**(1), e20193167 (2021). https://doi.org/10.1542/peds.2019-3167
16. Richardson-López Collada, V., Bautista-Márquez, A., Sánchez-Uribe, E., Esparza-Aguilar, M.: Impacto poblacional a 10 años de la vacunación contra rotavirus en México. Salud Pública de México **62**(1), 6 (2019). https://doi.org/10.21149/9936
17. Sánchez-Uribe, E., Esparza-Aguilar, M., Parashar, U.D., Richardson, V.: sustained reduction of childhood diarrhea-related mortality and hospitalizations in Mexico after Rotavirus vaccine universalization. Clin. Infect. Dis. **62**(suppl 2), S133–S139 (2016). https://doi.org/10.1093/cid/civ1205
18. Safe Drinking Water Foundation [SDWF]: What is chlorination? https://www.safewater.org/fact-sheets-1/2017/1/23/what-is-chlorination
19. Toro Monjaraz, E.M., Ignorosa Arellano, K.R., Loredo Mayer, A., Palacios-González, B., Cervantes Bustamante, R., Ramírez Mayans, J.A.: Gut microbiota in Mexican children with acute diarrhea: an observational study. Pediatr. Infect. Dis. J. **40**(8), 704–709 (2021). https://doi.org/10.1097/INF.0000000000003128
20. World Health Organization: Diarrheal disease (2024). https://www.who.int/es/news-room/fact-sheets/detail/diarrhoeal-disease
21. World Health Organization: The United Nations Children's Fund (UNICEF): Ending Preventable Child Deaths from Pneumonia and Diarrhoea by 2025: The Inte-

grated Global Action Plan for Pneumonia and Diarrhoea (GAPPD) - Executive Summary. WHO Press, Geneva (2013)
22. World Health Organization: Global Health Observatory data repository (2024). https://data.who.int/indicators/i/5131A52/1548EA3?m49=484
23. Palacio-Mejía, L.S., et al.: Leading causes of excess mortality in Mexico during the COVID-19 pandemic 2020–2021: a death certificates study in a middle-income country. Lancet Reg. Health-Am. **13**, 100303 (2022). https://doi.org/10.1016/j.lana.2022.100303
24. Torres-López, L., Serváñ-Mori, E., Wirtz, V.J., Reich, M.R., Bautista-Arredondo, S.: Increase of catastrophic and impoverishing health expenditures in Mexico associated to policy changes and the COVID-19 pandemic. Health Policy Plann. **38**(8), 891–901 (2023). https://doi.org/10.1093/heapol/czad065
25. Pan American Health Organization: Health overview - health in the Americas: Mexico country profile. PAHO, Washington, D.C. (2022). https://hia.paho.org/en/countries-22/mexico-country-profile
26. Chivardi, C., et al.: Understanding the social determinants of child mortality in Latin America over the last two decades: a machine learning approach. Sci. Rep. **13**, 20839 (2023). https://doi.org/10.1038/s41598-023-47994-w

Implementing AI in Mexico's Health Sector: A Strategic Framework

D. C. Lerma-Torres(✉)

Department of Medicine and Nutrition, University of Guanajuato, Guanajuato, Mexico
dc.lerma@ugto.mx

Abstract. Artificial intelligence (AI) promises substantial gains in healthcare, yet Mexico's adoption remains hindered by a mismatch between sophisticated algorithms and unresolved system fundamentals. This paper presents a clinically realistic, evidence-informed framework that distinguishes between use cases for screening, diagnosis/monitoring, and administrative optimization, arguing that the most significant near-term value lies in logistics and burden reduction. We inventory Mexico's conditions—significant "data debt" due to fragmented, non-interoperable records alongside underused strategic assets such as national clinical repositories and highly motivated human capital—and translate them into three actionable principles: (1) prioritize digital infrastructure and interoperability before advanced analytics; (2) foster a collaborative, open-source ecosystem and regulatory sandboxes for safe, rapid validation; and (3) design for the "augmented doctor" via explainable AI integrated into clinical workflows. Success should be measured not by algorithmic novelty but by reduced administrative load, improved interoperability, and a resilient digital health ecosystem that enables subsequent AI gains at scale.

Keywords: Artificial Intelligence in Health · Strategic Framework · Health Innovation · Clinical Informatics · Digital Transformation · Health Policy · Mexico

1 Introduction

The promise of Artificial Intelligence (AI) to revolutionize healthcare is undeniable, with advances ranging from diagnostic imaging to treatment optimization [1–3]. However, its translation into clinical and administrative practice in Mexico faces a profound paradox. While the global conversation focuses on increasingly complex AI models, the structural and fundamental problems of our healthcare system—such as fragmentation and a lack of data infrastructure—remain unresolved [4–6]. This disconnect fosters a fragmented innovation ecosystem [7,8], where well-intentioned projects often fail, not because of technical deficiencies, but due to a lack of alignment with clinical workflows, organizational culture, and the actual needs of end-users—a phenomenon amply documented in the literature on health technology implementation [5,6,9].

L. Martínez-Villaseñor et al. (Eds.): MICAI 2025, CCIS 2712, pp. 186–193, 2025.
https://doi.org/10.1007/978-3-032-08704-1_14

The recurring error is that of "solutionism": the development of technologically sophisticated tools that constitute a "solution in search of a problem". This approach ignores the operational realities of physicians and hospitals. Failing to address this gap has significant consequences, perpetuating systemic inefficiencies, exacerbating clinician burnout, and ultimately limiting potential improvements in patient outcomes. It is therefore crucial to reorient the strategy for technological innovation in the Mexican healthcare sector toward the most significant problems [10–12].

This position paper seeks to correct that course. To address the identified gap between AI's potential and its practical application in Mexico, a strategic framework is proposed based on the principle of "clinical realism." Rather than a prescriptive national strategy, this paper presents a set of principles for viable innovation, anchored in scientific evidence and the country's operational reality. The objective is to guide all ecosystem stakeholders—entrepreneurs, researchers, policymakers, and industry leaders—to focus their efforts on solving the correct problems, with the right tools, and on a solid infrastructural foundation, thereby ensuring that the technological transformation of medicine in Mexico is both successful and sustainable.

2 The Principle of Clinical Realism: Matching the Tool to the Problem

Any health technology project must begin with a thorough understanding of the clinical context. The viability of a tool does not depend on its algorithmic complexity, but on its appropriateness to the specific problem it seeks to solve [13].

2.1 The Essential Distinction: Screening, Diagnosis, and Optimization

Not all clinical problems are the same. Their technological approach must respect functional stratification. Screening, for example, must adhere to well-established epidemiological and health economics principles, such as the Wilson and Jungner criteria, which require that the test be low cost, acceptable to the population, and applicable at an early stage of the disease [14]. Proposing AI systems for population screening that replace advanced imaging or expensive biomarkers is inherently unfeasible in a public health system with limited resources, as it also induces severe bias by excluding those without access to such technology [15].

Diagnosis, on the other hand, is applied to a population that has already been selected, where clinical suspicion exists. In this scenario, higher costs and complexities can be justified if the information obtained is highly accurate and capable of modifying the physician's therapeutic plan. Ignoring this distinction leads to the development of "perfect" but inapplicable solutions [16–18].

2.2 The Real Bottleneck: The Administrative and Logistical Burden

While innovation in diagnostics is attractive, the area of most significant immediate potential impact for resource optimization lies in logistics and reducing administrative burdens. International studies show that physicians spend a substantial and increasing portion of their time on administrative and documentation tasks, which contributes to burnout and reduces the time available for direct patient care [19,20]. In Mexico, where the burden of care is high, this problem is magnified. Therefore, AI projects that aim to optimize surgery scheduling, predict demand for supplies, automate bed management, or simplify procedures represent the "low-hanging fruit" and can generate the most significant savings and systemic benefits [21].

3 An Inventory of the Mexican Reality: Data Debt and Strategic Assets

To innovate effectively, an honest inventory of the country's starting conditions is indispensable.

3.1 The Liability: The "Data Debt"

Mexico carries a significant "data debt". This debt is the result of a historically fragmented information recording culture and a health system segmented into subsystems (IMSS, ISSSTE, Ministry of Health, and the private sector) that rarely communicate [4]. Existing Electronic Health Records (EHRs), while a step forward, often operate as institutional silos, with limited or no interoperability, which prevents the creation of large, longitudinal, standardized datasets that are the fuel of AI [4,22,23]. Acknowledging this debt is not a call for pessimism, but the first step towards realistic solutions that do not assume the existence of pristine and integrated data.

3.2 Underutilized Strategic Assets

Despite the debt, Mexico possesses assets of immense value:

- **National Clinical Data Repositories:** Public institutions, such as the Mexican Social Security Institute (IMSS), serve millions of people and consequently possess some of the largest and most diverse archives in Latin America. These are not limited to medical imaging (e.g., X-rays, CT scans, mammograms) but also include massive, longitudinal volumes of laboratory results, clinical notes, pharmacy records, and pathology reports. Although consolidated public figures detailing this multimodal data are unavailable, the sheer volume of services reported annually suggests the existence of a massive data resource [24,25]. With an appropriate regulatory and collaborative framework that ensures anonymization and ethics, these repositories could become an invaluable source for training and validating next-generation AI models worldwide.

- **High Quality Human Capital:** Mexican healthcare personnel are resilient, highly trained, and, contrary to the perception that there is a "resistance to change", they are deeply motivated to adopt any tool that reduces their overwhelming administrative and cognitive burden and improves the quality of care [5,26,27]. They are not a barrier, but rather the primary force for validating, adopting, and iteratively improving useful technology.

4 Principles of the Strategic Framework for Viable Innovation

Considering the clinical context and the national inventory, any successful health technology project in Mexico should adhere to the following principles.

4.1 Principle 1: Prioritize Digital Infrastructure over Complex Algorithms

Digital transformation is the indispensable foundation for AI. A recurring error, driven by "solutionism," is to pursue complex predictive models while neglecting the fundamental digital infrastructure required to support them. To counter this tendency and provide a pragmatic roadmap, we propose a conceptual framework (Fig. 1) that envisions the technological prerequisites as a pyramid of needs. This model dictates a sequential, bottom-up approach to innovation.

The base of this pyramid—its widest and most essential part—is not software, but the enabling infrastructure. This includes widespread, functional access to electricity and internet connectivity. Resting upon it is the hardware layer, which involves the deployment of essential tools such as computers, tablets, and smartphones for both clinical staff and the general population. It is only when these socio-technical foundations are solid that we can begin to build the upper layers of software, such as Electronic Health Records (EHRs) and the interoperability systems needed to overcome the institutional silos that contribute to our national "data debt". At the apex of the pyramid, and only once the other layers are in place, do we find advanced applications that generate value from the data, such as business intelligence (BI), data analysis, and ultimately, artificial intelligence (AI).

Attempting to implement the apex without having built the base is a recipe for innovation failure. This bottom-up approach is the practical application of clinical realism: addressing these foundational needs not only solves immediate problems but also organically generates the structured data repositories that are the prerequisite for any future AI application, thus beginning to pay down the existing data debt rather than accruing more of it.

4.2 Principle 2: Foster a Collaborative and Open-Source Ecosystem

The "walled gardens" model presents a barrier to large-scale innovation in the public sector. A successful approach must be collaborative and open.

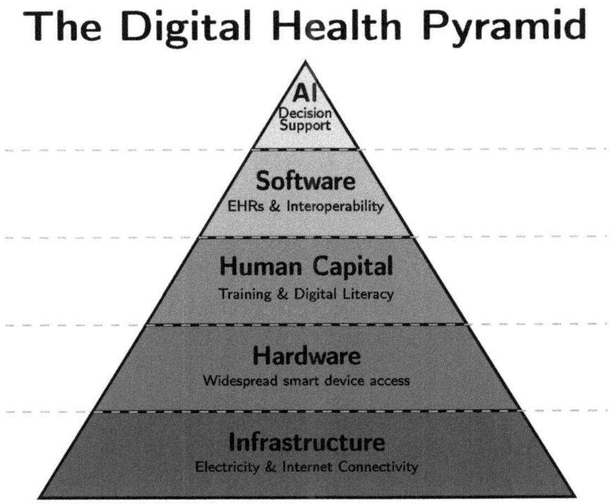

Fig. 1. The Digital Health Pyramid. The model illustrates the necessary bottom-up approach to innovation, where each layer is a prerequisite for the one above it, culminating in data-driven solutions such as AI.

- **Promote Open Source:** Especially for publicly funded initiatives, the use of open source software ensures sustainability, transparency, auditability, and continuity throughout policy cycles, avoiding dependence on a single vendor and cumulative licensing costs [28,29]. Projects such as OpenMRS and DHIS2 exemplify the power of this model in public health [30].
- **Create "Regulatory Sandboxes":** Innovation often outpaces regulation. To avoid being held back by existing legislation, controlled testing environments ("sandboxes") should be established where new technologies can be validated in a safe, ethical, and agile manner [31], in collaboration with entities such as COFEPRIS. This model, which has already been successfully tested in sectors such as the United Kingdom's financial sector, enables responsible technological development [32].

4.3 Principle 3: Design for the "Augmented Doctor" Through Explainable AI (XAI)

The narrative that AI will replace physicians is counterproductive and misguided. A more constructive and realistic paradigm is that of "augmented intelligence," where AI serves as a powerful tool that enhances the cognitive capabilities of clinicians. Any system should be designed as such, which implies:

- **Traceability and Explainability:** The clinician must be able to understand why an algorithm arrives at a recommendation or, failing that, know its limitations and systematic failure modes. This field, known as Explainable AI (XAI), is crucial for establishing trust, promoting adoption, and ensuring patient safety. "Black box" models, however accurate, face insurmountable ethical and practical barriers in the clinic [33,34].

- **Workflow Integration:** The tool should be fast, intuitive, and not require additional processes that disrupt care [35].
- **Clinical Accountability:** No decision is made "by AI". Each diagnosis and treatment is, and should remain, a non-transferable responsibility of the certified healthcare professional using the tool [36,37].

5 Conclusion and Future Directions

The path to a successful and equitable technological transformation in the Mexican healthcare sector does not lie in the pursuit of algorithmic novelty, but in the development of a pragmatic strategy grounded in our realities. The framework presented here, based on clinical realism, an honest inventory, and principles of viable innovation, offers a roadmap for entrepreneurs, researchers, and institutional leaders to focus their efforts on solving the correct problems, with the right tools and on a solid infrastructure base.

Success, in the first stage, will not be measured in the complexity of our algorithms, but in the vitality of our digital health ecosystem. It will manifest itself in increased interoperability between institutions, measurable reductions in the administrative burden on clinical staff, and the emergence of an ecosystem of companies and initiatives, many of which are open source, dedicated to strengthening the system. This is the first step in ensuring that the benefits of artificial intelligence finally trickle down from academic publications to patients across Mexico.

References

1. Bhagat, M.I.A., Wankhede, M.K.G., Kopawar, M.N.A., Sananse, P.D.A.: Artificial intelligence in healthcare: a review. Int. J. Sci. Res. Sci. Eng. Technol. **11**(4), 133–138 (2024)
2. Miyoshi, N.: Use of AI in diagnostic imaging and future prospects. JMA J. **8**(1), 198–203 (2025)
3. Basubrin, O., Basubrain, O.: Current status and future of artificial intelligence in medicine. Cureus **17**(1), (2025)
4. Gómez-Dantés, O., Flamand, L., Cerecero-García, D., Morales-Vazquez, M., Serván-Mori, E.: Origin, impacts, and potential solutions to the fragmentation of the Mexican health system: a consultation with key actors. Health Res. Policy Syst. **21**, 80 (2023)
5. Doubova, S.V., García-Saisó, S., Pérez-Cuevas, R., Sarabia-González, O., Pacheco-Estrello, P., Leslie, H.H., et al.: Barriers and opportunities to improve the foundations for high-quality healthcare in the Mexican Health System. Health Policy Plan. **33**(10), 1073–1082 (2018)
6. Madai, V.I., Higgins, D.C.: Artificial intelligence in healthcare: lost in translation? arXiv preprint arXiv:2107.13454 (2021)
7. Contreras-Hernández, I., Bonifaz-Alfonzo, L.C.: Redes Transversales de Investigación en Salud: estrategia para la medicina traslacional. Rev Médica Inst Mex Seguro Soc **60**(Suppl 2), S110–S118 (2022)

8. Hernández, M. del PMP.: Las organizaciones intermedias en los procesos de innovación en México. Rev Perfiles Latinoam **24**(48), 161–183 (2016)
9. Cresswell, K., Sheikh, A.: Organizational issues in the implementation and adoption of health information technology innovations: an interpretative review. Int. J. Med. Inf. **82**(5), e73–e86 (2013)
10. Wong, A., Otles, E., Donnelly, J.P., Krumm, A., McCullough, J., DeTroyer-Cooley, O., et al.: External validation of a widely implemented proprietary sepsis prediction model in hospitalized patients. JAMA Intern. Med. **181**(8), 1–6 (2021)
11. Swetlitz, C.R.I.: IBM's Watson supercomputer recommended "unsafe and incorrect" cancer treatments, internal documents show. STAT. https://www.statnews.com/2018/07/25/ibm-watson-recommended-unsafe-incorrect-treatments/. Accessed 20 Aug 2025
12. Landi, H.: IBM sells Watson Health assets to investment firm Francisco Partners. Fierce Healthcare. https://www.fiercehealthcare.com/tech/ibm-sells-watson-health-assets-to-investment-firm-francisco-partners. Accessed 20 Aug 2025
13. Coston, A., Kawakami, A., Zhu, H., Holstein, K., Heidari, H.: A validity perspective on evaluating the justified use of data-driven decision-making algorithms. arXiv preprint arXiv:2206.14983 (2023)
14. Wilson, J.M.G., Jungner, G.: Principles and Practice of Screening for Disease. Public Health Papers, No. 34, World Health Organization, Geneva (1968)
15. Norori, N., Hu, Q., Aellen, F.M., Faraci, F.D., Tzovara, A.: Addressing bias in big data and AI for health care: a call for open science. Patterns **2**(10), 100347 (2021)
16. Newman-Toker, D.E., McDonald, K.M., Meltzer, D.O.: How much diagnostic safety can we afford, and how should we decide? A health economics perspective. BMJ Qual. Saf. **22**(Suppl 2), ii11–ii20 (2013)
17. Winkens, R., Dinant, G.J.: Rational, cost effective use of investigations in clinical practice. BMJ **324**(7340), 783–785 (2002)
18. Knottnerus, J.A., van Weel, C., Muris, J.W.M.: Evaluation of diagnostic procedures. BMJ **324**(7335), 477–480 (2002)
19. Sinsky, C., Colligan, L., Li, L., Prgomet, M., Reynolds, S., Goeders, L., et al.: Allocation of physician time in ambulatory practice: a time and motion study in 4 specialties. Ann. Intern. Med. **165**(11), 753–760 (2016)
20. Arndt, B.G., Beasley, J.W., Watkinson, M.D., Temte, J.L., Tuan, W.J., Sinsky, C.A., et al.: Tethered to the EHR: primary care physician workload assessment using EHR event log data and time-motion observations. Ann. Fam. Med. **15**(5), 419–426 (2017)
21. Melo, T.: A note on challenges and opportunities for operations research in hospital logistics. Pesquisa Operacional **38**(1), 169–180 (2018)
22. Saturno-Hernández, P.J., Acosta-Ruíz, O., Bautista-Morales, A.C., Poblano-Verástegui, O., Vértiz-Ramírez, J.D.J.: Calidad de la información en salud de México en el contexto de la OCDE: 2017–2021. Gac. Sanit. **38**, 102372 (2024)
23. Meneses Navarro, S., Pelcastre-Villafuerte, B.E., Becerril-Montekio, V., Serván-Mori, E.: Overcoming the health systems' segmentation to achieve universal health coverage in Mexico. Int. J. Health Plann. Manage. **37**(6), 3357–3364 (2022)
24. Rojas, R.: IMSS contará con archivo digital de estudios de imagen. Saludiario. https://www.saludiario.com/archivo-digital-de-radiografias-la-nueva-herramienta-para-especialistas-del-imss/. Accessed 20 Aug 2025
25. IMSS: Derechohabiencia aumentó en 9.2 millones de usuarios por una mejor recaudación y nuevos programas de aseguramiento: Zoé Robledo. https://www.imss.gob.mx/prensa/archivo/202407/343. Accessed 20 Aug 2025

26. Juárez-Ramírez, C., Reyes-Morales, H., Gutiérrez-Alba, G.: Local health systems resilience in managing the COVID-19 pandemic: lessons from Mexico. Health Policy Plan. **37**(10), 1210–1220 (2022)
27. García, M. del C.L., Lugo, A.P., Soto, E.P.: Realización personal y resiliencia, factores protectores contra Burnout en trabajadores de la salud mexicanos durante la pandemia. Rev. Colomb. Salud. Ocupacional **14**(1), (2024)
28. Kharazmi, O.A., Dartoomi, S.: A systematic literature review on collaborative innovation in the public sector. Innov. Eur. J. Soc. Sci. Res. **36**(4), 602–630 (2023)
29. Wilson, W.A.: Collaborative Innovation in the Public Sector: Jacob Torfing. Georgetown University Press, Washington (2016). Soc. Sci. J. **57**(3), 399–400 (2020)
30. Paton, C., Braa, J., Muhire, A., Marco-Ruiz, L., Kobayashi, S., Fraser, H., et al.: Open source digital health software for resilient, accessible and equitable healthcare systems. Yearb. Med. Inform. **31**, 067–073 (2022)
31. Leckenby, E., Dawoud, D., Bouvy, J., Jónsson, P.: The sandbox approach and its potential for use in health technology assessment: a literature review. Appl. Health Econ. Health Policy **19**(6), 857–869 (2021). https://doi.org/10.1007/s40258-021-00665-1
32. Fahy, L.A.: Fostering regulator–innovator collaboration at the frontline: a case study of the UK's regulatory sandbox for fintech. Law Policy **44**(2), 162–184 (2022)
33. Ghassemi, M., Oakden-Rayner, L., Beam, A.L.: The false hope of current approaches to explainable artificial intelligence in health care. Lancet Digit. Health **3**(11), e745–e750 (2021)
34. Singhal, A., Pratap, P., Dixit, K.K., Kathuria, K.: Advancements in explainable AI: bridging the gap between model complexity and interpretability. In: 2024 2nd International Conference on Disruptive Technologies (ICDT), pp. 675–680. IEEE (2024)
35. Dibble, E.R., Iott, B.E., Flynn, A.J., King, D.P., MacEachern, M.P., Friedman, C.P., et al.: A rapid process for identifying and prioritizing technology-based tools for health system implementation. JMIR Cancer **4**(2), e11195 (2018)
36. Holm, S.: On the justified use of AI decision support in evidence-based medicine: validity, explainability, and responsibility. Camb. Q Healthc. Ethics, 1–7 (2023)
37. Lawton, T., Morgan, P., Porter, Z., Hickey, S., Cunningham, A., Hughes, N., et al.: Clinicians risk becoming "Liability Sinks" for artificial intelligence. Preprints. https://www.authorea.com/users/422244/articles/638984-clinicians-risk-becoming-liability-sinks-for-artificial-intelligence?commit=9a3eb8c3ce8744245ee856b77e65bd0eaaaf8c0f. Accessed 21 Aug 2025

Improving K-Means Algorithm Performance Through an Ant Colony Optimization Strategy

Sinuhé Ginés-Palestino[1](✉), Eduardo Roldán-Reyes[1], Marcela Quiroz-Castellanos[2], and Adilene Palma Asunción[3]

[1] Instituto Tecnológico de Orizaba, Avenida Oriente 9 No. 852. Col. Emiliano Zapata. Orizaba, 94320 Veracruz, México
sinuhe.gines@gmail.com, eduardo.rr@orizaba.tecnm.mx

[2] Instituto de Investigaciones en Inteligencia Artificial de la Universidad Veracruzana, Calle Paseo Lote II, Sección Segunda N° 112, Nuevo Xalapa, 91097 Xalapa, Ver., México
maquiroz@uv.mx

[3] Universidad Tencológica Bilingüe Internacional y Sustentable de Puebla, Boulevard Audi sur S/N, Ciudad Modelo, San José Chiapa, 75010 Puebla, México
adilene-asuncion@utbispuebla.edu.mx

Abstract. The K-means algorithm is one of the most widely used unsupervised learning methods for clustering data. This research is inspired by improving its performance using a Metaheuristic based on the collective work of ants. K-means is easy to use due to its simplicity and ease of application. However, it tends to present weaknesses in certain information domains, especially in the overlapping and correct assignment of groups, generating poor quality clusters. A strategy focused on improving the quality of the clusters and minimizing the computational cost is proposed through an initialization method, performing experiments on a given data set.

Keywords: K-means · Ant Colony Optimization · Entropy · Group overlapping

1 Introduccion

In data analysis and information mining, the K-means algorithm has been widely used as an efficient technique for clustering data due to its simplicity, ease of application and speed [1–3]. However, its performance can be limited by factors such as sensitivity to initial centroids, convergence to local optima and the generation of clusters with high overlap. These shortcomings directly impact the clustering quality, especially when the data has complex structures [4–6]. An optimization strategy based on collective intelligence is proposed to address these limitations, namely the Ant Colony Optimisation (ACO) approach, which has proven effective in search and adaptation problems in dynamic environments [7].

This research proposes the integration of ACO as a refinement mechanism after the initial clustering generated by K-means, allowing an artificial agent (ant) to redistribute the misclassified elements [8] dynamically. The primary purpose is to improve cohesion

L. Martínez-Villaseñor et al. (Eds.): MICAI 2025, CCIS 2712, pp. 194–203, 2025.
https://doi.org/10.1007/978-3-032-08704-1_15

and separation between clusters [9, 10], reducing overlap by analyzing entropy and Silhouette Index as performance metrics [11]. In addition, the necessary experimentation was carried out with the aim of minimizing the computational cost associated with this process, proposing an efficient model that combines the speed of K-means with the adaptability of ACO.

The means to achieve what was mentioned in the previous paragraphs is an efficient model based on a statistical centrality metric to minimize the computational cost of the clustering process. This approach combines the rapid convergence of the K-means algorithm with the adaptability of the ant colony optimization (ACO) method, achieving a balance between accuracy and efficiency. This research is divided into five sections: the first describes the introductory context of the work; the second discusses related research on this topic; the third describes the method used; the fourth analyzes the results; and the fifth presents the respective conclusions.

2 Related Work

In this section, the main objective is to make a brief analysis of the literature, associating the main documented contributions of the efforts made to augment the K-means algorithm with some method, metaheuristic, or strategy that directly impacts its performance variables, such as the quality of the groups and the execution time to achieve the best clustering result. First, the problem of cluster overlapping is addressed, as reported by [9] that the Projection Clustering Method and Consistent Fuzzy Samples Transformation (PCGDST-IE) is suggested to learn the information from overlapping class samples better and simultaneously deal with class imbalance and overlapping problems. Compared with existing related algorithms, PCGDST-IE can achieve significantly better performance.

This analysis [10] applied an improved k-means clustering method using medical data. A hybrid method combining K-Harmonic Means and Overlapping K-means algorithms (KHM-OKM) was used, where the initial points are selected according to the results of the KHM clustering algorithm. Experimental results using ten publicly available medical datasets show that the proposed hybrid method provides better or comparable results than the original OKM algorithm.

In the research proposed by [12], the cluster overlay method can also be used in legal tasks. Multi-view Overlay Clustering of Legal Judgments (MOSTA), a novel artificial intelligence method, can identify groups of legal judgments with similar characteristics, possibly corresponding to topics, thus reducing the human effort required to navigate, organize and classify large amounts of legal judgments. The first one aims to represent the semantics of the textual content, while the second one aims to represent citations of legal acts, also considering the granularity of the citations.

In [13], a hybrid clustering algorithm that synergistically combines K-means and Ant Colony Optimization (ACO) to address limitations of standalone methods. The primary contribution lies in leveraging ACO's stochastic, self-organizing properties to generate robust initial clusters for K-means, circumventing the latter's sensitivity to initial centroids while enhancing convergence speed and accuracy. The ACO implementation involves simulating ants on a grid, where objects are probabilistically picked or dropped based on colony similarity, calculated via a sigmoid-transformed local similarity metric (incorporating parameters like neighbourhood radius r and coefficient α). Performance is evaluated using F-measure and runtime on Iris datasets, demonstrating the hybrid method's superior accuracy (F-measure up to 88%) over K-means (83%) and ACO (58%), albeit with slightly higher computational cost than K-means alone.

In [14], an enhanced K-means algorithm integrated with Ant Colony Optimization (ACO) addresses traditional K-means' limitations, particularly its sensitivity to initial centroids and tendency to converge to local optima in high-dimensional data. The key contribution lies in employing ACO as a post-processing refinement step. The proposed ACO variant distinguishes itself by focusing solely on refinement post-K-means initialization, unlike hybrid approaches combining ACO with other metaheuristics (e.g., PSO or SA) found in the literature. The study highlights the method's efficacy in reducing misclustering errors and eliminating empty clusters, validated on benchmark datasets.

In [15], presents a hybrid K-means Ant Colony Optimization (K-ACO) algorithm to address the limitations of traditional K-means, particularly its sensitivity to centroid initialization and tendency to converge to local optima. The key contribution lies in integrating Ant Colony Optimization (ACO) with K-means, where ACO optimizes centroid selection by leveraging pheromone-based pathfinding inspired by ant behaviour, thus enhancing global search capabilities. The implementation involves three stages: initial K-means clustering, ACO-based centroid optimization (using transition rules and pheromone updates from the Travelling Salesman Problem framework), and final K-means refinement.

The paper [16] introduces HGA-FACO, a hybrid genetic-fuzzy ant colony optimization algorithm, addressing key limitations of traditional K-means by automating cluster number determination and optimizing initial centers through genetic algorithms (GA) and adaptive fuzzy systems (AFS). The implementation integrates Ant Colony Optimization (ACO) with K-means by leveraging pheromone-based search strategies and dynamic parameter tuning via AFS, enhancing global optimization and avoiding local optima. Performance is evaluated using metrics like Silhouette Coefficient (SC), Davies-Bouldin Index (DBI), and Sum of Squared Errors (SSE), demonstrating superior clustering compactness and separation compared to baseline methods (e.g., GA-KMeans, ACO-KMeans).

In [17], a hybrid Ant Colony Optimization (ACO) and K-means algorithm to enhance image segmentation by addressing the K-means algorithm's sensitivity to initial cluster centers and local optima. The contributions include integrating ACO's pheromone-based learning mechanism with K-means, employing two pheromone update methods: Method-1 incorporates spatial coordinate distances to favour compact and well-separated clusters, while Method-2 omits spatial distances to accommodate multispectral similarity across disparate locations. Performance is evaluated through cluster compactness, inter-cluster separation, and stability across runs, demonstrating improved robustness over traditional K-means, though visual results indicate partial success.

In retrospect, the review of the research in this section integrates Ant Colony Optimization (ACO) with K-means, either to optimize the initial selection of centroids, refine the subsequent clustering, or improve image segmentation, showing advances in compactness and cluster separation metrics. According to [18], overlap, group imbalance, and other weaknesses of K-means are recurrent, so it is advisable to resort to hybrid strategies that contemplate collective intelligence. In line with the above, the article's proposal stands out by incorporating ACO as a refinement mechanism after the execution of K-means, accompanied by an initialization strategy based on statistical mode detection. This not only improves the Silhouette Index and Entropy indices by reducing overlap between groups, but also minimizes the computational cost of initialization, providing a balance between accuracy and efficiency.

3 Improvement Strategy for the K-means Algorithm

This section describes in detail the algorithms to be used and the ACO-based strategy to improve the performance of the overlapping groups, as well as the performance measures used:

3.1 K-means Algorithm

The K-means algorithm has four fundamental stages, which in some cases may vary depending on the mode of use and the initialization technique to be used, based on [19], as described below:

1. Place K points in the space represented by the grouping objects. These points represent the initial centroids of the group.
2. Assign each object to the group with the closest centroid.
3. When all objects have been assigned, recalculate the positions of the K centroids.
4. Repeat steps 2 and 3 until the centroids stop moving. This produces a separation of the objects into groups from which the metric to be minimized can be calculated.

3.2 K-means Algorithm/ACO and Mode

This section of the research describes in detail each of the steps of the K-means algorithm and the incorporation of an ACO-based strategy to stimulate clustering improvement after having implemented a conventional K-means with the steps in the previous section, and a statistical metric to improve initialization as well as computational cost. Performance measurement calculations with Silhouette Index (SI) and Entropy are also included:

- Select several clusters.
- Define the maximum number of iterations.
- Calculate the first three modes of the data set.
- Assign each of the three modes, in order of occurrence, as the initial centroids.
- K-means. For each iteration up to the maximum number of iterations:
- Calculate distance from each point to each centroid.
- Assign each point to the cluster whose centroid is closest to it.
- Recalculate centroids as the average of the points in each cluster.
- If centroids do not change significantly, terminate iterations.

- Calculate Silhouette Index (4) to assess cluster quality.

$$a(x) = \frac{1}{|C| - 1} \sum_{y \in C, y \neq x} x - y^2 \tag{1}$$

$$b(x) = min_{G \neq C} \frac{1}{|C|} \sum_{y \in G} x - y^2 \tag{2}$$

$$s(x) = \frac{b(x) - a(x)}{max(b(x), a(x))} \tag{3}$$

$$\frac{1}{n} \sum_{x} s(x) \tag{4}$$

$$-1 \leq s(x) \leq 1 \tag{5}$$

II. ACO-based strategy:

a. Calculate entropy (7) based on membership probabilities

$$E_j = -\sum_i p_{ij} log\left(p_{ij}\right) \tag{6}$$

$$E_{CS} = -\sum_{j=1}^{m} \frac{n_j * E_j}{n} \tag{7}$$

b. Choose a cluster randomly
c. For i = 1 to N:
d. Calculate the probability of dropping and picking.

$$Pp = \left(\frac{k_1}{k_1 + f}\right)^2 \tag{8}$$

$$Pd = \left(\frac{f}{k_2 + f}\right)^2 \tag{9}$$

e. If Probability of Picking > Probability of Dropping.
f. Assign the data to a remaining random cluster.
g. Recalculate the entropy value.
h. If the entropy value after performing the swap is greater than the entropy value before performing it, then the data returns to its place.
i. Repeat until all data are evaluated.
j. Recalculate Silhouette Index and Entropy to evaluate cluster quality.

Table 1. Results of experimentation with the proposed Metaheuristic.

Performance measures	K-means	K-means/ACO	K-means/ACO/mode
Silhouette Index	0.43	0.71	0.71
Entropy	0.9	0.88	0.88
Time (seg.)	0.63	1.87	1.38

4 Experimentations and Results

In this level of the research, the result of implementing K-means based on an ACO approach is shown, for which the Iris dataset was selected, which has four classes for three types of plants. The algorithm was run without ACO, Entropy, and SI (Silhouette Index), and the time in seconds was measured. Subsequently, implementing the ACO-based strategy is considered, giving interesting results in the three performance measurement parameters. K-means/ACO and an initialization technique based on mode detection is implemented to estimate the cluster number and decrease the computational cost. The above description is shown in Table 1.

Table 1, shows the measurement results of both algorithms. On the one hand, a relatively low SI (Silhouette Index) parameter is observed, with 0.43 for a normal K-means. The non-normalized entropy indicates a susceptible ordering of 0.9 compared to the proposed strategy and the execution time of 0.63 s. Once K-means/ACO is implemented, a comparative analysis is performed, indicating that it is better, considering a value of 0.71 versus 0.43 obtained in the initial method. A minimal improvement is observed regarding entropy, since it is reduced from 0.9 to 0.88. Regarding time, an increase is observed with ACO from 0.63 to 1.87, since it is a complete and more robust algorithm.

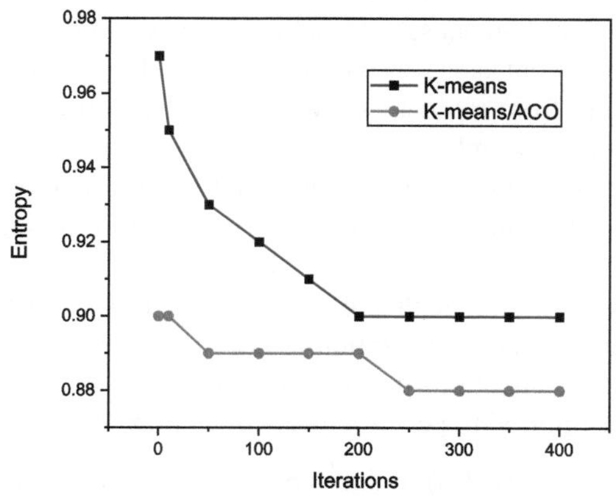

Fig. 1. Entropy trend according to K-means and K-means/ACO approach

It is important to highlight the behaviour of the entropy within the dataset, as a decrease is observed, especially in the transition of each cluster, which means that in larger instances, it can be a potential tool to minimize the overlapping of groups due to a bad centroid assignment in the traditional K-means algorithm (see Fig. 1). On the other hand, it is important to highlight the comparison of the Silhouette Index. This parameter evaluates the superposition of the groups specially. It can be seen that the implementation of K-means barely reaches a value of 0.43 compared to K-means with ACO, which shows a value of 0.71 up to 400 iterations (see Fig. 2).

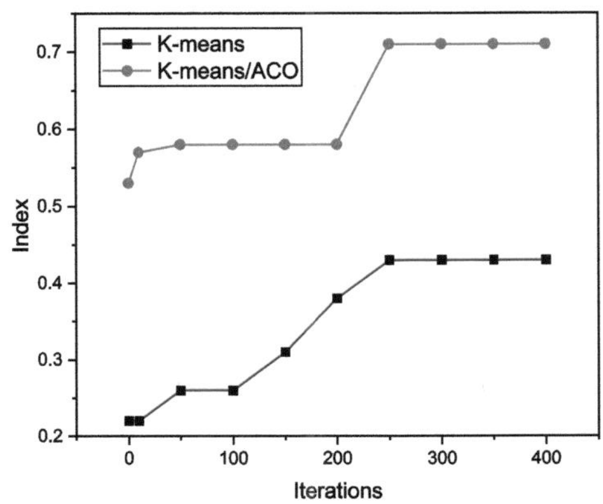

Fig. 2. Silhouette Index between K-means and K-means/ACO

The K-means algorithm yields an acceptable execution time, derived from its basic and not very complex Heuristics. However, to add K-means with an ACO approach the time increases from 0.63 to 1.87 s, therefore an initialization strategy is proposed that benefits the computational cost, without altering the results obtained with Entropy and SI (see Fig. 3). According to the computational cost, a strategy was designed to minimize the execution time of K-means/ACO, since it yielded a considerably high time compared to conventional K-means, an initialization was introduced to reduce this time. The random selection of centroids was omitted, and the idea of selecting centroids based on the modes resulting from the data set was considered, as this would considerably reduce the cluster number search. The results are shown in Fig. 3. The graph shows the decrease in the execution time of the conventional K-means algorithm from 0.63 s to 1.38 s with K-means/ACO/mode, with K-means/ACO the worst time considered in this research.

The above analyses highlight that ACO "is more robust" but increases the time compared to K-means; mode initialization is introduced precisely to reduce this cost while maintaining the same Entropy and Silhouette values (see Table 1). Practical recommendations for improving performance while balancing computational cost are:

1. Statistical initialization (modes): reduces previous iterations and the work that ACO must do.
2. ACO bounded by improvement: stop refinement (stopping criterion) if entropy does not improve after a number of moves or if the Silhouette Index converges.
3. Incremental Entropy and Silhouette calculations: update only the contributions affected (swaps) by a reassignment, avoiding global recomputation each time.

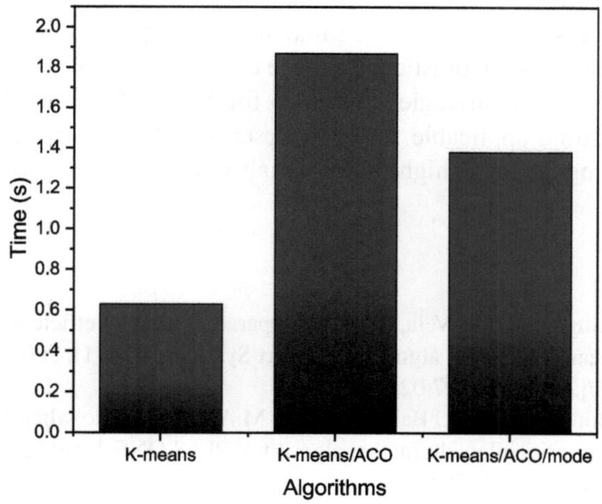

Fig. 3. Execution time of the three implemented algorithms

4. Sampling for Silhouette: calculate SI on a stratified subsample between ACO steps and calculate the complete SI only at the end. Equations (1)–(5) allow for partial estimation.

5 Conclusion

The hybridization of K-means with Ant Colony Optimization (ACO) introduced in this work addresses key limitations of traditional clustering methods. By incorporating a post-processing refinement phase inspired by collective ant behaviour, the model dynamically reassigns misclustered instances using entropy and Silhouette Index as feedback mechanisms. Integrating a statistical centrality metric during initialization reduces computational cost without compromising clustering quality. Experimental results using the Iris dataset reveal substantial cluster compactness and separation improvements. Although the ACO-enhanced model increases execution time from 0.63 s to 1.87 s, the proposed initialization technique effectively reduces this overhead to 1.38 s, offering a practical balance between accuracy and efficiency.

The research offers valuable contributions by bridging unsupervised learning with bioinspired optimization, providing a flexible and adaptive alternative for complex data scenarios prone to cluster overlap. The methodology demonstrates that biologically inspired algorithms can enhance traditional machine learning models in accuracy, robustness, and adaptability. Future work should focus on scaling the proposed model to higher-dimensional and imbalanced datasets, integrating advanced pheromone update rules, and exploring multi-objective formulations considering intra-cluster variance, compactness, and interpretability simultaneously. Additionally, embedding this hybrid approach into streaming data environments could expand its applicability in real-time systems, where clustering speed and adaptability are critical.

Additionally, to strengthen the proposal in other research, the incorporation of dynamic stopping criteria is proposed, which interrupt refinement when improvements are minimal, and the restriction of the search space by limiting the reassignment of instances to the nearest centroids. At the same time, the exploitation of parallelization in distributed environments can drastically reduce computation times, expanding the scalability of the model. These strategies will allow for the development of a more efficient, adaptive, and real-time applicable version, preserving the robustness of the proposed method and enabling its use in high-dimensionality scenarios and large data volumes.

References

1. Celebi, M.E., Kingravi, H.A., Vela, P.A.: A comparative study of efficient initialization methods for the k-means clustering algorithm. Expert Syst. Appl. **40**(1), 200–210 (2013). https://doi.org/10.1016/j.eswa.2012.07.021
2. Raykov, Y.P., Boukouvalas, A., Baig, F., Little, M.A.: What to do when K-means clustering fails: a simple yet principled alternative algorithm. PLoS ONE 11(9) (2016). https://doi.org/10.1371/journal.pone.0162259
3. Pitafi, S., Anwar, T., Sharif, Z.: A taxonomy of machine learning clustering algorithms, challenges, and future realms. Appl. Sci. **13**(6), 3529 (2023). https://doi.org/10.3390/app13063529
4. Fränti, P., Sieranoja, S.: K-means properties on six clustering benchmark datasets. Appl. Intell. **48**(12), 4743–4759 (2018). https://doi.org/10.1007/s10489-018-1238-7
5. Zou, P., Rajora, M., Liang, S.: Multimodal optimization of job-shop scheduling problems using a clustering-genetic algorithm based approach. Int. J. Ind. Eng. Theory Appl. Pract. **26**(5) (2019). https://doi.org/10.23055/ijietap.2019.26.5.4043
6. Zhao, Q., Fränti, P.: WB-index: a sum-of-squares based index for cluster validity. In: Data and Knowledge Engineering, pp. 77–89 (2014). https://doi.org/10.1016/j.datak.2014.07.008
7. Dorigo, M., Birattari, M., Stutzle, T.: Ant colony optimization. IEEE Comput. Intell. Mag. **1**(4), 28–39 (2006). https://doi.org/10.1109/MCI.2006.329691
8. Kuo, R.J., Wang, H.S., Hu, T.-L., Chou, S.H.: Application of ant K-means on clustering analysis. Comput. Math. Appl. **50**(10–12), 1709–1724 (2005). https://doi.org/10.1016/j.camwa.2005.05.009
9. Li, F., et al.: An overlapping oriented imbalanced ensemble learning algorithm with weighted projection clustering grouping and consistent fuzzy sample transformation. Inf. Sci. **637**, 118955 (2023). https://doi.org/10.1016/j.ins.2023.118955
10. Khanmohammadi, S., Adibeig, N., Shanehbandy, S.: An improved overlapping k-means clustering method for medical applications. Expert Syst. Appl. **67**, 12–18 (2017). https://doi.org/10.1016/j.eswa.2016.09.025
11. Toktas-Palut, P., Onan, K., Zahid Gürbüz, M., Gülden-Özdemir, B.: Moss Software: A New Tool for Multi-Objective Green Supplier Selection (2022). https://doi.org/10.23055/ijietap.2022.29.2.5903
12. De Martino, G., Pio, G., Ceci, M.: Multi-view overlapping clustering for the identification of the subject matter of legal judgments. Inf. Sci. **638**, 118956 (2023). https://doi.org/10.1016/j.ins.2023.118956
13. Lu, J., Hu, R.: A new hybrid clustering algorithm based on K-means and ant colony algorithm. In: Proceedings of the 2nd International Conference on Computer Science and Electronics Engineering (ICCSEE 2013), pp. 1718–1721. Atlantis Press (2013). https://doi.org/10.2991/iccsee.2013.430
14. Aparna, K., Nair, M.K.: Enhancement of K-means algorithm using ACO as an optimization technique on high dimensional data. In: International Conference on Electronics and Communication Systems (ICECS), Coimbatore, India, pp. 1–5 (2014). https://doi.org/10.1109/ECS.2014.6892561

15. Ratnaningsih, D.: Clustering with K-means hybridization ant colony optimization (K-ACO). Int. J. Math. Model. Comput. **12**(2), 143–152 (2022). https://doi.org/10.30495/ijm2c.2022.1953867.1249
16. Ran, X., Suyaroj, N., Tepsan, W., Ma, J., Zhou, X., Deng, W.: A hybrid genetic-fuzzy ant colony optimization algorithm for automatic K-means clustering in urban global positioning system. Eng. Appl. Artif. Intell. **137**, 109237 (2024). https://doi.org/10.1016/j.engappai.2024.109237
17. Hung, C.C., Sun, M.: Ant colony optimization for the k-means algorithm in image segmentation. In: Proceedings of the 48th Annual ACM Southeast Conference, pp. 1–4 (2010). https://doi.org/10.1145/1900008.1900075
18. Gines-Palestino, S., Roldan-Reyes, E., Quiroz-Castellanos, M., Cortes-Robles, G.: Evaluation of initialization methods for the performance of the K-means algorithm. DYNA **100**(3), 204–210 (2025). https://doi.org/10.52152/D11325
19. MacQueen, J.A.O.: Some methods for classification and analysis of multivariate observations. In: Proceedings of the Fifth Berkeley Symposium on Mathematical Statistics and Probability, Berkeley, California, pp. 281–297 (1967)

Classification of Myelocytic Leukemia by Simple Convolutional Neural Networks with Structural Variants

Rocio Ochoa-Montiel(✉), C. Sánchez-López, and Mauricio Hernández-Romano

Autonomous University of Tlaxcala, Tlaxcala de Xicohténcatl, Mexico
ma.rocio.ochoa@gmail.com , 20213873@uatx.mx

Abstract. In medical practice, morphological analysis presents multi-factorial drawbacks mainly related to the quality of the sample and the skill of the human expert. In this regard, artificial vision offers an alternative for the recognition of biological tissues as a support in medical diagnosis. For this reason, in this work we evaluate different architectures of simple convolutional networks for the classification of five types of acute myelocytic leukemia, which have been scarcely tested with these techniques. The results show that the depth of the models is not related to better performance.

Keywords: Leukemia · Convolutional neural network · Structural variants

1 Introduction

A common problem in medicine is the recognition of pathologies such as cancer. Acute leukemias (AL) are a type of cancer with an average annual lethality of 3 to 5 cases per 100,000 population and a marked upward trend, [1]. The types of leukemia relevant to its study are lymphocytic and monocytic leukemia, whose category derives from the type of cells that are affected. The visual analysis of bone marrow smears is a common practice for the cell abnormalities diagnosis. Although morphological classification of AL is useful in the early stages of diagnosis, there is generally a percentage of misclassification cases due to human error. [2], so the use of computer vision and pattern recognition techniques is useful to decrease these errors.

The problem of blood cell recognition and classification has been worked on extensively using image processing techniques [3,4], machine learning [5,6], or deep learning models [7,8]. However, most focus on lymphocytic leukemia while myelocytic leukemia has been little studied. This can be noted in literature reviews [9–11] and various proposals that commonly address lymphocytic leukemia. Therefore, in this work we propose using simple convolutional neural networksf (CNNs) with structural variants for classification of five types of Myelocytic Leukemia.

L. Martínez-Villaseñor et al. (Eds.): MICAI 2025, CCIS 2712, pp. 204–215, 2025.
https://doi.org/10.1007/978-3-032-08704-1_16

Finally, it is important to mention that the use of medical approaches [12] based on large language models (LLMs) has been little explored due to the limited availability of image sets suitable for training these models.

In the next section, the materials and methods are described. Section 3 presents the methodology of the proposed scheme to the classification of myelocytic leukemia by convolutional neural networks. In Sect. 4, Experiments and Results are shown. Conclusions are included in Sect. 5.

2 Background

A convolutional neural network (CNN) is a multilayer perceptron designed to recognize two-dimensional shapes with high translation, scale and rotation invariance, among other forms of distortion. These actions are learned in a supervised manner using a neural network whose structure has the following characteristics [13]:

1. **Feature extraction**. Each neuron takes its synaptic inputs from a local *receptive field* in the previous layer, forcing it to extract local features. Once a feature has been extracted, its exact location is irrelevant, however, its position relative to other features is moderately preserved.
2. **Feature mapping**. Each computational layer of the network is composed of multiple *feature maps*, where each feature map has the form of a plane within which individual neurons are constrained to share the same set of synaptic weights. This second form of structural constraint has the following advantages:
   - *Invariance to motion*, forcing the operation of a feature map through the use of *convolution* with a small kernel size, followed by a sigmoid function.
   - reduction in the number of free parameters, realized through the use of *weight sharing*.
3. **Subsampling**. Each convolutional layer is followed by a computational layer that performs a *local averaging* and a *subsampling* by which the resolution of the feature map is reduced. This operation has the effect of reducing the sensitivity of the feature map output to motion and other forms of distortion.

2.1 LeNet

The LeNet architecture is one of the basic forms of convolutional neural networks that was used for handwritten digit identification. LeNet-5 is a variant of this architecture and owes its name to the fact that it compresses 5 layers of weights in total. Its architecture consists of two convolution layers followed by a subsampling (max-pooling) layer to extract features. Then, a single convolution layer, followed by a set of two fully connected layers that act as a classifier on the extracted features. It is worth mentioning that the activations after the weight layers are also flattened by means of a nolinearity *tanh*. The model architecture is shown in Fig. 1. In this work, we use LeNet as a basic model to evaluate the structural variants in the CNNs.

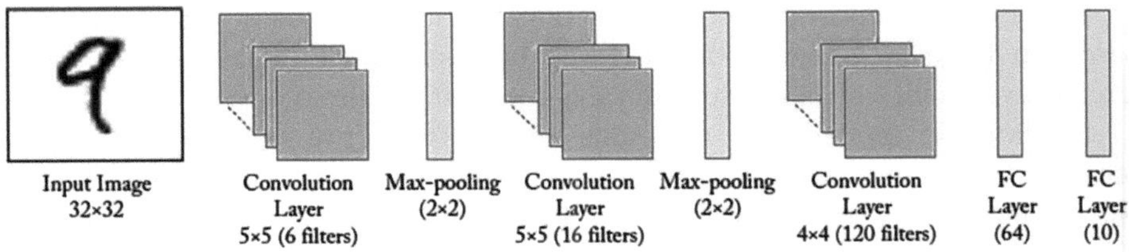

Fig. 1. Architecture LeNet-5 [14].

3 Methodology

This section provides a general overview of the proposed methodology for classification of myelocytic leukemia by simple CNNs with structural variants.

3.1 Simple Convolutional Neural Networks with Structural Variants

Leukemia classification is addressed by means of three convolutional neural network models: LeNet, model 1 and model 2. Models 1 and 2 are convolutional networks with an architecture similar to LeNet. Thus, the structural variants refer to the differences in the architecture of models 1 and 2 with respect to LeNet.

Figures 2 and 3 show the structure of models, in which the main differences are the number of layers and the use of dropout. One of the purposes of the proposed variants is to identify the relationship between the depth of a model and its performance in the leukemia classification problem.

The classification of leukemia types M0, M2, M3, M4 and M5 is performed with the LeNet models, Model 1, and Model 2, and their performance is evaluated. The criteria for this assessment are described in detail in the following section.

Layer (type)	Output Shape	Param #
conv2d_3 (Conv2D)	(None, 320, 256, 16)	160
max_pooling2d_2 (MaxPooling2D)	(None, 160, 128, 16)	0
conv2d_4 (Conv2D)	(None, 160, 128, 32)	4,640
max_pooling2d_3 (MaxPooling2D)	(None, 80, 64, 32)	0
conv2d_5 (Conv2D)	(None, 80, 64, 64)	18,496
flatten_1 (Flatten)	(None, 327680)	0
dense_2 (Dense)	(None, 64)	20,971,584
dense_3 (Dense)	(None, 5)	325

Fig. 2. LeNet

Layer (type)	Output Shape	Param #
conv2d (Conv2D)	(None, 318, 254, 32)	320
max_pooling2d (MaxPooling2D)	(None, 159, 127, 32)	0
conv2d_1 (Conv2D)	(None, 157, 125, 64)	18,496
max_pooling2d_1 (MaxPooling2D)	(None, 78, 62, 64)	0
conv2d_2 (Conv2D)	(None, 76, 60, 128)	73,856
max_pooling2d_2 (MaxPooling2D)	(None, 38, 30, 128)	0
conv2d_3 (Conv2D)	(None, 36, 28, 256)	295,168
max_pooling2d_3 (MaxPooling2D)	(None, 18, 14, 256)	0
conv2d_4 (Conv2D)	(None, 16, 12, 512)	1,180,160
max_pooling2d_4 (MaxPooling2D)	(None, 8, 6, 512)	0
flatten (Flatten)	(None, 24576)	0
dropout (Dropout)	(None, 24576)	0
dense (Dense)	(None, 5)	122,885

(a) Model 1

Layer (type)	Output Shape	Param #
conv2d (Conv2D)	(None, 160, 128, 32)	320
max_pooling2d (MaxPooling2D)	(None, 80, 64, 32)	0
conv2d_1 (Conv2D)	(None, 78, 62, 64)	18,496
max_pooling2d_1 (MaxPooling2D)	(None, 39, 31, 64)	0
conv2d_2 (Conv2D)	(None, 37, 29, 128)	73,856
max_pooling2d_2 (MaxPooling2D)	(None, 18, 14, 128)	0
conv2d_3 (Conv2D)	(None, 16, 12, 256)	295,168
max_pooling2d_3 (MaxPooling2D)	(None, 8, 6, 256)	0
flatten (Flatten)	(None, 12288)	0
dropout (Dropout)	(None, 12288)	0
dense (Dense)	(None, 5)	61,445

(b) Model 2

Fig. 3. Structure of models 1 and 2, respectively.

4 Experiments and Results

The experiments were performed on a CPU Xeon 2670V3, 16GB RAM, Windows10 Home Edition operating system, graphics processing unit (GPU) GTX 1070 TI, and Phyton 3.8.

For learning validation, two sets were used: training and testing, whose percentages were 70% and 30%, respectively. The training used a learning rate of 0.001, the Adam optimizer, and the cross-entropy loss function. The metric for evaluating learning was accuracy, the number of epochs for LeNet training was 30, while 15 epochs were used for models 1 and 2. Both values were determined by experimentation. In addition, in all cases 15 runs were performed to statistically evaluate the performance of each model, varying the batch size in each experiment of these 15 runs.

4.1 Dataset

In this work, a dataset containing 1085 images of 5 types of acute leukemia is used, whose class is determined by the morphological characteristics of each type of leukemia [15]. Table 1 shows the 11 types of acute leukemia currently recognized by the FAB group. The datasets used in this work consist of sets of 217 images of leukemia classes M0, M2, M3, M4, and M5.

The original images have a size of 1280×1024., which were resized to a size of 256×320 and converted to .png format. Figure 4 shows examples of the types of acute myelocytic leukemia used in this work.

4.2 Results

The Lenet results are shown in Fig. 5, where it can be noted that the best average performance was obtained with a batch size of 128. However, overall, a minimum of 80% in average accuracy was not achieved.

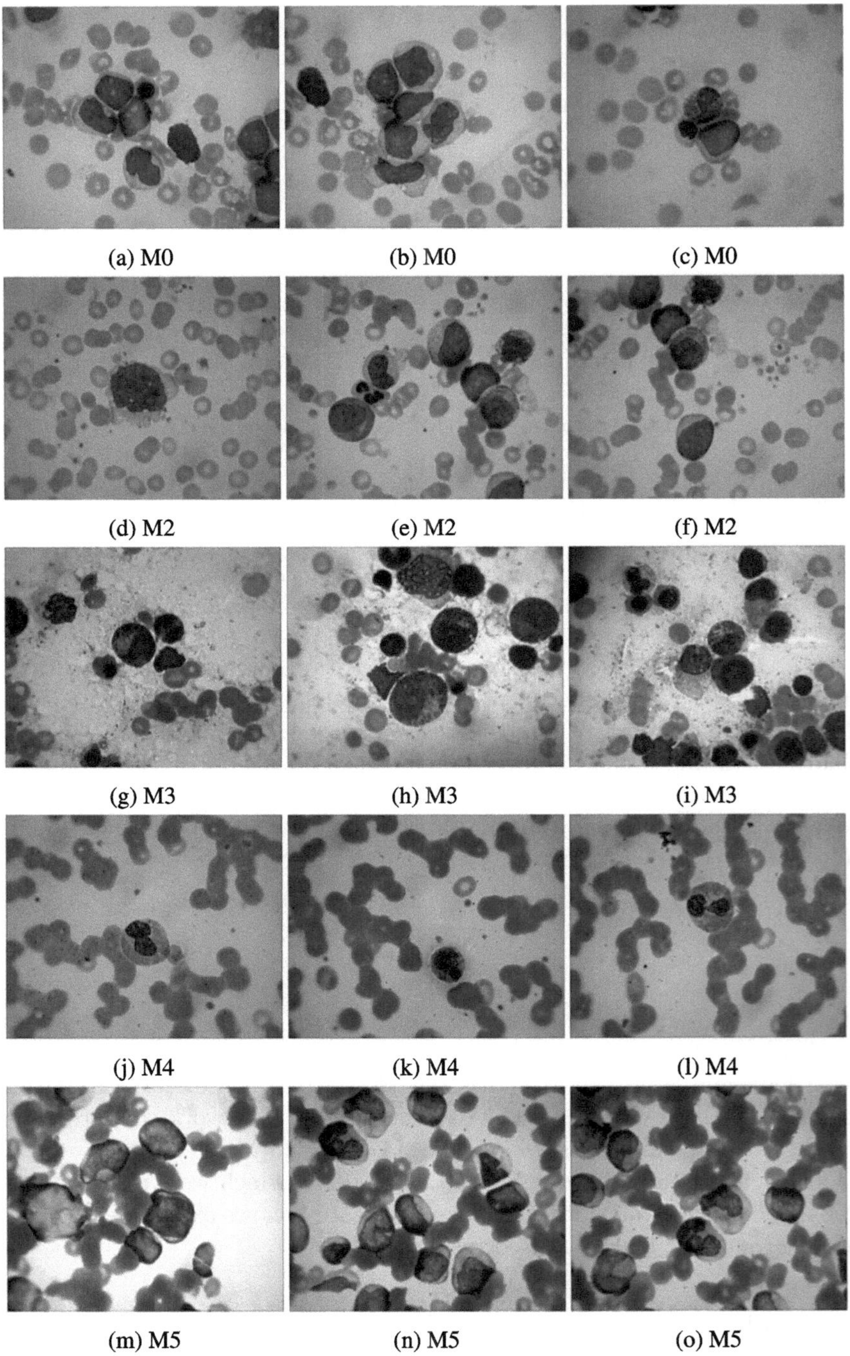

Fig. 4. Five types of acute myelocytic leukemia.

Table 1. Types of leukemia according to FAB classification [2].

	Leukemia type	Description
Acute lymphocytic leukemia (ALL)		
1	L1	Typical lymphoblastic
2	L2	Atypical lymphoblastic
3	L3	Similar to Burkitt's lymphoma
Acute myeloid leukemia (AML)		
4	**M0**	Minimally differentiated myeloblastic
5	M1	Immature myeloblastic
6	**M2**	Mature myeloblastic
7	**M3**	Hypergranular Promyelocytic
8	**M4**	Myelomonoblastic
9	**M5**	Pure monoblastic
10	M6	Erythroleukemia
11	M7	Megakaryoblastic

For Model 1, the results are shown in Fig. 6. In this case, the best performance was obtained with a batch size of 32, since an average accuracy of 89% was achieved. It can also be noted that although a maximum accuracy of 97% was achieved with a batch size of 64, the average accuracy was lower.

Finally, the results of model 2 are presented in Fig. 7 . This model showed better performance in most of the tests. Particularly, with a batch size of 16, a higher average accuracy was achieved than in the rest of the evaluated models.

Figures 8 and 9 show the training plots and confusion matrix for the best performing model run 2 (batch size=16). As shown in the confusion matrix, it is worth noting that class M5 achieved the lowest classification accuracy, primarily due to the presence of mislabeled cases within class M3. This suggests that the visual characteristics of classes M3 and M5 are similar, which can be distinguished in the images in Fig. 4.

Noteworthy that the classification results for all classes are good, since the classification accuracy ranges from 90.77% for class M5 to 98.46% for class M4. Meanwhile, the precision, recall, and F1 are 95.08, 95.08, and 0.95, respectively.

No_exec	Acc_TRAIN	Acc_TEST	TIME
1	0.9692	0.7907	506.2841
2	0.9415	0.6553	502.517
3	0.9459	0.6984	505.7032
4	0.8581	0.6061	502.6081
5	0.9605	0.7476	502.4702
6	0.9488	0.7292	501.7256
7	0.9722	0.7815	502.7617
8	0.9605	0.7415	510.7191
9	0.9561	0.7384	516.2753
10	0.671	0.4492	515.3761
11	0.9488	0.7292	514.522
12	0.9576	0.7015	514.5643
13	0.9663	0.7384	514.8402
14	0.9692	0.8307	514.3629
15	0.9371	0.7169	515.071
Min	0.67	0.45	501.73
Max	0.97	**0.83**	516.28
Var	0.01	0.01	38.49
Std	0.08	0.09	5.93
Avg	0.93	**0.71**	509.32

(a) Batch size= 16

No_exec	Acc_TRAIN	Acc_TEST	TIME
1	0.9371	0.683	393.9515
2	0.8486	0.5507	409.3736
3	0.8567	0.6338	400.3955
4	0.9736	0.7723	398.9284
5	0.9473	0.723	398.7678
6	0.9612	0.7599	399.3769
7	0.9429	0.7107	406.5807
8	0.9488	0.7323	408.1167
9	0.9532	0.72	418.8152
10	0.9561	0.7446	417.5491
11	0.9298	0.683	417.3803
12	0.9634	0.7476	416.6347
13	0.9568	0.7446	411.796
14	0.9444	0.6984	398.0107
15	0.9532	0.7446	397.6688
Min	0.85	0.55	393.95
Max	0.97	**0.77**	418.82
Var	0.00	0.00	74.66
Std	0.04	0.06	8.64
Avg	0.94	**0.71**	406.22

(b) Batch size= 32

No_exec	Acc_TRAIN	Acc_TEST	TIME
1	0.9327	0.7323	314.1194
2	0.9692	0.7661	318.6339
3	0.97	0.72	318.2162
4	0.9576	0.7046	316.1394
5	0.9422	0.7076	316.1978
6	0.9524	0.7507	315.9191
7	0.948	0.7353	316.9843
8	0.9429	0.723	323.6148
9	0.9605	0.7169	319.1336
10	0.9619	0.7784	317.7672
11	0.9619	0.7569	317.1548
12	0.9356	0.6584	316.2575
13	0.9488	0.7599	315.716
14	0.9612	0.72	316.1894
15	0.9532	0.723	315.9625
Min	0.93	0.66	314.12
Max	0.97	**0.78**	323.61
Var	0.00	0.00	4.80
Std	0.01	0.03	2.19
Avg	0.95	**0.73**	317.20

(c) Batch size= 64

No_exec	Acc_TRAIN	Acc_TEST	TIME
1	0.8932	0.6523	296.907
2	0.9181	0.6523	299.8682
3	0.8815	0.643	298.508
4	0.9217	0.6646	295.0002
5	0.9349	0.72	297.8094
6	0.9437	0.72	299.1129
7	0.891	0.6738	295.5762
8	0.9422	0.723	296.3791
9	0.9195	0.7076	309.979
10	0.9517	0.7353	314.4828
11	0.9605	0.7969	315.8121
12	0.9583	0.7907	324.8187
13	0.9385	0.72	316.4133
14	0.9576	0.7292	309.6476
15	0.9671	0.763	313.3621
Min	0.88	0.67	295.00
Max	0.97	**0.80**	324.82
Var	0.00	0.00	97.22
Std	0.03	0.04	9.73
Avg	0.93	**0.74**	305.58

(d) Batch size= 128

Fig. 5. Results for LeNet.

No_exec	Acc_TRAIN	Acc_TEST	TIME
1	0.9697	0.9107	266.965
2	0.9789	0.8953	264.3455
3	0.8802	0.803	264.072
4	0.9302	0.8307	262.8229
5	0.9842	0.8769	263.668
6	0.9828	0.9138	263.8687
7	0.9223	0.8861	264.8117
8	0.9657	0.8923	264.8401
9	0.9868	0.8923	266.0506
10	0.8697	0.8523	264.0286
11	0.896	0.8338	264.1447
12	0.9486	0.923	264.1005
13	0.9815	0.92	264.1773
14	0.9789	0.8953	265.3866
15	0.9894	0.8953	264.1071
Min	0.87	0.80	262.82
Max	0.99	**0.92**	266.97
Var	0.00	0.00	0.71
Std	0.04	0.04	1.01
Avg	0.95	**0.88**	264.49

(a) Batch size= 16

No_exec	Acc_TRAIN	Acc_TEST	TIME
1	0.9565	0.9169	262.7967
2	0.9105	0.8553	264.1439
3	0.9868	0.92	264.4037
4	0.9605	0.9076	263.2365
5	0.9684	0.9076	262.9511
6	0.9671	0.8799	263.3896
7	0.9631	0.8769	265.7251
8	0.9539	0.9076	265.266
9	0.9065	0.8769	265.9806
10	0.9592	0.8707	266.2761
11	0.9671	0.8799	267.0971
12	0.9078	0.8553	265.546
13	0.9631	0.8923	264.7643
14	0.971	0.9076	265.1385
15	0.9697	0.923	265.8151
Min	0.91	0.86	262.80
Max	0.99	**0.92**	267.10
Var	0.00	0.00	1.72
Std	0.02	0.02	1.31
Avg	0.95	**0.89**	264.84

(b) Batch size= 32

No_exec	Acc_TRAIN	Acc_TEST	TIME
1	0.8565	0.8246	290.4287
2	0.8723	0.8523	291.7185
3	0.9105	0.8646	293.6809
4	0.9184	0.8676	292.1637
5	0.8828	0.8246	293.0348
6	0.9144	0.8646	293.5294
7	0.9671	0.9661	292.1375
8	0.921	0.8799	294.1785
9	0.9184	0.8923	291.3307
10	0.7605	0.7815	293.5234
11	0.9381	0.8676	290.7531
12	0.9197	0.8215	291.1772
13	0.9447	0.8769	292.0459
14	0.9486	0.8615	291.7126
15	0.9052	0.8769	293.2285
Min	0.76	0.78	290.43
Max	0.97	**0.97**	294.18
Var	0.00	0.00	1.34
Std	0.05	0.04	1.16
Avg	0.91	**0.86**	292.31

(c) Batch size= 64

No_exec	Acc_TRAIN	Acc_TEST	TIME
1	0.7776	0.7261	293.6359
2	0.6697	0.6615	301.7995
3	0.7565	0.6923	299.4035
4	0.7302	0.7261	300.5239
5	0.8486	0.8092	301.8531
6	0.7605	0.7046	300.7722
7	0.7092	0.6953	304.007
8	0.75	0.7015	302.598
9	0.8236	0.7753	308.5647
10	0.7065	0.6523	304.0505
11	0.8947	0.8184	301.4822
12	0.8618	0.8246	300.4483
13	0.8092	0.7938	302.7716
14	0.82368	0.7876	303.6466
15	0.7092	0.643	302.5915
Min	0.67	0.64	293.64
Max	0.89	**0.82**	308.56
Var	0.01	0.01	9.87
Std	0.07	0.07	3.14
Avg	0.78	**0.74**	301.88

(d) Batch size= 128

Fig. 6. Results for Model 1.

No_exec	Acc_TRAIN	Acc_TEST	TIME
1	0.90789473	0.91076922	65.2189498
2	0.98815787	0.92923075	64.9543204
3	0.98421055	0.90769231	64.5473583
4	0.9657895	0.86769229	64.4285924
5	0.98421055	0.91076922	67.3966579
6	0.96447366	0.90153849	66.2182376
7	0.9763158	0.94153845	66.5613687
8	0.97236842	0.91076922	65.8697474
9	0.96184212	0.90769231	65.9876499
10	0.97105265	0.93230772	65.731385
11	0.95789474	0.91384614	64.5779066
12	0.8986842	0.88307691	65.4034231
13	0.9763158	0.92923075	64.8318045
14	0.96447366	0.92923075	66.5047526
15	0.98289472	0.92923075	65.8426743
Min	0.90	0.87	64.43
Max	0.99	**0.94**	67.40
Var	0.00	0.00	0.83
Std	0.03	0.02	0.86
Avg	0.96	**0.91**	65.60

(a) Batch size= 16

No_exec	Acc_TRAIN	Acc_TEST	TIME
1	0.97105265	0.94153845	62.0078721
2	0.95526314	0.93846154	61.3452535
3	0.94868422	0.93538463	61.7805762
4	0.96184212	0.91692311	62.1963418
5	0.92500001	0.9046154	61.450227
6	0.96052629	0.9046154	61.5326016
7	0.77499998	0.77230769	61.5658166
8	0.95921052	0.90769231	61.9080338
9	0.93552631	0.88615382	61.247102
10	0.93684208	0.89538461	61.9400146
11	0.79736841	0.76615387	63.1757822
12	0.95921052	0.91384614	63.2312534
13	0.97236842	0.91692311	63.9426827
14	0.9763158	0.94153845	66.9839065
15	0.93421054	0.89538461	66.9425085
Min	0.77	0.77	61.25
Max	0.98	**0.94**	66.98
Var	0.01	0.00	3.64
Std	0.06	0.05	1.88
Avg	0.93	**0.90**	62.75

(b) Batch size= 32

No_exec	Acc_TRAIN	Acc_TEST	TIME
1	0.86578947	0.78769231	67.9199538
2	0.8618421	0.84923077	68.8404348
3	0.94078946	0.91076922	68.8070717
4	0.83552629	0.80615383	69.6037621
5	0.89342105	0.88307691	69.2394218
6	0.90789473	0.89846152	69.1958022
7	0.92763156	0.92615384	69.3888378
8	0.87105262	0.82769233	68.6544271
9	0.92631578	0.92615384	68.6020246
10	0.79210526	0.75999999	68.7415636
11	0.91052634	0.90153849	69.1464899
12	0.86052632	0.7846154	68.8831427
13	0.88684213	0.84923077	68.7637067
14	0.8855263	0.85538459	69.8296013
15	0.82763159	0.83076924	69.0124376
Min	0.79	0.76	67.92
Max	0.94	**0.93**	69.83
Var	0.00	0.00	0.21
Std	0.04	0.05	0.46
Avg	0.88	**0.85**	68.98

(c) Batch size= 64

No_exec	Acc_TRAIN	Acc_TEST	TIME
1	0.67105263	0.6215385	66.5745919
2	0.7473684	0.7076923	67.2540073
3	0.72894734	0.7015384	63.1551795
4	0.66578948	0.64	60.5079324
5	0.76973683	0.7415385	60.0303063
6	0.78947371	0.7415385	60.0647807
7	0.72894734	0.7230769	60.5609796
8	0.64736843	0.6307693	60.3584092
9	0.80921054	0.7630769	59.8927817
10	0.83947366	0.8123077	61.5830967
11	0.80789477	0.7815385	60.589385
12	0.81973684	0.7969231	60.7447453
13	0.82368422	0.8184615	60.0803928
14	0.74473685	0.7230769	60.7234592
15	0.75526315	0.6984615	60.1751523
Min	0.65	0.63	59.89
Max	0.84	**0.82**	67.25
Var	0.00	0.01	3.64
Std	0.06	0.06	2.35
Avg	0.76	**0.75**	61.49

(d) Batch size= 128

Fig. 7. Results for Model 1.

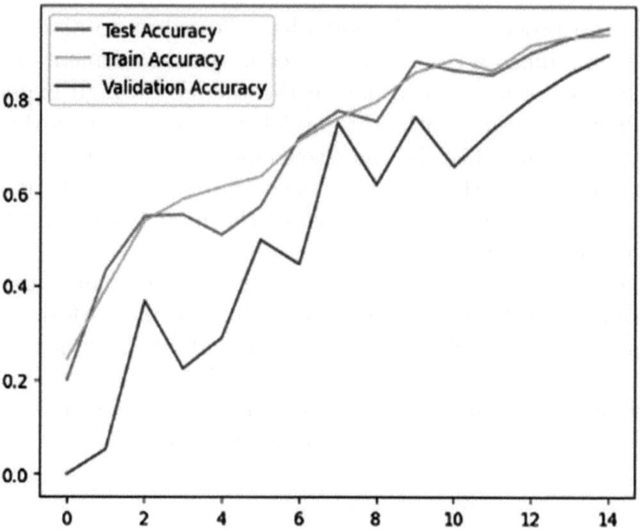

Fig. 8. Training graph of Model 2. The X-axis represents the number of epochs, and the Y-axis is the accuracy.

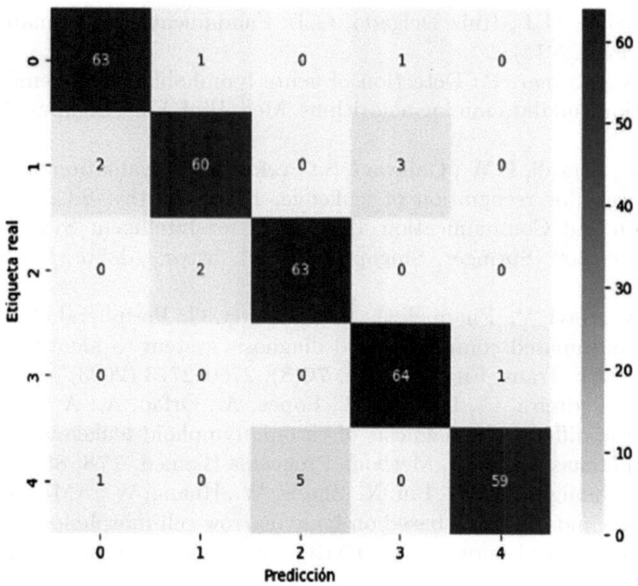

Fig. 9. Confusion matrix of the Model 2 with batch size= 16

5 Conclusions

This paper presents an experimental review of three basic convolutional neural network architectures applied to myelocytic leukemia classification.

The evaluation process of each model has allowed us to distinguish the differences in performance and the influence of particular elements in each architecture, which enables us to corroborate the theory through experimentation. The results show that the depth of a model does not imply a direct relationship with better performance. It was also found that the dropout may slightly favor the performance of these architectures. Furthermore, statistical analysis is important to evaluate the performance of the models to avoid biases in the interpretation of the results.

Based on the above, as future work, pre-trained models can be used to address the classification of myelocytic leukemia and compare the performance of simple and pre-trained models in different visual explainability techniques.

Acknowledgements. Authors would like to acknowledge the support provided by the Applied Computational Intelligence Network (RedICA).

References

1. The Global Center Observatory: International Agency for Research on Cancer (2023)
2. Ruiz Argüelles, G.J., Ruiz Delgado, G.J.: Fundamentos de Hematología, 5 edn. Panamericana (2014)
3. Acharya, V., Kumar, P.: Detection of acute lymphoblastic leukemia using image segmentation and data mining algorithms. Med. Biol. Eng. Comput. **57**, 1783–1811 (2019)
4. Rege, M.V., Gawali, B.W., Gaikwad, S.: Performance evaluation of image segmentation process for recognition of leukemia. In: Satapathy, S.C., Joshi, A. (eds.) Information and Communication Technology for Intelligent Systems. SIST, vol. 107, pp. 499–509. Springer, Singapore (2019). https://doi.org/10.1007/978-981-13-1747-7_48
5. Acharya, V., Ravi, V., Pham, T.D., Chakraborty, C.: Peripheral blood smear analysis using automated computer-aided diagnosis system to identify acute myeloid leukemia. IEEE Trans. Eng. Manage. **70**(8), 2760–2773 (2023)
6. Moraes, L., Pedreira, C., Barrena, S., Lopez, A., Orfao, A.: A decision-tree approach for the differential diagnosis of chronic lymphoid leukemias and peripheral b-cell lymphomas. Comput. Methods Programs Biomed. **178**, 85–90 (2019)
7. Huang, F., Guang, P., Li, F., Liu, X., Zhang, W., Huang, W.: AML, ALL, and CML classification and diagnosis based on bone marrow cell morphology combined with convolutional neural network: a STARD compliant diagnosis research. Medicine **99**, e23154 (2020)
8. Schouten, J., Matek, C., Jacobs, L.F.P., Buck, M., Bosnacki, D., Marr, C.: Tens of images can suffice to train neural networks for malignant leukocyte detection. Sci. Rep. **11** (2021)
9. Fu, Y., et al.: Artificial intelligence in lymphoma histopathology: systematic review. J. Med. Internet Res. **27**, e62851 (2025)
10. Mustaqim, T., Fatichah, C., Suciati, N.: Deep learning for the detection of acute lymphoblastic leukemia subtypes on microscopic images: a systematic literature review. IEEE Access **11**, 16108–16127 (2023)

11. Ramaneswaran, S., Srinivasan, K., Vincent, P., Chang, C.Y.: Hybrid inception v3 XGBoost model for acute lymphoblastic leukemia classification. Comput. Math. Methods Med. **2021**(1), 2577375 (2021)
12. Li, C., et al.: LLaVA-Med: large language and vision assistant for biomedicine (2025)
13. LeCun, Y., Bengio, Y.: Convolutional networks for images, speech, and time series. In: The Handbook of Brain Theory and Neural Networks (2003)
14. Khan, S., Rahmani, H., Ali-Shah, S.A., Bennamoun, M.: A guide to convolutional neural networks for computer vision. In: Synthesis Lectures on Computer Vision (2018)
15. Ochoa-Montiel, R., Sossa, H., Olague, G.: Dataset leukemia (2021)

Natural Language Processing

Sentiment Classification of Sexist Comments: A Comparative Study of Supervised Models

Karen Esmeralda Delgado Pérez(✉), Néstor David García Franco, Darnes Vilariño Ayala, Beatriz Beltrán Martínez, David Eduardo Pinto Avendaño, and Yolanda Moyao Martínez

Benemérita Universidad Autónoma de Puebla, Puebla, Mexico
{dp224470254,gf224470255}@alm.buap.mx,
{darnes.vilarino,beatriz.beltran,david.pinto,
yolanda.moyao}@correo.buap.mx

Abstract. Sexism detection is still considered a challenging task because of the linguistic expressions of many online comments. In this study we present a comparative analysis between three supervised learning models: Random Forest, Gradient Boosting and Multilayer Perceptron (MLP). These models were applied to the classification: positive, negative and neutral, in texts with sexist content. The dataset was constructed from one million comments collected from Reddit and Gab platforms, along with 20,000 instances manually labeled by the EDOS team as part of the SemEval 2023 competition. The texts were preprocessed and vectorized using word embeddings that were generated with Word2Vec, thus preserving the semantic relationships between terms. The results obtained indicate that, although the decision tree-based models offered acceptable initial performance, the MLP with 7 hidden layers achieved the best overall performance, outperforming the other models in terms of accuracy, recall and F1-score. Based on the results, the effectiveness of using deep neural networks to capture complex patterns in textual data is shown with this result. Finally, the potential of using more efficient models, such as MLPs, as a viable alternative to more expensive architectures such as transformers, especially in environments with limited computational capacity, is highlighted.

Keywords: Sexism · MLP · Random Forest · Text classification

1 Introduction

Internet access has become an everyday occurrence for most people, which has led to a remarkable increase in digital interactions. As a result, users can now share, comment and react to any content they encounter. However, this amplified connectivity also facilitates the spread of harmful and prejudicial behaviors, such as sexism. The Oxford English Dictionary defines sexism as prejudice, stereotyping or discrimination, typically against women, on the basis of sex. Similarly,

L. Martínez-Villaseñor et al. (Eds.): MICAI 2025, CCIS 2712, pp. 219–229, 2025.
https://doi.org/10.1007/978-3-032-08704-1_17

the Real Academia Española defines it as discrimination against people on the basis of sex [9].

However, detecting sexism on the Internet is a difficult task, since it expresses itself in so many different ways. Sexism can sound "friendly": the statement "You have to love and respect women, always treat them as a fragile vessel" may seem positive, but in reality it is considering women to be weaker than men. Also, it can be expressed in a "funny" way, as is the case with sexist jokes or humor ("You have to love women... just that... You will never understand them"). Added to this is "offensive" and "hateful" content, as in "Humiliate yourself, expose yourself and degrade yourself like the shit you are if you want attention". Consequently, sexism affects people and causes a series of psychological pressures; this factor significantly increases the likelihood of increased levels of anxiety, depression and suicidal tendencies [10].

The objective of this research is to identify all types of sexist comments from the context, using a classification of negative, positive or neutral comments, which is determined by searching each word within the dataset, applying natural language processing (NLP) techniques, with supervised learning models such as Random Forest, Gradient Boost and Multilayer Perceptron (MLP). Although transformer-based models such as BERT have proven to be highly efficient, this study focuses on evaluating the ability of classical models and MLP neural networks to solve the task with lower computational cost and higher interpretability, relevant aspects for use in resource-limited platforms.

The remaining sections of this article are organized as follows: Sect. 2 discusses the work related to the research, Sect. 3 breaks down the proposed methodology of the work, while Sect. 4 shows the analysis of the results; ending with the conclusions and future work in the Sect. 5.

2 Related Work

Online sexism is a relevant issue within social media networking platforms due to the fact that users misuse these tools, giving a negative impact on gender equality. Faced with the problem, several recent studies have proposed different approaches based on machine learning and natural language processing techniques to detect sexist expressions and promote safer digital spaces.

One of the most representative research projects is that proposed by the EDOS task (Explainable Detection of Online Sexism) [2], which proposes a hierarchical classification of sexism and provides a finely labeled dataset that allows for a more accurate analysis of the various proposed sexist discourse tasks. This work not only introduces a new corpus of 20,000 labeled comments but also evaluates base models and analyzes their errors, encouraging the development of explainable systems. In [6], a dual vision is offered that combines sexism detection with automatic generation of a Wikipedia article in Indian languages. While its focus also encompasses multilingual knowledge generation, its contributions to the use of techniques such as adaptive retraining and data segmentation in task such as EDOS show substantial improvements in the performances of BERT classifiers over conventional approaches.

In another study, [1] explores transformers models such as RoBERTa. Through a combination of embeddings and Long Short-Term Memory (LSTM) models, it is shown that an integration of approaches improves the accuracy of sexism detection, achieving an F1-score higher than 84%. This research emphasizes the value of hybrid models and voting strategies to refine the results.

On the other hand, [4] introduces the first Chinese corpus for sexism on Sina Weibo, along with a lexicon of offensive gender terms. Also, initiatives such as the EXIST task, described in [5], put into practice the development of systems to identify and categorize sexism in English and Spanish. This international competition demonstrated the effectiveness of using models such as BERT, which have outperformed other approaches in classification tasks, mainly in learning for multilingual environments.

Now, a multitask learning strategy in Spanish [7] has been explored, combining hate detection with polarity and emotion classification. These related tasks improve the detection of offensive content, showing the relevance of including affective dimensions in the modeling of offensive language. Unlike what happens in the MeTwo [9] corpus, which gives a key contribution in the analysis of subtle sexist expressions in Spanish. This work highlights that sexism is not always presented explicitly but can manifest itself through stereotypes and normalized attitudes. Through the use of deep learning models, it validates the possibility of identifying different types of sexism and of generalizing the methods to other forms of gender-based violence, such as misogyny.

In parallel, approaches have been developed that consider sexism as a manifestation of broader hate speech. On the other hand, work such as [8,10] uses deep learning techniques, which include multilayer perceptron (MLP), Bi-GRU and Bi-LSTM, to detect offensive language and cyberbullying. These studies reveal that neural models with embedding techniques, such as TF-IDF or GloVe, outperform traditional methods, such as logistic regression, in precision and recall, with F1-score rates higher than 95%, suggesting that embedding architectures can boost precision.

The present work is supported by the results of previous studies, which show a promising use of machine learning algorithms and neural networks to advance the automatic detection of online sexism.

3 Methodology

This section describes the steps for the development of sentiment classification: positive, negative and neutral. Dataset preparation, text vectorization using Word2Vec and implementation of three supervised models: Random Forest, Multilayer Perceptron and Gradient Boosting were included in the process. All were evaluated with 10-fold cross validation. Finally, the performance of each model is evaluated with standard classification metrics. The diagram of the process is shown in Fig. 1.

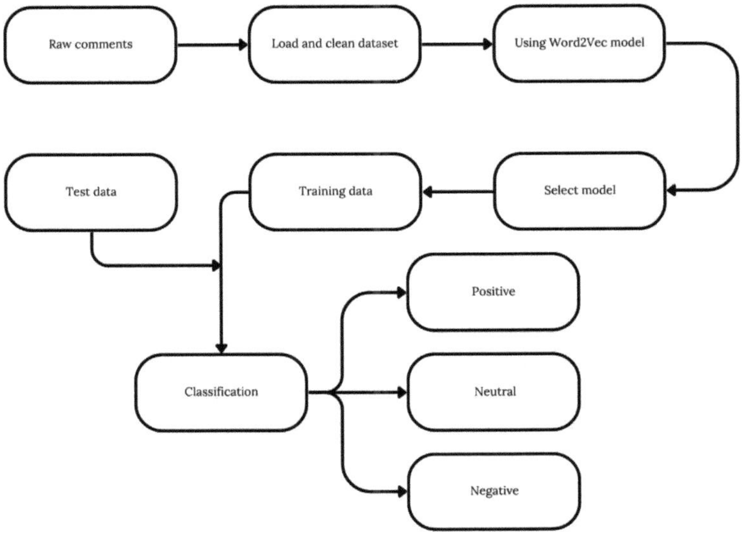

Fig. 1. Workflow of the model.

3.1 Dataset

For this work, a dataset composed of one million comments in English is used, which were collected from two social platforms: Reddit and Gab. This selection seeks to ensure a linguistic approach in which some sexist opinion can be presented online. In addition, in order to strengthen the reliability of the labels, 20,000 additional comments in English are incorporated, which were manually classified by the SemEval 2023 competition organizing team, within the EDOS (Explainable Detection of Online Sexism) task.

3.2 Preprocessing

The first step in the preprocessing process is to clean up the text. Initially, all comments were converted to lowercase to avoid duplicate words. Subsequently, emojis, apostrophes, numbers, ats, underscores, punctuation marks and unwanted Unicode characters are removed, as they do not contribute semantic value to the classification task.

During the review of the dataset, the presence of concatenated words within some sentences was identified, which represents a problem for tokenization. To solve this situation, the Python WordNinja library is used, which allows automatic and accurate splitting of words joined without spaces. An example of this problem is the string "metoostrongbend", which was segmented into "metoo strong bend". In the same way, the elimination of stopwords, lemmatization and exclusion of tokens with a length of less than three characters continues, with the aim of preserving the most significant terms. Finally, the Word2Vec model is applied, which generates word embeddings capable of capturing semantic and syntactic relationships, resulting in a better interpretation of the linguistic context present in the comments.

3.3 Model Selection

For the development of this research, three supervised learning models were selected. The selected models are Random Forest, Gradient Boosting and Multilayer Perceptron. Each of these models was trained under the same experimental conditions and using the vector representations generated by Word2Vec, which allows a fair and controlled comparison of their performance.

Random Forest. As a first analysis, this model is used because of its training speed and its ability to handle high-dimensional data without requiring extensive parameter optimization. This model allows us to obtain the first predictions on the real labels, starting from an initial baseline for the evaluation.

Gradient Boosting. This model seeks to improve on the performance achieved by Random Forest. Its stepwise learning approach, known for its higher tunability and error correction, allows us to explore whether a more sophisticated ensemble technique can offer significant improvement in evaluation metrics.

Multilayer Perceptron. The evaluation of Random Forest and Gradient Boosting models, while providing acceptable results, also have limitations in capturing complex nonlinear relationships between vectorized text features. Multilayer Perceptron (MLP) is implemented for this purpose,because it has the ability to model deeper, nonlinear dependencies within the data. In general, machine learning algorithms perform best when their capacity is adequate for the actual complexity of the task to be performed and the amount of training data available to them. Models with high capacity can solve complex tasks, but when their capacity is higher than needed to solve the actual task, they may overfit [3].

3.4 Model Evaluation

The dataset was divided into 80% for the training set and 20% for the test set. Thus, the metrics considered are accuracy, precision, recall and F1-score, with which it is possible to evaluate the performance of the models. The column *text* is used to identify the preprocessed text, and the *true_label* column contains the true labels, and the *predicted_label* column saves the predictions.

The million dataset is divided into 150,213 comments labeled as positive, 471,097 as negative, and 380,638 as neutral, which were used as true labels for evaluating model performance. Because of this, we observe that the classes are unbalanced, which indicates that the detection of negative words is accurate, contrary to what happens with positive classification.

If a comment has a positive label, it means that the content is not sexist, such as *"The dog is more intelligent, too"*, or *"I definately will. A few months maybe. Apart from my chin i look decent. Clear skin thick hair, ok eyes, good symmetry. Etc"*. If the classification is negative, it means that it shows sexist content, for example *"White girls can have such a victim complex. They could downplay racism and equal it to their sexism which are often their first world problems. Also trying to blame the white male when white people in general are the topic"*, or *"Nah, Metoo will always be strong when men are bending over backwards and spreading their ass open for women. The damage has been done and people are now afraid to speak out lest they be punished by losing their jobs"*. In the case of a neutral label, it refers to a comment that does not distinguish between genders, such as: *"Truth time find life tolerable brief moment think head start feel like miss"*, or *"At some point in your life, even jf just once, you have had a nonrelated woman act positively towards you. so your entire rant was based on this assumption"*.

4 Results

This section presents the results obtained after the application of the sentiment classification models described in the methodology. Random Forest model was the first model to address the sentiment classification task. Figure 2 shows the confusion matrix, which allows visualizing the number of correct and incorrect predictions for each of the three classes.

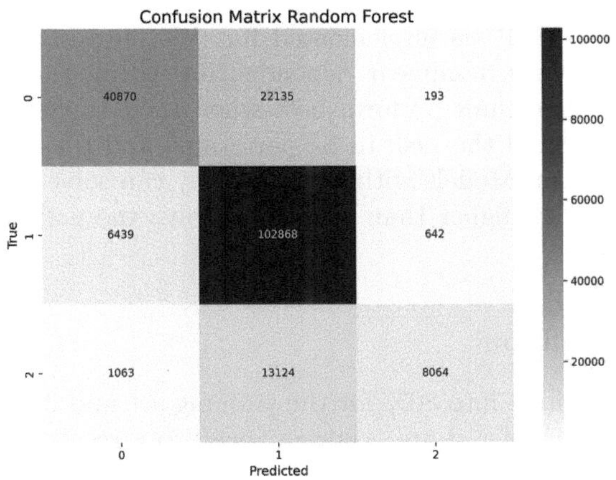

Fig. 2. Confusion matrix for Random Forest model.

The model achieves an accuracy of 77.7%, more than three quarters of the predictions were correct, and it is good at avoiding false positives, with 83.2% of the cases being correct. However, it has trouble identifying all the examples in each class. With a recall of 64.8%, it indicates difficulty in detecting true positives, especially in the positive class. With an F1-score of 69.3%, it shows an acceptable balance, but with room for improvement, especially in the recall of true instances of minority classes. Due to these limitations in the recovery of minority classes, it was necessary to evaluate other models, such as Gradient Boosting and later MLP, looking for a better balance between precision and recall. Gradient Boosting was the second model implemented. Figure 3 shows the confusion matrix with the predictions made.

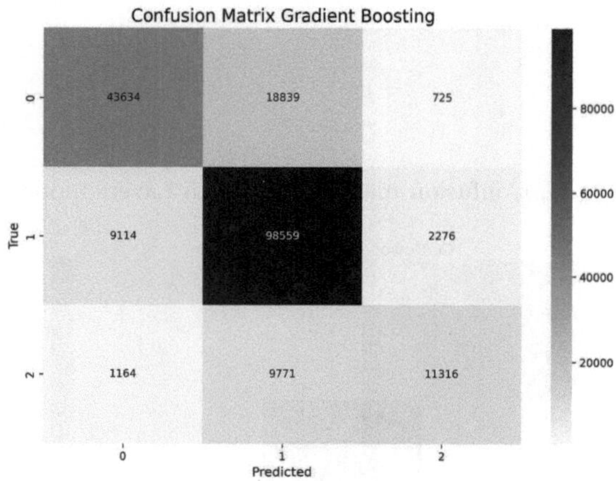

Fig. 3. Confusion matrix for Gradient Boosting model.

This model achieves an accuracy of 78.6%, which represents a slight improvement over Random Forest. In precision, 79.2% was obtained, while recall reached 69.8%, reflecting a better capacity to recover true positives, especially in the positive class, which had shown difficulties in the previous model. The F1-score obtained was 73.2%, however, despite these improvements, the model continues to show differences between the neutral and positive classes.

The Multilayer Perceptron model with 5 layers is the first one evaluated within the neural network category. Figure 4 shows its confusion matrix, where a significant improvement in the classification of the three labels is observed with respect to the previous models.

This model achieves an accuracy of 82.4%, outperforming Random Forest and Gradient Boosting. With an accuracy of 80.3%, an F1-score of 80.1% and a recall of 79.9%, it indicates a greater ability to recover true positives in all classes. These results marked an important advance in classification quality, motivating further evaluation of networks. In order to explore the impact of greater depth in the architecture, an MLP with 7 hidden layers was trained. The corresponding confusion matrix is presented in Fig. 5.

This model achieves an accuracy of 83.4%, being the highest value reached up to this point. The accuracy reaches 81.7%, while the recall is 80.8% and the

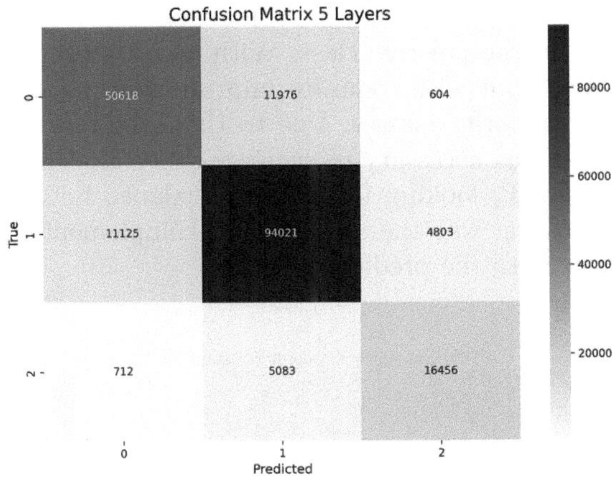

Fig. 4. Confusion matrix for MLP 5 Layers model.

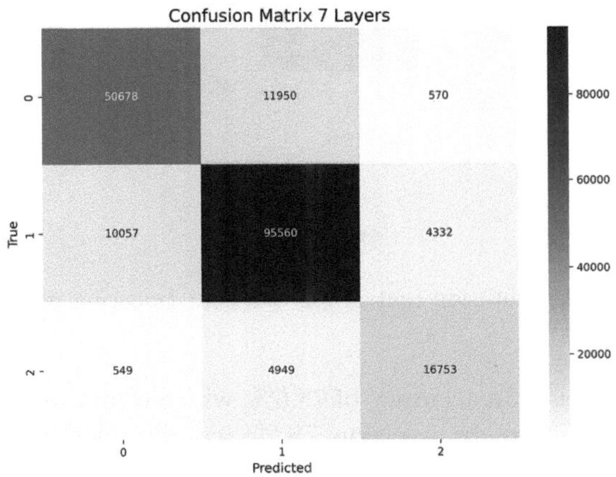

Fig. 5. Confusion matrix for MLP 7 Layers model.

F1-score was 81.2%, evidencing the best overall balance between the main metrics. These results confirmed that increasing the number of layers improves the model's capability, further reducing classification errors. Finally, an MLP with 9 hidden layers is evaluated, seeking to determine whether greater depth would continue to provide significant improvements. The relevant confusion matrix is visualized in Fig. 6.

The model maintains an accuracy of 83.4%, similar to that obtained with 7 layers, indicating that further increasing the number of layers did not generate a noticeable increase in overall accuracy. Accuracy reached 81.9%, while recall was 80.4%. The F1-score stands at 81.1%, showing stable performance compared to the previous model. These results suggest that, while the additional depth does not hurt performance, it does not bring significant additional benefits either,

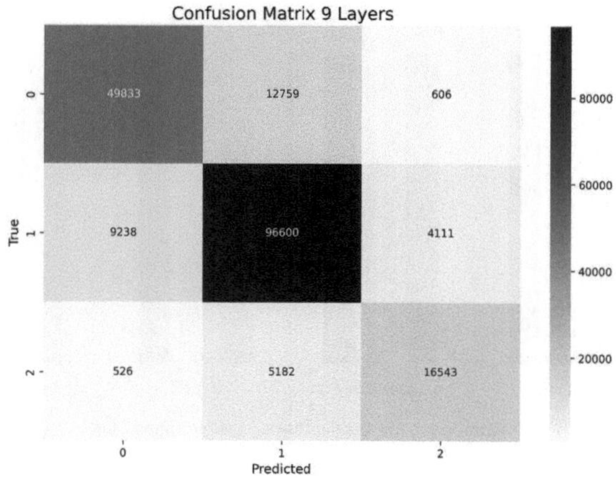

Fig. 6. Confusion matrix for MLP 9 Layers model.

demonstrating that a 7-layer architecture represents the best performance when classifying positive, negative and neutral feedback.

A summary of the metrics observed in the Random Forest, Gradiant Boosting and Multilayer Perceptron models (5, 7 and 9 layers) is presented in Table 1 below. The results show that the Multilayer Perceptron models outperformed the decision tree based approaches in almost all metrics.

Table 1. Comparative summary of the models.

Model	Accuracy	Precision	Recall	F1-score
Random Forest	0.777	**0.832**	0.648	0.693
Gradient Boosting	0.786	0.792	0.698	0.732
MLP 5 Layers	0.824	0.803	0.799	0.801
MLP 7 Layers	**0.834**	0.817	**0.808**	**0.812**
MLP 9 Layers	**0.834**	0.819	0.804	0.811

In particular, the 7-layer Multilayer Perceptron stands out as the model with the best overall performance, achieving the highest recall and F1-score values. Although the 9-layer Multilayer Perceptron obtained similar metrics, it does not represent a significant improvement over the 7-layer model. On the other hand, Random Forest presents a high accuracy, but with a low recall, while Gradient Boosting offers a better balance, but without surpassing the performance achieved by the neural networks.

Finally, Fig. 7 shows a comparative plot of the key metrics between Random Forest, Gradient Boosting and 7-layer Multilayer Perceptron. This representation allows to clearly observe the positive evolution in all metrics as the complexity of the models increases.

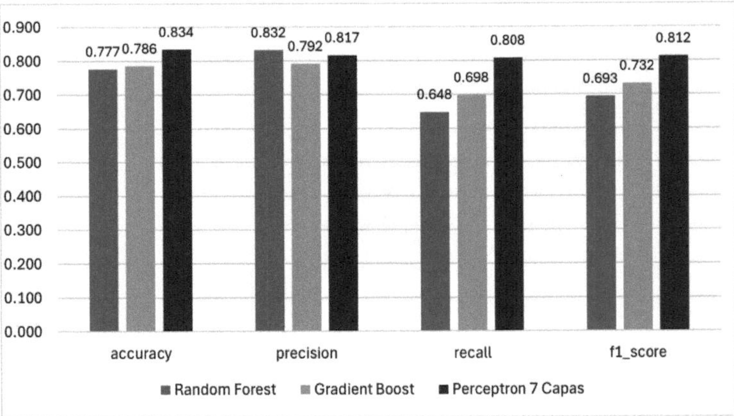

Fig. 7. Comparison of metrics between the 3 models.

5 Conclusion and Future Work

In conclusion, this study analyzed and compared different machine learning models. The objective was to classify emotions in online comments that have to do with sexism. For this purpose, models such as Random Forest, Gradient Boosting and Multilayer Perceptron with different configurations were tested, and Wor2Vec was used to understand the meaning of the words.

In short, it is observed that although the simpler models based on decision trees performed well, the neural networks, especially the 7-layer one, were the best performers, achieved a superior balance between precision, recall and F1-score, and outperformed the previous models in all key aspects. This shows us that if we use more complex models capable of understanding subtle connections, we can better classify sentiment in this type of feedback. In addition, it is important to note that despite not using the latest technologies such as transformer models, this approach achieves very good results and with lower computational cost. This is crucial when resources are limited.

For future work, we seek to use the results obtained in this work to be able to perform the subcategories of offensive languages, as shown in task B of the research mentioned by the EDOS SemEval 2023 team.

Acknowledgments. The authors would like to thank the Secretaría de Ciencia, Humanidades, Tecnología e Innovación (SECIHTI) for the support provided through the national graduate scholarship. We also express our appreciation to the anonymous reviewers for their valuable feedback and suggestions to improve this work.

Disclosure of Interests. The authors declare that there are no conflicts of interest related to the publication of this article.

References

1. Belbachir, F., Roustan, T., Soukane, A.: Detecting online sexism: integrating sentiment analysis with contextual language models. AI **5**(4), 2852–2863 (2024). https://doi.org/10.3390/ai5040137
2. Deb, P., et al.: Evaluating online sexism detection: a comparative study of machine learning models using the EDOS dataset. In: 2024 IEEE 9th International Conference for Convergence in Technology (I2CT), pp. 1–6. IEEE (2024)
3. Goodfellow, I., Bengio, Y., Courville, A., Bengio, Y.: Deep Learning, vol. 1. MIT Press, Cambridge (2016)
4. Jiang, A., Yang, X., Liu, Y., Zubiaga, A.: Swsr: a Chinese dataset and lexicon for online sexism detection. Online Soc. Netw. Media **27**, 100182 (2022)
5. Maqbool, N.: Sexism identification in social networks: advances in automated detection–a report on the exist task at CLEF. Working Notes of CLEF (2024)
6. Panwar, J.: Techniques for text classification and text generation: enhanced online sexism detection and template driven Wikipedia article generation, Ph.D. thesis, International Institute of Information Technology Hyderabad-500 032, India (2024)
7. Plaza-Del-Arco, F.M., González, M.D., Urena-Lopez, L., Martín-Valdivia, M.: A multi-task learning approach to hate speech detection leveraging sentiment analysis. IEEE Access **9**, 112478–112489 (2021). https://doi.org/10.1109/ACCESS.2021.3103697
8. Raj, C., Agarwal, A., Bharathy, G., Narayan, B., Prasad, M.: Cyberbullying detection: hybrid models based on machine learning and natural language processing techniques. Electronics **10**(22), 2810 (2021)
9. Rodríguez-Sánchez, F., Carrillo-de Albornoz, J., Plaza, L.: Automatic classification of sexism in social networks: an empirical study on twitter data. IEEE Access **8**, 219563–219576 (2020). https://doi.org/10.1109/ACCESS.2020.3042604
10. Sharma, R., Kaur, K.: Hate speech detection using MLP and random forest. In: 2024 7th International Conference on Contemporary Computing and Informatics (IC3I), vol. 7, pp. 91–96 (2024). https://doi.org/10.1109/IC3I61595.2024.10829319

User-Centered Approach for AI-Powered Pitch Deck Creation

Claudia Anahí Guzmán-Solano[1](✉), Bogdan Kaleb García Rivera[1], Ignacio Arroyo-Fernández[1], Mario Alberto Moreno Rocha[2,3], Cesar Felipe Martínez Cisneros[1], and Jesús Ulises Quiroz Bautista[1]

[1] Universidad Tecnológica de la Mixteca, División de Estudios de Posgrado, Huajuapan de León, Oaxaca, Mexico
claudia.guzmansolano@gmail.com, {iaf,qubj980830}@gs.utm.mx
[2] UsaLab Laboratorio de Usabilidad, Huajuapan de León, Oaxaca, Mexico
mmoreno@gs.utm.mx
[3] Universidad Tecnológica de la Mixteca, UsaLab Usability Laboratory, Huajuapan de León, Mexico

Abstract. This study explores the use of Generative AI, specifically Large Language Models (LLM), to create cost-effective and impactful Pitch Decks for entrepreneurs. Using a User-Centered Design (UCD) approach, prompts were designed to generate persuasive content. A prototype system was developed and tested with real entrepreneurs, receiving positive feedback with only minor improvements needed. The results demonstrate the potential of AI-driven tools, guided by UCD principles, to assist early-stage startups by producing high-quality marketing materials and generating business opportunities.

Keywords: Pitch Deck · Generative AI · Large language models (llm) · User-Centered Design (UCD) · Usability Testing · Persuasion

1 Introduction

Generative marketing, powered by AI, offers startups a low-cost, high-impact strategy for campaigns and personalized experiences. By integrating AI into agile strategies, early-stage ventures can optimize ideas efficiently, reducing reliance on human intuition [1]. User-Centered Design (UCD) ensures these solutions are practical and memorable, aligning with budget constraints. LLM further amplify this potential, transforming marketing and business innovation [2].

Generative marketing is explored for creating AI-powered Pitch Decks using LLMs and UCD principles. This study compares AI-generated vs. human-made decks, assessing similarity, persuasion, and effectiveness (see Fig. 1). Pitch decks are crucial for entrepreneurs to secure funding [3].

Oaxacan entrepreneurs need practical, low-cost AI (LLM) marketing tools. This study fills a gap by comparing LLM-generated vs human Pitch Decks' effectiveness, asking: Can AI match human persuasion for investors/clients?.

L. Martínez-Villaseñor et al. (Eds.): MICAI 2025, CCIS 2712, pp. 230–244, 2025.
https://doi.org/10.1007/978-3-032-08704-1_18

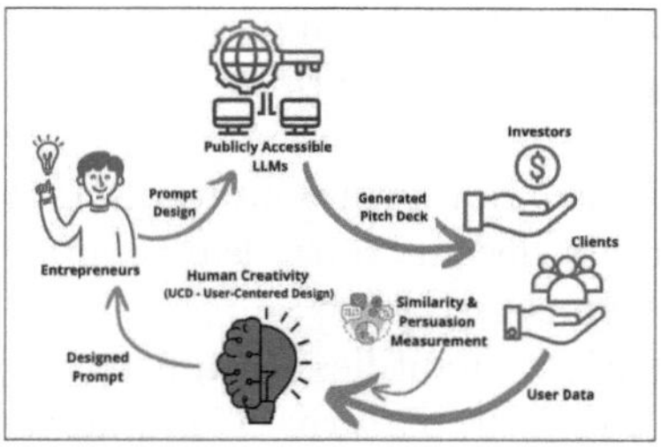

Fig. 1. Diagram illustrating the proposed study's process, integrating UCD and AI.

UCD is key for creating impactful generative marketing strategies that meet startups' early-stage needs, helping them compete for investors/clients.

This study followed key phases: 1) user/market research, 2) UCD-based prompt template design, 3) evaluation via semantic metrics and entrepreneur testing. Results of initial usability showed high satisfaction with AI-generated Pitch Decks (coherent, professional), requiring only minor improvements. As of this development stage, the findings confirm that UCD-guided AI tools can effectively support startup fundraising.

2 Related Literature

Focusing on Generative Marketing with AI/NLP, this section highlights key research on LLM for entrepreneurial content creation, featuring practical strategies to attract investors.

In [4] shows LLM persuasive power in public opinion, while [5] enhances argumentation styles with LLM's, considering emotional and evidence-based styles. [6] examines GPT's impact on entrepreneurial decisions, and [7] presents an AI chatbot startup-idea evaluator.

Similar to our approach, [8] demonstrates LLMs' effectiveness for business pitches, while [9] examines AI integration challenges in startup ideation. Finally, the research in [10] is based on predicting the success of crowdfunding campaigns through the analysis of textual, visual, and linguistic signals.

This work addresses a research gap: no prior study combines user-centered prompt design with generating human-like, proven-effective persuasive pitches.

2.1 Theoretical Background

The evolution of Artificial Intelligence (AI) allows machines to process and produce human language more fluently, which triggers significant changes in multiple sectors [11]. This is rapidly transforming various industries, including the field of marketing; the latter is one of the business areas that has begun to adopt these innovative technologies to optimize and streamline its fundamental operations [12].

Next, key concepts optimal for this study are highlighted:

LLM as deep neural networks that can process and generate text very similar to that produced by humans, through learning from large volumes of textual data [13].

Pitch Decks are concise funding presentations that communicate business value effectively [14]. Prompt design crafts clear inputs (textual/visual) for LLM to generate precise AI responses [15].

Semantic text similarity quantifies meaning alignment between texts, enabling AI to identify linguistic patterns. Computational methods use vector representations to measure sentence-level semantic similarity [16].

Finally, Persuasion detection uses AI to analyze persuasive techniques, employing text mining for ML models and multilingual data for automated detection [17]. Our hierarchical, cross-lingual approach detects persuasion by mining text while encoding rhetorical strategy taxonomies [34]. An mBART-50 model learns hierarchical persuasion strategies (e.g., Ethos/Pathos) and specific techniques (e.g., Loaded Language) to measure human-LLM pitch deck alignment.

3 Methods and Implementation

Using UCD methodology, we develop AI tools to help entrepreneurs create effective Pitch Decks. UCD, established in HCI since the 1980s by Norman and Draper [18], guides the focus of this research.

Figure 2 shows UCD's iterative process, informed by user feedback, ensuring Generative AI meets seed-stage founders' needs effectively.

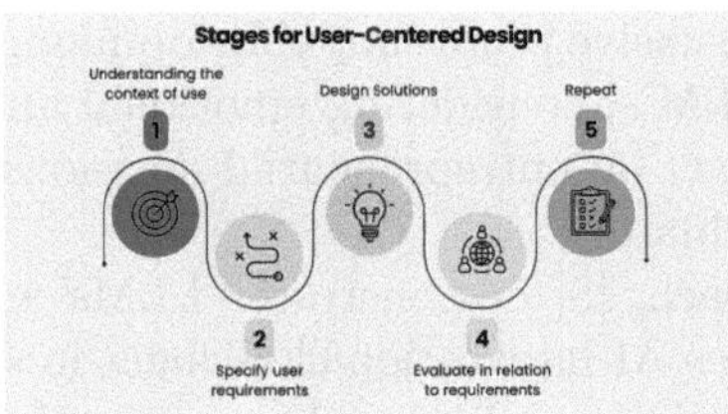

Fig. 2. Stages established in User-Centered Design. With information from [19].

UCD principles engage entrepreneurs throughout design, using research techniques to understand their Pitch Deck challenges and knowledge gaps in crowdfunding contexts.

Startup founders seeking crowdfunding are our users. We design prompts to create investor-attracting Pitch Decks, centering user needs in the process [20]. Multidisciplinary collaboration enables deep user understanding, with continuous iteration ensuring designs meet expectations [19]. Applied to tech entrepreneurs, this methodology adapts Generative AI for marketing needs, creating investor-ready presentations to secure funding.

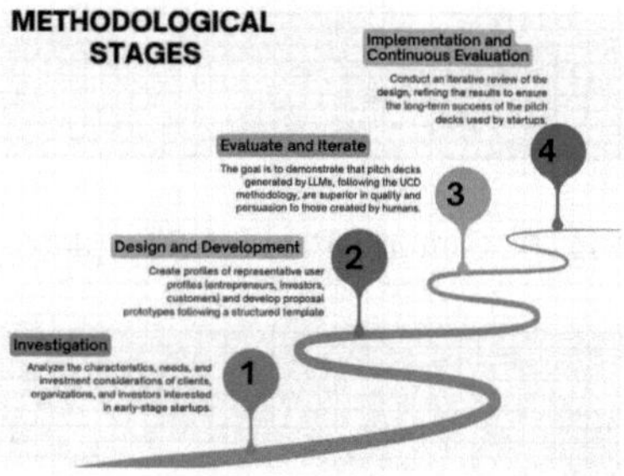

Fig. 3. Specific development objectives.

The Fig. 3, summarizes the development of the methodological stages:

1. Research: Studied AI in marketing and startup needs, analyzing literature and crowdfunding campaigns to understand investor preferences.

2. Design: User profiles entrepreneurs (Fig. 4), were developed to guide service design, following the systematic approach from [21].

Fig. 4. Entrepreneurs User profile.

Prototype templates were then created for the LLM to generate startup-tailored presentations, based on criteria derived from the literature. Three entrepreneur profiles were considered to help guide the system and prompt design, based on an understanding of entrepreneurs' needs, following the stages of the UCD methodology and the generic prompt design was developed.

3. Evaluation and Iteration: We test the prompts using text analysis, persuasion checks, and real user feedback, comparing results with crowdfunding data. We then refine the templates to improve the AI's ability to create successful pitches, focusing on what language works best. For logging prompt iterations, an example of a prompt template for a specific slide, such as the "Problem and Solution" slide, is shown. Below, we describe how this prompt evolved based on user feedback. See Fig. 5, 6, 7.

The product to be evaluated will be the output generated by the designed system, Fig. 8 which shows an interface created for the user to input specific business data (particular elements from Table 1).

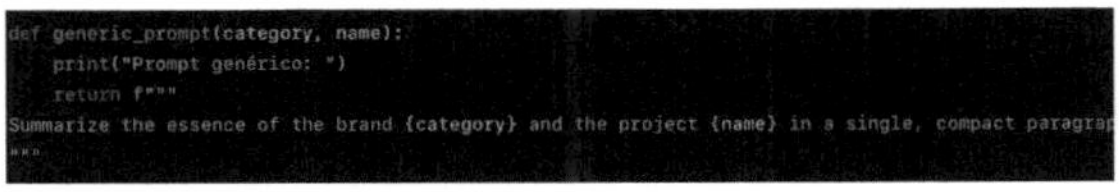

Fig. 5. Generic Prompt Template.

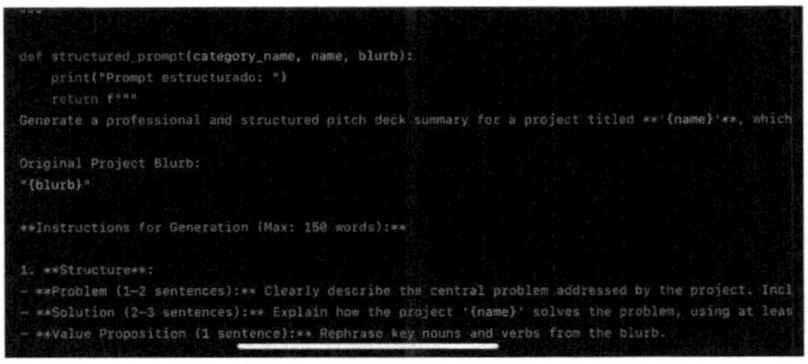

Fig. 6. Structured Prompt Template (Part 1).

4. Implementation and Continuous Evaluation: Final prompt templates are integrated into a user-friendly system for quick pitch deck generation, ensuring effectiveness through continuous refinement for startup success.

3.1 Implementation

For the design of the system to be implemented with users, the system uses NVIDIA's free, unlimited API for model testing and Jupyter Notebook (Python) to analyze Pitch Decks from scraped datasets [26,27].

The cleaning process initially consisted of selecting the variables. The following were established:

- **category_name:** Indicates the category to which the project belongs.
- **blurb:** Variable established to add a brief description or a concise slogan of the project. It is a quick summary of the content or value proposition, designed to capture attention.
- **name:** Represents the full title or name of the project. It is its main identification.
- **backers_count:** This numerical value indicates the number of sponsors or "backers" the project has received. It is a metric of financial support or community participation.
- **staff_pick:** Boolean value (True/False) that indicates whether the project has been selected or featured by the platform's team (in this case, Kickstarter). True indicates it was selected, while False means the opposite.

To exemplify, Table 2 shows a portion of the acquired database, displaying the columns used.

Three instruct-based LLMs were selected for Pitch Deck generation: 'Marin-8b-instruct', 'Deepseek-r1', and 'Qwen3-235b-a22b'. Their diverse NLP capabili-

```
    def structured_prompt(category_name, name, blurb):

2. **Lexical Guidelines**:
- At least 70% lexical overlap.
- Preserve verbs/nouns/adjectives; add synonyms.
- Avoid redundancy.

3. **Style**:
- Natural, persuasive, concise.
- Ensure coherence and logical flow.
"""
```

Fig. 7. Structured Prompt Template (Part 2).

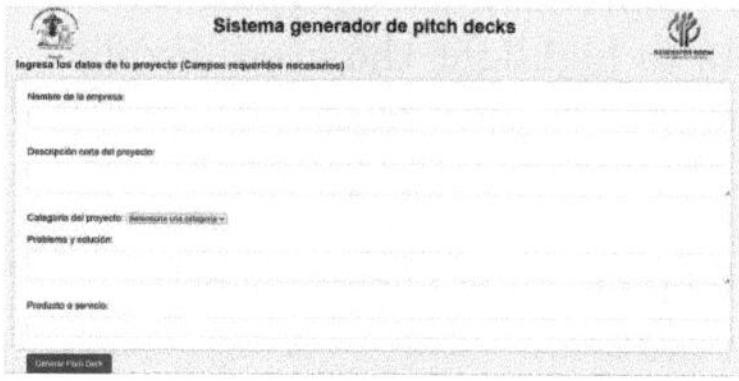

Fig. 8. Interface of our Pitch Deck generation system used during usability tests.

ties ensure precise responses and task versatility, combining strengths to optimize results.

The parameters recommended by the NVIDIA API for each model were used, as described below: For "Marin/Marin-8b-instruct", a temperature of 0.7, top of 0.9, and a maximum of 512 tokens were configured. In the case of "Deepseek-ai/Deepseek-r1", the parameters were a temperature of 0.6, top of 0.7, and up to 4096 tokens. Finally, "Qwen/Qwen3-235b-a22b" used a temperature of 0.2, top of 0.7, a limit of 8192 tokens, and an extra body with "chat template kwargs": "thinking": True.

It is detailed that, for the generation of Pitch Decks, the language used was English to facilitate comparison. After the established prompts, a new dataframe was generated (See Fig. 3).

3.2 Comparison Metrics Between Texts

Four metrics were used for text comparison: Rouge-L, BLEU, Embeddings + Cosine Similarity and Meteor Score.

Rouge-L: Measures the Longest Common Subsequence (LCS) between generated and reference texts, where $Z = [z_1, ..., z_n]$ is a subsequence of $X = [x_1, ..., x_m]$ if there exists an increasing index sequence in X $([i_1, ..., i_k])$ with $z_j = x_{ij}$ [28].

BLEU: Computes the geometric mean of n-gram precision (1–4 words), with a brevity penalty. Precision counts n-grams in machine output that match reference translations, divided by total output words [29].

Table 1. Essential matching elements by authors for creating a Pitch Deck.

Element	Characteristics	Authors Referencing It
Title Slide	First visible slide, direct impact on funders' first impression	[14]
Purpose and Vision	Company's purpose, history, and mission. Emotions to reinforce rational mission. Enthymemes to project future vision	[14, 22, 23]
Value Proposition	Unique benefit offered by the product or service	[24]
Problem and Solution	The problem or "difficulty", unmet need and "why" a problem exists. Rational arguments to highlight the need. Explicit statements about the current market. Solution: Technology and product "solution". Emotions supporting the rational viability and solution to the identified problem	[14, 22, 23, 25]
Product	Rational arguments about benefits.	[22, 23]
Market and Competition	Market analysis, identification of target audience, customer or market. Opportunity (key economic data to demonstrate potential and project growth and competitiveness)	[14, 22–25]
Business Model and Strategy	Priority on economic arguments and data to support revenue strategy. Describe your business model and scalability strategy	[14, 22–25]
Finances and Ask	Detailed, rational projections and key metrics. Proforma projections and funding "ask" (demand or purchase price). Request and use of funds that justify it and persuasive discourse to project investment impact	[14, 22–25]
Entrepreneurial Team	Experience and competencies of the leadership team. Explicit statements about experience	[14, 22–24]
Summary	A clear, concise, and persuasive conclusion of the reasons to invest	[14, 24, 25]

Cosine Similarity + Word Embeddings: Measures vector similarity by calculating the angle between them. Aligned vectors (small angle) indicate similar documents, while divergent vectors show dissimilarity. Documents are represented as points in multidimensional space [30]. Supported by [31] for determining document orientation and information content analysis.

Table 2. Sample of the acquired database.

category_name	blurb	name	backers_count	staff_pick
3D Printing	Organize anything with our innovative 3D printing solution...	Thread Boards 2.0 | 3D printable peg boards with...	2389	True
Animation	Alyson confronts her perfectionism as she struggles to...	Alyssum - A 2D Animated Short Film	75	True

Table 3. Sample of the new dataframe created.

Category	Original Text	Generated Text	Name	Model	Prompt Type
3D Printing	Organize anything with our innovative 3D printing solution...	Thread Boards 2.0 | 3D printable peg boards with...	Thread Boards 2.0	Marin-8b-instruct	generic
3D Printing	Organize anything with our innovative 3D print...	<think>Ok, I need to summarize...	Thread Boards 2.0	Deepseek-r1	generic

Meteor Score: This is an evaluation metric for translations that compares a translation with a reference through word alignments. If there are multiple references, the best match is chosen [32].

4 Results

Initial system development followed an iterative, user-centered approach. A cognitive walkthrough and Expert Usability Analysis by a UX/UI specialist identified key improvement areas in early iterations.

Key findings focused on: interface category clarity, intuitive Pitch Deck audience profiling, screen layout/ergonomics, and a heuristic analysis [33] to identify usability issues. This refined both the interface design and defined tasks/metrics for end-user testing.

4.1 Usability Study Details

After expert-driven improvements, initial usability tests were conducted with diverse entrepreneurs in a controlled lab environment.

The usability tests involved three entrepreneurs from the following industries: healthcare technology, sustainable and environmental development, and technology and product development. They were recruited through university entrepreneurship forums in the state of Oaxaca and interviewed in person, which is where the tests were also conducted. Participants performed two tasks:

1) Completing interface fields (Fig. 8) to generate a pitch deck.
2) Evaluating the AI-generated output (Fig. 9).

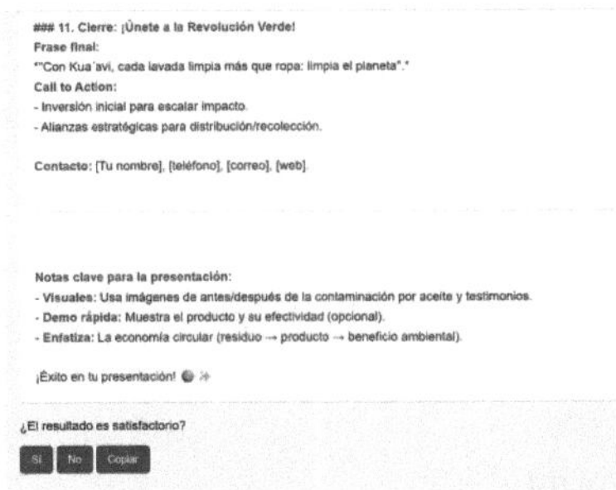

Fig. 9. Result of Pitch Deck generated in usability test with information provided by a user.

The study also assessed interface usability, speed, and pitch deck effectiveness, with data collected for future iterations.

Usability tests yielded highly positive results. Entrepreneurs found the interface intuitive and easy to use, with strong approval for the AI-generated Pitch Decks which were rated as coherent, complete, and professionally surprising - exceeding expectations for an AI tool.

Furthermore, the results showed a high degree of accuracy when compared to the pre-test interviews. The entrepreneurs praised the system's ability to transform their ideas into persuasive narratives, highlighting the clarity of the messaging, logical structure, and an appropriate tone for investors.

At the end of the feedback session, participants were asked to rate their satisfaction with the results on a scale of 1 (minimum) to 10 (maximum). The average satisfaction score was 9/10, with a standard deviation of ± 0.5. This indicates that the ratings were consistently high and close to the average, confirming the system's effectiveness at meeting entrepreneurs' core needs for creating accessible, fast, and effective pitch decks.

Identified improvements were minor, focusing on: refining on-screen instructions, adding customization options, optimizing loading times, and ensuring Spanish-language support for Oaxacan users. These confirm the system's effectiveness in meeting entrepreneurs' core needs for accessible, quick, and effective Pitch Deck creation.

In this work, a total of 1,379 pitch decks were generated and tested at different points in time, consistently yielding very similar outputs across multiple runs using the same prompts.

4.2 Metrics for Human/LLM-Generated Pitch Decks

Table 4 shows results from 690 AI-generated pitch decks using generic prompts. BLEU metrics revealed semantic misalignment with original blurbs, indicating room for improvement. While recall captured key terms, high standard deviation showed inconsistency. Smaller models outperformed larger ones in BLEU, Semantic Similarity, METEOR, and ROUGE F1, while Qwen3 excelled in recall.

Similarly, Table 5 shows structured prompts improved all metrics versus generic ones. Marin-8b-instruct doubled its BLEU score (0.0126→0.0266) and led in semantic similarity, emerging as the most balanced model. Larger models (Deepseek/Qwen) achieved >90.

While the AI generated coherent presentations, in some cases, the larger models (Deepseek and Qwen) showed lower semantic similarity compared to Marin-8B. This is despite their high information recall (Rouge Recall) and could be due to a greater diversity in their output, which sometimes caused them to stray from the key points of the original text.

On the other hand, the AI's strengths were its ability to transform ideas into compelling narratives with a logical structure and a tone appropriate for investors. Figure 10 compares model performance using generic vs. structured prompts across three metrics. With generic prompts, Marin-8b led in semantic similarity and ROUGE F1, showing better content alignment. BLEU scores stayed below 0.02 - acceptable for creative tasks valuing lexical diversity. In con-

Table 4. Average results and standard deviation (±) of the metrics for generic prompts.

Métrics	Marin-8b-instruct	Deepseek-r1	Qwen3-235b	Average
BLEU	0.0126 ± 0.0159	0.0034 ± 0.0027	0.0030 ± 0.0023	0.0063
Semantic Similarity	0.5067 ± 0.1791	0.4688 ± 0.1491	0.4498 ± 0.1436	0.4751
METEOR Score	0.1881 ± 0.0757	0.1086 ± 0.0436	0.0964 ± 0.0386	0.1310
Rouge Precision	0.0737 ± 0.0400	0.0219 ± 0.0087	0.0194 ± 0.0083	0.0383
Rouge Recall	0.2959 ± 0.1208	0.4671 ± 0.1547	0.4843 ± 0.1508	0.4158
Rouge F1	0.1135 ± 0.0504	0.0416 ± 0.0161	0.0370 ± 0.0155	0.0640

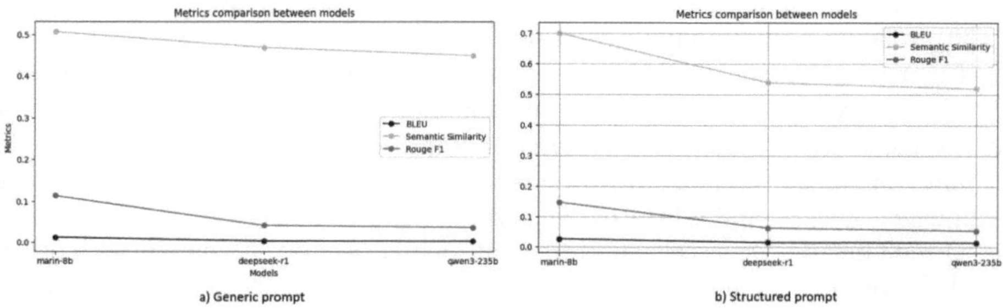

Fig. 10. Metrics comparison between models for a) Generic prompt and b) Structured prompt.

Table 5. Average results and standard deviation (±) of the metrics for structured prompts.

Métrica	Marin-8b-instruct	Deepseek-r1	Qwen3-235b	Average
BLEU	0.0266 ± 0.0232	0.0151 ± 0.0091	0.0144 ± 0.0088	0.0187
Semantic Similarity	0.7004 ± 0.1145	0.5388 ± 0.0926	0.5192 ± 0.1015	0.5861
METEOR Score	0.3091 ± 0.1056	0.1600 ± 0.0530	0.1378 ± 0.0496	0.2023
Rouge Precision	0.0845 ± 0.0321	0.0330 ± 0.0113	0.0278 ± 0.0106	0.0484
Rouge Recall	0.6653 ± 0.1794	0.9208 ± 0.0882	0.9247 ± 0.0959	0.8369
Rouge F1	0.1476 ± 0.0507	0.0634 ± 0.0212	0.0538 ± 0.0199	0.0883

trast, structured prompts improved all metrics, especially semantic similarity, confirming that user-centered designs produce outputs closer to original content. Results demonstrate UCD's direct impact on text generation quality.

Comparing Tables 4 and 5, structured prompts boost Rouge Recall while lowering its deviation, showing UCD-based prompts better capture human-written pitch deck content and reduce generation noise. In particular, larger models (Deepseek-R1 32B, Qwen3 235B) show higher ROUGE recall but lower semantic similarity versus Marin-8B, likely due to greater output diversity. Structured prompts work best with these larger models, reducing performance gaps between them. While ROUGE precision remains low (possibly from size mismatches between human and AI decks), ROUGE recall effectively measures content completeness against human benchmarks. Semantic similarity results showed significant improvements, particularly for the smaller Marin-8B model (16.2% gain vs. larger models). All models displayed higher mean similarity and lower deviation with structured prompts, demonstrating more consistent human-reference alignment. The 0.11-point average gain ([0,1] scale) confirms user-centric prompts substantially improve content generation quality.

4.3 Persuasion Detection in Human/LLM-Generated Pitch Decks

Human pitch decks show diverse persuasion techniques (Fig 11), with Loaded Language and Name Calling most frequent (>40 uses), followed by Smears (>30), reflecting emotionally rich rhetorical styles.

Figure 12 presents the outputs generated using generic prompts for each of the models evaluated in this study. In subfigure (a), Loaded Language emerges as the most dominant label by a large margin, followed by Smears and Name Calling/Labeling. Subfigure (b) reveals an increase in the occurrence of Loaded Language, Smears, and Glittering Generalities (Virtue).

Qwen3 mirrors Deepseek's patterns but focuses heavily on Smears, with other labels being less frequent. This suggests large models share similar persuasive strategies, while smaller ones show more limited rhetorical distributions.

Meanwhile, in the texts generated using structured prompts (Fig. 13), Loaded Language remains highly prevalent across all three models. Qwen3-235b and

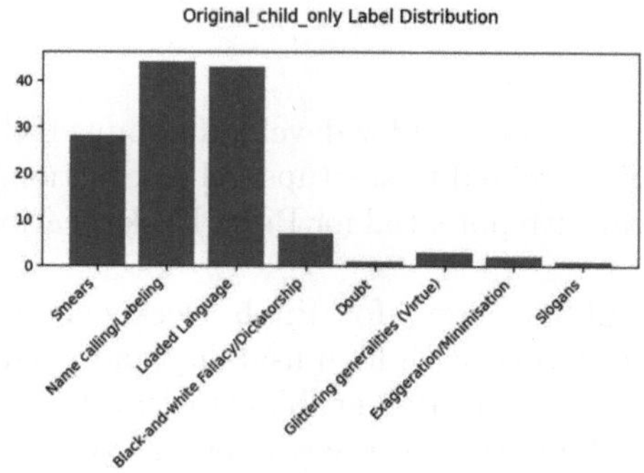

Fig. 11. Histogram of the persuasion techniques detected by the persuasion identification model in the human-created (original) samples.

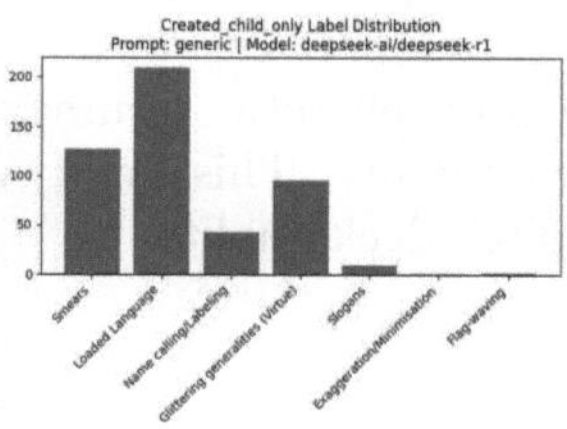

(a) Deepseek-R1

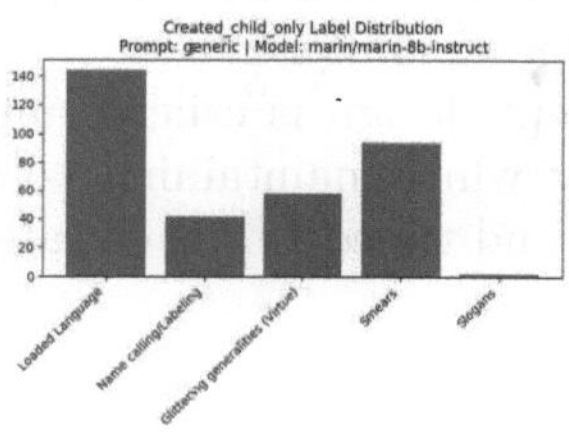

(b) Marin-8b-instruct

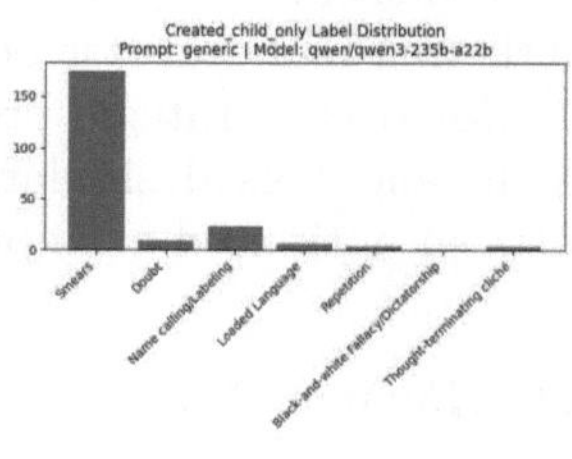

(c) Qwen3-235b-a22b

Fig. 12. Child-only persuasion technique distributions for `created_text` under the **generic** prompt type.

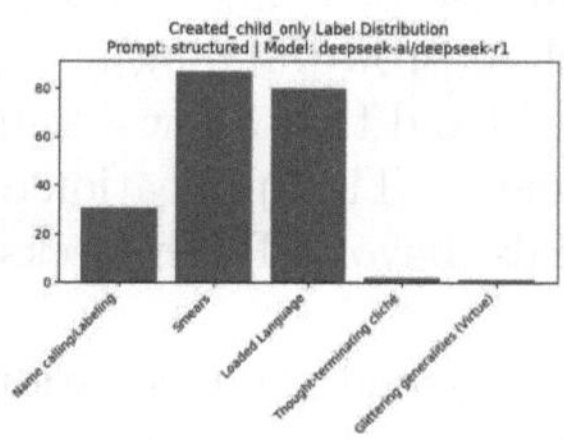

(a) Deepseek-R1

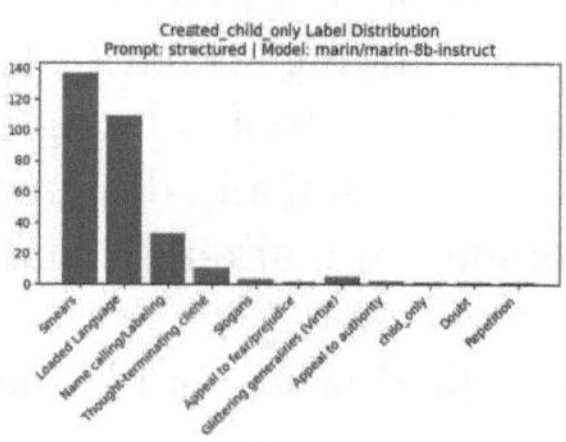

(b) Marin-8b-instruct

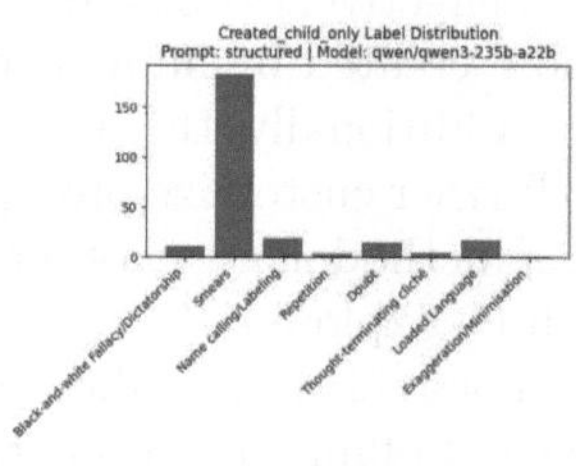

(c) Qwen3-235b-a22b

Fig. 13. Child-only persuasion technique distributions for `created_text` under the **structured** prompt type.

Deepseek-R1 employ this strategy most dominantly, whereas Marin-8b-instruct exhibits a more varied distribution. This model incorporates additional techniques such as Name Calling, Glittering Generalities, Slogans, and others–though to a lesser extent–suggesting a broader rhetorical range.

5 Conclusions

In particular, UCD proves essential for developing impactful, text-based generative marketing strategies tailored to startups. AI integration, particularly LLMs, demonstrates transformative potential for Pitch Deck creation and business marketing.

The UCD-guided LLM system for Pitch Deck generation showed strong results in entrepreneur testing, with high usability and positive feedback requiring only minor tweaks. This approach enables startups to quickly create effective marketing materials with limited resources, offering a practical, low-cost AI solution for fundraising and investor engagement.

Throughout the analysis, AI-generated pitch decks prove feasible and effective, offering entrepreneurs a valuable tool to create compelling, coherent presentations efficiently. This enhances idea communication and provides impactful marketing materials for better visibility.

Moreover, strategic prompt design is crucial–enhancing semantic accuracy, recall, and lexical similarity while maintaining content fidelity. This synergy between optimized prompts and tuned LLMs elevates pitch deck quality.

5.1 Future Work

This work proposes a continuous improvement approach for the developed tools. Future research will focus on expanding the study through a deeper analysis of similarity and persuasion metrics, including experimentation with more language models and parameter configurations to further optimize Pitch Deck generation. The effectiveness of these AI-generated Pitch Decks will also be compared with those created by humans in real funding scenarios (such as crowdfunding).

Additionally, the development of a tool is being considered that allows users to further customize prompts with visual and design elements. The application of this methodology to other persuasive marketing materials, beyond Pitch Decks, will be explored.

For real-world validation, a field study is planned to extend the evaluation beyond offline metrics and laboratory impressions. The goal is to directly compare the effectiveness of AI-generated pitch decks with those created by humans. This validation will be conducted through an A/B test on a crowdfunding platform or at an investment simulation event.

Finally, longitudinal studies will be sought to evaluate the long-term impact of AI-generated Pitch Decks on startup success and the evolution of investor and client preferences regarding AI-generated content.

References

1. Martínez-Ortega, A.G., Medina-Chicaiza, R.P.: Tecnologías en la inteligencia artificial para el marketing: una revisión de la literatura. Pro Sci. **4**(30), 36–47 (2020)

2. Verma, S., Sharma, R., Deb, S., Maitra, D.: Inteligencia artificial en marketing: revisión sistemática y dirección futura de la investigación. Int. J. Inf. Manag. Data Insights (2021). https://doi.org/10.1016/j.jjimei.2020.100002
3. Sabaj, O., Cabezas, P., Varas, G., González-Vergara, C., Pina-Stranger, Á.: Empirical literature on the business pitch: classes, critiques, and future trends. J. Technol. Manag. Innov. **15**(1), 55–63 (2020). https://doi.org/10.4067/S0718-27242020000100055
4. Breum, S.M., Egdal, D.V., Mortensen, V.G., Møller, A.G., Aiello, L.M.: The persuasive power of large language models. In: Proceedings of the International AAAI Conference on Web and Social Media, vol. 18, no. 1, pp. 152–163 (2024). https://doi.org/10.1609/icwsm.v18i1.31304
5. Bordia, S.: Using large language models to assist content generation in persuasive speaking. Intersect Stanford J. Sci. Technol. Soc. (2023)
6. Lallee, A., Muco, N.: Hello! How can I assist you today? An analysis of GPT technology in supporting international entrepreneurship (dissertation). Linnéuniversitetet, Växjö (2023). https://urn.kb.se/resolve?urn=urn:nbn:se:lnu:diva-125787
7. Ilagan, J.B.R., Ilagan, J.R.: A prototype of a chatbot for evaluating and refining student startup ideas using a large language model (2023)
8. Short, C. E., Short, J. C.: The artificially intelligent entrepreneur: ChatGPT, prompt engineering, and entrepreneurial rhetoric creation. J. Bus. Ventur. Insights **19**, e00388 (2023). https://www.sciencedirect.com/science/article/abs/pii/S2352673423000173
9. Puapongsakorn, P., Brazdeikyte, E.: Exploring the Integration of Artificial Intelligence in the Ideation Stage of Product Development in Swedish Startups: Challenges, Opportunities, and Tool Utilization. Lund University Publications (LUP) (2023). https://lup.lub.lu.se/luur
10. Kaminski, J.C., Hopp, C.: Predicting outcomes in crowdfunding campaigns with textual, visual, and linguistic signals. Small Bus. Econ. **55**, 627–649 (2020)
11. Gutiérrez, K.: Generative artificial intelligence: disruption and challenges. Rev. Enfoques **4**(2), 57 (2023). https://revistasdigitales.uniboyaca.edu.co/index.php/EFQ/article/view/1075/838
12. Chintalapati, S., Pandey, S.K.: Inteligencia artificial en marketing: una revisión sistemática de la literatura. Rev. Int. Investigación de Mercado **64**(1), 38–68 (2022). https://doi.org/10.1177/14707853211018428
13. Arroyo Fernández, I.: A very simple introduction to large language models (2024)
14. Shimasaki, C.: Chapter 23 - investor presentations: what do you need in an investor pitch deck? In: Biotechnology Entrepreneurship (Second Edition), Academic Press, pp. 325–336 (2020). https://doi.org/10.1016/B978-0-12-815585-1.00023-1
15. Doria, M.V., Korzeniewski, M.I., Flores, C.V., Del Prado, A.M.: Herramientas y tips para generar prompts con Inteligencia Artificial (2023)
16. Arroyo-Fernández, I., Méndez-Cruz, C.F., Sierra, G., Torres-Moreno, J.M., Sidorov, G.: Unsupervised sentence representations as word information series: revisiting TF–IDF. Comput. Speech Lang., 107–129 (2019). https://doi.org/10.1016/j.csl.2019.01.005
17. Piskorski, J., et al.: News Categorization, Framing and Persuasion Techniques: Annotation Guidelines. European Commission, Ispra (2023)
18. Interaction Design Foundation - IxDF: What is User Centered Design (UCD)? (2016). https://www.interaction-design.org/literature/topics/user-centered-design
19. Norman, D.A., Draper, S.W. (eds.): User-Centered System Design: New Perspectives on Human-Computer Interaction. Lawrence Erlbaum Associates (1986)

20. Mao, J.Y., Vredenburg, K., Smith, P.W., Carey, T.: The state of user-centered design practice. Commun. ACM **48**(3), 105–109 (2005). https://doi.org/10.1145/1047671.1047677
21. Hernández Salazar, P.: El perfil del usuario de información. Investigación bibliotecológica: Archivonomía, bibliotecología e información **7**(15) (1993). https://doi.org/10.22201/iibi.0187358xp.1993.15.3816
22. Fernández-Vázquez, J.S., Álvarez-Delgado, R.C.: Persuasive strategies in the SME entrepreneurial pitch: functional and discursive considerations. Econ. Res.-Ekonomska Istraživanja **33**(1), 2342–2359 (2019). https://doi.org/10.1080/1331677X.2019.1683462
23. van Werven, R., Bouwmeester, O., Cornelissen, J.P.: Pitching a business idea to investors: how new venture founders use micro-level rhetoric to achieve narrative plausibility and resonance. Int. Small Bus. J. **37**(3), 193–214 (2019). https://doi.org/10.1177/0266242618818249
24. Cabezas, P., Bateman, J.: Estructura de diapositivas de presentaciones de un programa de aceleración. Bus. Prof. Commun. Q. (2024). https://doi.org/10.1177/23294906241257448
25. Baehr, E., Loomis, E.: Get Backed: Craft Your Story, Build the Perfect Pitch Deck, and Launch the Venture of Your Dreams. Harvard Business Review Press (2015)
26. Kickstarter. https://www.kickstarter.com/
27. WebRobots.io: Kickstarter Datasets. https://webrobots.io/kickstarter-datasets/
28. Lin, C.Y.: Rouge: a package for automatic evaluation of summaries. In: Text Summarization Branches Out, pp. 74–81 (2004). https://www.microsoft.com/en-us/research/wp-content/uploads/2016/07/
29. Mayor, A., Alegria, I., de Ilarraza, A.D., Labaka, G., Lersundi, M., Sarasola, K.: Evaluación de un sistema de traducción automática basado en reglas o por qué BLEU sólo sirve para lo que sirve. Procesamiento del Lenguaje Nat. **43**, 197–205 (2009)
30. Genc, Z., Babieva, N.S., Zarembo, G.V., Lobanova, E.V., Malakhova, V.Y.: The views of special education department students on the use of assistive technologies in special education. Int. J. Emerg. Technol. Learn. **16**(19), 69–80 (2021). https://online-journals.org/index.php/i-jet/article/view/26025
31. Januzaj, Y., Luma, A.: Cosine similarity-a computing approach to match similarity between higher education programs and job market demands based on maximum number of common words. IJET **17**, 258–268 (2022). https://doi.org/10.3991/ijet.v17i12.30375
32. Agarwal, A., Lavie, A.: METEOR, M-BLEU and M-TER: evaluation metrics for high-correlation with human rankings of machine translation output. In: Proceedings of the Third Workshop on Statistical Machine Translation (StatMT '08), Association for Computational Linguistics, USA, pp. 115–118 (2008). https://doi.org/10.5555/1626394.1626406
33. Nielsen, J.: Usability Engineering. Morgan Kaufmann, San Francisco (1994)
34. Chatterjee, N., Pranjić, M., Koloski, B., Pivovarova, L., Pollak, S.: Whatdoyoumeme at SemEval-2024 task 4: hierarchical-label-aware persuasion detection using translated texts. In: Kr. Ojha, A., Seza Doŭruöz, A., Tayyar Madabushi, H., Da San Martino, G., Rosenthal, S., Rosá, A. (eds.), Proceedings of the 18th International Workshop on Semantic Evaluation (SemEval-2024), pp. 1537–1543. Association for Computational Linguistics, Mexico City, Mexico (2024). https://doi.org/10.18653/v1/2024.semeval-1.220

A Natural Language Processing Approach for Early Detection of Suicide and Depression Risk on Social Media Platforms

Estefanía De la Cruz-Bautista(✉)

Universidad Mundo Maya,
Campus Villahermosa, Jefatura Académica de Arquitectura, Ingenierías y Computación, Villahermosa, México
vlicd2231002@universidadmundomaya.edu.mx, fanydlacruzb@gmail.com

Abstract. This paper presents an NLP-based approach for the early detection of mental health risks, focusing on depression and suicidal ideation. The study uses publicly available datasets from Reddit, Kaggle, and Mendeley, applying a dual scoring strategy (cleaned vs. original text) to enhance interpretability. The model demonstrates solid performance: when classifying texts into two categories (risk/no risk), it achieves an accuracy of 86.02% with an F1-score of 0.84 and recall of 0.85. When expanded into three categories (depression/suicide/none), accuracy decreases to 71.09%, with an average F1-score of 0.70. These results highlight the challenge of differentiating closely related emotional states while ensuring explainability. Beyond technical contributions, the study emphasizes the ethical use of NLP in mental health, underlining that such models should serve as supportive tools and not replacements for professional intervention.

Keywords: Natural Languaje Processing · Mental Health · Suicide Detection · Depression · Tokenizacion · Lemmatization

1 Introduction

In the digital age, millions of individuals turn daily to platforms like Reddit to express their thoughts, emotions, and personal experiences. This continuous stream of spontaneous, emotionally charged textual content represents a valuable source of data for studying users' mental states, particularly for the early detection of risk signals associated with depression and suicidal ideation.

Mental health is a global priority, and the rising rates of affective disorders and suicide highlight the urgent need for automated monitoring tools that can complement the work of clinical professionals. In this context, Natural Language Processing (NLP) has emerged as a key discipline for analyzing human language for diagnostic purposes, thanks to its ability to extract semantic, syntactic, and emotional patterns from large volumes of text.

This study proposes a supervised text classification approach aimed at identifying signs of depression and suicide risk in anonymous Reddit posts. By collecting, cleaning,

L. Martínez-Villaseñor et al. (Eds.): MICAI 2025, CCIS 2712, pp. 245–256, 2025.
https://doi.org/10.1007/978-3-032-08704-1_19

and analyzing public datasets, we developed a logistic regression model capable not only of assigning risk labels but also of pinpointing the specific phrases that triggered the classification, thereby enhancing the interpretability of the system.

The research question guiding this study is: Can NLP techniques, combined with an interpretability layer, contribute to the early detection of depressive and suicidal language in online platforms? Accordingly, the objectives of this work are: (1) to build a classification model capable of distinguishing between risk and non-risk content with acceptable accuracy; (2) to extend the classification to three categories (depression, suicide, none) while analyzing the associated performance trade-offs; and (3) to propose a transparent and interpretable framework that can later be integrated into real-world applications in collaboration with mental health professionals.

2 Related Works

The application of Natural Language Processing (NLP) in the context of mental health has seen steady growth in recent years. Various studies have demonstrated that machine learning algorithms can identify linguistic patterns associated with emotional states such as sadness, anxiety, or hopelessness—common indicators among individuals at risk of depression or suicide [1, 2].

On social platforms like Reddit, previous research has leveraged the unique characteristics of thematic subreddits such as r/depression or r/SuicideWatch to develop risk detection models. Recent approaches often combine classical NLP techniques—such as tokenization, lemmatization, and TF-IDF vectorization—with classification algorithms like support vector machines, random forests, or logistic regression to capture both the explicit content and the emotional context of user posts [3, 4].

However, one of the most common limitations lies in the limited interpretability of the results, particularly when using complex models. To address this, the present study proposes an alternative that aims to balance accuracy with human interpretability. This is achieved through a supervised model that not only classifies text but also highlights specific phrases associated with emotional risk. Such an approach facilitates practical implementation in clinical or digital moderation settings, where transparency and explainability are essential for informed decision-making [5].

Recent research in NLP and mental health has increasingly adopted deep learning and transformer-based models (e.g., BERT, RoBERTa, DistilBERT) for text classification. These approaches have shown improvements in capturing contextual embeddings but often lack transparency, which limits their clinical applicability.

3 Materials and Methods

This study is based on the analysis of textual data extracted from various Reddit communities focused on mental health, particularly **r/depression** and **r/SuicideWatch**. These forums provide a valuable source of user-generated content for the automatic detection of suicidal ideation and depressive symptoms using **Natural Language Processing (NLP)** techniques. The data were compiled from two main public repositories: the **Kaggle** platform (dataset: *Reddit Dataset: r/depression and r/SuicideWatch*) [6], and **Mendeley**

Data, which hosts the *Suicidal Ideation Detection Reddit Dataset*, consisting of two complementary parts [7]. In total, three CSV files were used as raw material for preprocessing, each with distinct structures that required thorough cleaning, standardization, and integration procedures.

The entire processing pipeline was implemented using **Python 3**, within the **Google Colab** environment. This cloud-based platform facilitates large-scale data manipulation without the need for local setup and supports a wide range of powerful libraries for data handling (pandas, numpy) and text processing (nltk, scikit-learn).

Dataset Cleaning and Integration

- **Column normalization:** Due to inconsistencies in column names across datasets (e.g., some using "text" and "label", others "Post" and "Label"), a harmonization step was necessary. Core columns were standardized as "Title", "Post", and "Label". The Mendeley datasets included a "Title" field, while the Kaggle dataset did not. Additionally, the Mendeley files had two classes in the Label column (suicidal, non-suicidal), whereas the Kaggle dataset used suicidewatch and depression.
- **Datasets unification:** To maximize the volume and utility of the available data, we decided to construct three integrated datasets, each structured to facilitate subsequent analysis and classification:

  o Post dataset: This dataset retains the full textual content of all posts along with their original labels. It includes three categories: non-suicidal, suicidewatch, and depression.
  o Title dataset: This dataset contains only the titles of the posts and their corresponding labels. Since only the Mendeley datasets included titles, this set comprises only two categories: non-suicidal and suicidal.
  o The Big Dataset: This is a comprehensive dataset in which both titles and post texts were considered as individual entries. The union of the previous two datasets resulted in a more robust and extensive corpus.

- **Column selection:** To streamline downstream processing, all datasets were structured using only two core columns: Post (text) and Label. For modeling purposes, the Label column was further transformed into binary classification variables, resulting in three separate fields: non_suicidal, suicidal_watch, and depression. The original categorical label was removed after that conversion.
- **Textual cleaning:** During preprocessing, several errors patterns were identified and corrected manually, as these introduced significant noise into the model. One of the most frequent issues involved corrupted characters where apostrophes (') were replaced with sequences such as â€™, likely due to character encoding mismatches. A custom function was implemented to automatically correct these instances.

```
df_post['non_suicidal'] = df_post['Label'].eq('Non-Suicidal').astype(int)
df_post['suicidal_watch'] = df_post['Label'].isin(['Suicidal', 'SuicideWatch']).astype(int)
df_post['depression'] = df_post['Label'].str.lower().eq('depression').astype(int)
```

Fig. 1. Presents the code used to perform this multi-label binarization.

```
                                                Post  non_suicidal  \
0  I recently went through a breakup and she said...             0
1  I do not know how to navigate these feelings, ...             0
2  So I have been with my bf for 5 months , and h...             0
3  I am so exhausted of this. Just when I think I...             0
4  I have been severly bullied since i was 5 till...             0

   suicidal_watch  depression
0               0           1
1               0           1
2               0           1
3               1           0
4               0           1
```

Fig. 2. Illustrates the final structure of the three resulting datasets.

```
df_post_final['Post'] = df_post_final['Post'].str.replace('â€™', "'")
```

Fig. 3. Shows the snippet used to address this character-level error

Another major challenge was the frequent use of contractions (e.g., "can't", "won't"), typical in informal language on social media. To improve semantic consistency and enhance tokenization, these contractions were manually expanded to their full forms (e.g., "can't" → "cannot") [8] (Figs. 1, 2, and 3).

```
df_post_final['Post'] = df_post_final['Post'].str.replace("won't", "will not", regex=False)
df_post_final['Post'] = df_post_final['Post'].str.replace("can't", "cannot", regex=False)
df_post_final['Post'] = df_post_final['Post'].str.replace("n't", " not", regex=False)
df_post_final['Post'] = df_post_final['Post'].str.replace("'re", " are", regex=False)
df_post_final['Post'] = df_post_final['Post'].str.replace("'ve", " have", regex=False)
df_post_final['Post'] = df_post_final['Post'].str.replace("'ll", " will", regex=False)
df_post_final['Post'] = df_post_final['Post'].str.replace("'d", " would", regex=False)
df_post_final['Post'] = df_post_final['Post'].str.replace("'m", " am", regex=False)
df_post_final['Post'] = df_post_final['Post'].str.replace("'s", " is", regex=False)
```

Fig. 4. Demonstrates the code implementation for expanding these textual contractions.

To conduct the tasks of data cleaning, text processing, analysis, and modeling, several specialized Python libraries were employed within the collaborative environment of Google Colab. Each tool played a key role in the different stages of this study (Fig. 4).

The pandas library was the backbone for structured data manipulation. It enabled the loading of CSV files, dataset merging, normalization of column names, label transformation, and the creation of coherent tabular structures for analysis. In parallel, numpy facilitated efficient numerical and logical operations, supporting streamlined processing of data arrays.

For text cleaning tasks, re (Python's regular expressions module) was essential in identifying and correcting encoding issues, removing unwanted or corrupted characters, and expanding common contractions to their full forms, thereby improving the quality of the textual data. Additionally, the string library provided targeted functions for removing punctuation and filtering non-alphabetic characters, contributing to more precise text sanitation.

Natural Language Processing (NLP) was handled through nltk (Natural Language Toolkit), which offered robust tools for sentence and word tokenization, stopword removal (i.e., filtering out semantically insignificant words), and lemmatization—the reduction of words to their base forms. These preprocessing steps were vital for converting free-form text into structured input suitable for machine learning algorithms.

For modeling and evaluation, scikit-learn (sklearn) was used. This widely adopted library allowed for splitting the dataset into training and testing sets, transforming text into numerical vectors using the TfidfVectorizer method, training a logistic regression classifier, and evaluating its performance through metrics such as precision, recall, F1-score, and confusion matrix.

Finally, for the visualization stage, matplotlib and seaborn were utilized to generate insightful plots that illustrated model performance and word distributions across categories. Additionally, wordcloud was applied to create word clouds segmented by class (suicidal, depressive, and non-suicidal), offering a visual perspective on the most frequent terms within each emotional category.

Together, these tools built a comprehensive and rigorous analytical pipeline, ensuring that the processing and modeling respected both the semantic integrity and the emotional context embedded in user-generated Reddit content.

4 Experimental Procedure

The objective of this study was to develop a supervised text classification model for early detection of suicidal ideation and depressive symptoms from Reddit posts. Implementation was carried out in Python 3 within Google Colab, leveraging NLP techniques. The main training dataset used was the Post Dataset, which was thoroughly cleaned and structured before model development.

1 **Text Preprocessing and Initial Analysis**: The first phase involved thorough text normalization involved correcting encoding anomalies, particularly sequences like 'â€™' which had erroneously replaced apostrophes ('). These distortions, commonly resulting from character encoding mismatches, were systematically addressed. Moreover, informal contractions were expanded into their complete forms to reduce linguistic ambiguity. These corrections were vital due to the high occurrence of colloquial and emotionally nuanced language typical of social media discourse.

Linguistic preprocessing followed, using tools from the NLTK library. This included tokenization, stopword removal, and lemmatization, which allowed for semantically uniform representations by reducing words to their base forms. These preprocessing steps facilitated a more accurate downstream classification.

2 **Exploratory Data Analysis and Visual Support:** Exploratory analysis was fundamental to understanding the dataset and developing initial insights. Word frequency analysis was conducted using Counter and nltk.FreqDist to identify key terms within

each risk category: non-suicidal, suicidal_watch, and depression. These frequent terms supported the construction of a preliminary keyword dictionary for each class.

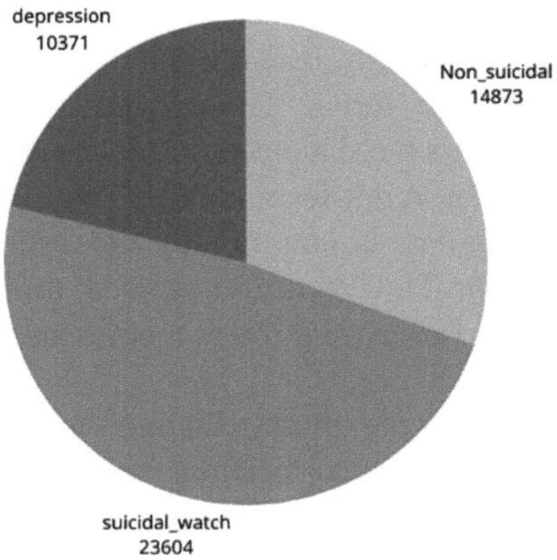

Fig. 5. Post Dataset Distribution by Category

Word clouds were generated for each category to provide a visual representation of dominant terms. These, along with frequency bar plots, were essential not only for exploratory interpretation but also for validating and enriching the manually curated dictionaries used in the classification logic (Fig. 5).

Additionally, these visualizations played a central role in contextualizing language usage within each class. Although many terms appeared across categories—particularly between suicidal and depressive content—their relative frequency and co-occurrence patterns provided deeper semantic cues. This prompted the construction of a secondary frequency analysis per term, in which each word's context and proximity to high-risk expressions were measured to determine their discriminative value. This step was critical to disambiguating emotionally intense but semantically overlapping posts. The final keyword dictionaries were refined based on both absolute frequency and contextual relevance, strengthening the classification model's sensitivity and interpretability (Fig. 6).

As observed, both the depression and suicidal categories shared many high-frequency terms, complicating their distinction through word frequency alone. Therefore, contextual analysis was necessary to differentiate between these closely related categories (Figs. 7 and 8).

3 **Text Vectorization:** After preprocessing, the text data were transformed into numerical format using the TF-IDF (Term Frequency-Inverse Document Frequency) technique via TfidfVectorizer from scikit-learn. This approach weighed each word based on its frequency relative to other documents in the corpus, thus penalizing overly common terms and highlighting those with higher discriminative power across classes.

Fig. 6. WordClouds for each category in the dataset

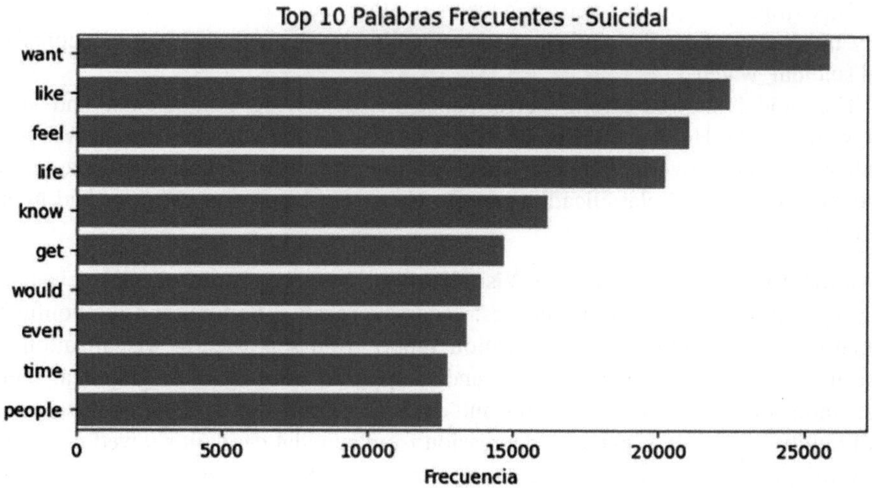

Fig. 7. Top 10 most frequent words in texts labeled as *Suicidal.*

4 **Model Construction and Training:** The core classifier used was logistic regression, implemented using scikit-learn. The dataset was split into training (80%) and testing (20%) subsets. A dual cross-validation strategy was adopted to improve model reliability:

- Internal validation was performed using cross_val_score during training.
- External evaluation was applied to the reserved test set.

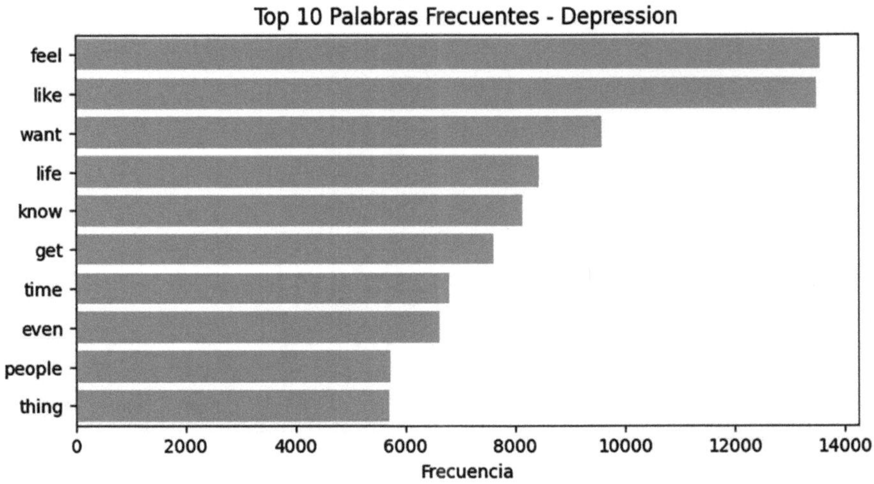

Fig. 8. Top 10 most frequent words in texts labeled as *Depression.*

This strategy improved performance estimation and reduced overfitting—particularly important when distinguishing semantically close categories such as depression and suicidal_watch.

The model showed strong performance in identifying non-suicidal and suicidal_watch posts. However, differentiating depression from suicidal content was more challenging due to overlapping emotional and linguistic cues. This was reflected in the confusion matrix and classification report, where the depression category had higher misclassification rates.

5 **Model Evaluation and Result Visualization:** Model performance was evaluated using standard classification metrics: accuracy, recall, F1-score, and the confusion matrix, all computed via classification_report from scikit-learn. Visualizations of results were created using seaborn and matplotlib, offering clear graphical representations of the model's strengths and areas for improvement. Despite the model's difficulty in sharply separating depression from suicidal cases, it showed promising overall performance and potential as a supportive tool for monitoring emotional risk in digital communities.

5 Results and Discussion

The model trained on the Post Dataset demonstrates a promising ability to identify and classify textual content related to mental health risks, particularly depression and suicidal ideation, through natural language processing techniques. The logistic regression classifier exhibited high overall accuracy when distinguishing between non-suicidal content and emotionally vulnerable posts, aligning with previous findings in NLP-based suicide detection studies [9].

A key enhancement in this study was the incorporation of a dual-scoring interpretability layer. After classification, each user input was further broken into sentences, which were evaluated both in their original form and in a lemmatized, cleaned version. A custom-built function analyzed the presence of terms related to suicide or depression using a domain-informed dictionary. Scores were assigned to each sentence based on whether key terms appeared in both original and lemmatized versions (2 points), only one (1 point), or neither (0 points). This allowed the system not only to assign an overall category to the input but also to highlight specific risk-related sentences, enhancing the model's explainability and usefulness in real-world applications.

Although the model shows strong results in detecting risk overall, it still faces challenges in distinguishing between depression and suicidal ideation. These categories often overlap semantically, as individuals experiencing depression may also use language suggestive of suicidal thoughts, even if no immediate risk is present. This semantic blur leads to occasional misclassifications between these two classes. However, this issue reflects the complexity of human psychology and highlights the need for more context-aware representations in future versions of the system.

To address this, an additional step was integrated into the analytical pipeline: after identifying the most frequent terms per category, a second-layer contextual analysis was conducted. Each word was evaluated not just by how often it appeared, but by the nature of the surrounding phrases and the emotional polarity of the sentences where it occurred. This process allowed the model to infer subtle distinctions between expressions of chronic sadness and imminent risk. These insights emerged partly from the visual inspection of the word clouds and frequency graphs, which highlighted lexical convergence between depression and suicide classes but also hinted at differentiated narrative structures. This analytical depth improved the model's decision logic and informed the scoring function used to evaluate sentence-level risk.

Despite its technical nature, this project is not merely a data science exercise; it is conceived as a tool of practical value in support of mental health professionals. By automatically flagging content that may indicate distress, the system could one day assist clinicians or online moderators in identifying individuals who may benefit from early intervention. In this sense, the model could contribute to saving lives, offering rapid, scalable, and explainable detection of warning signs in open digital conversations.

Moreover, Reddit as a data source adds several strengths to the model's real-world applicability:

- Its topic-specific subreddits (like r/depression or r/SuicideWatch) enable precise data targeting.
- The anonymity encourages honest, emotionally raw self-disclosure.
- Public datasets and API access facilitate ethical, large-scale research.
- The natural, non-clinical language in Reddit posts mirrors how people genuinely express distress.
- Reddit's use in prior scientific work provides a strong precedent for methodological validation.

Together, these factors ensure that the model is trained not only on simulated examples but on authentic linguistic patterns associated with real mental health concerns. This strengthens its potential for deployment in preventive care systems, where it can serve as a supportive assistant to professionals, not as a replacement. Its role is to enhance human capacity to detect subtle signs in overwhelming volumes of text data task otherwise unfeasible through manual review alone.

In the binary classification setup (risk/no risk), the model reached an accuracy of 86.02%, with precision = 0.83, recall = 0.85, and F1-score = 0.84. The confusion matrix indicated balanced performance, with relatively few false positives (8%) and false negatives (6%).

In the multiclass scenario (depression/suicide/none), performance decreased, achieving an accuracy of 71.09%. Class-wise results showed F1 = 0.72 for depression, F1 = 0.68 for suicide, and F1 = 0.70 for none. Misclassifications were most frequent between depression and suicide, reflecting their overlapping linguistic signals.

These findings underline the inherent difficulty of distinguishing between depressive and suicidal expressions, which often share overlapping linguistic markers. From a clinical perspective, it is crucial to minimize false negatives, as undetected risk may delay necessary intervention. False positives, while less harmful, may lead to unnecessary alerts that could overwhelm professionals. Future work should therefore prioritize techniques that balance sensitivity and specificity, possibly through hybrid models integrating linguistic and behavioral features. Beyond technical improvements such as transformers, future research must also include cultural adaptation, professional validation, and responsible deployment strategies to ensure ethical and context-sensitive use.

6 Conclusions

This study confirms that NLP techniques can provide valuable support in the early detection of depression and suicide risk. The dual scoring approach improved interpretability, offering both original and cleaned text perspectives. While results are encouraging (86.02% accuracy in binary tasks, 71.09% in multiclass tasks), the model is not intended to replace mental health professionals but to serve as a supportive tool. Responsible integration into real-world settings requires clinical validation, explicit handling of false positives and negatives, and collaboration with professionals to ensure that such systems are used ethically and effectively.

The primary strength of the model lies not only in its technical performance but also in its interpretability. The segmentation of input into sentences, combined with a domain-informed scoring system based on keyword matching, enabled the model to highlight not only the overall risk classification but also the specific parts of the text that triggered it. This approach marks a substantial improvement over traditional “black-box” models by enhancing the transparency and clinical usability of predictions.

Nonetheless, the model also faces limitations. The distinction between depressive and suicidal content remains a persistent challenge, as the two categories often overlap in language. Many depressive posts contain ambiguous, hopeless, or emotionally heavy expressions that can be misinterpreted as suicidal cues. These misclassifications are not necessarily errors of the model, but rather reflections of the intrinsic complexity of human emotional states and the nuanced nature of natural language.

Nevertheless, by incorporating visual tools such as word clouds and frequency bar graphs during the exploratory phase, this study managed to identify key linguistic similarities and differences between the two risk categories. This insight led to the creation of a refined context-sensitive keyword dictionary, which was not based solely on frequency but also on semantic behavior. These methodological choices enhanced the model's interpretability and its ability to detect nuanced emotional shifts. The use of a dual-frequency approach—first for identifying high-occurrence words, then for analyzing their contextual embedding—was fundamental in achieving more reliable risk stratification.

Importantly, this project was never intended as a purely academic or technical exercise. Its broader objective is to support mental health professionals by providing automated tools that may assist in the early detection of individuals at risk. If properly integrated into ethical, human-supervised systems, models like this could serve as early warning mechanisms, complementing the efforts of psychologists, psychiatrists, counselors, or digital platform moderators. Rather than replacing human intervention, the system is meant to enhance human capabilities, allowing for scalable monitoring and faster responses.

Moreover, the use of real, unfiltered, and emotionally rich data from Reddit strengthens the model's applicability to real-world conditions. Unlike artificial or clinical datasets, Reddit provides an environment where individuals express their emotions freely, informally, and with significant variation in language style. Training on such data ensures that the model is grounded in the actual linguistic landscape of those who are suffering, rather than an idealized or sanitized version.

This work also opens several avenues for future research. Promising directions include the use of deep semantic models such as BERT or RoBERTa, the refinement of multiclass classification strategies, and the development of interactive dashboards that allow mental health professionals to visualize and interpret model results with clarity. Thus, while the current system demonstrates strong performance, it also lays the groundwork for future advancements that combine technical rigor, ethical responsibility, and human-centered design in the service of emotional well-being.

References

1. Martinez-Romo, J., Reneses, B., Martínez-Capella, I., Araujo, L., Sevilla-Llewellyn-Jones, J., Seara-Aguilar, G.: Detecting signs of non-suicidal self-injury in psychiatric medical reports using language analysis. Procesamiento del Lenguaje Natural **69**, 129–140 (2022). https://doi.org/10.26342/2022-69-11
2. De Choudhury, M., Gamon, M., Counts, S., Horvitz, E.: Predicting Depression via Social Media (2013). www.aaai.org
3. De Carvalho Cardoso, V., Fhillipi, A., Silva, M., Sinoara, R.A., Rezende, S.O., Calçada, D.B.: Detecting Suicidal Ideation on Tweets
4. Yeskuatov, E., Chua, S.-L., Foo, L.K.: Leveraging Reddit for suicidal ideation detection: a review of machine learning and natural language processing techniques. Int. J. Environ. Res. Public Health **19**(16), 10347 (2022). https://doi.org/10.3390/ijerph191610347
5. Gupta, C., Jogdand, S., Kumar, M.: Reviewing the impact of social media on the mental health of adolescents and young adults. Cureus (2022). https://doi.org/10.7759/cureus.30143

6. Rogoulet, X.: Reddit dataset: r/depression and r/SuicideWatch
7. Matin Mafi, M.M.H., Alam, M.S.: Suicidal Ideation Detection Reddit Dataset
8. Slagoski, J.D.: Professional Learning Practices and Beliefs of an Online Community of English Language Teachers
9. Akhtar, K., Yaseen, M.U., Imran, M., Khattak, S.B.A., Nasralla, M.M.: Predicting inmate suicidal behavior with an interpretable ensemble machine learning approach in smart prisons. PeerJ Comput. Sci. **10** (2024). https://doi.org/10.7717/peerj-cs.2051

Automatic Classification of BI-RADS in Spanish Radiology Reports Using Transformers and Traditional Machine Learning Approaches

Dimitri Semenov-Flores[1], Jesús-Alejandro Torres-Hurtado[2], Helena Gomez-Adorno[2](✉), José Luis Vázquez Noguera[3], and Julio César Mello-Román[3]

[1] Facultad de Ciencias, Universidad Nacional Autónoma de México, Coyoacán, 04510 Mexico City, Mexico
dimavita@ciencias.unam.mx

[2] Instituto de Investigaciones en Matemáticas Aplicadas y en Sistemas, Universidad Nacional Autónoma de México, Coyoacán, 04510 Mexico City, Mexico
jesusalejandro030803@gmail.com, helena.gomez@iimas.unam.mx

[3] Universidad Americana, Asunción 1029, Paraguay
{jose.vazquez,julio.mello}@ua.edu.py

Abstract. Mammography reports are crucial for the early detection of breast cancer; however, their unstructured format and high volume pose challenges for automated evaluation. This study aims to classify mammography reports by BI-RADS scores using both transformer-based models and classical machine learning approaches. We used a dataset of 4,357 annotated reports to train and evaluate the models. Three classification tasks were explored: (1) binary classification of reports into high- and low-priority groups, (2) multiclass classification based on BI-RADS categories, and (3) a cascaded approach that combines both. Model performance was assessed using F1-score, precision, and recall, with the F1-score serving as the primary comparison metric. Results show that classical machine learning and transformer-based models achieved comparable performance across all tasks. For Task 1, we found that models struggled to correctly classify underrepresented classes. In contrast, Task 2 showed improved results across all models and the highest scores in the F1-score metric. Task 3 demonstrated that the cascaded approach improves multiclass classification performance, but it depends a lot in the first binary classification.

Keywords: Mammography reports · Breast cancer · BI-RADS

1 Introduction

Breast cancer is one of the most common oncological diseases worldwide, and early detection can mean the difference between life and death for patients [10]. In this detection step, mammography reports play a key role, especially those

L. Martínez-Villaseñor et al. (Eds.): MICAI 2025, CCIS 2712, pp. 257–273, 2025.
https://doi.org/10.1007/978-3-032-08704-1_20

that follow the BI-RADS (Breast Imaging Reporting and Data System) classification, a system designed to standardize information and thus facilitate diagnosis and treatment [1]. However, manually reviewing and classifying reports is time-consuming, and since it depends heavily on the specialist's judgment, this can lead to errors. With the advancement of technology, a possible solution emerges: automated tools that allow for the rapid and accurate processing of these types of clinical texts [2]. This challenge becomes even greater in Spanish-speaking countries, where natural language processing (NLP) resources focused on the medical field are still scarce compared to those developed in English.

Natural Language Processing (NLP) techniques have been applied in the medical field, with transformer-based models proving particularly effective in text classification [7]. Compared to traditional rule-based systems or classic machine learning models, transformers are quite good at identifying linguistic patterns within texts and, as a result, better understanding the medical context, allowing for considerably better performance [3]. In this project, two different strategies were applied: first, a traditional approach that utilizes machine learning models along with a search for the best hyperparameters; and second, more advanced transformer-based models, which were specifically trained to work with Spanish medical texts. With this comparison, we gain a clearer understanding of the performance and advantages of each approach in solving this type of task.

We propose a methodology consisting of three key tasks to analyze the performance of our models that will perform the BI-RADS classification of medical texts: (1) The first task is a multiclass BI-RADS categorization (0–6), (2) The second task is a binary classification; in these two classifications, the 7 BI-RADS categories are distributed based on how much priority they have to be given, and (3) the third task consists of the union of the previous ones, first performing the binary classification and then the multiclass classification. Our experiments will be performed on a carefully selected dataset of 4,357 real mammography reports written in Spanish. To ensure a robust evaluation, we implement stratified sampling of the data and a rigorous hyperparameter optimization, with special attention to a current challenge: the BI-RADS class imbalance in mammographic reports.

The key contributions of the paper are summarized as follows:

- We leverage the publicly available dataset from Noguera et al. [9] and propose three tasks to address BI-RADS classification in Spanish-language mammography reports.
- We conduct a systematic comparison between general-purpose and domain-specific transformer models for the Spanish medical domain.
- We incorporate hyperparameter optimization and techniques to mitigate class imbalance.

The structure of this article is as follows: Sect. 2 presents a review of related work on medical report classification and the application of NLP in Spanish within the medical field. Section 4 describes the methodology we applied, including a brief description of the dataset we used, the preprocessing process, and the setup of the experiments performed in both approaches. Section 5 presents and analyzes the results obtained, and finally, Sect. 7 discusses the conclusions of the work carried out and some possible future lines of research.

2 Related Work

One application of Natural Language Processing techniques in the medical area is the automated classification of radiology reports, particularly those related to breast imaging, using the BI-RADS standard. Several works in English have explored this task. For example, Castro et al. [2] developed a system to annotate and classify the BI-RADS categories from free-text radiology reports with NLP techniques. Their approach involved combining information extracted using rule-based methods with supervised machine learning to map unstructured textual descriptions to standardized BI-RADS assessments. This approach yielded significant results in terms of accuracy and demonstrated promising clinical utility for large-scale studies.

More recent work by Liu et al. [5] uses a specifically fine-tuned large language model (LLM) to convert free-text mammographic reports into a structured format. After this, they used one transformer model to make a binary classification of the BI-RADS categories. They demonstrated with their results a better performance than GPT-4o and applied their proposal to an external test set.

In contrast, we found a lack of work in this area, particularly concerning BI-RADS classification, in Spanish mammographic reports. For example, [6] applied both general-purpose and medically trained language models to classify BI-RADS reports in Spanish; however, the dataset is not public which makes it difficult to reproduce the results or further train on new data.

An important challenge in this area is the widespread use of private, inaccessible datasets. The aforementioned studies [2,6,8] all rely on private data, which prevents the reproduction and verification of their findings.

Our work directly addresses these gaps. We focus on the BI-RADS classification of mammography reports written in Spanish, leveraging the publicly available dataset from Noguera et al. [9] to ensure reproducibility. Our primary focus includes: (1) a comparative analysis between general-purpose and medical domain-specific transformer models for Spanish; and (2) a robust methodology involving hyperparameter optimization and techniques to mitigate class imbalance, providing a rigorous performance evaluation.

3 Dataset

The dataset used in this study consists of 4,357 mammography reports provided by the OXADES company[1]. All reports were collected between January 2019 and August 2024. For more detailed information about the dataset, we recommend consulting the original publication [9].

[1] https://oxades.com.py.

The dataset contains approximately 15 variables; however, we only used three of them. The Observations variable contains the findings of the exam, the Reason variable contains the explanations of the reason for the mammogram, and the BI-RADS variable contains the risk category based on the findings. For a complete description of each variable, see [9].

The reason why we selected only these three variables and not all of the fifteen available in the dataset is behind the main goal of this study: to be able to classify the BI-RADS category of each study using only the mammography report. In the dataset, there are only 4 variables that contain the raw text of the reports: Full_Report, Observations, Conclusions, and Recommendations. These last 3 variables are the sections in which the complete report is composed. We focused on the variable "Observations" because it is in this variable where the findings of the mammography study are recorded; the section "Conclusions" was not considered since the BI-RADS classification assigned by the clinician is already in this, and the section "Recommendations" was not considered either since it does not provide any relevant information for the models.

The variable Reasons was decided to use because, although most records only mention the reason for the study, several records also mention the patient's clinical history. This additional information is crucial for the performance in the classification of the highest categories. We used the *BI-RADS* section to identify and label each report with its corresponding BI-RADS category.

One of the main challenges in this dataset is the class imbalance. Most reports are concentrated in four BI-RADS categories, while the remaining three have significantly fewer examples. Figure 1a shows the distribution of reports across the different BI-RADS classes. As shown, the majority of reports are labeled as BI-RADS 0 to 2, while BI-RADS 3 to 6 are underrepresented.

Due to the significant class imbalance among BI-RADS categories, previous studies [5,6] have simplified the multi-class classification problem by reformulating it as a binary classification task. In this formulation, the various BI-RADS categories are grouped into two classes to mitigate the effects of class imbalance.

To also address this class imbalance, we made a new feature that we used to filter the BI-RADS categories based on their priority to be attended, high or low. The high priority cases consist of the 0, 3, 4 and 5 BI-RADS categories and the low priority cases consist of the 1, 2, and 6 BI-RADS categories. This high/low priority filter was made based on the work of Lopez et al. [6]. Figure 1b shows the distribution of reports across the classes *high priority* and *low priority*. In contrast to task 1, this task features a more balanced distribution and a less pronounced class skew.

4 Methodology

Our methodology involves addressing three distinct classification tasks. For each task, we apply two classification approach: one based on transformer-based language models and another using traditional machine learning classifiers.

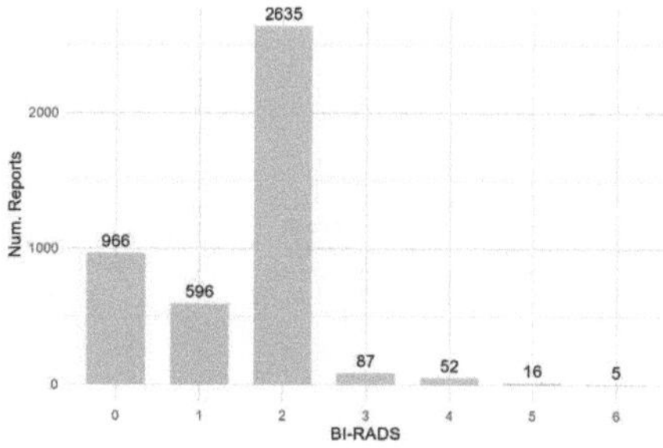

(a) Reports Distribution per BI-RADS Class.

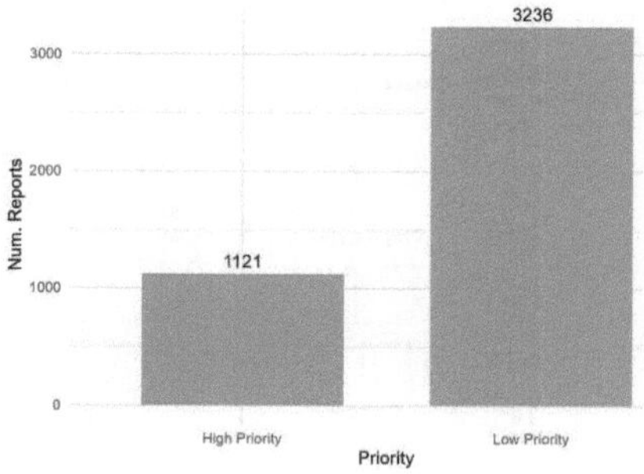

(b) Reports Distribution per Priority.

Fig. 1. Dataset Distributions

In our work, we address both the BI-RADS multi-class classification task and the binary priority classification task. Additionally, we introduce a third task that combines both approaches. The three tasks are described as follows:

- **Task 1. BI-RADS Classification.** Multi-class classification task. Given the report's observations, the goal is to predict the BI-RADS category. Each class corresponds to a BI-RADS number (0 to 6)
- **Task 2. Priority Classification.** Binary classification task. Given the report's observations, the goal is to determine whether a report is *high priority* or *low priority*. We consider a report to be *High Priority* if its corresponding BI-RADS is 0, 3, 4, 5 and we consider a report to be *Low Priority* if its corresponding BI-RADS is 1, 2, 6
- **Task 3. Cascade classification** A combination of the first two tasks. This consists of performing binary classification as a first step, thus obtaining two subsets of classifications: high-priority reports and low-priority reports. Once this step is completed, the exact bi-rads category of each report will be searched for in each priority set.

For each task and model, we implemented the pipeline illustrated in Fig. 2 to conduct the experiments.

First, we select the model we are going to test and the task for which the model will be trained. We then perform feature processing depending on the task we are going to do.

For Tasks 2 and 3, we categorized all reports into *high priority* or *low priority*. We then split the dataset provided by OXADES [9] into a training set and a test set, with the test set reserved exclusively for evaluating model performance, and we used a train–test ratio of 80%–20%. To ensure balanced class distributions, we employed stratified sampling. For Task 1, stratification was based on BI-RADS categories, while for Tasks 2 and 3, it was based on report priority.

We employed grid search for hyperparameter tuning and then selected the best combination of hyperparameters to train the model using the training set.

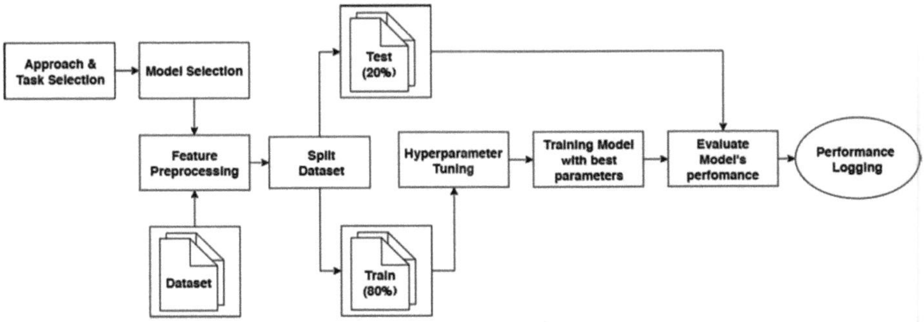

Fig. 2. Pipeline of the classification process.

Evaluation metrics included precision, accuracy, recall, and F1-score. While all metrics were recorded, the F1-score was prioritized in reporting results due to its balance between precision and recall.

Finally, we logged the performance of each model to facilitate comparisons across different hyperparameter settings and model types.

4.1 Traditional Machine Learning Experiments

The first step was to prepare the text to input into the models. We used the "Reason" and "Observations" fields, which were combined into a new field. We consider these two as essential fields because they capture the context of each case. To be able to pass the texts to the machine learning models, we vectorized them using the Term Frequency-Inverse Document Frequency (TF-IDF) transformation. With this, we generated a sparse matrix which contains the numerical representation of each document; this matrix assigns weights to words based on their importance within the texts. We also decided to remove Spanish stop words, such as "el," "la," and "y," from the texts, as they didn't provide relevant information, allowing the models to focus on more relevant terms. Once vectorized, the dataset was split into training and testing subsets using a stratified 80%–20% split. Using the stratification in the split was crucial in the multiclass task because, without it, the test set did not have any register for the category 6 which only has five registers. We trained and evaluated a wide range of machine learning models to assess their ability to classify the reports. These included traditional classifiers like Logistic Regression, K-nearest Neighbours, and SVM, as well as tree-based classifiers like Decision Tree and Random Forest and also we used boosted ensemble classifiers like XGBoost, LightGBM and CatBoost.

In order to make a better evaluation of the performance of these models, we experimented with various scenarios in terms of different n-gram configurations: unigrams, bigrams, trigrams, and four-grams. For each one of these configurations, all models were trained initially with their default hyperparameters, and after, we optimized them through hyperparameter tuning via grid search. This process allowed us to see how the n-gram configuration and the tuned version of the models influence classification performance compared with the default models.

These hyperparameter tunings were performed only in the first two tasks; in the third task, we utilized the best-optimized model of the other tasks. Table 1 shows the hyperparameters we tested and the values of the model with the best performance for each n-gram configuration after the training experiments for tasks 1 and 2, respectively.

Table 1. Best Hyper Parameters Values for Traditional Machine Learning Models

Grid Search					
Model	Hyperparameters Tested	Unigram [Task 1, Task 2]	Bigram [Task 1, Task 2]	Trigram [Task 1, Task 2]	Four-gram [Task 1, Task 2]
Catboost	Border Count: [32, 64, 128]	[64, 32]	[32, 32]	[64, 64]	[32, 64]
	Depth: [4, 6, 8]	[8, 8]	[8, 8]	[4, 8]	[6, 8]
	Iteration: [100, 200]	[200, 200]	[200, 100]	[200, 100]	[200, 200]
	L2 Leaf Reg: [1, 3, 5]	[1, 1]	[1, 3]	[1, 5]	[1, 3]
	Learning Rate: [0.01, 0.1, 0.2]	[0.2, 0.2]	[0.2, 0.1]	[0.2, 0.2]	[0.2, 0.2]
Decision Tree	Criterion: [Gini, Entropy, Log_loss]	[Entropy, Gini]	[Gini, Gini]	[Entropy, Entropy]	[Gini, Gini]
	Max Depth: [None, 5, 10, 20, 30]	[None, 5]	[10, 5]	[None, 10]	[30, 10]
	Max Features: [None, sqrt, log2]	[None, None]	[None, None]	[None, None]	[None, None]
	Min Samples Leaf: [1, 2, 4]	[4, 4]	[2, 2]	[1, 1]	[1, 2]
	Min Samples Split: [2, 5, 10]	[2, 10]	[5, 10]	[2, 10]	[10, 2]
KNN	Metric: [Euclidean, Manhattan, Minkowski]	[Manhattan, Manhattan]	[Euclidean, Manhattan]	[Manhattan, Manhattan]	[Euclidean, Manhattan]
	N Neighbors: [3, 5, 7, 9, 11]	[5, 5]	[3, 3]	[3, 3]	[3, 3]
	Weights: [Uniform, Distance]	[Distance, Distance]	[Distance, Uniform]	[Distance, Distance]	[Distance, Distance]
LightGBM	Colsample Bytree: [0.7, 1.0]	[1.0, 1.0]	[1.0, 0.7]	[0.7, 0.7]	[0.7, 0.7]
	Learning Rate: [0.01, 0.1, 0.2]	[0.1, 0.1]	[0.1, 0.1]	[0.1, 0.2]	[0.1, 0.1]
	Max Depth: [−1, 5, 10]	[−1, −1]	[10, 10]	[5, −1]	[5, 5]
	Num Estimators: [100, 200]	[200, 100]	[200, 100]	[100, 200]	[200, 200]
	Num Leaves: [31, 63]	[63, 63]	[63, 31]	[31, 31]	[31, 31]
	Subsample: [0.7, 0.9, 1.0]	[0.7, 1.0]	[1.0, 0.7]	[0.7, 0.7]	[0.7, 0.7]
Logistic Regression	C: [0.01, 0.1, 1, 10, 100]	[100, 10]	[100, 10]	[10, 10]	[10, 10]
	L1 Ratio: [None, 0.3, 0.5, 0.7]	[0.7, 0.3]	[None, None]	[None, 0.3]	[None, 0.3]
	Penalty: [L1, L2, Elasticnet, None]	[Elasticnet, Elasticnet]	[L1, L2]	[L1, Elasticnet]	[L1, Elasticnet]
	Solver: [Saga+]	[Saga, Saga]	[Saga, Saga]	[Saga, Saga]	[Saga, Saga]
Random Forest	Max Depth: [3, 5, 7, 10]	[10, 10]	[10, 10]	[10, 10]	[10, 10]
	Max Features: [10, 20, 30, 40]	[40, 40]	[40, 40]	[40, 40]	[40, 40]
	Min Samples Leaf: [1, 2, 4]	[1, 1]	[1, 1]	[1, 1]	[1, 1]
	N Estimators: [100, 200, 300, 400, 500]	[100, 200]	[500, 200]	[200, 500]	[300, 200]
SVM	C: [0.1, 1, 10, 100]	[1, 1]	[1, 1]	[1, 1]	[1, 1]
	Decision Function Shape: [Ovr, Ovr]	[Ovr, Ovr]	[Ovr, Ovr]	[Ovr, Ovr]	[Ovr, Ovr]
	Degree: [3, 4]	[3, 3]	[3, 3]	[3, 3]	[3, 3]
	Gamma: [Scale, Auto]	[Scale, Scale]	[Scale, Scale]	[Scale, Scale]	[Scale, Scale]
	Kernel: [Linear, Rbf, Poly]	[Linear, Linear]	[Linear, Linear]	[Linear, Linear]	[Linear, Linear]
XGBoost	Colsample Bytree: [0.7, 1.0]	[0.7, 0.7]	[1.0, 0.7]	[1.0, 1.0]	[1.0, 1.0]
	Gamma: [0, 1, 5]	[0, 0]	[0, 0]	[1, 0]	[1, 1]
	Learning Rate: [0.01, 0.1, 0.2]	[0.1, 0.1]	[0.2, 0.1]	[0.1, 0.1]	[0.2, 0.1]
	Max Depth: [3, 6, 10]	[10, 6]	[6, 3]	[3, 6]	[3, 10]
	N Estimators: [100, 200]	[200, 100]	[200, 200]	[100, 100]	[100, 100]
	Subsample: [0.7, 0.9, 1.0]	[1.0, 0.7]	[0.7, 0.9]	[0.7, 0.9]	[0.7, 1.0]

This process was made in all tasks, but as task 3 is a fusion of tasks 1 and 2, it had some extra steps; First, we made the binary classification with the best hyperparameters of each model of Task 2 and after this, we filtered the predictions leaving only the correct predictions (true high priority and true low priority) to start the process of the multiclass classification with the best models of Task 1.

As in the data is present this imbalance between classes, we centered our evaluation process mostly in the macro F1-score metric in all of the tasks we made, but in task 3 we analyzed this metric in two scenarios; The first is evaluating the F1-score macro without considering the erroneous predictions made by the binary model, this with the objective of observing if there is any improvement in the multiclass classification if it is done focusing only on high or low priority respectively, and the second scenario is evaluating the F1-score macro but this time including in it the errors in the prediction of the binary model to observe the real performance of the models (binary and multiclass) in this task.

4.2 Transformer-Based Experiments

We tested two transformer architectures, BERT and RoBERTa. In total, we tested four different transformer models, three of which are RoBERTa-based and one of which is BERT-based. All four models are Spanish models, with three being medical domain-specific and one being a general-purpose model.

The tested models are:

- Medical Domain: `PlanTL-GOB-ES/roberta-base-biomedical-clinical-es`
- Medical Domain: `serdarcaglar/roberta-base-biomedical-es`
- General Purpose: `PlanTL-GOB-ES/roberta-base-bne`
- Medical Domain: `beto-clinical-wl-es`

Table 2. Best Hyper Parameters Values for Transformer Models

Grid Search		
Model	Hyperparameters Tested	[Task 1, Task 2]
PlanTL-GOB-ES/roberta-base-bne	Num. Epochs : $[3, 5]$	$[3, 3]$
	Batch Size : $[4, 8]$	$[4, 4]$
	Learning Rate : $[1 \times 10^{-5}, 2 \times 10^{-5}, 4 \times 10^{-5}, 5 \times 10^{-5}]$	$[1 \times 10^{-5}, 3 \times 10^{-5}]$
	Weight Decay: $[0.01, 0.001]$	$[0.001, 0.01]$
serdarcaglar/roberta-base-biomedical-es	Num. Epochs : $[3, 5]$	$[3, 3]$
	Batch Size : $[4, 8]$	$[4, 4]$
	Learning Rate : $[1 \times 10^{-5}, 2 \times 10^{-5}, 4 \times 10^{-5}, 5 \times 10^{-5}]$	$[4 \times 10^{-5}, 5 \times 10^{-5}]$
	Weight Decay: $[0.01, 0.001]$	$[0.001, 0.001]$
PlanTL-GOB-ES/roberta-base-biomedical-clinical-es	Num. Epochs : $[3, 5]$	$[3, 3]$
	Batch Size : $[4, 8]$	$[4, 4]$
	Learning Rate : $[1 \times 10^{-5}, 2 \times 10^{-5}, 4 \times 10^{-5}, 5 \times 10^{-5}]$	$[2 \times 10^{-5}, 3 \times 10^{-5}]$
	Weight Decay: $[0.01, 0.001]$	$[0.001, 0.001]$
plncmm/beto-clinical-wl-es	Num. Epochs : $[3, 5]$	$[3, 3]$
	Batch Size : $[4, 8]$	$[4, 4]$
	Learning Rate : $[1 \times 10^{-5}, 2 \times 10^{-5}, 4 \times 10^{-5}, 5 \times 10^{-5}]$	$[1 \times 10^{-5}, 2 \times 10^{-5}]$
	Weight Decay: $[0.01, 0.001]$	$[0.001, 0.01]$

To fine-tune each model, we consider the following parameters: number of epochs, batch size, learning rate, and weight decay. Table 2 shows the values used for each parameter in the grid search, and it also shows the best values for each model for Task 1 and Task 2.

For task 3 we need to consider the binary classification and multi-class classification in one of the de BI-RADS classes. For the binary classification, we selected the model that achieved the best performance in Task 2 and classified the reports into the classes high priority and low priority.

After the binary classification, we train each of the four models to classify the reports in the high-priority class in the corresponding BI-RADS class, separately we follow the same procedure for the low-priority class. For this approach, we consider the erroneous predictions made by the binary model

Table 3 shows the values used for each parameter in the grid search, and it also shows the best values for each model for the high-priority and low-priority classes.

Table 3. Best Hyper Parameters Values for Transformer Models Task 3

Grid Search		
Model	Hyperparameters Tested	[High, Low]
PlanTL-GOB-ES/roberta-base-bne	Num. Epochs : [3, 5]	[5, 5]
	Batch Size : [4, 8]	[4, 4]
	Learning Rate : $[1 \times 10^{-5}, 2 \times 10^{-5}, 4 \times 10^{-5}, 5 \times 10^{-5}]$	$[1 \times 10^{-5}, 2 \times 10^{-5}]$
	Weight Decay: [0.01, 0.001]	[0.01, 0.01]
serdarcaglar/roberta-base-biomedical-es	Num. Epochs : [3, 5]	[5, 5]
	Batch Size : [4, 8]	[8, 8]
	Learning Rate : $[1 \times 10^{-5}, 2 \times 10^{-5}, 4 \times 10^{-5}, 5 \times 10^{-5}]$	$[3 \times 10^{-5}, 3 \times 10^{-5}]$
	Weight Decay: [0.01, 0.001]	[0.001, 0.01]
PlanTL-GOB-ES/roberta-base-biomedical-clinical-es	Num. Epochs : [3, 5]	[5, 3]
	Batch Size : [4, 8]	[4, 4]
	Learning Rate : $[1 \times 10^{-5}, 2 \times 10^{-5}, 4 \times 10^{-5}, 5 \times 10^{-5}]$	$[3 \times 10^{-5}, 1 \times 10^{-5}]$
	Weight Decay: [0.01, 0.001]	[0.01, 0.01]
plncmm/beto-clinical-wl-es	Num. Epochs : [3, 5]	[5, 5]
	Batch Size : [4, 8]	[8, 8]
	Learning Rate : $[1 \times 10^{-5}, 2 \times 10^{-5}, 4 \times 10^{-5}, 5 \times 10^{-5}]$	$[1 \times 10^{-5}, 1 \times 10^{-5}]$
	Weight Decay: [0.01, 0.001]	[0.01, 0.001]

We used the "observations" section of each report as input for the model; all the reports were tokenized using the corresponding model's tokenizer. Since the text in the observation did not exceed the maximum sequence length of the models, there was no need to truncate the inputs; in the case of shorter inputs, all were padded to the maximum sequence length.

The dataset was randomly split into training (80%) and test (20%). Stratification ensured that the distribution of classes remained consistent across both sets.

To account for class imbalance in the dataset, we implement the loss functions described in [4]. These functions take into account class imbalance and use weights to avoid model bias towards the most represented classes in the dataset.

5 Results

In this section, we present the results we obtained from all the classification task experiments using both traditional machine-learning models and transformer-based approaches. For each model, its evaluation will be presented in terms of F1-score, due to the imbalance of classes present in the dataset. The comparison between the results of both approaches aims to assess the performance of each approach to handle the complexity and class imbalance inherent in this Spanish mammography report dataset.

5.1 Traditional Machine Learning Results

Table 4 shows the best performance achieved by the Machine Learning models in terms of F1-score in tasks 1 and 2. These results were obtained with the hyperparameters configuration presented in Table 1.

Table 4. F1-scores for Machine Learning Models on Tasks 1 and 2 (Observations + Reasons).

Model	Task 1				Task 2			
	N-grams							
	1	2	3	4	1	2	3	4
Catboost	0.51	0.58	0.65	0.58	**0.93**	0.91	0.91	0.92
Decision Tree	0.50	0.59	0.67	0.58	0.90	0.90	0.90	0.90
KNN	0.52	0.63	0.42	0.47	0.90	0.90	0.89	0.87
LightGBM	0.45	0.44	0.54	0.49	0.91	0.92	0.92	0.92
Logistic Regression	0.68	0.69	0.67	0.53	0.91	0.92	**0.93**	0.92
Random Forest	0.38	0.33	0.32	0.33	0.90	0.89	0.88	0.86
SVM	0.67	0.62	0.69	0.63	0.92	**0.93**	**0.93**	0.92
XGBoost	0.47	**0.73**	0.71	0.63	0.91	0.92	0.92	0.92

The results in Table 4 show a clear performance gap between the two classification tasks. In Task 1, performance is generally lower and more variable than in Task 2, with an F1-score ranging from 0.32 to 0.73. XGBoost performed the highest score, followed by Logistic Regression and SVM, indicating that these models handle quite effectively the complexity of multi-class labels. In contrast, Task 2 shows consistently high performance, with most models achieving F1-scores above 0.90; handling the imbalance problem using binary classification shows to be quite effective. It can be seen that in both tasks, the n-gram configuration had quite an impact on model performance: in the scenarios where we used bigrams and trigrams, the models generally improved their scores, but using a four-gram configuration declined the scores for some models, hinting at overfitting or sparsity issues. Overall, XGBoost, SVM, and Logistic Regression demonstrated strong and stable performance across both tasks.

To visualize the error pattern, Fig. 3 compares the confusion matrices of the worst and best models under the same bigram scheme. On the left, the Random Forest model is shown; on the right, the XGBoost model.

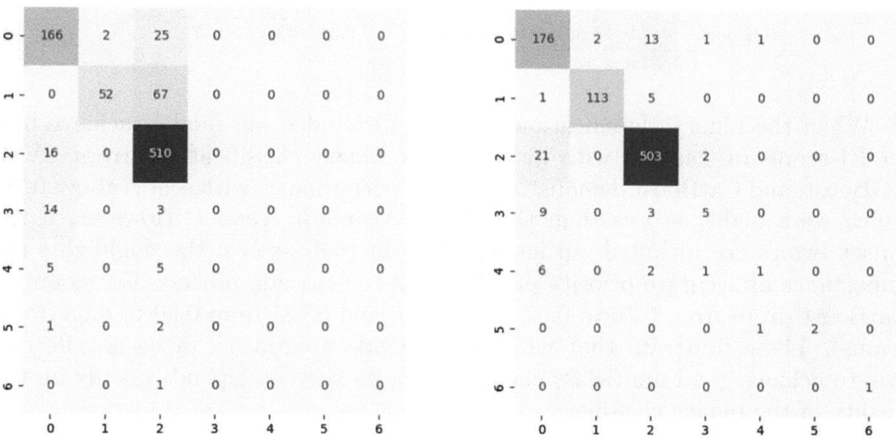

(a) Random Forest (b) XGBoost

Fig. 3. (a) worst-performing model (Random Forest) and (b) best-performing model (XGBoost), both using TF–IDF bigram representation.

When comparing matrices, Random Forest concentrates predictions on the most frequent classes and barely recognizes the high classes, with an error pattern that leans towards the 0–2 block. In contrast, XGBoost presents a more defined diagonal and hits distributed across the entire class spectrum, with less systematic drift between the low classes and the presence of true positives in the high classes. The result is more balanced behavior between classes and, therefore, a higher macro F1. However, interpretation should be cautious: several of the highest severity classes have very low support, so the per-class metrics and matrix counts can be unstable and sensitive to data partitioning.

Table 5 shows the performance of the models in terms of the F1-score in task 3; as we mentioned in the 4 section, this task first makes a priority (high or low) prediction and, using only the correctly predicted cases, performs the multiclass classification. The table is separated into two sections, the left section is the performance of the task without the errors in the prediction made by the binary classifier, and the right section is the real overall performance of the task (including the errors in the binary classifier).

Table 5. F1-scores for Machine Learning Models on Tasks 3 (Observations + Reasons).

Model	F1-score Excl. Bin. Errors				F1-score Incl. Bin. Errors			
	N-grams							
	1	2	3	4	1	2	3	4
Catboost	0.75	0.64	0.76	0.70	0.67	0.59	0.67	0.67
Decision Tree	0.59	0.65	0.62	0.60	0.52	0.55	0.56	0.51
KNN	0.60	0.56	0.53	0.51	0.56	0.44	0.49	0.48
LightGBM	0.60	0.61	0.61	0.45	0.58	0.58	0.59	0.43
Logistic Regression	0.61	0.65	0.66	0.66	0.56	0.62	0.62	0.61
Random Forest	0.50	0.37	0.38	0.37	0.44	0.34	0.33	0.32
SVM	0.60	0.65	0.69	**0.80**	0.54	0.61	0.58	**0.68**
XGBoost	0.50	0.70	0.61	0.61	0.47	0.63	0.57	0.57

When the binary classification errors are excluded, all models achieve better F1-scores in contrast with including the binary classification errors. SVM, XGBoost, and CatBoost demonstrated good performance with scores above 0.70, which were higher scores than the highest scores in Task 1. However, if the binary errors are included, all models drop in their scores; this highlights the importance of accurate priority prediction in the cascade process. For example, CatBoost drops from 0.76 to 0.67 (trigrams), and SVM from 0.80 to 0.68 (fourgrams). These illustrate that while the cascade approach can be an effective way to achieve good multiclass classification, its success depends mainly on the quality of the binary classifier.

5.2 Transformer-Based Results

Table 6 presents the best F1-score achieved by each model on Task 1 and Task 2, using the optimal hyperparameter values presented in Table 2.

Table 6. F1-scores for Transformer Models on Tasks 1 and 2 (Observations vs. Observations + Reasons).

Model (input: Observations)	Task 1	Task 2
plncmm/beto-clinical-wl-es	**0.564**	**0.944**
PlanTL-GOB-ES/roberta-base-biomedical-clinical-es	0.557	0.942
serdarcaglar/roberta-base-biomedical-es	0.561	0.938
PlanTL-GOB-ES/roberta-base-bne	0.560	0.935
Model (input: Observations + Reason)	**Task 1**	**Task 2**
plncmm/beto-clinical-wl-es	**0.571**	**0.946**
PlanTL-GOB-ES/roberta-base-biomedical-clinical-es	0.560	0.944
serdarcaglar/roberta-base-biomedical-es	0.563	0.940
PlanTL-GOB-ES/roberta-base-bne	0.566	0.934

A key observation is that all transformer models perform significantly better on Task 2. We hypothesize that this improved performance is due to the less severe class imbalance in Task 2, which provides a sufficient number of training examples for each class compared to Task 1.

Across both tasks, the models' performances plateau at similar levels, indicating no single model holds a distinct advantage. The diminished performance in Task 1 appears to stem from the models' difficulty in classifying reports from underrepresented BI-RADS classes. The BI-RADS 5 and 6 classes are of particular concern, with only 16 and 5 reports available, respectively. Consequently, only 13 and 4 of these reports were used for training, which presents a significant challenge for the models to learn relevant features for these classes.

Figure 4 compares the confusion matrices of the worst and best models for Task 1. On the left, the `PlanTL-GOB-ES/roberta-base-biomedical-clinical-es` model is shown; on the right, the `plncmm/beto-clinical-wl-es model`.

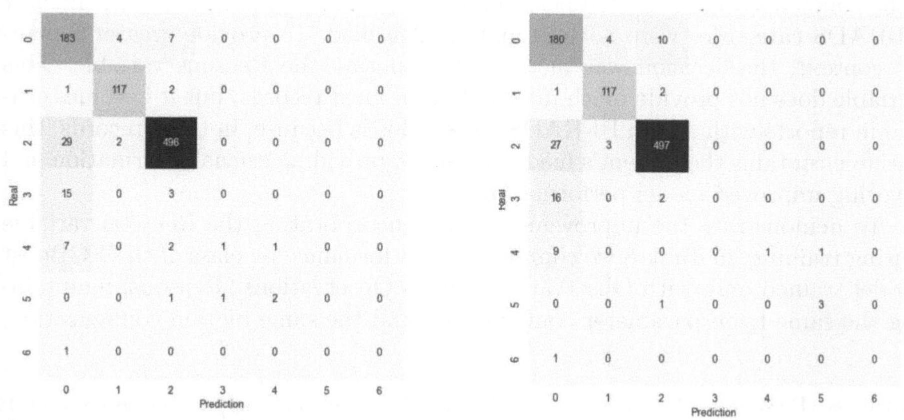

(a) PlanTL-GOB-ES/roberta-base-biomedical-clinical-es

(b) plncmm/beto-clinical-wl-es

Fig. 4. (a) worst-performing model and (b) best-performing model.

Table 7 presents the best F1-score achieved by each model on task 3 for both the high-priority class and the low-priority class, using the optimal hyperparameter values presented in Table 3.

We can observe that the performance of most models improves considerably concerning their performance in Task 1. These results show promise that a cascade approach for multiclass classification could be an effective way to address the problems of class imbalance present in Task 1. Further work is required to evaluate how the accuracy of the binary classification affects the performance of the multiclass classification in task 3.

Table 7. F1-scores for Transformer models on Task 3 (Observations + Reasons).

Model	High Priority	Low Priority
plncmm/beto-clinical-wl-es	**0.691**	**0.668**
PlanTL-GOB-ES/roberta-base-biomedical-clinical-es	0.662	0.664
serdarcaglar/roberta-base-biomedical-es	0.578	0.654
PlanTL-GOB-ES/roberta-base-bne	0.670	0.667

6 Discussion

6.1 Performance Adding the Reasons Variable

In the initial stage, the models were trained using only the Observations variable, which resulted in limited performance: reports corresponding to the highest BI-RADS categories were not adequately identified. To provide greater semantic context, the decision was made to incorporate the Reasons variable. This variable does not provide much information in most records, but it becomes crucial in reports with a high BI-RADS score. This is because, in these records, this variable contains the patient's medical history, providing crucial information and favoring improved model performance.

To demonstrate the improvement when incorporating the Reasons variable during training, in Table 8 we compare the performance by class of the XGBoost model trained only with Observations versus Observations+Reasons, maintaining the same hyperparameter configuration and the same bigram configuration.

Table 8. Per-class F1 scores for the XGBoost model on Task 1 (bigram setting): Observations vs. Observations+Reasons.

Class	Support	Observations	Observations + Reasons
0	193	0.87	0.87
1	119	0.96	0.97
2	526	0.96	0.96
3	17	0.31	0.38
4	10	0.15	0.15
5	3	0.40	0.80
6	1	0.00	1.00

Adding the Reasons variable during training does not alter performance in the most frequent classes where the model was already robust, and instead clearly improves the less represented and more difficult classes. This gain is concentrated precisely in cases where the additional clinical text provides discriminative context, while the remaining classes remain stable, with no signs of degradation.

Although some classes have very little support, the general pattern is consistent: Reasons contribute to disambiguating and better recovering difficult cases, improving performance per class without penalizing the majority classes.

For the transformer models (Table 6), adding the Reasons field produces a modest but consistent improvement in Task 1 across all architectures, while Task 2 remains essentially unchanged at a high level. This pattern suggests that pretrained encoders already capture much of the signal from Observations alone and only benefit slightly from the extra context, whereas the binary task appears close to saturation with either input. Importantly, the trend is uniformly positive—there is no degradation when Reasons is included—indicating that the auxiliary clinical context can help resolve borderline cases without harming performance on the majority.

6.2 Limitations of the Cascaded Approach: Gate Errors and Rare Classes

Table 5 deliberately reports two regimes: an upper bound that excludes the binary stage's errors and an end-to-end score that includes them. The consistent gap between these columns shows that the cascade is constrained by the priority gate: when a study is routed to the wrong branch, the multiclass classifier never "sees" the correct label space and cannot recover downstream. This fragility is amplified by class imbalance in the low-priority branch (BI-RADS 1/2/6). In particular, BI-RADS 6 has extremely low support in our corpus; a single correctly or incorrectly routed case can visibly move macro-F1. We also observe that some priority models struggle precisely on such rare categories, which reduces the pool of valid examples reaching the second stage and further depresses the end-to-end score—even when the branch-specific multiclass model performs well when evaluated in isolation.

The "Excl. Bin. Errors" columns reflect the intrinsic capacity of the branch classifiers given correct routing, whereas the "Incl. Bin. Errors" columns reflect the operational outcome of the full pipeline. The drop between them therefore quantifies how misrouting in the first stage propagates to the final metric. Because rare classes carry disproportionate influence under macro-averaging and are the most likely to be misrouted, the end-to-end score is inherently sensitive in our data setting.

Taken together, our results suggest that the "prioritized" classification strategy is effective: when we look only at the performance of multiclass classifiers (i.e., excluding errors in the binary step), most models outperform their Task 1 scores. This makes sense because each branch faces a smaller, more homogeneous problem (fewer classes to distinguish), which makes it easier to learn sharper decision boundaries. That said, the real benefit depends on the success of the binary classifier: if it fails to route, overall performance suffers. That's why we report both metrics and ask that the "pure" branch performance always be interpreted alongside the cost of routing errors. Still, cascading appears to be a promising approach when classes can be naturally grouped by priority.

7 Conclusions

This work explored different strategies for automatically classifying mammography reports using the BI-RADS standard. We designed three tasks with the aim of evaluating both traditional machine-learning models and transformer-based approaches.

In the machine learning approach, all three tasks were evaluated with different n-gram configurations to assess their impact on model performance; this indicated that trigram and bigram configurations were generally more effective for this problem. Logistic Regression, SVM, and XGBoost achieved better performance across all tasks.

In the transformer-based approach, we tested two architectures, along with both domain-specific and general-purpose models. No model showed a clear advantage across all tasks, suggesting that the specific architecture does not provide a consistent benefit for the tasks proposed. The main limitation faced by the transformer models appears to be the limited number of examples in underrepresented classes.

In Task 3, we implemented a cascaded classification process combining the best models of the binary and multiclass classifications. While this process proved to be a good approach for classifying the BI-RADS categories, it also introduced a clear vulnerability: the final performance is highly sensitive to errors in the initial binary stage. This can be seen in the drop of the F1-score when binary misclassifications were included.

Across all tasks, we observed that a traditional machine learning model, when well-optimized and paired with effective feature engineering (e.g., n-grams and TF-IDF), can rival more complex approaches.

The class imbalance affected the F1-score and should be better addressed in future work.

Acknowledgements. This research was partially funded by the CONACYT, Paraguay, under Grant PINV01-922 and PAPIIT-UNAM project IN104424.

References

1. Burnside, E.S., et al.: The ACR BI-RADS® experience: learning from history. J. Am. Coll. Radiol. **6**(12), 851–860 (2009). https://www.sciencedirect.com/science/article/abs/pii/S1546144009003901
2. Castro, S.M., et al.: Automated annotation and classification of BI-RADS assessment from radiology reports. J. Biomed. Inf. **69**, 177–187 (2017). https://doi.org/10.1016/j.jbi.2017.04.011. https://www.sciencedirect.com/science/article/pii/S1532046417300813
3. Cho, H.N., et al.: Task-specific transformer-based language models in health care: scoping review. JMIR Med. Inform. **12**, e49724 (2024)
4. Huang, Y., Giledereli, B., Köksal, A., Özgür, A., Ozkirimli, E.: Balancing methods for multi-label text classification with long-tailed class distribution. arXiv preprint arXiv:2109.04712 (2021). https://arxiv.org/abs/2109.04712

5. Liu, Y., et al.: Bootstrapping BI-RADS classification using large language models and transformers in breast magnetic resonance imaging reports. Vis. Comput. Ind. Biomed. Art **8**(1), 8 (2025). https://doi.org/10.1186/s42492-025-00189-8
6. López-Úbeda, P., Martín-Noguerol, T., Luna, A.: Automatic classification and prioritisation of actionable BI-RADS categories using natural language processing models. Clin. Radiol. **79**(1), e1–e7 (2024). https://doi.org/10.1016/j.crad.2023.09.009. https://www.sciencedirect.com/science/article/pii/S0009926023004233
7. Madan, S., Lentzen, M., Brandt, J., Rueckert, D., Hofmann-Apitius, M., Fröhlich, H.: Transformer models in biomedicine. BMC Med. Inf. Decis. Making **24**(1), 214 (2024). https://doi.org/10.1186/s12911-024-02600-5
8. Miao, S., et al.: Extraction of BI-RADS findings from breast ultrasound reports in Chinese using deep learning approaches. Int. J. Med. Inf. **119**, 17–21 (2018). https://doi.org/10.1016/j.ijmedinf.2018.08.009
9. Noguera, J.L.V., et al.: Mammography reporting dataset with BI-RADS system for natural language processing applications: addressing public data gaps in Spanish. Data Brief, 111761 (2025). https://doi.org/10.1016/j.dib.2025.111761. https://www.sciencedirect.com/science/article/pii/S2352340925004883
10. World Health Organization: Breast cancer, March 2024. https://www.who.int/news-room/fact-sheets/detail/breast-cancer. Fact sheet published on 13 March 2024

Neural Networks

Adaptation of Object Detection Models Using Transfer Learning for Navigation in Urban Environments

Aldo Yael Hernández Flores[1], Jorge Alonso Vasquez Trujillo[1], Daniel Sánchez-Ruiz[1], and Jesús García-Ramírez[1,2](✉)

[1] Unidad Profesional Interdisciplinaria de Ingeniería Campus Tlaxcala, Instituto Politécnico Nacional, Tlaxcala, Mexico
{ahernandezf2102,jvazquezt2200}@alumno.ipn.mx,
{dsanchezro,jegarciara}@ipn.mx
[2] Universidad Poltécnica Metropolitana de Hidalgo, Hidalgo, Mexico

Abstract. Most navigation algorithms are developed for controlled environments, such as warehouses and factories, or for autonomous vehicles, where the challenge lies in fast decision-making over a limited set of obstacles. These conditions differ significantly from pedestrian spaces, which are highly unstructured and low-speed in nature. This work focuses on the adaptation of object detection algorithms for pedestrian navigation via transfer learning. Several models were fine-tuned using the VIDVIP dataset. While all the trained models showed similar performance, YOLOv12x managed to achieve a mAP50-95 score higher than 0.6, which shows a visibly better performance on test environments. This work highlights the potential of transfer learning with urban datasets for enhancing pedestrian navigation systems.

1 Introduction

Modern object detection models have demonstrated strong performance in structured, high-speed environments, such as autonomous driving [1] or robotic automation [2,3]. However, these approaches do not transfer well to navigating pedestrian-centric spaces. Many current solutions assume either high-speed dynamics or highly predictable spatial layouts, conditions not typically present in urban pedestrian settings.

In response, research has focused on adapting object detection models for navigational tasks. The YOLO architecture and its variants have been widely adopted, with efforts focusing on improving performance in dense areas and under adverse weather conditions [4]. Other studies aim to optimize efficiency with techniques like quantization [5], often at the cost of reduced accuracy in complex scenarios. Some systems have utilized models like YOLOv3 as the foundation for autonomous navigation aids for the visually impaired, often creating hybrid systems to achieve better real-world performance. Emerging research also explores new architectures like Vision Transformers, which have demonstrated

L. Martínez-Villaseñor et al. (Eds.): MICAI 2025, CCIS 2712, pp. 277–288, 2025.
https://doi.org/10.1007/978-3-032-08704-1_21

a strong balance between performance and computational cost for pedestrian detection [6].

As for fully formed projects that similarly aim to aid visually impaired persons, [7,8] provide on on-demand detailed scene descriptions, and [9] has rudimentary pedestrian detection, instead concerning itself with problems of mass adoption and potential privacy problems. The inability to provide real time detection of objects make these systems unfit for fast paced environments, and the always online requirement of the more complex algorithms makes them unreliable and restricts their usability to areas with a constant stable internet connection. In summary, we have so far failed to find any single project that can analyze an urban scene with enough precision and speed to be reliably used to navigate these spaces.

This study addresses this gap by focusing on the development and evaluation of object detection models suitable for low-speed, highly variable pedestrian navigation. Through the use of transfer learning, pretrained models are adapted to better suit urban conditions by using the pedestrian-perspective VIDVIP dataset.

The training evaluation will focus on outdoors environments, both because the VIDVIP dataset rarely features indoors environments, and because these are better handled by other methods such as LiDAR or ultrasonic sensors.

Evaluating the metrics obtained from training the selected models, similar results were obtained across the board, but the YOLOv12x model was declared the best performing as it had the best score on the strict mAP50-95 metric, meaning it not only frequently detected objects correctly, but was also able to overlap a bounding box over its detections with at least 95% accuracy around 60% of the time.

This paper is organized as follows: Sect. 2 presents related work relevant to the proposed approach. Section 3 introduces the proposed methodology for model fine-tuning. The results are described in Sect. 4. Finally, Sect. 5 presents the conclusions and outlines future work.

2 Related Works

Real-time object detection is essential for guiding autonomous instruments, and currently, the state-of-the-art model is YOLO (You Only Look Once) [4]. For example, one study uses YOLOv4 for detecting urban objects in densely populated areas, achieving 90% accuracy at short distances, making it ideal for congested zones [10]. Due to certain limitations, modifications have been made to YOLO itself, such as DCYOLO, which is based on YOLOv4 and designed for outdoor environments. It achieved 9.1% more accuracy than YOLOv4 in complex urban areas [11]. One of the most common challenges is adverse weather conditions, which have been mitigated by training on multiple images of the same object in different climatic conditions, as well as through the creation of synthetic noise [12]. These studies share the use of YOLO as the base model while aiming to improve it or enhance the detection processes. Although these models are still in development, the most advanced ones report up to 70% accuracy in dynamic environments, suggesting potential for urban applications.

Other types of models attempt to improve computational cost. For instance, smaller models using quantization reduce data size from 32 bits to 8 bits. This provides a notable improvement in computational efficiency, but accuracy tends to drop in complex or dynamic environments [5]. These optimization techniques could be applied to the YOLO model to assess whether results are maintained while improving computational cost. Despite the impact on accuracy, studies have been conducted using hybrid systems that integrate YOLO with specialized hardware, leading to significant performance improvements.

There exists research focused on autonomous navigation for people with disabilities. One system based on YOLOv3 estimates distances and focal angles to facilitate navigation using a dataset collected from real environments with no preprocessing [13]. Combinations of odometry and vision have also been explored, such as BBeep, which helps detect pedestrians and avoid collisions [14]. Both systems use YOLO and integrate additional technologies to create hybrid systems that give the model more context, expanding the capabilities of pure vision alternatives. Beyond hybrid systems, research has also explored dynamic environments and outdoor navigation.

Reinforcement learning has been used with raw images to enable models to operate in uncontrolled, dynamic environments [15]. Research has also focused on indoor, controlled environments using LiDAR and BLE signals, processed with CNNs like PoseNet [16]. This demonstrates the existence and utility of hybrid systems for navigation, which have proven effective indoors and potentially outdoors. It also highlights how hybrid systems enable YOLO to be applied in real-world settings with strong performance. Recently, a new approach is emerging through the use of multimodal architectures like transformers.

New types of multimodal architectures are being introduced. Research on pedestrian detection using transformers has achieved a good balance between performance and cost [17]. Similarly, other multimodal systems use video sensors to detect pedestrians, reaching 92% accuracy [18]. These new approaches, beyond traditional CNNs, have delivered better results. Another line of improvement is in training methods, particularly using image-text pairs, following a similar paradigm to large language models (LLMs) for zero-shot classification.

Training with image-text pairs is being conducted to create models capable of labeling objects they were never explicitly trained on, outperforming models like ResNet50 [19]. While this method differs in approach, it shares with [17,18] the demonstration of extensive research aimed at surpassing models like YOLO.

3 Methodology

The evaluated models are different versions of YOLOv9 (versions m, c, e), YOLOv12 (versions m, l, x), and RT-DETR-L. As all the models to be compared are provided by Ultralytics implementation, and due to the selected dataset already being in the format required by the library, no additional preprocessing is needed and the models can train on it right out of the box.

However, since there is no significant amount of articles using the VIDVIP dataset [20], its usage must first be justified through an analysis of some of its basic features to ensure it contains quality data, more specifically: class distribution, class distinctiveness (how much each class features differ from each other), and each class spatial distribution in dataset images were analyzed; all these features may cause poor accuracy or overfitting if poor in quality.

After confirming the suitability of the data, a single training environment (300 epochs, image resizing to 640 × 640, batch size of 64, AdamW optimizer, learning rate of 0.0001, and early stopping patience of 50) was set in order to compare their precision, recall, mAP50 and mAP50-95. After determining the best model via mAP50-95 performance, a more detailed analysis will be made on graphs of its training behavior, such as the loss of its bounding box accuracy and its classification accuracy.

3.1 VIDVIP (Visual Dataset for Visually Impaired Persons)

The VIDVIP dataset [20] contains 32,036 pedestrian-perspective images labeled with urban navigation-relevant classes such as people, steps, vehicles, and safety cones. Although the dataset is underutilized in existing literature, its focus aligns closely with the goals of this project.

An analysis over the dataset revealed:

- **Class Distribution**: Notable imbalance in class frequency (Fig. 1), deemed acceptable for initial model development after augmentation through variation of HSV values, rotation, translation, scale, shearing and perspective warping.
- **Class Distinctiveness**: High separability between classes, as shown in Fig. 2.
- **Spatial Bias**: Minimal vertical bias (e.g., trees in upper image regions), considered non-problematic due to consistent camera orientation.

To assess class distinctiveness, an embedding-based t-SNE visualization was used (Fig. 2), with embeddings extracted via EfficientNet [21]. Most classes formed well-separated clusters, indicating low ambiguity among the labeled categories. For this reason, we consider the VIDVIP dataset a suitable choice for our experiments.

A spatial distribution analysis (Fig. 3) was performed to identify potential positional biases. Some heatmaps indicated a vertical positional bias; for example, trees were mostly spotted in the upper half of the picture, and escalators rarely appeared outside the center. However, this bias was deemed unproblematic due to the consistent camera orientation in the target application.

Horizontal distribution, which is far more critical for this study's purposes, showed minimal bias. Most classes had an even spread from the left to the right border. The few classes that did show a concerning bias (such as elevators or the aforementioned escalators) are of least concern for outdoor environments.

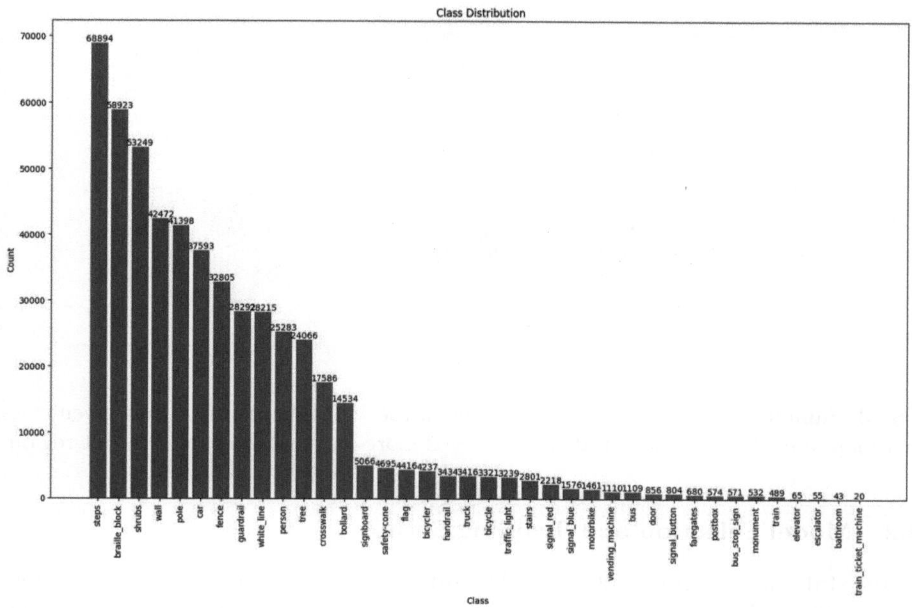

Fig. 1. Class distribution of the VIDVIP dataset, there exists a clear imbalance in the classes of the dataset.

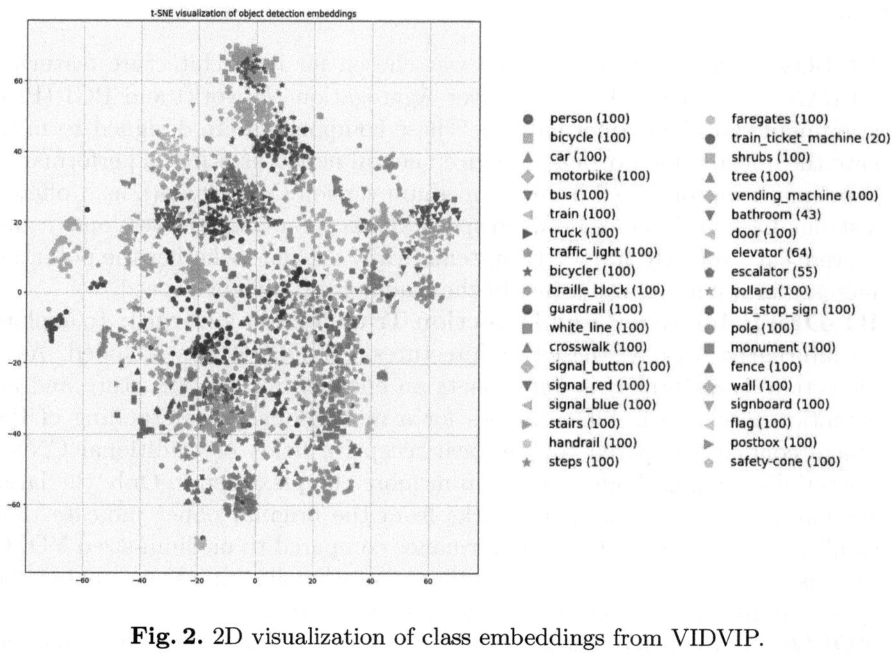

Fig. 2. 2D visualization of class embeddings from VIDVIP.

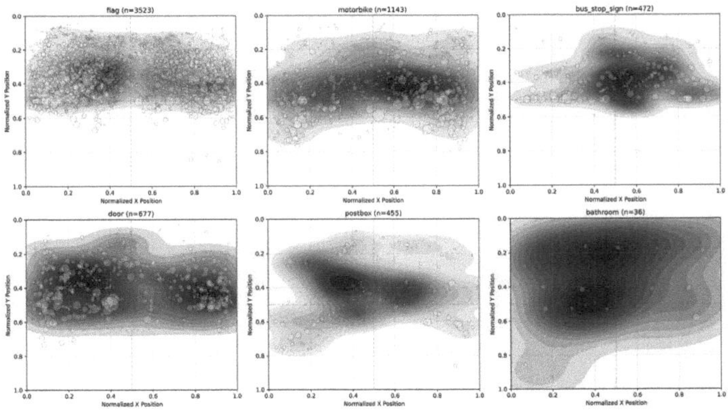

Fig. 3. Sample heatmaps of object locations in the VIDVIP dataset. For a given class heatmap, a darker region indicates the class is more frequently located in that region.

3.2 Model Selection and Training Setup

Three state-of-the-art detection model families were selected, leveraging a transfer learning scheme. Each model, pretrained on the COCO dataset, was fine-tuned using the VIDVIP dataset to adapt its capabilities to the specific challenges of pedestrian navigation by detecting common objects in an urban environment. The selection criteria were based on architectural innovations and their potential to address the accuracy and efficiency trade-offs crucial for this application.

- **YOLOv9 (m, c, e):** This model was chosen for its architecture featuring GELAN (Generalized Efficient Layer Aggregation Network) and PGI (Programmable Gradient Information). These components are designed to mitigate the information bottleneck in deep neural networks. First, a performance benchmark was obtained from the medium version (YOLOv9m), as it offered a strong baseline balance between speed and accuracy. Larger versions (c and e) were subsequently trained to systematically evaluate whether the potential increase in accuracy would justify the trade-off in inference speed.
- **RT-DETR-L (Real-Time Detection Transformer - Large):** To explore an alternative to CNN-based architectures, RT-DETR was included. As a Detection Transformer, it implements an encoder-decoder structure and an attention mechanism, which allows for a more global understanding of the image context compared to the local receptive fields of traditional CNNs, potentially yielding higher precision in more complex scenes. Only the large version was selected, as benchmarks from the original paper indicate that smaller versions have inferior performance compared to medium-sized YOLO models, while larger models are too computationally intensive, making the speed sacrifice impractical for a real-time application.
- **YOLOv12 (m, l, x):** These models were selected due to their implementation of an attention mechanism, a feature embedded in the model's architec-

ture that was previously unimplemented in the YOLO platform. The hypothesis was that this feature would enable the model to focus on the most relevant visual cues for the target objects, leading to more robust and accurate detection. Similar to the strategy for YOLOv9, the medium, large, and extra-large models were trained to analyze the trade-off between performance and inference speed.

A special focus was given to YOLO models due to their generally good performance compared to the resources needed to train and use them, whereas vision transformers ask for more resources while giving similar results.

3.3 Training Configurations

The fine-tuning strategy involved training the entire network by unfreezing all layers of the pre-trained models. This common practice allows the network to fully adapt to the new data distribution. To enhance generalization and prevent overfitting, standard data augmentation techniques were applied, including random scaling, color jitter, and horizontal flips. The chosen hyperparameters, such as image dimensions and learning rate, are based on established practices from previous works [22].

The configuration of the training environment is as follows:

- Epochs: 300
- Image dimensions: 640×640
- Batch size: 64
- Optimizer: AdamW
- Learning rate: 0.0001
- Early stopping patience: 50

The chosen image dimensions strike a good balance between capturing sufficient detail and maintaining performance. We selected a specific number of epochs and patience limit to allow for thorough exploration of each model's potential without risking overfitting or excessively long training times. The AdamW optimizer was used due to its consistent strong performance across various model types. While the learning rate is deliberately slow, it enables the models to converge to more finely tuned values.

Finally, a batch size of 64 was chosen as the maximum capacity supported by our hardware.

3.4 Evaluation Metrics

Performance was assessed using:

- **Precision**: Proportion of correct positive predictions relative to total positive predictions.

- **Recall**: Proportion of correct positive predictions relative to total actual positives.
- **mAP@50**: Mean Average Precision at an IoU threshold of 0.5.
- **mAP@50-95**: Mean Average Precision across IoU thresholds from 0.5 to 0.95, emphasizing precise bounding box localization.

4 Results

Training was conducted on a high-performance computing system equipped with an Nvidia A100 GPU (80 GB VRAM), two Intel Xeon Gold processors (2.8 GHz, 24 cores each), and 1024 GB of RAM. The pre-trained models–YOLOv9m, YOLOv9c, YOLOv9e, YOLOv12m, YOLOv12c, YOLOv12e, and RT-DETR-L–were fine-tuned on the VIDVIP dataset with an 80/20 train/validation split, using the Ultralytics library for implementation.

The models selected in Sect. 3.2 were trained on the VIDVIP dataset with a 80/20 train/validation ratio, using the configuration described in Sect. 3.3. We use ultralytics library that provide us a train function with that implement the used models. Performance metrics for the training results can be seen in Table 1.

Table 1. Precisión, Recall, mAP@50 and mAP@50-95 comparison for trained models.

Model	Precision	Recall	mAP@50	mAP@50-95
YOLOv9m	0.80756	0.79630	0.83605	0.57280
YOLOv9c	0.81110	0.82300	0.84910	0.58060
YOLOv9e	0.80789	0.81414	0.84583	0.59122
YOLOv12m	**0.81830**	0.81820	**0.85760**	0.58070
YOLOv12l	0.81190	0.80990	0.84960	0.58360
YOLOv12x	0.80075	0.82589	0.85450	**0.60081**
RTDETR L	0.80566	**0.84509**	0.85232	0.56025

All evaluated models showed very similar performances across precision, recall, and mAP50. However, the YOLOv12x model's performance was particularly remarkable, surpassing the 0.6 mark for mAP50-95. This is notable, as most COCO-based object detection models typically achieve scores of around 0.4 to 0.5, with the base YOLOv12x model only reaching 0.552. While other models might outperform YOLOv12x in different metrics, we consider it the best due to its superior performance in mAP@50-95, as it means more precise bounding box detection, allowing for the navigation of crowded spaces while avoiding collisions with finer instructions, and comparing it to the highest scorer in the more commonly prioritized mAP50 (YOLOv12m) the difference is less than 0.05, meaning an insignificant loss in general detection, this cannot be said for the next best scorer for mAP@50-95 YOLOv9e, which sees a loss greater than 0.1, a significant value given the standard deviation is 0.0064.

Figure 4 illustrates the general training behavior of this model. We observe a steady improvement across all metrics until approximately epoch 50. At this point, some overfitting becomes apparent for bounding box positioning and the classification of less common classes, for this reason, an early stopping measure was implemented at the 50 epoch mark. Overfitting for the classification of common classes only begins around epoch 100. Scores for mAP50, recall, and mAP50-95 plateau around epoch 60, while precision continues to increase until the very end of training.

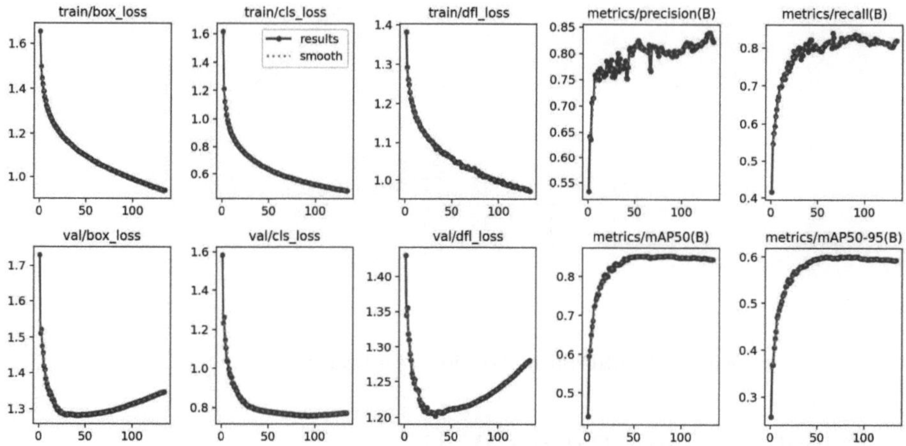

Fig. 4. General training behavior graphs for YOLOv12x.

Figure 5 presents the normalized confusion matrix for the model's inferences. As indicated by the model's precision score, most instances were correctly classified. The majority of misclassifications occurred when the model failed to recognize classes entirely, with only a minimal number of instances being completely misclassified. The background class achieved performance similar to other approaches.

A more human centric test was also done by running the trained model on test videos which can be seen in the next link.

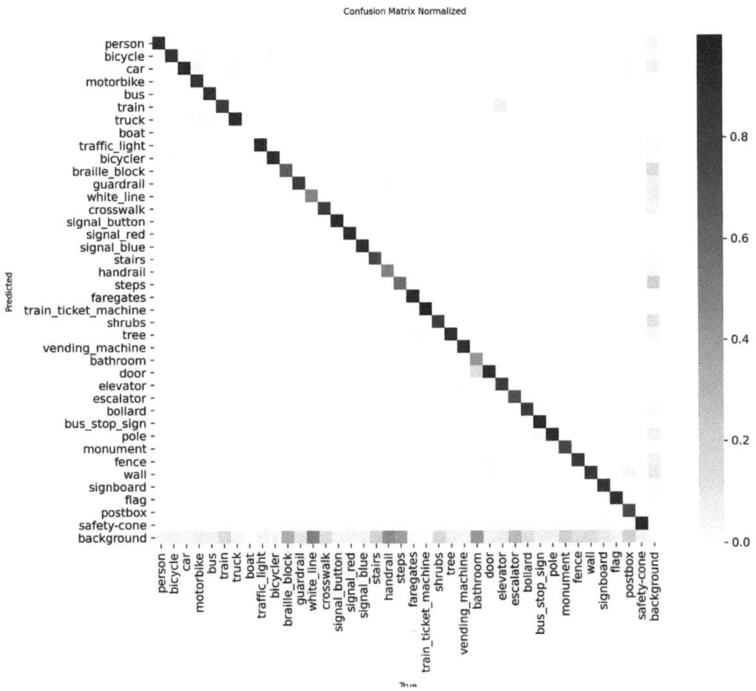

Fig. 5. Confusion matrix for YOLOv12x inferences.

5 Conclusion and Future Work

In this paper we compare the performance of different pre-trained models in order to obtain a model that can be used for object detection in novel scenarios including datasets created from different parts of the world.

The experiments indicate that all tested models achieved acceptable performance. The top-performing models surpassed the others by extremely small margins, and their metrics suggest significant promise for applications outside of testing environments. While this article primarily focused on bounding box precision, an argument could be made for using any of the other models if comparing different metrics, such as speed.

This performance stems partly from the creators' significant efforts in developing architectures capable of precisely determining the position of trained classes within a given image. Equally important, however, is the high quality of the VIDVIP dataset. Its distinct and varied classes and class instances prove its competence for object detection applications.

As for the reason for the difference in performance between models, while precision and recall seem to bounce around with no clear trend, the prioritized mAP50-95 seems to increase with larger and more complex models, so the YOLOv12x model being the best scoring can be partially attributed to its size, allowing it to extract more detail from each image, but its attention mechanism also allows it to better abstract the features of any given class, especially given the variety they present in urban environments.

Future work will focus on several key areas to build upon the findings of this study. This includes:

- hyperparameter optimization to further fine-tune model performance and exploring generalization across more diverse datasets to enhance real-world applicability.
- Distance estimation and path-planning modules with the object detection system to develop comprehensive pedestrian navigation solutions.
- Statistical significance tests (e.g., ANOVA) to rigorously validate performance differences between models and to report inference speeds to assess computational efficiency for real-time deployment.

Acknowledgments. The authors thankfully acknowledge computer resources, technical advice and support provided by Laboratorio Nacional de Supercómputo del Sureste de México (LNS), a member of the SECIHTI national laboratories, with project No. 202501029N.

References

1. Dong, X., Cappuccio, M., Jassmi, H.A., et al.: Why autonomous vehicles are not ready yet: a multi-disciplinary review of problems, attempted solutions, and future directions. arXiv preprint arXiv:2311.09093 (2025)
2. Krnjaic, A., Steleac, R.D., Thomas, J.D., et al.: Scalable multi-agent reinforcement learning for warehouse logistics with robotic and human coworkers. arXiv preprint arXiv:2212.11498 (2024)
3. Peyas, I.S., Hasan, Z., Tushar, M.R.R., Musabbir, A., Azni, R.M., Siddique, S.: Autonomous warehouse robot using deep q-learning. In: TENCON 2021—2021 IEEE Region 10 Conference (TENCON), pp. 857–862. IEEE (2021). https://doi.org/10.1109/tencon54134.2021.9707256
4. Redmon, J., Divvala, S., Girshick, R., Farhadi, A.: You only look once: unified, real-time object detection. arXiv preprint arXiv:1506.02640 (2015)
5. Wang, J.: Lightweight and real-time object detection model on edge devices with model quantization. J. Phys. (2021)
6. Zhao, Y., Lv, W., Xu, S., et al.: DETRs beat YOLOs on real-time object detection. arXiv preprint arXiv:2304.08069 (2024)
7. Rao, S.U., Ranganath, S., Ashwin, T.S., Reddy, G.R.M.: A Google glass based real-time scene analysis for the visually impaired. IEEE Access **9**, 166351–166369 (2021). https://doi.org/10.1109/ACCESS.2021.3135024
8. Brilli, D.D., Georgaras, E., Tsilivaki, S., Melanitis, N., Nikita, K.: Airis: an AI-powered wearable assistive device for the visually impaired. arXiv preprint arXiv:2405.07606 (2024)
9. Lee, K., Sato, D., Asakawa, S., Kacorri, H., Asakawa, C.: Pedestrian detection with wearable cameras for the blind: a two-way perspective. In: Proceedings of the 2020 CHI Conference on Human Factors in Computing Systems, ser. CHI '20. Association for Computing Machinery, New York, NY, USA, pp. 1–12 (2020). https://doi.org/10.1145/3313831.3376398.

10. Villegas, W.E., Sanchez-Vitteri, S., Lujan-Mora, S.: Real-time recognition and tracking in urban spaces through deep learning: a case study. IEEE (2024)
11. Jiang, S., Luo, B., Jiang, H., Zhou, Z., Sun, S.: Research on dense object detection methods in congested environments of urban streets and roads based on DCYOLO. MDPI (2023)
12. Gupta, H., Kotlyar, O., Andreasson, H., Lilienthal, A.J.: Robust object detection in challenging weather conditions. IEEE (2021)
13. Hasan, M.Z., Sikder, S., Rahaman, M.A.: Real-time computer vision based autonomous navigation system for assisting visually impaired people using machine learning. IEEE (2022)
14. Kayukawa, S., Higuchi, K., Guerreiro, J., et al.: BBeep: a sonic collision avoidance system for blind travellers and nearby pedestrians. ACM (2019)
15. Kulhanek, J., Derner, E., de Bruin1, T., Babuška, R.: Vision-based navigation using deep reinforcement learning. arXiv preprint arXiv:1908.03627 (2019)
16. Ishihara, T., Kitani, K.M., Asakawa, C., Hirose, M.: Deep learning and geometry-based image localization enhanced by Bluetooth signals. J-Stage (2018)
17. Yuan, J., Barmpoutis, P., Stathaki, T.: Effectiveness of vision transformer for fast and accurate single-stage pedestrian detection. NeurIPS (2022)
18. Xu, D., Ouyang, W., Ricci, E., Wang, X., Sebe, N.: Learning cross-modal deep representations for robust pedestrian detection. arXiv preprint arXiv:1704.02431 (2017)
19. Radford, A., Kim, J.W., Hallacy, C., et al.: Learning transferable visual models from natural language supervision. arXiv preprint arXiv:2103.00020 (2021)
20. Baba, T.: VIDVIP dataset (2023). https://tetsuakibaba.jp/project/vidvip/
21. Tan, M., Le, Q.: EfficientNet: rethinking model scaling for convolutional neural networks. In: International Conference on Machine Learning, pp. 6105–6114. PMLR (2019)
22. Tian, Y., Ye, Q., Doermann, D.: YOLOv12: attention-centric real-time object detectors. arXiv preprint arXiv:2502.12524 (2025)

Deep Mutual Information Meets Segmentation: Enhancing Neural Network Segmentation via Mutual Information Regularization

Felipe de Jesús Félix Arredondo, Nezih Nieto Gutiérrez(✉), Gustavo De Los Ríos Alatorre, Arturo José Murra López, Manuel Alejandro Ucan-Puc, and Luis Alberto Muñoz Ubando

Tecnológico de Monterrey, Monterrey, N.L., Mexico
nezihniegu@tec.mx

Abstract. This paper presents a novel regularization method that enhances segmentation in neural networks by refining the learning process rather than modifying the architecture. The approach incorporates mutual information as an auxiliary learning objective, where an additional network maximizes shared information between input and output representations. This optimization improves weight adjustments during training, enabling the model to capture structural and contextual relationships more effectively. Experiments on multiple benchmarks demonstrate that this method significantly improves segmentation accuracy, enhancing both large objects and smaller, densely crowded regions. By mitigating the tendency of neural networks to produce overly linear segmentations, it encourages more adaptive, nonlinear contours. Consequently, segmentation masks achieve superior object delineation, improving precision and coherence in separated segments. These findings highlight the efficacy of mutual information in guiding efficient weight updates, enhancing the precision of convolutional segmentation models such as U-Net, and improving the learning of nonlinear features without requiring architectural modifications.

Keywords: Mutual Information · Neural Networks · Image Segmentation

1 Introduction

Segmentation tasks have been extensively studied over the years, leading to the development of various neural architectures that address this complex problem using different mathematical approaches [10,15]. Notable models, such as U-Net and variants, have significantly advanced the field of segmentation, representing a key milestone in deep learning-based computer vision approaches [18,22]. Theoretical research in computer vision, particularly incorporating information

L. Martínez-Villaseñor et al. (Eds.): MICAI 2025, CCIS 2712, pp. 289–302, 2025.
https://doi.org/10.1007/978-3-032-08704-1_22

theory, stands out from traditional approaches and is crucial for further advancements in model optimization [25]. The approach presented in this paper addresses the problem of information loss between the input X and the output Y during the segmentation process: internal features of a model often retain far more information from the input than the final prediction does, failing to preserve that information in the output, a common issue in the information-maximization perspective [14] that, despite it's long history in information theory [3], has only recently been studied in neural networks. Indeed, an analysis of mutual information across U-Net layers after training showed that shared information between intermediate representations and the output is significantly smaller than between the input and output [12], indicating that traditional segmentation models prioritize transforming rather than preserving input information. Earlier work on MINE(Mutual Information Neural Estimator) explored maximization of mutual information between a purely random latent space $\mathcal{S}$ and the data domain $\mathcal{X}$ in GANs [2], but did not consider downstream, supervised tasks such as segmentation. In contrast, our work reconceptualizes the objective to learn a latent, input-dependent representation that suppresses irrelevant information from $\mathcal{X}$ while preserving features necessary to generate the structured output $\mathcal{X}'$ (i.e., segmentation maps), arguing that naïvely conditioning MINE on an input image oversimplifies the problem geometry and neglects critical mutual dependencies in dense prediction settings. To extend MINE beyond unsupervised generative modeling and apply it directly as an auxiliary learning objective in image segmentation, we integrate MINE into the U-Net optimization pipeline without adding noise to the latent space as a new loss regularizer, and evaluate its performance on datasets with varied segmentation targets (bodies of water, cells, nails) to assess robustness to different shapes, sizes, and occlusions, and compare the resulting U-Net + MINE model against the traditional U-Net baseline performance as an initial test to verify it's effectiveness in segmentation methods and as a starting point for more computationally intensive applications with bigger architectures.

2 Background and Related Work

Recent advances in computer vision have favored U-Net in a variety of contexts, including image segmentation [1], a fundamental task and a crucial technique for many applications such as medical imaging, autonomous driving, and remote sensing [19,23]. The adoption of deep learning techniques, particularly convolutional neural networks (CNNs), has revolutionized segmentation by improving both accuracy and efficiency [6]. Recent developments in information-theoretic approaches and mutual information estimation have provided additional insights into improving segmentation performance. A notable contribution is the use of Mutual Information Neural Estimation (MINE) as a regularization term in the U-Net architecture, enhancing feature learning by capturing dependencies between latent space input and output distributions, thus refining the image generation process for the GANs and improving the information flow of the Decoder [2].

2.1 Image Segmentation Methods

Image segmentation techniques have evolved significantly from early classical approaches to modern deep learning-based methods. Early works by [5] framed segmentation as an estimation problem, while [20] introduced mathematical morphology and lattice theory for segmentation tasks. The U-Net architecture, proposed by [18], played a pivotal role in advancing segmentation, particularly with its encoder-decoder structure featuring skip connections that preserve spatial information and improve boundary delineation, making it highly effective for both medical and non-medical segmentation tasks. The paper [15] further expanded on this, noting how deep learning methods have surpassed traditional techniques in segmentation performance, especially in domains that require high precision, such as autonomous driving and satellite imagery, but there still remains the need for models that can generalize robustly across datasets, handle small or ambiguous structures, and leverage additional information such as contextual or relational dependencies to improve segmentation quality beyond what standard pixel-wise losses capture.

2.2 Information-Theoretic Approaches to Segmentation and Information Flow

Information theory has provided a robust mathematical framework for improving image segmentation. It quantifies the relationships between image features and segmentation masks, leading to better performance in complex tasks. For example, [17] applied mutual information maximization to segment medical images by structuring the image into homogeneous regions and clustering histogram intensity bins. Information-theoretic methods have also been extended to other fields, such as image clustering and satellite imagery analysis, where mutual information plays a key role in improving the accuracy of feature extraction and object detection. Understanding how information flows through segmentation networks is essential for improving their performance. Lee and Bajić [12,13] explored information propagation in U-Net architectures, highlighting the importance of skip connections in transferring spatial information from the encoder to the decoder. These studies are fundamental for optimizing architectures for specific tasks in both medical and non-medical image segmentation, as they provide insights into the theoretical foundations of how information is processed through the network.

2.3 Mutual Information Neural Estimation

Traditional mutual information estimation techniques often struggle with high-dimensional, complex data distributions. [2] introduced Mutual Information Neural Estimation (MINE), a neural network-based approach that overcomes these limitations, making it particularly well-suited for high-dimensional image analysis tasks. MINE estimates mutual information between continuous random variables and discrete variables and has been used effectively across different domains, but in this case serves as the main key of the paper for improve the representation learning of the model. Further applications, such as deep comprehensive correlation mining [24] and deep adaptive clustering [4], demonstrate the versatility of neural mutual information estimation in tasks beyond traditional image segmentation and let making even more complex feature analysis.

2.4 Criterion Function

To evaluate whether a labeling function f produces a meaningful segmentation, we define a *criterion function* σ. This function assesses the quality of the labeling by associating a real-valued score to a predicted subset $A \subseteq E$ under f.

Formally, let $\mathcal{P}(E)$ denote the power set of E. Then the criterion function is defined as:

$$\sigma : \mathcal{F} \times \mathcal{P}(E) \to \mathbb{R}, \quad \sigma(f, A) = \mathbb{E}_{x \in E}[\hat{\sigma}(f, A)]. \tag{1}$$

Here, $\hat{\sigma}(f, A)$ denotes a per-element measure of classification correctness for the subset A, and the expectation is taken over the image domain. In probabilistic segmentation, $\hat{\sigma}$ is typically defined via a conditional probability:

$$\hat{\sigma}(f, A) = \mathbb{P}(A = A^* \mid E) = \mathbb{P}(A \mid E) \tag{2}$$

where $A^* \subseteq E$ is the ground-truth foreground region, and $A = f^{-1}(1)$ is the predicted foreground under f and it became useful to determine the joint probability in future sections, in this case A being the prediction and E the original image and $P(A|E)$ as the probability of the generated segmentation be the correct mask for the given image.

2.5 Likelihood Model and Binary Cross-Entropy

The quantity $\mathbb{P}(A = A^* \mid E)$ can be modeled using the likelihood of independent Bernoulli predictions over pixels. For each pixel $x \in E$, let $c_x \in \{0, 1\}$ denote the ground-truth class, and $f(x) \in [0, 1]$ the model's estimated probability of class 1. The likelihood becomes:

$$\mathbb{P}(A^* \mid E)_f = \prod_{x \in E} f(x)^{c_x} (1 - f(x))^{1 - c_x}. \tag{3}$$

The segmentation task is therefore reframed as a maximum likelihood estimation (MLE) problem:

$$\max_{f \in \mathcal{F}} \mathbb{P}(A^* \mid E)_f. \tag{4}$$

To facilitate optimization, we minimize the negative log-likelihood, yielding the binary cross-entropy loss:

$$\mathcal{L}_{\text{BCE}}(f) = -\sum_{x \in E} \left[c_x \log f(x) + (1 - c_x) \log(1 - f(x)) \right]. \tag{5}$$

This loss measures the divergence between the true labels and the predicted probabilities, penalizing uncertainty and incorrect predictions. Minimizing this loss reduces classification entropy and sharpens decision boundaries. However, this formulation lacks a mechanism to enforce global structural consistency.

2.6 Mutual Information as Regularization

To improve the semantic alignment between input and output, one can regularize the loss using *mutual information* (MI), which quantifies statistical dependence between random variables.

Given random variables X and Y, the mutual information is:

$$I(X;Y) = \mathbb{E}_{p(x,y)}\left[\log \frac{p(x,y)}{p(x)p(y)}\right]. \tag{6}$$

This can also be interpreted via intersection likelihoods:

$$I(X_1;Y_1) > I(X_2;Y_2) \quad \Leftrightarrow \quad p(X_1 \cap Y_1) > p(X_2 \cap Y_2), \tag{7}$$

assuming all marginals are fixed, which makes the inequality valid under symmetric divergence assumptions. Mutual information provides a robust criterion for enforcing consistency between input image features and output segmentations. This is illustrated in Fig. 1.

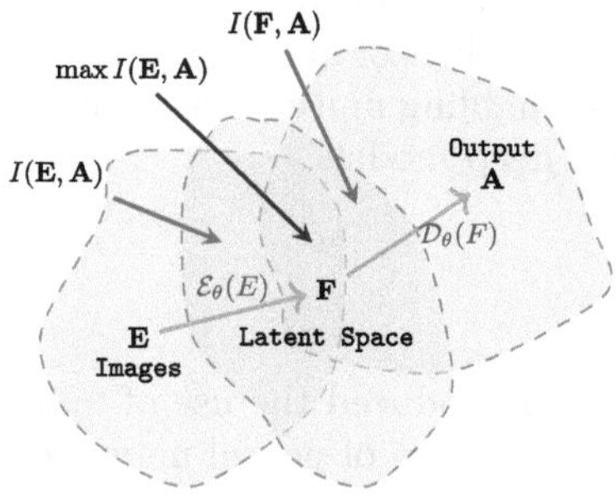

Fig. 1. This illustration represents the concept of mutual information between the input (the images) and the output (the masks). The intersection of these information sets corresponds to the mutual information. Specifically, there is some information, denoted as $\mathcal{I}(E,F)$, that flows through the input and the latent space, but only a small portion of it is transferred to the output, represented as $\mathcal{I}(E,A)$. Maximizing this transferred information is the main objective.

Mutual information is a powerful measure to quantify statistical dependence between input and output, but it presents significant computational challenges. Specifically, computing $I(X;Y)$ requires access to the joint distribution $p(x,y)$ and the marginals $p(x)$ and $p(y)$, which are often unknown or intractable to estimate in high-dimensional settings such as computer vision. The joint distribution $p(x,y)$ reflects the co-occurrence of input features and output predictions across the data distribution. In practice, estimating this joint directly requires either full knowledge of the data-generating process or density estimation in high-dimensional spaces, both of which are typically infeasible. Therefore, approximations or lower bounds are necessary. A standard approach is to express mutual information as a Kullback-Leibler divergence:

$$I(X;Y) = D_{KL}(p(x,y) \,\|\, p(x)p(y)), \tag{8}$$

which measures how far the joint distribution is from the product of the marginals. To make this quantity tractable, we employ the Donsker-Varadhan variational formulation [2,8].

Theorem 1. ***(Donsker-Varadhan Representation).*** *Let $\mathbb{J} = \mathbb{P}_{XY}$ be the joint distribution, and $\mathbb{Q} = \mathbb{P}_X \otimes \mathbb{P}_Y$ be the product of marginals. Then:*

$$D_{KL}(\mathbb{J} \,\|\, \mathbb{Q}) = \sup_{T \in \Omega} \mathbb{E}_{\mathbb{J}}[T] - \log \mathbb{E}_{\mathbb{Q}}[e^T], \tag{9}$$

where Ω is the set of measurable, integrable functions $T : \mathcal{X} \times \mathcal{Y} \to \mathbb{R}$.

This representation allows us to optimize a lower bound of the mutual information using a parameterized critic function $T_\omega(x,y)$. In practice, this function is implemented as a neural network trained to distinguish between samples drawn from the joint and from the product of marginals. This bypasses the need to estimate the full distributions, enabling mutual information to serve as a regularizer during training in complex deep models.

3 Methodology

The method proposed in [2] introduced the use of mutual information as a regularization term in the loss function of neural networks. The motivation behind incorporating mutual information is to enable the model to learn richer, non-linear representations that go beyond the limited expressivity of traditional objectives such as cross-entropy. This is particularly beneficial in complex tasks like segmentation, where spatial and semantic consistency play a key role. In that work, the authors proposed the Mutual Information Neural Estimator (MINE), which estimates mutual information between the input and the output of a model by parameterizing the DonskerâĂŞVaradhan representation through a neural network $T_\phi(x,y)$:

$$\hat{\mathcal{I}}_\phi(X;Y) = \mathbb{E}_{\mathbb{P}_{XY}}[T_\phi(x,y)] - \log \mathbb{E}_{\mathbb{P}_X \otimes \mathbb{P}_Y}[e^{T_\phi(x,y)}] \tag{10}$$

This formulation transforms mutual information estimation into a trainable objective. Since neural networks are typically optimized through minimization, the negative of the estimated mutual information is added to the total loss, encouraging the model to maximize dependence between X and Y. Moreover, the accuracy of the estimator improves with larger batch sizes, as they allow better approximation of the expectations involved in both the joint and product of marginals with the lower uncertainty and the more accurate became with the real mutual information. The total loss function becomes:

$$\min_{\theta} \mathcal{L}(\phi) = \mathcal{L}_{\text{CE}} - \lambda \hat{\mathcal{I}}_{\phi}(X;Y) \tag{11}$$

Here, $\mathcal{L}_{\text{CE}}$ is the binary cross-entropy loss, $\hat{\mathcal{I}}_{\phi}$ is the estimated mutual information, and λ is a hyperparameter that controls the contribution of the mutual information term by choosing a value equivalent to $\lambda = 1/d$ with d as the number of neurons in the final layer due to the average amount of information in the final layer $d = H(T) \approx d$. This regularization encourages the model to align its predictions with latent dependencies in the data, complementing the discriminative objective of cross-entropy. Intuitively, this is aligned with maximizing the joint probability $P(X,Y)$, or equivalently, maximizing the conditional likelihood $P(Y|X)$ via information-theoretic means. However, directly optimizing $\hat{\mathcal{I}}_{\phi}$ introduces challenges. The mini-batch based estimation of the expectations introduces bias, and the exponential term can cause instability during training. To address this, a moving average $\bar{\mu}_{\mathcal{I}}$ of the exponential expectation is maintained, following the update rule:

$$\bar{\mu}_{\mathcal{I}} \leftarrow \alpha \bar{\mu}_{\mathcal{I}} + (1-\alpha)\mathbb{E}_{\mathbb{P}_X \otimes \mathbb{P}_Y}[e^{T_{\phi}(\bar{x},\bar{y})}] \tag{12}$$

This exponentially weighted average stabilizes the log term and controls the variance across training iterations. Given the estimator's bias, an adjusted gradient is employed to reduce the variance of the gradient estimator and allow convergence:

$$\hat{G} = \mathbb{E}_{\mathbb{B}}[\nabla_{\phi} T_{\phi}(x,y)] - \frac{\mathbb{E}_{\mathbb{B}}[e^{T_{\phi}(\bar{x},\bar{y})} \nabla_{\phi} T_{\phi}(\bar{x},\bar{y})]}{\bar{\mu}_{\mathcal{I}}} \tag{13}$$

This corrected gradient balances bias-variance tradeoffs introduced by mini-batching. Training proceeds using this formulation, optimizing both segmentation performance and mutual dependency between input and output. The optimization process is summarized in Algorithm 1 and can be seen in the Fig. 2, where batch size and computational constraints are adjusted depending on the available hardware, the batch size was a result of the computational limit of the equipment used for training, so there was a hardware limitation for larger tests. In this approach, we test and collect data using a U-Net model, replacing its standard convolutional modules with residual blocks inspired by the ResNet modules and setting the parameters to a initial value of 32 filters and neurons per layer and duplicating the value through every value on the encoder and then dividing it by 2 in the decoder like the original U-Net amount [1] and repeating the process for the MINE network, the training was made with the Adam optimizer with a learning rate induced by $\eta = \sqrt{|W|} \approx 0.001$, where $|W|$ is the amount of parameters. The model's performance is evaluated using three different metrics: one to minimize and two to maximize. These metrics are commonly used in segmentation tasks, specifically the Binary Cross-Entropy (BCE) loss, the Dice Sørensen coefficient, and the Jaccard coefficient (Also known as IoU or Intersection over Union). For convenience, we will refer to these performance metrics as $\mathcal{L}(X,Y)$, $D(X,Y)$, and $J(X,Y)$ for BCE, Dice, and Jaccard, respectively. The model is evaluated using the Nail Segmentation dataset [16], the Flood Area Segmentation dataset [11], the Colorectal Cancer WSI (EBHI-Seg) dataset [9,21], and the Blood Cell Dataset (BCCD) [7]. Usinge diverse datasets like those selected here allow for a comprehensive assessment of the model's performance, due to their characteristics. They include cases of sparsely distributed masks, highly crowded object distributions, and masks with highly non-convex shapes.

Algorithm 1. Mutual Information Neural Estimation Training with U-Net Segmentation

1: **Data:** $\mathbb{B}$: Dataset of images $(\mathbf{E}, \mathbf{S}) \sim \mathbb{B}$, where $\mathbf{E}$ is an image and $\mathbf{S}$ its segmentation mask.
2: **Models:** $\mathcal{I}_\phi$: MINE estimator, P_θ: U-Net segmentation model.
3: **for** each batch $b \in \mathbb{B}$ **do**
4: Sample batch: $(\mathbf{E}, \mathbf{S}) \sim b$, shuffled batch: $(\bar{\mathbf{E}}, \bar{\mathbf{S}}) \sim \text{Shuffle}(b)$.
5: Define distributions: $z \leftarrow (\mathbf{E}, \mathbf{S})$, $\bar{z} \leftarrow (\bar{\mathbf{E}}, \bar{\mathbf{S}})$.
6: Compute mutual information lower bound:

$$\mathcal{L}_\mathcal{I}(\phi) = \mathbb{E}_{\mathbb{P}_{\text{XY}}}[T_\phi(z)] - \log(\mathbb{E}_{\mathbb{P}_{X \otimes Y}}[e^{T_\phi(\bar{z})}]) \tag{14}$$

7: Update $\mathcal{I}_\phi$ using Adam and EMA definition in Eq. 12 G: $\phi \leftarrow \phi - \alpha\hat{G}$.
8: Predict segmentation: $\mathbf{A} \leftarrow P_\theta(\mathbf{E})$, shuffled batch: $(\bar{\mathbf{E}}, \bar{\mathbf{A}}) \sim \text{Shuffle}(\mathbb{B})$.
9: Define new distributions: $z_\theta \leftarrow (\mathbf{E}, \mathbf{A})$, $\bar{z}_\theta \leftarrow (\bar{\mathbf{E}}, \bar{\mathbf{A}})$.
10: Compute the mutual information of U-Net:

$$\mathcal{I}_\phi(\theta) = \mathbb{E}_{\mathbb{P}_{\text{XY}}}[T_\phi(z_\theta)] - \log(\mathbb{E}_{\mathbb{P}_{X \otimes Y}}[e^{T_\phi(\bar{z}_\theta)}]) \tag{15}$$

11: Compute loss for U-Net:

$$\mathcal{L}_P(\theta) = \mathcal{L}_{\text{BCE}}(S, P_\theta(E)) - \lambda \mathcal{I}_\phi(\theta) \tag{16}$$

12: Update P_θ using Adam to minimize $\mathcal{L}_P(\theta)$.
13: **end for**

4 Results

This model demonstrated strong performance across four datasets: Flood, Cancer, Nails, and Blood. Despite the biased data in the Flood Area Segmentation dataset, the model effectively resisted learning these biases and instead focused on relevant features. It successfully corrected missed or incorrectly annotated regions, particularly in the flood and cancer datasets. The model showed resilience in segmenting sparse regions that were overlooked in the original data, prioritizing accurate segmentation over learning incorrect features. These results

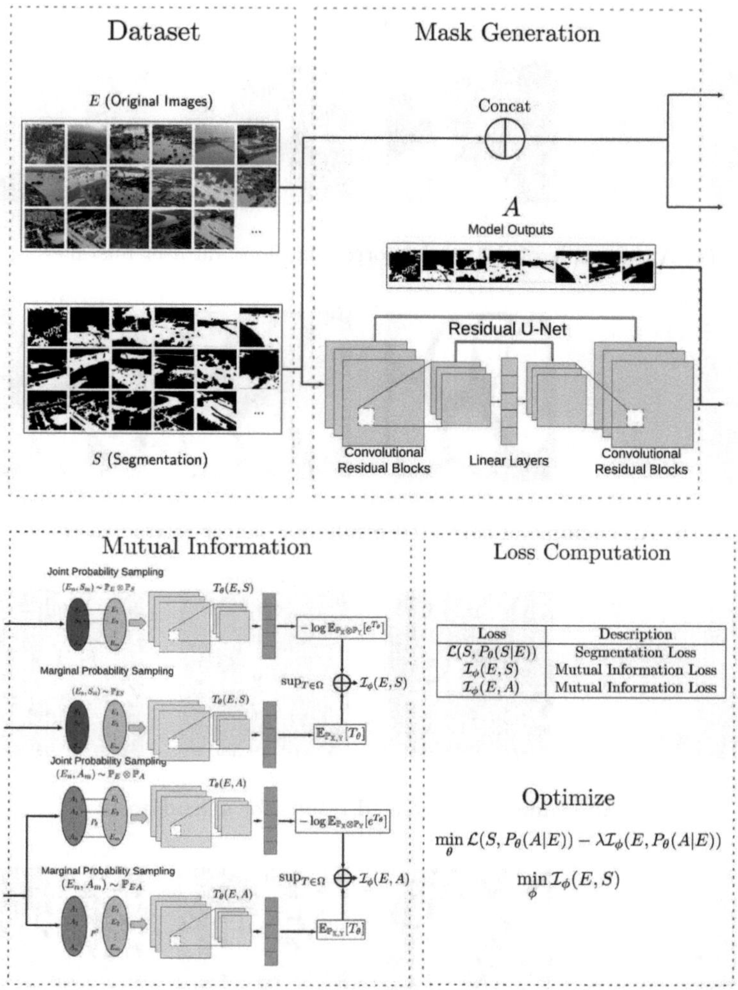

Fig. 2. The main pipeline takes the dataset as input, then passes the input $\mathbf{E}$ through the U-Net $\mathbf{P}_\theta$ to obtain the mask $\mathbf{A}$. Once $\mathbf{A}$ is obtained, two processes take place. The first trains the MINE network to learn $\mathcal{I}(\mathbf{E};\mathbf{S})$. Then, with MINE fixed, the U-Net is evaluated to maximize $\mathcal{I}(\mathbf{E};\mathbf{P}_\theta(\mathbf{A} \mid \mathbf{E}))$ between its output $\mathbf{A}$ and input $\mathbf{E}$, using the loss map for guidance.

highlight the model's ability to generalize well across varied segmentation tasks. A commonly used metric to define model performance is accuracy, which depends on the performance metric. However, one observed behavior during testing was that, despite the bias in the data of the Flood Area Segmentation [11], the model with MINE showed strong resistance to learning the biased features, as seen in the fourth image in Fig. 3a.

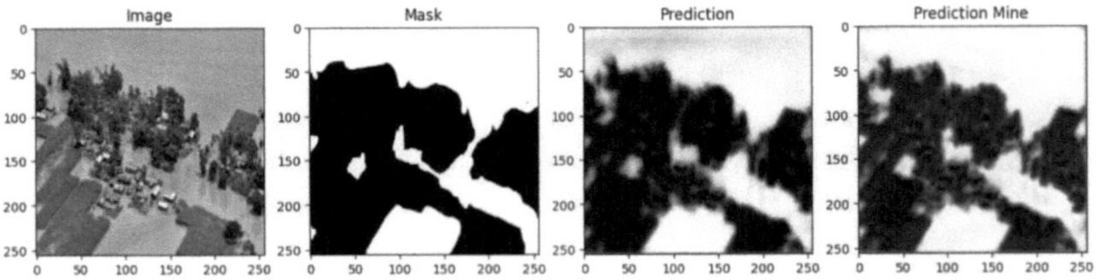

(a) An example of the model correcting flood dataset mistakes

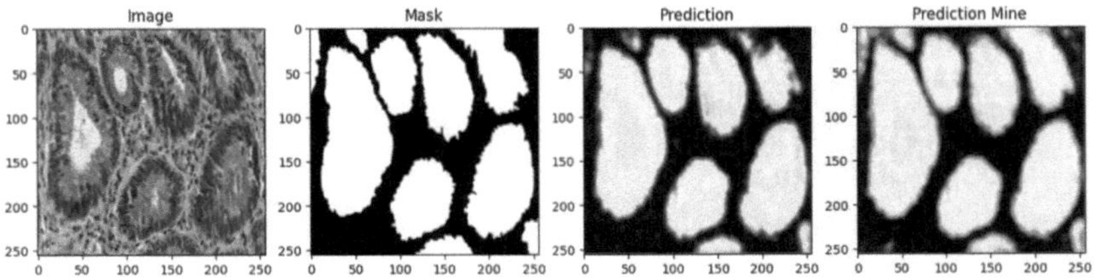

(b) An example of corrected results for cancer-related cases

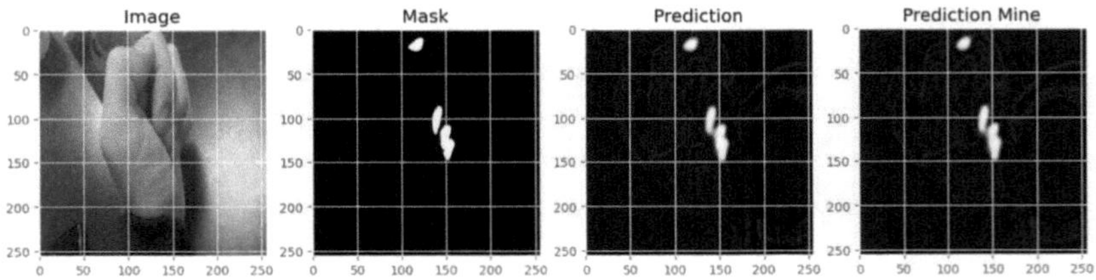

(c) An example of corrected results for nails dataset

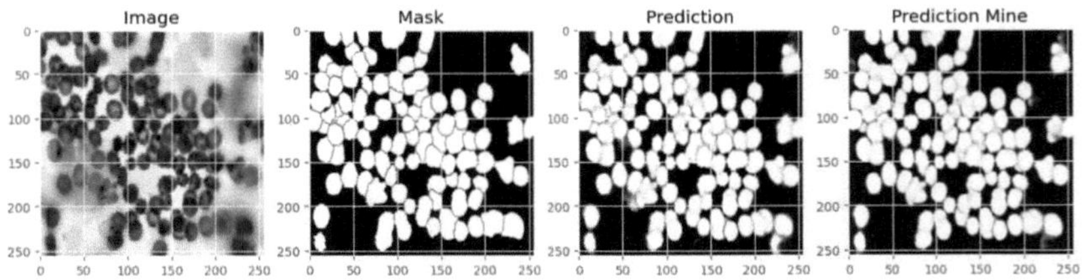

(d) An example of corrected results for blood dataset

Fig. 3. Comparison of model corrections on different datasets: Flood, Cancer, Nails, and Blood. Improvement on the definition and the images, with more defined borders and generating and generalizing things that the original data was not detected. A good example on the images is the Fig. 3a when the ground truth make a simplification but the generated model has a improve on the generation of small and thin segmentation masks and with crowded images.

In the original flood images, certain small elements such as narrow paths and minor rivers were omitted, since they are difficult to annotate consistently when the ground truth is manually generated. These areas should ideally have been included in the binary masks but were overlooked. Interestingly, the MINE model tended to recover and include these neglected details in its outputs, demonstrating a higher degree of generalization over the dataset and resisting the bias introduced by incorrect annotations in the training set. This behavior suggests that MINE achieved a more robust training process, even though such improvements were not fully captured by the accuracy and loss metrics reported in Tables 1. To validate these findings, each model was trained and tested 12 times, and the results consistently passed mean-difference significance tests (two-sample t-test), confirming that the observed differences in performance are statistically meaningful. A plausible explanation is that the model leveraged the additional structural information it learned, which was reinforced by the mutual information regularization applied between input and output representations, thereby aligning similarities across feature spaces.

The model effectively prioritizes relevant features in the images it was trained on, highlighting key regions based not only on their size but also on the information they provide. For example, in the flood dataset [11], the model accurately identified and segmented sparse water regions that were overlooked in the original masks. This suggests that the model generated masks that more accurately reflected the actual regions of interest. Additionally, it was not biased by densely populated areas and successfully distinguished water-filled regions that required segmentation from the rest of the image. This same phenomenon was also observed in the blood cell segmentation dataset [7]. The results presented in Fig. 5 highlight the impact of incorporating the MINE (Mutual Information Neural Estimation) method into the U-Net backbone across different segmentation tasks and batch sizes. Generally, models utilizing MINE exhibit improved performance metrics, particularly in Log Loss, Dice Accuracy, and Jaccard Coefficient (IoU), suggesting that optimizing mutual information contributes to better segmentation quality. The evaluation of the model on the four datasets in the collection yields the obtained values, as seen in Table 1 (Fig. 4).

Table 1. Performance comparison of segmentation models with and without the MINE method using different batch sizes (Bs). The best-performing models are highlighted in bold. Each experiment was repeated 16 times, and the results were averaged across all runs.

Model Backbone	U-net			U-net + MINE		
	Log. Loss	Dice Acc.	Jacc. Coef. (IoU)	Log. Loss	Dice Acc.	Jacc. Coef. (IoU)
Flood Seg. (Bs = 16)	0.3762	0.8392	0.7230	**0.3749**	**0.8474**	**0.7365**
Blood Cell Seg. (Bs = 8)	0.1212	0.9271	0.8652	**0.1018**	**0.9503**	**0.9054**
Colorectal Cancer (Bs = 16)	0.3103	0.9482	0.9065	**0.2935**	**0.9527**	**0.9148**
Hand Nails Seg. (Bs = 4)	**0.1130**	**0.8777**	**0.7868**	0.1207	0.8736	0.7803

Across four segmentation tasks, integrating MINE into U-Net yielded clear gains in most cases. With a batch size of 16 on Flood and Colorectal Cancer datasets, the MINE-enhanced model achieved lower log loss and higher Dice

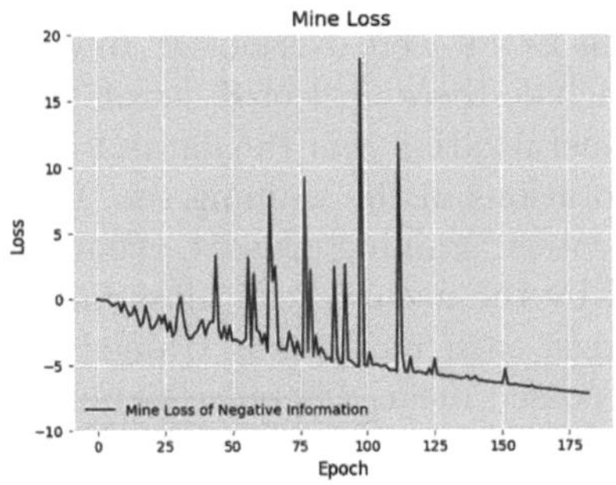

Fig. 4. Minimization of the loss over time, converging to a point of maximum information using only the database data.

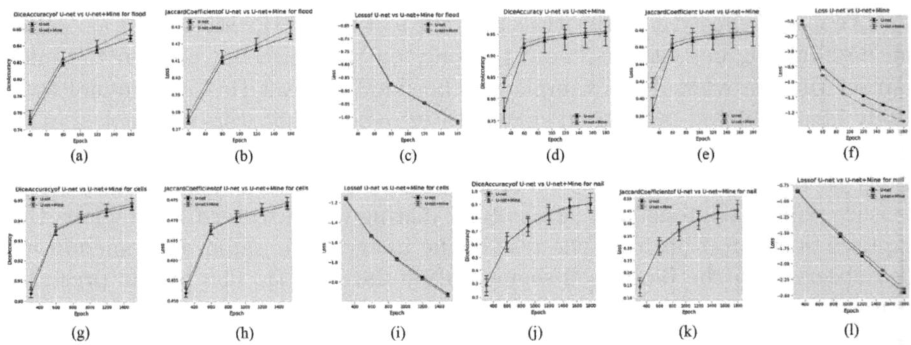

Fig. 5. Performance metrics across datasets: (a-c) Flood, (d-f) Cancer, (g-i) Cells, and (j-l) Nails.

and Jaccard scores (IoU) than the standard U-Net, demonstrating a more informative latent representation. On Blood Cell segmentation (batch size 8), MINE again substantially reduced log loss (0.1018) and boosted Dice accuracy (0.9503), underscoring its value in medical imaging. However, for Hand Nail segmentation (batch size 4), MINE slightly worsened all metrics, suggesting that small batches may undermine reliable mutual information estimation. These results highlight that MINE's benefit varies with batch size and data characteristics, and point toward exploring pre-training the mutual information estimator before U-Net training to strengthen early gradients and potentially improve mid-stage performance.

5 Conclusions and Future Work

The results highlight the positive impact of preserving mutual information in deep learning-based segmentation applications. Regularizing the U-Net architecture with MINE enabled it to successfully segment diverse shapes and features across multiple datasets, each representing a unique segmentation challenge. The addition of mutual information can enhance every model, as it acts as a regularization method. It allows for an increase in the inner complexity of modern models by adding nonlinear features with this focus. In the flood dataset, the model accurately delineated large, interconnected bodies of water. In the cancer dataset, it effectively handled varying distances and large circular regions. For the nails dataset, it managed small separations between objects of interest, while in the cells dataset, it successfully outlined individual objects in crowded scenes but does not have a greater performance due to the impossibility of increasing the batch size for training a neural network due to not having enough RAM on the equipment used and the large size of the dataset images. Also there is a need to explore the application on more specific models of neural networks made for the task and even bigger architectures to prove if the model have the ability to generalize the behavior, but the advantage of the model it is that is compatible with new architectures and there is no indication that it could conflict with other training techniques.

References

1. Azad, R., et al.: Medical image segmentation review: the success of u-net. IEEE Trans. Pattern Anal. Mach. Intell. **46**(12), 10076–10095 (2024). https://doi.org/10.1109/TPAMI.2024.3435571
2. Belghazi, M.I., et al.: Mine: mutual information neural estimation. arXiv preprint arXiv:1801.04062 (2018)
3. Bell, A.J., Sejnowski, T.J.: An information-maximization approach to blind separation and blind deconvolution. Neural Comput. **7**(6), 1129–1159 (1995)
4. Chang, J., Wang, L., Meng, G., Xiang, S., Pan, C.: Deep adaptive image clustering. In: Proceedings of the IEEE International Conference on Computer Vision, pp. 5879–5887 (2017)
5. Chen, P., Pavlidis, T.: Image segmentation as an estimation problem. Comput. Graph. Image Process. **12**(2), 153–172 (1980)
6. Crowley, J.L.: Convolutional neural networks. In: ECCAI Advanced Course on Artificial Intelligence, pp. 67–80. Springer (2021)
7. Depto, D.S., et al.: Blood cell segmentation dataset (2023). https://doi.org/10.34740/KAGGLE/DSV/6107556
8. Donsker, M.D., Varadhan, S.S.: Asymptotic evaluation of certain Markov process expectations for large time, I. Commun. Pure Appl. Math. **28**(1), 1–47 (1975)
9. MIaMIA Group: EBHI-SEG (2022). https://doi.org/10.6084/m9.figshare.21540159.v1
10. Hornegger, J., Paulus, D., Niemann, H.: 15 - probabilistic modeling in computer vision. In: Jähne, B., Haußecker, H. (eds.) Computer Vision and Applications, pp. 517–540. Academic Press, San Diego (2000). https://doi.org/10.1016/B978-012379777-3/50016-9
11. Karim, M.F., Sharma, K., Barman, N.R.: Flood area segmentation (2022). https://doi.org/10.34740/KAGGLE/DSV/4732950
12. Lee, S., Bajic, I.V.: Analysis of information flow through u-nets. arXiv preprint arXiv:2101.08427 (2021)
13. Lee, S., Bajić, I.V.: Information flow through u-nets. In: 2021 IEEE 18th International Symposium on Biomedical Imaging (ISBI), pp. 812–816. IEEE (2021)

14. Mazoure, B., des Combes, R.T., Doan, T., Bachman, P., Hjelm, R.D.: Deep reinforcement and infomax learning. arXiv preprint arXiv:2006.07217 (2020)
15. Minaee, S., Boykov, Y., Porikli, F., Plaza, A., Kehtarnavaz, N., Terzopoulos, D.: Image segmentation using deep learning: a survey. IEEE Trans. Pattern Anal. Mach. Intell. **44**(7), 3523–3542 (2021)
16. Papenko, V.: Nails segmentation (2018). https://www.kaggle.com/datasets/vpapenko/nails-segmentation/data
17. Rigau, J., Feixas, M., Sbert, M., Bardera, A., Boada, I.: Medical image segmentation based on mutual information maximization. In: Barillot, C., Haynor, D.R., Hellier, P. (eds.) MICCAI 2004. LNCS, vol. 3216, pp. 135–142. Springer, Heidelberg (2004). https://doi.org/10.1007/978-3-540-30135-6_17
18. Ronneberger, O., Fischer, P., Brox, T.: U-net: convolutional networks for biomedical image segmentation. In: Medical Image Computing and Computer-assisted Intervention–MICCAI 2015: 18th inteRnational Conference, Munich, Germany, October 5–9, 2015, Proceedings, Part III 18, pp. 234–241. Springer (2015)
19. Ruiwen, N., et al.: Segmentation of remote sensing images based on u-net multi-task learning. Comput. Mater. Continua **73**, 3263–3274 (2022). https://doi.org/10.32604/cmc.2022.026881 https://doi.org/10.32604/cmc.2022.026881 https://doi.org/10.32604/cmc.2022.026881 https://doi.org/10.32604/cmc.2022.026881 https://doi.org/10.32604/cmc.2022.026881 https://doi.org/10.32604/cmc.2022.026881 https://doi.org/10.32604/cmc.2022.026881
20. Serra, J.: A lattice approach to image segmentation. J. Math. Imag. Vis. **24**, 83–130 (2006)
21. Shi, L., et al.: EBHI-SEG: a novel enteroscope biopsy histopathological haematoxylin and eosin image dataset for image segmentation tasks. arXiv preprint arXiv:2212.00532 (2022)
22. Tai, X.C., Liu, H., Chan, R.H., Li, L.: A mathematical explanation of UNet. Math. Found. Comput. (2024). https://doi.org/10.3934/mfc.2024040
23. Tangestanizadeh, M., Tezerjani, M.D., Jazi, S.Y.: Attention-based U-Net method for autonomous lane detection. arXiv preprint arXiv:2411.10902 (2024)
24. Wu, J., et al.: Deep comprehensive correlation mining for image clustering. In: Proceedings of the IEEE/CVF International Conference on Computer Vision, pp. 8150–8159 (2019)
25. Xu, X., Huang, S.L., Zheng, L., Wornell, G.W.: An information theoretic interpretation to deep neural networks. Entropy **24**(1) (2022).https://doi.org/10.3390/e24010135

Rice (*Oryza Sativa*) Leaf Disease Classification Using Convolutional Neural Networks: Comparing Deep Learning Techniques with Custom Architecture and Xception

Antonio Velázquez-Beltrán[1], Juan Carlos Olguín-Rojas[2](✉), and Gilberto de Jesús López-Canteñs[1,2]

[1] Universidad Autonóma Chapingo, Posgrado en Ingeniería Agrícola y Uso Integral del Agua, Texcoco, Estado de México, Mexico
[2] Universidad Autonóma Chapingo, Departamento de Ingeniería Mecánica Agrícola, Texcoco, Estado de México, Mexico
{glopezc,jolguinr}@chapingo.mx

Abstract. Currently, in rice production areas, the detection and classification of leaf diseases is often performed manually by technical personnel, which can lead to identification errors and affect crop yield. These drawbacks can be reduced through the use of computer vision systems integrated with deep learning algorithms. In this study, different techniques based on convolutional neural networks (CNNs) were analyzed to classify rice leaf diseases, and two approaches were selected: a custom architecture and the pre-trained Xception model. The classes considered were: leaf with brown spot, healthy leaf, leaf with hispa, leaf with blight, and scald leaf. The performance of both architectures was evaluated under different configurations. For each treatment, their performance in precision, recall, and accuracy were measured. In the end, the best performance was obtained by the Xception model with fine-tuning and the RMSprop optimizer, reaching an accuracy of 93.8 %. These findings may be useful for automated agricultural applications, such as the application of crop protection products.

Keywords: Precision Agriculture · Computer Vision · Deep Learning · Crop Monitoring · Transfer Learning

1 Introduction

Early detection and accurate classification of crop diseases is a critical need in modern agriculture, especially in the case of rice.(*Oryza sativa*), One of the most cultivated and consumed cereals worldwide. Currently, visual inspection by technical personnel remains the predominant practice in agricultural areas, which can lead to diagnostic errors, inappropriate treatments, and significant

L. Martínez-Villaseñor et al. (Eds.): MICAI 2025, CCIS 2712, pp. 303–312, 2025.
https://doi.org/10.1007/978-3-032-08704-1_23

yield losses [1]. These limitations have driven the development of automated tools based on computer vision and deep learning [2] Convolutional neural networks (CNNs) have demonstrated outstanding performance in multi-class image classification tasks, including applications in the agro-industrial field [3]. Its ability to extract and learn hierarchical features directly from images allows for the detection of subtle patterns related to the symptomatology of foliar diseases, even under variable visual conditions. Previous studies have reported successful results using CNNs in the detection of pests and diseases in fruits and vegetables, frequently exceeding 90 % accuracy [4].

2 Materials and Methods

This section outlines the methodological framework of the study. It includes dataset characteristics, preprocessing procedures, and the experimental design used to evaluate different deep learning architectures. Both the exploratory and final training phases are described, with emphasis on the selection of models and hyperparameters. The implementation environment is specified to ensure reproducibility. In addition, the evaluation metrics are presented to provide a rigorous basis for performance assessment across multiple configurations.

2.1 Dataset

An RGB image dataset of rice leaves was used, obtained from the online platform Kaggle [4], comprising 10,000 samples equally distributed among five categories: healthy leaf, leaf with brown spot, leaf with hispa, leaf with blight, and leaf with scald. All images were resized to 200×200 pixels. The dataset was partitioned into 5,000 samples for training, 2,500 for validation, and 2,500 for testing, as shown in Fig. 1.

Preprocessing included pixel value normalization and data augmentation using transformations such as rotation, shifting, zooming, horizontal flipping, and shearing, aimed at improving the model's generalization capabilities [6].

2.2 Experimental Design

The experimental design was structured into two phases to evaluate the impact of different configurations on model performance.

Proposed Architectures:

VGG16. A deep neural network developed by the Visual Geometry Group at the University of Oxford, widely used in transfer learning tasks [7]. In this study, it was adapted by fine-tuning its final layers to meet the classification objectives.

VGG19. An extension of VGG16 with additional convolutional layers, enabling deeper feature extraction [7], aiming to balance depth and computational efficiency.

A) Healthy Leaf Class.

B) Brown Spot Class.

C) Hispa-Affected Class.

D) Blight-Affected Class.

E) Scald-Affected Class.

Fig. 1. Representative examples from the rice leaf dataset, classified into five categories.

Xception. Proposed by Chollet [8], Xception replaces standard convolutions with depthwise separable convolutions, enhancing both efficiency and performance.

Exploratory Phase: Initially, the architectures tested included a custom CNN, VGG16, VGG19, and Xception. Each model was trained for 10 epochs under various strategies: from scratch, feature extraction, and fine-tuning. Learning rates and optimizers were also varied. Configurations with an accuracy below 50 % were discarded during this phase to narrow the search space.

Final Training Phase: The best-performing configurations were selected for a final training session lasting 100 epochs. Early stopping was applied with a patience threshold of 10 epochs. The final evaluation was conducted on an independent test set that was not used during training or validation. Cross-validation was not applied due to the high computational demands of the models.

Model implementation was carried out using Google Colaboratory with GPU L4 acceleration, running Python 3.10, TensorFlow 2.18.0, and Keras 3.8.0.

2.3 Evaluated Architectures

Custom CNN. A convolutional neural network was built from scratch, consisting of four convolutional layers (with 32, 64, 128, and 128 filters), followed by MaxPooling2D layers, a `Flatten` layer, a dense layer with 512 neurons (`ReLU`), and an output layer with `softmax` activation. The model was trained using RMSprop (lr = 1e−4) for 100 epochs, with early stopping to prevent overfitting [9].

Xception Model. Pretrained weights from ImageNet were used, and two training strategies were implemented:

Feature Extraction: The Xception model was used with `include_top=False` and a 200×200 input shape. All layers were explicitly frozen (`layer.trainable = False`). A custom classification head was added: `Flatten` → `Dense(512, ReLU)` → `Dense(5, Softmax)`. Dropout was not applied. This configuration was trained using a learning rate of 1e-4.

Fine-Tuning: The same base Xception model was reused, but with selective unfreezing of the upper layers (`layer.trainable = True`). The classification head included a `Dropout(0.5)` layer following `Dense(512, ReLU)`. Training was performed with a reduced learning rate (1e-5) to preserve pretrained weights.

2.4 Evaluation Metrics

To assess the model performance, standard metrics commonly used in multiclass classification tasks were applied:

Accuracy: The proportion of correct predictions over the total number of samples.

Precision: The proportion of true positives among all positive predictions.

Recall (Sensitivity): The proportion of true positives relative to the actual positives.

F1-Score: The harmonic mean of precision and recall, balancing both metrics especially in imbalanced datasets.

Confusion Matrix: A visual representation of classification outcomes per class, useful for identifying misclassification patterns [10].

3 Results

The analysis of the learning curves (see Fig. 2) demonstrated clear differences in the behavior of the evaluated models. The custom CNN architecture trained from scratch showed an acceptable improvement in accuracy across epochs; however, its loss curve exhibited greater fluctuations, suggesting limited convergence and a tendency toward overfitting. In contrast, the Xception model with feature extraction achieved a more stable evolution, but its validation accuracy plateaued earlier, indicating that frozen layers restricted the network's ability to capture discriminative features in the dataset. The fine-tuned Xception model outperformed both alternatives, reaching the highest accuracy values while maintaining smoother convergence in both training and validation, which evidences a superior generalization capability.

The confusion matrices (see Fig. 3) provide additional insights into classification behavior. The fine-tuned Xception configuration yielded the largest number of true positives across all classes, reducing misclassifications particularly between visually similar diseases such as brown spot and blight. Meanwhile, the custom CNN showed more dispersion of errors, reflecting its limited representational capacity compared to transfer learning approaches.

A direct comparison of accuracy and loss across the three models is illustrated in Fig. 4. This analysis highlights the superior convergence of the fine-tuned Xception model, which not only achieved higher accuracy but also maintained consistently lower validation loss. In contrast, the CNN trained from scratch exhibited higher variance in both curves, while the feature extraction strategy, although more stable, underperformed in terms of final accuracy.

Finally, the quantitative comparison summarized in Table 1 reinforces these findings. While the baseline CNN achieved 92.58% validation accuracy and 89.80% test accuracy, and the Xception with feature extraction reached 93.36% and 93.20%, respectively, the fine-tuned Xception clearly surpassed them with

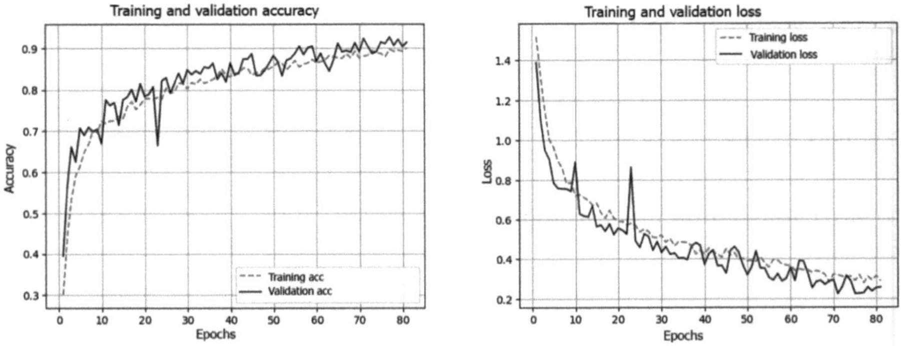

A) Custom CNN Architecture (trained from scratch).

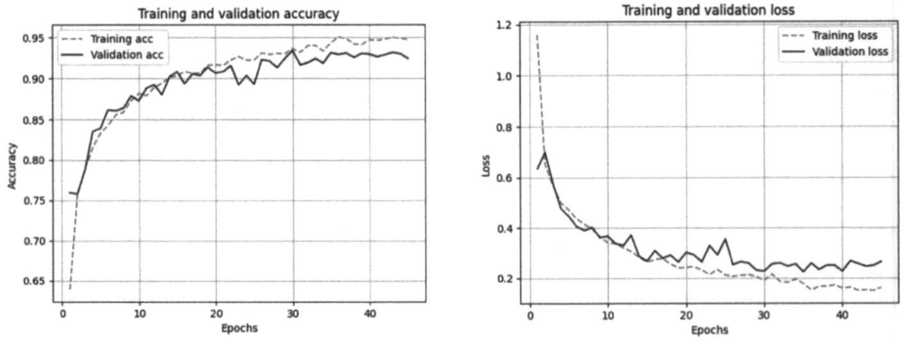

B) Xception Model with Feature Extraction.

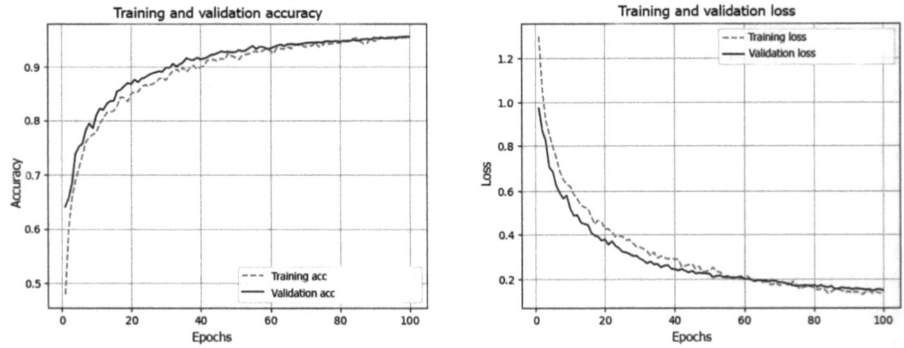

C) Xception Model with Fine-Tuning.

Fig. 2. Accuracy and loss evolution during training for the three evaluated models. The fine-tuned model achieved the best convergence and generalization.

94.16% validation accuracy and 95.40% test accuracy. These results confirm that leveraging pretrained weights and selectively retraining upper layers allows the model to adapt more effectively to the rice leaf disease dataset, providing a robust framework for computer vision–based agricultural applications.

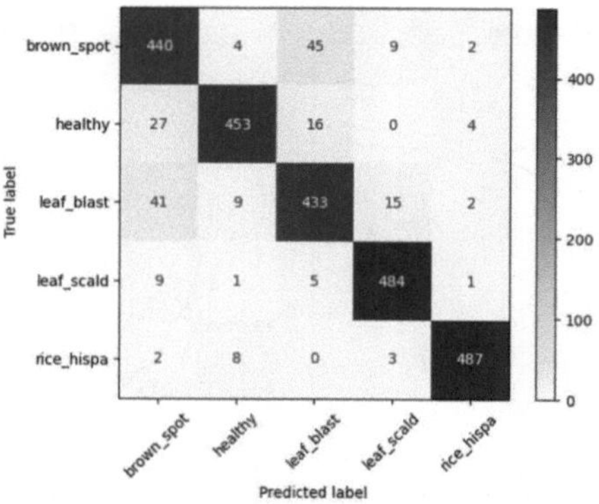

A) Custom CNN Architecture (trained from scratch)

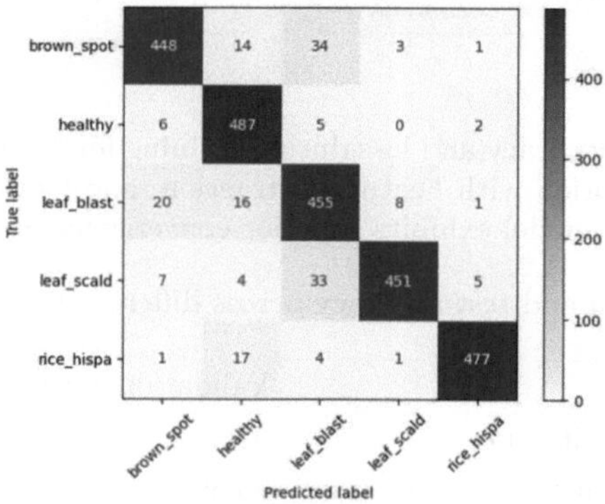

B) Xception Model with Feature Extraction

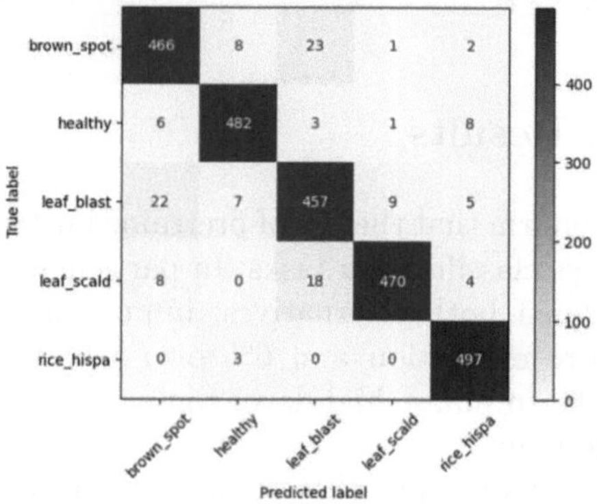

C) Xception Model with Fine-Tuning

Fig. 3. Confusion matrices for the three evaluated models. A higher number of true positives was observed in the fine-tuning configuration.

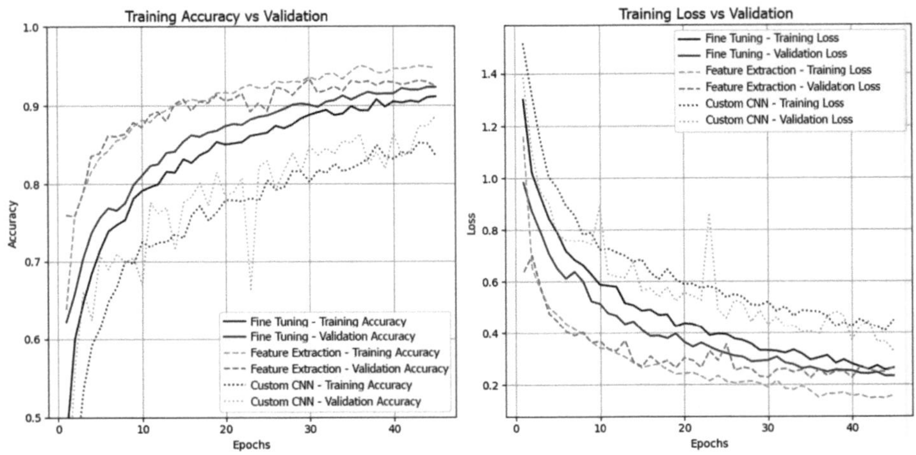

Fig. 4. Comparison of accuracy and loss during training for the three models: Xception with Fine-Tuning, Xception with Feature Extraction, and Custom CNN trained from scratch. The fine-tuned model exhibits superior convergence and lower loss.

Table 1. Validation and test accuracy across different training configurations

Model	Validation Accuracy	Test Accuracy
Custom CNN Architecture	92.58%	89.80%
Xception Model with Feature Extractio	93.36%	93.20%
Xception Model with Fine-Tuning	**94.16%**	**95.40%**

4 Discussion of Results

The results obtained confirm that the use of pretrained networks offers significant advantages in multiclass classification tasks. In particular, the fine-tuned model consistently outperformed both alternatives, improving accuracy by approximately 2% over feature extraction and 6% over training from scratch. This demonstrates its ability to adapt high-level representations from ImageNet to the rice leaf disease domain.

The feature extraction strategy, while slightly less accurate, proved computationally more efficient, representing a viable trade-off when resources are limited. Conversely, training from scratch with data augmentation yielded the lowest performance, yet still highlighted the importance of augmentation in mitigating overfitting when pretrained models are unavailable.

Overall, these findings align with the conclusions of Yosinski et al. [11], who emphasized that deep network features are transferable and can be effectively fine-tuned to new contexts. In this sense, the present study validates the relevance of transfer learning approaches for agricultural computer vision applications, particularly when datasets are limited in size or class variability.

5 Conclusions

This study demonstrated that transfer learning, particularly the fine-tuned Xception model, provides a robust and accurate framework for the automatic classification of rice leaf diseases. By selectively retraining upper layers, the model successfully adapted generic ImageNet representations to the agricultural domain, achieving the highest accuracy in both validation (94.16%) and testing (95.40%).

Although training from scratch yielded lower performance, the integration of data augmentation proved beneficial in mitigating overfitting. Likewise, the feature extraction strategy, despite achieving slightly lower accuracy, emerged as a computationally efficient alternative that may be advantageous in resource-constrained environments.

Overall, these findings reinforce the value of pretrained models for agricultural computer vision applications, where data scarcity is a common limitation. Future work may extend this approach by exploring more diverse datasets, integrating attention mechanisms, or deploying the trained models in real-world decision-support systems for precision agriculture.

References

1. Kamilaris, A., Prenafeta-Boldú, F.X.: Deep learning in agriculture: a survey. Comput. Electron. Agric. **147**, 70–90 (2018). https://doi.org/10.1016/j.compag.2018.01.009
2. Barbedo, A.G.: Plant disease identification from individual lesions and spots using deep learning. Biosyst. Eng. **180**, 96–107 (2019). https://doi.org/10.1016/j.biosystemseng.2019.02.003
3. Krizhevsky, A., Sutskever, I., Hinton, G.E.: ImageNet classification with deep convolutional neural networks. In: Advances in Neural Information Processing Systems (NeurIPS), vol. 25, pp. 1097–1105 (2012). https://doi.org/10.1145/3065386
4. Ferentinos, K.P.: Deep learning models for plant disease detection and diagnosis. Comput. Electron. Agric. **145**, 311–318 (2018). https://doi.org/10.1016/j.compag.2018.01.009
5. Kaggle: Classification datasets. https://www.kaggle.com/datasets?tags=13302-Classification. Accessed 19 June 2025
6. Mohanty, S.P., Hughes, D.P., Salathé, M.: Using deep learning for image-based plant disease detection. Front. Plant Sci. **7**, 1419 (2016). https://doi.org/10.3389/fpls.2016.01419
7. Simonyan, K., Zisserman, A.: Very deep convolutional networks for large-scale image recognition. arXiv preprint arXiv:1409.1556 (2014)
8. Chollet, F.: Xception: deep learning with depthwise separable convolutions. In: IEEE Conference on Computer Vision and Pattern Recognition (CVPR), pp. 1251–1258 (2017). https://doi.org/10.1109/CVPR.2017.195
9. Deng, J., Dong, W., Socher, R., Li, L.-J., Li, K., Fei-Fei, L.: ImageNet: a large-scale hierarchical image database. In: IEEE Conference on Computer Vision and Pattern Recognition (CVPR), pp. 248–255 (2009). https://doi.org/10.1109/CVPR.2009.5206848

10. Pedregosa, F., Varoquaux, G., Gramfort, A., et al.: Scikit-learn: machine learning in Python. J. Mach. Learn. Res. **12**, 2825–2830 (2011)
11. Yosinski, J., Clune, J., Bengio, Y., Lipson, H.: How transferable are features in deep neural networks? In: Advances in Neural Information Processing Systems (NeurIPS), vol. 27, pp. 3320–3328 (2014)

An Analysis of Spatio-Temporal Graph Neural Networks Based on Synthetic Time Series with Known Structural Dependencies

Armando Martinez-Ruiz[1(✉)], Pilar Gomez-Gil[1], and Rigoberto Fonseca-Delgado[2]

[1] Computer Science Department, National Institute of Astrophysics, Optics and Electronics, Puebla, Mexico
{armandomtzruiz,pgomez}@inaoep.mx

[2] School of Mathematical and Computational Sciences, Yachay Tech University, San Miguel de Urcuquí, Ecuador
rfonseca@yachaytech.edu.ec

Abstract. Spatio-temporal data modeling is a crucial component of many real-world systems, such as traffic prediction, environmental monitoring, and energy forecasting. Spatio-Temporal Graph Neural Networks (ST-GNNs) have recently emerged as powerful models for learning complex temporal and spatial dependencies simultaneously. However, existing evaluations primarily rely on real-world datasets with fixed characteristics, which limits our understanding of model behavior under varying conditions. This paper proposes a systematic empirical analysis of ST-GNNs using controlled synthetic benchmarks with tunable noise and structural dependencies. Synthetic datasets of sinusoidal time series with known inter-node correlations were designed and used to evaluate a diffusion-based ST-GNN architecture against classical baselines including ARIMA and LSTM. The experiments showed that the ST-GNN model outperformed traditional models in a multi-step forecasting task, particularly when leveraging spatial correlations. Our findings offer insight into the strengths and limitations of ST-GNNs and highlight the value of synthetic benchmarks for analyzing model generalization and robustness.

Keywords: Graph Neural Networks · Time Series Forecasting · Synthetic Data · Spatio-Temporal Graph Neural Networks

1 Introduction

Spatio-temporal data is central to a wide range of real-world applications, including traffic forecasting, energy consumption prediction, and environmental monitoring. Effectively modeling this type of data requires capturing both temporal patterns and the spatial structure that naturally arises from interconnected entities, such as sensors, roads, or power grids.

L. Martínez-Villaseñor et al. (Eds.): MICAI 2025, CCIS 2712, pp. 313–324, 2025.
https://doi.org/10.1007/978-3-032-08704-1_24

Deep learning techniques, particularly Recurrent Neural Networks (RNNs) and their variants like Long Short-Term Memory networks (LSTMs), have demonstrated strong performance in time series forecasting [1]. However, these models typically focus on temporal dependencies and often neglect spatial dependencies, limiting their ability to fully exploit the structure of spatio-temporal data.

Graph Neural Networks (GNNs) provide an effective framework for learning from relational or topological data structures. Extending this approach, Spatio-Temporal Graph Neural Networks (ST-GNNs) combine spatial modeling via GNNs with temporal modeling through RNNs or convolutional methods [2]. This enables joint learning of both spatial and temporal dependencies in complex dynamic systems.ST-GNNs have demonstrated strong potential in real-world applications where structured time series are involved, including traffic forecasting [12], energy demand prediction [10], and environmental monitoring [11].

Despite their increasing adoption, most ST-GNN architectures are evaluated using real-world datasets from narrow application domains. This limits our understanding of their generalization ability under different structural and noise conditions. In particular, real datasets rarely allow for precise control over the spatio-temporal properties being tested, making systematic evaluation difficult.

The goal of this work is to simulate structural relationships between different time series to analyze the advantages and limitations of ST-GNNs in long term forecasting. By generating synthetic multivariate time series with tunable noise and explicit inter-node dependencies, the model performance was rigorously analyzed. The ultimate purpose of this work is to offer deeper insights into the robustness and generalization of spatio-temporal models. The key contributions are as follows:

- The introduction of synthetic spatio-temporal datasets with known structure and noise characteristics, to be considered as benchmarks.
- A representative ST-GNN architecture was evaluated, based on graph diffusion and GRU-based temporal modeling comparing its behavior with two traditional baselines, ARIMA and LSTM under three synthetic scenarios: additive, multiplicative and average-based temporal dependency.
- Systematic analysis of spatial modeling impact, by varying the dependency structure of the target node (sum, mean, and product of neighbors).

2 Background

2.1 Time Series Forecasting

A time series is a sequence of time-ordered observations which describe how a system or a phenomenon evolves over time. Formally, a multivariate time series X is a sequence of N-dimensional vector observations collected over time, i.e., $X \in \mathbb{R}^{N \times T}$ [4].

Time series forecasting can be defined as the prediction of future values of it given past historical observations. There can be two types of forecasting: *single-step-ahead forecasting*, which consists in predicting single future observations of the time series once at a time, i.e., the target is $Y = X_{t+H}$ at time t for some $H \in \mathbb{N}$, and *multi-step-ahead forecasting*, with target $Y = X_{t+1:t+H}$ where the prediction is an interval of multiple time steps [3].

2.2 Graph Neural Networks

A Graph Neural Network (GNN) is a deep learning model designed to process graph-structured data which has an inherent graph structure. The first model was proposed by Scarselli et al. [6]. Let $G = (N, E)$ be a graph where N is the set of nodes and E is the set of edges. The set $N(i) = \{j \in N | (n, m) \in E\}$ is called the neighborhood of node i and the set $co(i) = \{(i, j) \in E | j \in N\}$ denotes the set of arcs having node i as the vertex. In their fundamental work, each node of a graph is represented as a state $x_i \in \mathbb{R}^s$, which contains all the information of the neighborhood of node i, including the labels of each adjacent node and edge. With a function f_w, usually called transition or aggregation function, the dependence of a node i with its neighborhood can be expressed, and a function g_w usually called output function describes how the information regarding node i will be processed [2].

If the function f_w is a contraction function with respect to the state, i.e., $\exists \mu \in [0, 1)$ such that $||f_w(x) - f_w(y)|| \leq \mu||x - y||, \forall x, y$ states, then according to Banach's Fixed Point Theorem [7], if the function f_w is applied iteratively, it will converge to a unique fixed state x'. Then, the GNN model can formally be described with the following expressions:

$$x_i(t+1) = f_w(l_i, l_{co(i)}, x_{N(i)}(t), l_{N(i)}) \quad (1)$$
$$o_i(t) = g_w(x_i(t), l_i) \quad (2)$$

where l denotes the labels of the nodes and arcs and o_i is the output about the concept that represents node i. This iterative method allows message passing between nodes so they share similarities in their embeddings [8] until a fixed point is reached.

2.3 Spatial-Temporal Graph Neural Networks

Spatial-Temporal Graph Neural Networks (ST-GNNs) are a class of models designed to capture both spatial and temporal dependencies in structured time series data [2]. They leverage the connectivity of nodes in a graph to model spatial relationships and track the evolution of node features over time to learn temporal dynamics. These architectures are particularly effective for forecasting tasks where the data naturally reside on graphs—such as traffic networks, sensor grids, or energy distribution systems.

A typical ST-GNN architecture has three components and can be observed in Fig. 1:

1. Data processing module: Constructs the spatio-temporal graph from raw inputs, including defining the graph structure and aligning temporal sequences.

2. Spatio-temporal graph learning module: Learns joint spatial and temporal dependencies from the data. This is typically achieved by combining spatial modeling through GNN variants (e.g., Spectral Graph Convolutional Networks (Spectral GCN), Spatial GNNs, or Graph Attention Networks) with temporal modeling through Recurrent Neural Networks (RNNs) or Temporal Convolutional Networks (TCNs).
3. Task-specific prediction module: Maps the learned spatio-temporal representations to outputs suitable for the downstream task, such as forecasting future values.

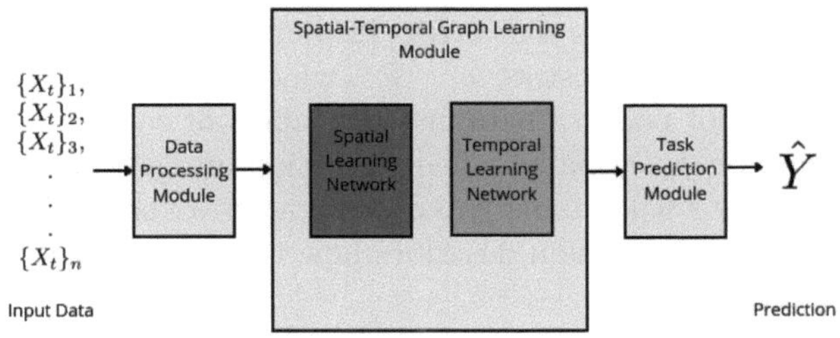

Fig. 1. Basic architecture of a Spatio-Temporal Graph Neural Network (ST-GNN) for time series forecasting. The model integrates spatial dependencies through graph convolutional layers and temporal dynamics through recurrent or convolutional modules.

The most common model utilized for processing the spatial dependencies is the Spectral GCN [5], based on the graph convolution, which takes the graph Fourier transform and the Inverse graph Fourier transform to achieve the transformation from the spatial domain to the spectral domain. Both transforms are defined as follows:

$$\mathcal{F}(x) = U^T x, \tag{3}$$

$$\mathcal{F}^{-1}(x) = Ux, \tag{4}$$

where $x \in \mathbb{R}^N$ denotes the signal defined on the nodes of the graph and U is the eigenvector matrix of the normalized Laplacian of the graph. Based on this idea, the graph convolution is defined with the following equation:

$$g \star x = \mathcal{F}^{-1}(\mathcal{F}(g) \odot \mathcal{F}(x)) = U(U^T g \odot U^T x), \tag{5}$$

where $\odot$ is the element-wise multiplication, $g \in \mathbb{R}^N$ is the vector of spectral coefficients of the filter, and the operation $U(U^T g \odot U^T x)$ applies the filter in the spectral domain.

3 Related Work

Although there is abundant work on time series forecasting through deep learning models, some recent works utilizes several GNNs architectures for time series forecasting.

The fundamental work of Wang et al. [9] focuses on the temporal classification/regression problem, which consists on building a function that maps a multivariate time series to a discrete class label or real value response. They propose a model called sparse functional multilayer perceptron (SFMLP) for handling missing values in time series covariates. Simeunovic et al. [10] propose to take a graph signal processing perspective to model multi-site photovoltaic production time series as signals on a graph to capture their spatio-temporal dependencies. There are two approaches in this work: the graph-convolutional long short term memory (GCLSTM) and the graph convolutional transformer (GCTrafo) models. Moreover, Oskarsson et al. [11] proposed a temporal graph neural network model for forecasting of graph structured irregularly observed time series. This approach introduces a time-continuous, latent state in each node, following a linear ordinary differential equation defined by the output of a Gated Recurrent Unit (GRU).

Finally, the work of Kim et al. [12] proposed a new method for multivariate time series forecasting with missing values, called temporal matrix factorization-based graph neural network (TMF-GNN). The concept of temporal matrix factorization is used to reconstruct partially observed MTS data.

4 Proposed Approach

4.1 Proposed Synthetic Datasets

To evaluate the performance of ST-GNNs under controlled conditions, five synthetic time series were generated based on sinusoidal functions with additive Gaussian noise, where four time series are independent, and the fifth exhibits a star graph relationship that depends on all other time series. Different dependency scenarios were established to define the independent time series as follows:

$$x_i(t) = \sin(\frac{10t}{T} + i) + \epsilon_i(t), \text{for } i \in \{1, 2, 3, 4\}, \tag{6}$$

where $T = 1000$ are the time steps, $x_i(t)$ is the value of the time series associated to node i at time step t and $\epsilon_i(t) \sim \mathcal{N}(0, \sigma^2)$.

The additional dependent time series, $x_0(t)$, was constructed using three different schemes to reflect varying degrees of inter-node dependency and to incorporate linear and non-linear relationships:

1. **Sum-based dependency:**

$$x_0(t) = \sum_{i=1}^{4} x_i(t). \tag{7}$$

2. **Mean-based dependency:**

$$x_0(t) = \frac{1}{4}\sum_{i=1}^{4} x_i(t). \tag{8}$$

3. **Product-based dependency:**

$$x_0(t) = \prod_{i=1}^{4} x_i(t). \tag{9}$$

This setup introduces an explicit dependency structure, considering both linear and non linear dependencies, allowing us to test the model's ability to capture node relationships and exploit spatial correlations in the data.

The graph structure was defined by computing the Pearson correlation coefficient between each pair of time series; an edge was included for statistically significant correlations (see Fig. 2). This synthetic setup provides complete control over spatial and temporal properties, enabling reproducible and detailed analysis of model robustness and generalization.

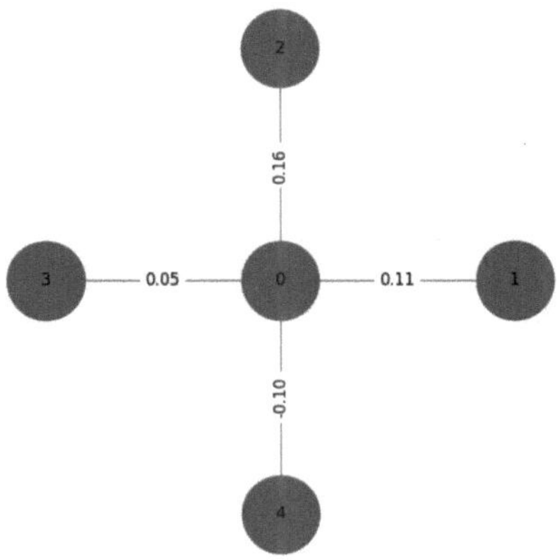

Fig. 2. The graph associated to the synthetic data. Each node represents a time series, edges represent statistically significant Pearson correlations between node pairs. Edge labels indicate the correlation coefficients, reflecting the strength of pairwise dependencies.

4.2 Spatio-Temporal GNN Model

The spatio-temporal forecasting model evaluated in this study is based on the architecture proposed by Li et al. [13], which integrates temporal encoding via Gated Recurrent Units (GRUs) and spatial modeling using Spectral Graph Convolutional Networks (Spectral GCNs) informed by diffusion processes.

The model processes inputs sequences in two stages:

1. **Temporal encoding:** For each node, a GRU processes its historical time series to extract latent temporal features.

2. **Graph-based spatial encoding:** The node embeddings are passed through a spectral graph convolution layer, which propagates information across the graph based on the connectivity defined by the similarity matrix.

This approach enables the model to jointly learn temporal dynamics and spatial correlations encoded in the graph structure. Training is performed end-to-end, using a mean squared error loss between the predicted and ground-truth future values.

4.3 Experimental Setup

The experiment was done in two phases: first, the evaluation of the models was done by defining the first time series as the mean of the rest of the time series. Each model was trained using the splitting convention for the dataset.

The models were trained for 100 epochs, to eventually calculate the metrics RMSE and MAE using the test set. The second phase of the experiment consisted on repeating the training of the models with the difference that the first time series is the sum of the rest of the time series.

Table 1 summarizes the key hyper-parameters used for training the LSTM and ST-GNN models. Both models were trained using the same learning rate, batch size, and number of epochs to ensure a fair comparison. While the LSTM uses a larger hidden size (64 vs. 32), the ST-GNN compensates by incorporating node embeddings and a graph convolutional layer with a kernel size of 2. This architectural design allows ST-GNN to model spatial relationships between nodes in addition to temporal dependencies. Additionally, the ST-GNN had fewer trainable parameters (12.1k) compared to the LSTM (17.9k), resulting in faster training times.

Table 1. Summary of hyperparameters used for the LSTM and ST-GNN models. Both models were trained under identical learning conditions to ensure a fair comparison.

Hyperparameter	LSTM	ST-GNN
Input size	1	1
Hidden size	64	32
Horizon	12	12
RNN layers	1 (LSTM)	1 (GRU)
GNN kernel size	–	2
Node embeddings	–	Yes
Learning rate	0.001	0.001
Batch size	32	32
Max epochs	100	100

4.4 Baseline Models and Metrics

To contextualize the performance of the ST-GNN model, two widely-used forecasting baselines were implemented:

- **ARIMA**: A classical autoregressive integrated moving average model [1], fit independently to each series.
- **LSTM**: A deep learning model based on Long Short-Term Memory units, which models temporal dependencies but do not consider spatial dependencies [2].

All models are evaluated on a multi-step-ahead forecasting task, where the objective is to predict future values of node 0 given historical data from all nodes. The dataset is split into training (70%), validation (15%), and test (15%) subsets. Each model is trained for 100 epochs with a forecasting horizon of $H = 12$.

Two standard regression metrics were used to evaluate forecasting accuracy:

$$\text{RMSE} = \sqrt{\frac{1}{n}\sum_{i=1}^{n}(y_i - \hat{y}_i)^2} \tag{10}$$

$$\text{MAE} = \frac{1}{n}\sum_{i=1}^{n}|y_i - \hat{y}_i| \tag{11}$$

These metrics quantify both average and squared prediction errors across different model types and dependency scenarios.

5 Experimental Results

5.1 Discussion

Table 2 summarizes the forecasting accuracy across both synthetic settings. The reported values for the deep learning models (LSTM and ST-GNN) represent the mean and standard deviation computed over 10 independent training runs. For the ARIMA model, the forecast was computed independently for each of the five time series, and the final metrics were obtained by averaging the results, followed by calculating the overall standard deviation.

The results showed that the ST-GNN outperforms the ARIMA model by a large margin in all synthetic scenarios, highlighting the limitations of traditional statistical methods when handling multivariate and spatially dependent time series. Figure 3 illustrates the predicted versus true values of the target time series (Node 0, which is dependent of the rest of the nodes) across the three dependency settings.

The comparison between ST-GNN and LSTM revealed the following findings:

- Mean-based setting: LSTM achieved slightly lower RMSE than ST-GNN, suggesting that in scenarios with weak spatial dependencies, temporal models be enough for the forecasting task.

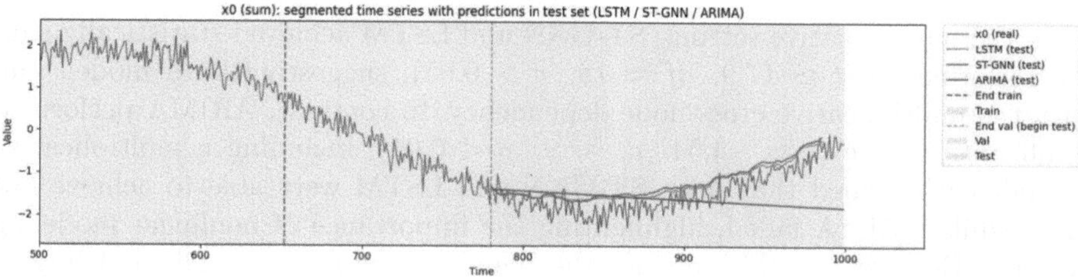

(a) Sum-based time series.

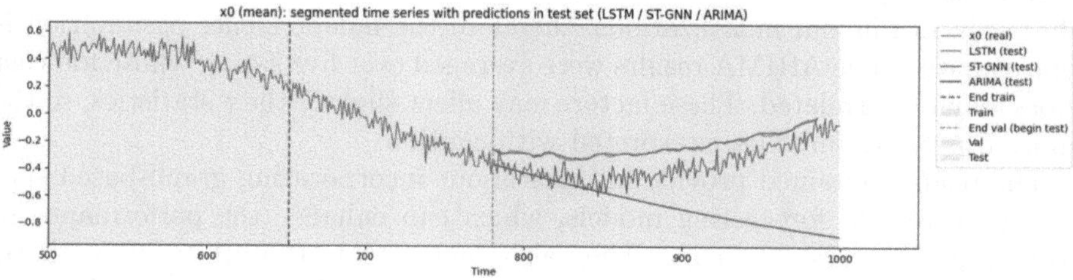

(b) Mean-based time series.

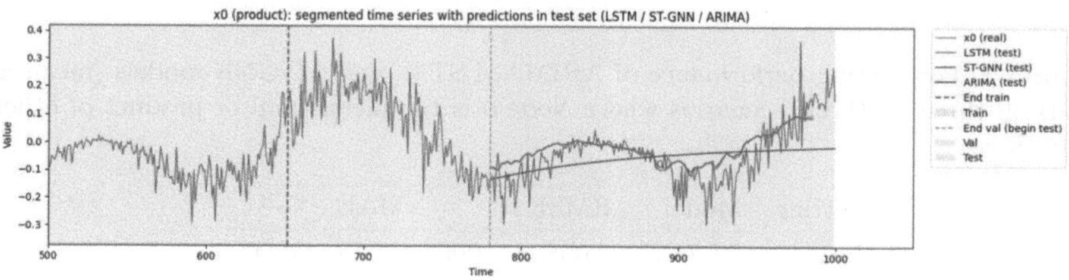

(c) Product-based time series.

Fig. 3. Forecasting results for the dependent time series under three synthetic dependency settings: (a) sum-based, (b) mean-based, and (c) product-based. The plots illustrate the ground truth versus model predictions.

- Sum-based setting: ST-GNN significantly outperformed LSTM, indicating that spatial modeling is crucial when the target series aggregates multiple sources.
- Product-based setting: Both deep learning models performed comparably, showing that they could capture nonlinear dependencies. However, the benefit of spatial modeling was less pronounced in this case.

To assess that the observed performance gaps were statistically significant, a Welch's independent-sample t test was conducted on the ten repeated runs of the deep-learning models and the five ARIMA models. For the RMSE in the mean-based scenario, ST-GNN vs LSTM yielded $t = 61.4$ ($df \approx 15.7$, $p < 10^{-18}$); ST-GNN vs ARIMA yielded $t = 36$ ($df \approx 4.2$, $p < 10^{-4}$). Similar results were obtained for the MAE score and the sum-based scenario, confirming that the improvements are statistically significant.

In the multiplicative setting, ST-GNN and LSTM achieved statistically similar performance ($t \approx 17.9$, $df \approx 18$, $p > 0.05$), suggesting both models can learn the multiplicative cross-node dependency. In contrast, ARIMA performed significantly worse ($t \approx -4.54$, $df \approx 9$, $p < 0.01$); including a multiplicative dependency revealed that both ST-GNN and LSTM were able to achieve low error, while ARIMA failed, highlighting the importance of nonlinear modeling capacity. However, in this setting, the benefit of explicit spatial modeling in ST-GNN was not as pronounced as in the sum-based scenario.

It is also important to mention that the ten runs for each deep learning model differ only in random initializations; therefore the independence assumption is approximated. The ARIMA results were averaged over five series, whose forecast errors may be correlated. These factors may affect slightly the t-statistics, so the reported p-values must be interpreted with caution.

The results obtained provide insights about incorporating graph-based spatial structure into forecasting models, which can enhance the performance in structured time series domains. They also demonstrate the utility of synthetic benchmarks for identifying model strengths and limitations in controlled experiments.

Table 2. Forecasting performance of ARIMA, LSTM, and ST-GNN models (mean ± std) on three synthetic scenarios where Node 0 is the mean, sum or product of other time series.

Setting	Model	RMSE	MAE
Mean	ST-GNN	0.098 ± 0.0003	0.076 ± 0.0003
	ARIMA	1.073 ± 0.640	1.038 ± 0.650
	LSTM	0.091 ± 0.0002	0.091 ± 0.002
Sum	ST-GNN	0.131 ± 0.0005	0.098 ± 0.0005
	ARIMA	1.230 ± 0.450	1.190 ± 0.480
	LSTM	0.117 ± 0.001	0.116 ± 0.001
Product	ST-GNN	0.095 ± 0.001	0.074 ± 0.001
	ARIMA	1.053 ± 0.667	1.017 ± 0.679
	LSTM	0.087 ± 0.001	0.087 ± 0.001

6 Conclusions

In this work, an empirical evaluation of Spatio-Temporal Graph Neural Networks (ST-GNNs) is presented using a synthetic dataset designed to simulate controlled spatio-temporal relationships. By creating time series with explicit inter-node relationships —ranging from linear (sum and mean) to nonlinear (product)—and additive noise, it was possible to assess the forecasting capabilities of a diffusion-based ST-GNN model under three structural settings. The results indicate that the ST-GNN consistently outperformed traditional models such as ARIMA and

LSTM, especially in scenarios where spatial structure is significant. However, the presented results are limited by the simplicity of the graph and small scale of the designed datasets.

This analysis highlights the advantages of using synthetic data for stress-testing deep learning models, providing valuable insights into their generalization capabilities. Future work includes extending the evaluation to more diverse synthetic graphs and real-world spatio-temporal datasets. Additional directions involve exploring alternative graph structures and assessing the robustness of ST-GNNs in the presence of missing data and structural perturbations. This line of research aims to contribute to the development of more reliable and interpretable spatio-temporal forecasting models for real-world applications.

Acknowledgment. The authors would like to thank the Department of Science, Humanities, Technology and Innovation for the support offered for the realization of this project.

References

1. Kasun, M., et al.: Multivariate time series forecasting: a review. In: Proceedings of the 2024 2nd Asia Conference on Computer Vision, Image Processing and Pattern Recognition, pp. 1–9. ACM (2024). https://doi.org/10.1145/3663976.3664241
2. Jin, G., et al.: Spatio-temporal graph neural networks for predictive learning in urban computing: a survey. IEEE Trans. Knowl. Data Eng. **36**(10), 5388–5408 (2024). https://doi.org/10.1109/TKDE.2023.3333824
3. Bontempi, G., Ben Taieb, S., Le Borgne, Y.-A.: Machine learning strategies for time series forecasting. In: Aufaure, M.-A., Zimányi, E. (eds.) eBISS 2012. LNBIP, vol. 138, pp. 62–77. Springer, Heidelberg (2013). https://doi.org/10.1007/978-3-642-36318-4_3
4. Jin, M.: A survey on graph neural networks for time series: Forecasting, classification, imputation and anomaly detection. IEEE Trans. Pattern Anal. Mach. Intell. **46**(12), 10466–10485 (2024)
5. Wu, F., Souza, A., Zhang, T., Fifty, C., Yu, T., Weinberger, K.: Simplifying graph convolutional networks. In: Proceedings of the 36th International Conference on Machine Learning, in Proceedings of Machine Learning Research, vol. 97, pp. 6861–6871 (2019). https://proceedings.mlr.press/v97/wu19e.html
6. Scarselli, F.: The graph neural network model. IEEE Trans. Neural Netw. **20**(1), 61–80 (2009)
7. Rudin, W.: Principles of Mathematical Analysis. McGraw Hill (1976)
8. Hamilton, W.L., Ying, R., Leskovec, J.: Representation learning on graphs: methods and applications. IEEE Data Eng. Bull. **40**, 52–74 (2017)
9. Wang, Q.: Deep time series models for scarce data. Neurocomputing **456**, 504–518 (2021)
10. Simeunovic, J.: Spatio-temporal graph neural networks for multi-site PV power forecasting. IEEE Trans. Sustain. Energy **13**(2), 1210–1220 (2022)
11. Oskarsson, J., Sidén, P., Lindsten, F.: Temporal graph neural networks for irregular data. In: Proceedings of The 26th International Conference on Artificial Intelligence and Statistics, in Proceedings of Machine Learning Research, vol. 206, pp. 4515–4531 (2023). https://proceedings.mlr.press/v206/oskarsson23a.html

12. Kim, S.: TMF-GNN: temporal matrix factorization-based graph neural network for multivariate time series forecasting with missing values. Syst. Appl. **275** (2025)
13. Li, Y., Yu, R., Shahabi, C., Liu, Y.: Diffusion convolutional recurrent neural network: data-driven traffic forecasting. In: International Conference on Learning Representations (2018)

Author Index

L. Martínez-Villaseñor et al. (Eds.): MICAI 2025, CCIS 2712, pp. 325–326, 2025.
https://doi.org/10.1007/978-3-032-08704-1

MIX
Papier aus verantwortungsvollen Quellen
Paper from responsible sources
FSC® C105338

If you have any concerns about our products,
you can contact us on
ProductSafety@springernature.com

In case Publisher is established outside the EU,
the EU authorized representative is:
Springer Nature Customer Service Center GmbH
Europaplatz 3, 69115 Heidelberg, Germany

Printed by Libri Plureos GmbH
in Hamburg, Germany